THUCYDIDES

Thucydides

W. Robert Connor

PRINCETON UNIVERSITY PRESS

PRINCETON, NEW JERSEY

Published by Princeton University Press, 41 William Street,
Princeton, New Jersey 08540
In the United Kingdom: Princeton University Press,
Oxford

All Rights Reserved

Library of Congress Cataloging in Publication Data will
be found on the last printed page of this book

ISBN 0-691-03569-5

Publication of this book has been aided by a grant from
The Whitney Darrow Fund of Princeton University Press

This book has been composed in Linotron Times Roman type

Clothbound editions of Princeton University Press books
are printed on acid-free paper, and binding materials are chosen
for strength and durability.

Printed in the United States of America by Princeton
University Press, Princeton, New Jersey

Second printing, with corrections, 1985

9   8   7   6   5   4

To Steve and his grandparents

Contents

Acknowledgments

ON COMPLETING this manuscript I find that it has been almost exactly twenty-seven years—the length of the Peloponnesian War—since I first read Thucydides. For almost half of that time I have been at work on this book. The debts one accumulates over such a period one cannot accurately calculate or adequately acknowledge. If I leave nameless the teachers, colleagues, students, readers and listeners, editors, research assistants and typists, all friends and fellow inquirers, it is not from want of gratitude. To name the institutions that have assisted me is more feasible—the libraries of the American School of Classical Studies at Athens, Dartmouth College, the University of Melbourne, and Stanford University, and fellowships from the American Council of Learned Societies, the American School of Classical Studies, the Australian-American Educational Foundation, and the National Endowment for the Humanities. Princeton University and its Press have sustained me in every possible way. To the named and the unnamed my warmest thanks.

Abbreviations

THE ABBREVIATIONS are those commonly used in American classical scholarship. They include:

AJAH   *American Journal of Ancient History*
AJP   *American Journal of Philology*
AntCl   *L'Antiquité Classique*
BICSL   *Bulletin of the Institute of Classical Studies of the University of London*
Classen- *Thukydides.* Elucidated by J. Classen. Edited by J. Steup. Berlin 1908-
  Steup   1922.
ClMed   *Classica et Mediaevalia*
CP   *Classical Philology*
CQ   *Classical Quarterly*
CR   *Classical Review*
Crawley   R. Crawley. *Thucydides' Peloponnesian War.* 1st ed. London 1974.
FGrHist   *Fragmente der griechischen Historiker.* Edited by F. Jacoby. Leiden
          1957—.
GRBS   *Greek Roman and Byzantine Studies*
HCT   *Historical Commentary on Thucydides.* Edited by A. W. Gomme,
          A. Andrewes, and K. J. Dover. Oxford 1945-1981.
HSCP   *Harvard Studies in Classical Philology*
IG i³   *Inscriptiones Graecae.* 3rd ed., fasc. 1. Edited by D. M. Lewis. Berlin
          1981.
LSJ   *Greek-English Lexicon.* Compiled by H. G. Liddell and Robert Scott,
          revised by H. S. Jones. 9th ed. Oxford 1940. With supplement, Oxford
          1968.
ML   R. Meiggs and D. M. Lewis. *Greek Historical Inscriptions.* Oxford
          1969.
OCT   *Oxford Classical Text*
Poppo-   E. F. Poppo. *Thukydides.* Revised by J. M. Stahl. Leipzig 1876-1885.
  Stahl
RE   *Realencyclopädie der classischen Altertumswissenschaft.* Stuttgart
          1894-1980.
REA   *Revue des Études Anciennes*

REG	*Revue des Études Grecques*
RhMus	*Rheinisches Museum*
SEG	*Supplementum Epigraphicum Graecum*
TAPA	*Transactions and Proceedings of the American Philological Association*
TGrF[2]	*Tragicorum Graecorum Fragmenta*. 2nd ed. Edited by A. Nauck. Leipzig 1888. Reprinted with a supplement by B. Snell, Hildesheim 1964.
VS	H. Diels. *Die Fragmente der Vorsokratiker*. 9th ed. Edited by W. Kranz. Berlin 1959-1960.
Warner	Rex Warner, trans. *Thucydides, The Peloponnesian War*. Hammondsworth 1954.
WS	*Wiener Studien*
YCS	*Yale Classical Studies*

THUCYDIDES

Introduction

I FIRST READ Thucydides in the 1950s—that strange decade in which we Americans enjoyed such national power and stability and yet assumed the imminence of such disaster. During the first Cold War it seemed self-evident that the world was dividing into two camps. The great anti-democratic continental powers, the Soviet Union and what was called "Mainland China," each with its "satellites" and co-ordinated plans for world conquest, seemed to be driving closer to a conflict with "the free world" whose strength derived from control of the seas and the air. That earlier struggle, the Peloponnesian War, in which democratic, naval Athens fought totalitarian, land-based Sparta provided a simple but awesome allegory for our own times. Thucydides' work revealed a precedent for our own polarized world, and might, we hoped, provide a guide through the perils of contemporary international affairs. In 1947 Secretary of State George Marshall had called attention to the significance of the Peloponnesian War for an understanding of the contemporary world: "I doubt seriously whether a man can think with full wisdom and with deep convictions regarding certain of the basic international issues today who has not at least reviewed in his mind the period of the Peloponnesian War and the Fall of Athens." And his views were widely echoed.[1]

For me, and I believe for many other students of the classics in my generation, Thucydides possessed an immediate applicability. Despite the obscurity of his style and undeniable complexity of thought, he was one of the most lucid of ancient writers. Our own historical situation provided

[1] Secretary Marshall's remarks were made in a speech at Princeton University on February 22, 1947. I am grateful to the George C. Marshall Research Foundation in Lexington Virginia for assistance in finding the quotation. In August 1952 the *Foreign Service Journal* carried an article entitled "A Message from Thucydides" by Louis J. Halle, of the policy planning staff of the Department of State. It contained the following section: "The present, in which our country finds herself, like Athens after the Persian Wars, called upon to assume the leadership of the free world brings him [Thucydides] virtually to our side. . . . It seems to me that since World War II Thucydides has come still closer to us so that he now speaks to our ear." The article is reprinted in L. J. Halle, *Civilization and Foreign Policy* (New York 1952) 261-277. These sentences are excerpted from pages 262-265.

ample confirmation of his claim to have written a possession for all time. That situation also eclipsed many of the unresolved questions and interpretive problems in Thucydidean studies. It was easy to feel that we knew what Thucydides was saying, even if the form of his expression, the origin and development of his thought, and many other issues remained to be resolved. Paradoxically, the great significance of Thucydides deflected attention elsewhere. He was a writer who spoke directly to our own condition; to enrich his account by careful study of the epigraphical and other evidence about Athens and her empire seemed to me a more pressing task for classical scholarship than further exegesis of his *Histories*.

This assessment, which appears in retrospect to have been based largely on reactions to contemporary events, was strengthened by two more academic considerations. First, what scholarship had long designated ''the Thucydidean question'' seemed, if not dead, at least moribund. The chief intellectual justification of attempts to determine the stages by which the work was composed had always been the hope of constructing an intellectual biography of the author and of recording thereby the responses of an intelligent and well-informed Athenian to the immense changes of his lifetime. Despite occasional essays by separatist critics, it was clear by the 1950s that this effort had bogged down and was unlikely ever to fulfill its promise. The most illuminating Thucydidean studies were works such as John Finley's that emphasized the fundamental unity and coherence of the work. Madame de Romilly's new approach in *Thucydides and Athenian Imperialism*[2] seemed to me much more revealing about the coherence of Thucydides' analysis of imperialism than about the stages in which the work had been composed. ''Unitarian'' criticism seemed to be carrying the day against the Separatists.

A second confirmation came from the New Criticism then so dominant in American studies of literature. These critics taught us to look at the ''work as work, rather than the processes by which a work came into being—the background, the creative process, or, on the other hand, the way in which one reads or misreads it.''[3] We believed in an immanent reading of texts, one devoid of all externals such as the author's biography and the history of his time.[4] The New Criticism told us such a reading

---

[2] J. de Romilly, *Thucydide et l'imperialisme athénien* (Paris 1947; 2nd ed. 1951; English ed., trans. P. Thody, Oxford 1963).

[3] Cleanth Brooks quoted in *The National Humanities Center Newsletter* 2 (Fall 1980) 21.

[4] Cf. T. Todorov, ''On Literary Genesis,'' *Yale French Studies* 58 (1979) 221: ''An immanent reading is an illusion. However great our good will, when we read a text we always have at our disposal information that is exterior to the text. . . . This information is absolutely indispensable to the intellection of a work.''

was possible and Unitarianism freed us from the distractions and limitations of trying to reconstruct the changes in the author's attitudes and the stages of the growth of his work.

Scholarship makes strange carrell mates. The antihistorical tendency within the New Criticism was not entirely uncongenial to some of us with strong historical interests. It liberated us from the effort to construct an intellectual biography of Thucydides, reinforced those interpretations of the text that emphasized its unity and made it possible to get on with the pressing task of synthesizing Thucydides and the other evidence for the period. We could hope to extract from Thucydides data that could be compared to and tested by the evidence from inscriptions and other sources; we could thereby determine just how "objective" he was and use him in new reconstructions of the past.

In the same way the prevalent assumptions about the text made it easy for political philosophers and political scientists to extract from the work a series of propositions about his political views on the empire, democracy, Realpolitik, and the like. If this sounded suspiciously like the construction of the prose-paraphrases that the New Critics so deplored, it was at least a convenient approach, one that made it possible to treat Thucydides as a thinker and to extract some useful messages from his work: that peace and freedom required power and preparedness; that great powers had to be tough and constantly alert, that sea powers ought, if properly directed, to have a great strategic advantage over continental powers. These and other inferences could be debated, of course, and none was explicitly stated by Thucydides, but it seemed fully appropriate to view his text as containing propositions that could be explicated and brought into a coherent system and identified as "Thucydides' Political Philosophy," or even as a series of laws about the science of politics.

Strange, and wondrous synthesis this—Thucydides simultaneously the prophet of our own age, the quarry for historical constructions, the scientist and the political philosopher! Behind it stood assumptions about the homogeneity of the text and a paradigm of how history (and even science) works. The objective and dispassionate observer, carefully gathering and presenting the facts about a phenomenon, could induce—or make it possible for others to induce—general laws. The historian was not far from the scientist, if, like Thucydides, he was willing to detach himself from personal involvement about the events he described. The result would be a cool and objective account, carefully excluding bias and emotion, and leading ultimately to truths of general applicability.

Now we all recognize this paradigm was naive and simplistic. It does not describe what scientists do, still less what historians do, nor does it account for the recurring paradox of the *Histories*: the intense emotional power of a work ostensibly so detached. Thucydidean scholarship in the 1960s and 1970s became intensely aware of this paradox. Scholars increasingly emphasized the emotional intensity of the *Histories* and the signs of the author's personal involvement in the sufferings he related. We began to confront a Thucydides who profoundly cared about the events of the war and who, it appeared, wanted his readers to share the intensity of his own reactions.[5]

But if this was the case, what became of "objectivity?" As we came to realize that "objectivity" was unattainable both in theory and in practice, we naturally wondered whether Thucydides had indeed set this as the goal of his work. The suspicion began to grow that objectivity was for Thucydides not a principle or a goal but an authorial stance, a device, a mode by which the author presented himself to the reader. It was a relationship between reader and author, not one between author and his subject matter. The initial reaction of classical scholars to this suspicion was shock and complaint: "When you can say, 'so and so gave me this account of what happened, and it seems a likely version', you are objective about your relation to history. But when, without discussing sources, you present everything as *auta ta erga* (I.21.2), the way it really happened, you are forcing the reader to look through your eyes, imposing your own assumptions and interpretations of events."[6] Other scholars were even more explicit in their displeasure. "No totalitarian meeting of voters assembled to elect a single slate of candidates has ever been more unanimous than the readers of Thucydides in assessing the issues of the Peloponnesian War."[7] Some felt cheated of the old Thucydides, the objective reporter, the scientist, the convenient source for historical facts.

We lost a great deal in the 1960s and 1970s, including many of the old certainties and assumptions about Thucydides, objectivity, and the process of writing history. The synthesis that many American classicists of my generation had relied upon in forming an approach to Thucydides now seemed dubious. Yet even more significant than the changes in our intellectual outlook were, I strongly suspect, the changes in politics and world affairs. At least that was the case for me. The wonderful smugness of our Cold War view of foreign policy disintegrated. The polarization that had

    [5] This shift in Thucydidean criticism is discussed in greater detail in "A Post Modernist Thucydides?" *Classical Journal* 72 (1977) 289-298.

    [6] A. M. Parry, "Thucydides' Historical Perspective," *YCS* 22 (1972) 48.

    [7] W. P. Wallace, "Thucydides," *Phoenix* 18 (1964) 258.

seemed so evident and so ominous in the 1950s and such a striking analogue to the world Thucydides described, no longer provided an adequate way to view a world in which Chinese and Russians had become antagonists, in which "The Third World" forced itself upon our attention, and in which the difficulties and contradictions of our own system were becoming increasingly evident. But above all it was the shattering experience of the Vietnam War that made me reconsider the *Histories*. I had long been struggling with the tensions between detachment and involvement, optimism and pessimism, morality and power in Thucydides, and had become increasingly puzzled about the way the text worked. But I can be quite precise about the moment when I began to think about Thucydides in a new way. In the middle of the Vietnamese War, when it seemed impossible to think of almost anything else, I remember reading an essay in the *New Yorker* on the destruction of Vietnam. The issue was dated March 9, 1968— the very height of the conflict. Five hundred and forty-two American soldiers had been killed in the previous week; the following day the papers reported General Westmoreland's request for 206,000 troops to be added to the existing American force of 510,000. The essay, by Jonathan Schell, began: "The following article is about what is happening to Vietnam—to the people and the land—as a result of the American military presence. I shall not discuss the moral ramifications of that presence. I shall simply try to set down what I saw and heard first hand during several weeks I spent with our armed forces in South Vietnam last summer. . . . I have no wish to pass judgment on the individual Americans fighting in Vietnam. I wish merely to record what I witnessed."[8] As I read on in the article I was repeatedly reminded of Thucydides[9] and his descriptions that avoided moral rhetoric and made the audience visualize what was happening. Impressed by Schell's account, reminded of Thucydides' powerful and compassionate treatment of the suffering of the war, for example at Mycalessus (7.29-30), I was drawn back to some remarks by Friedrich Meinecke, written in 1928, which I had read before but never fully assimilated:

The historian selects his material . . . as something having more or less of value and in this he is evaluating it. The presentation and exposition of culturally im-

---

[8] J. Schell, "Quang Ngai and Quang Tin," *The New Yorker* (March 9, 1968) 37. The article was later expanded into a book, *The Military Half: an Account of Destruction in Quang Ngai and Quang Tin* (New York 1968).

[9] In the passage above, for example, note the similarity to some features of the beginning of the *Histories*: the emphasis on the national identity of the author: "*our* armed forces":: Thoukydides *Athenaios*; the modesty of the verb of reporting: "merely to record":: ξυνέγραψε and the avoidance of any moral judgment.

portant facts is utterly impossible without a lively sensitivity to the values they reveal. Although the historian may, in form, abstain from value judgments of his own, they are there between the lines, and act as such upon the reader. The effect, then, as in Ranke, for example, is often more profound and moving than if the evaluation were to appear directly in the guise of moralizing, and therefore it is even to be recommended as an artifice. The historian's implicit value judgment arouses the reader's own evaluating activity more strongly than one which is explicit.[10]

Meinecke seemed in many respects to be describing the kind of history Thucydides had written and to be pointing out that objectivity is an impossible goal for the historian but a legitimate means by which the reader can be helped to an understanding of the events narrated.

As I tried to test this new approach to Thucydides, I was no longer troubled by the feeling that there was something wrong in using objectivity as an authorial stance rather than as a principle or goal. It now became possible to give passages their full emotional force and to recognize the role of suffering in the work. I could read Thucydides with an understanding and a fullness of response that hitherto had seemed impossible. But at the same time many old questions about the work were re-opened. Two examples will suffice: first, the relationship between power and morality. During the Cold War it had been easy to read Thucydides as the recorder, perhaps even the advocate, of a law of the stronger. Great Powers naturally imposed their wills; lesser powers accommodated or were crushed. Now, as I began to look at the detachment and irony in the text in a new way, what was I to make of its emphasis on the inexorable operations of power? Various answers to this question were proposed in the scholarship of the 1960s and 1970s. Some represented Thucydides as the spokesman for a very traditional, almost archaic, morality. Others, following Geoffrey de Ste. Croix in his *Origins of the Peloponnesian War*, drew a distinction between the treatment of personal and domestic affairs, in which Thucydides implicitly advocated a conventional morality, and the treatment of foreign affairs, in which he recognized totally amoral processes. This seemed to me to account for the intensity of the account of the Corcyrean revolution but not for the tone of episodes such as the punishments of Plataea and Mytilene. But there was always the nagging fear that misled by the spirit of the times I was imposing my own views and preferences upon Thucydides. The words of Ben Perry troubled me: "There can be no real appreciation of Thucydides and his type of mind, if, owing to your

[10] The quotation is from his essay "Values and Causalities in History," trans. J. H. Franklin in *Varieties of History*, 2nd ed., ed. F. Stern (New York 1970) 272.

cordial disapproval of imperial ruthlessness, you fail to see that in the Melian Dialogue, for instance, the folly of the Melians rather than the cruelty of the Athenians is the chief subject of contemplation. Thucydides has the strange faculty of seeing and telling the plain truth of a matter without trying in any way to bring it into line with the cherished beliefs of men. For that reason he has often escaped comprehension."[11] In a period in which classical scholars were increasingly recognizing the distance between their own civilization and that of the Greeks, the accusation of anachronistic and sentimental misinterpretation was intimidating. Was the moral and emotional intensity that so many readers, ancient and modern, have found in the *Histories* simply "the product of the moral sensitivity of his readers?"[12] An honest answer to this question seemed to me to require a careful examination of the ways in which the work involved its readers and elicited their reactions to the events depicted. It drove me to look more critically at the role of the reader in the text.

A second set of questions, equally if less obviously connected with the climate of the time, concerned the role of reason, its ability to predict and shape the future, and the relative optimism or pessimism of the work. Linked to this were numerous other issues, the function of historical writing, the extent to which Thucydides believed in the recurrence of events or cycles of history, his claim about the utility of his work. The 1960s saw many challenges to the view that Thucydides was essentially a rationalist who felt that by careful observation one could determine laws of history that, in turn, would make possible predictions and perhaps even some control of the future. The most powerful critique was the pessimistic work by Hans-Peter Stahl, *Thukydides: Die Stellung des Menschen im geschichtlichen Prozess* (Munich 1966), a monograph that has earned a central place among the most important recent discussions of Thucydides.[13]

Behind questions such as these stand even more fundamental issues about the nature of the text and the relationship between the work and its readers. Indeed any serious attempt to resolve the problems that currently

[11] B. E. Perry, "The Early Greek Capacity for Viewing Things Separately," *TAPA* 68 (1937) 427.

[12] G. Kennedy, *The Art of Persuasion in Greece* (Princeton 1963) 50. Kennedy's comment is directed to those who claim to detect in the text a "dogmatic morality," for which, to be sure, there is no evidence.

[13] Stahl's views contrast most sharply with those of Jacqueline de Romilly, see especially "L'utilité de l'histoire selon Thucydide," in *Histoire et Historiens dans l'antiquité*, vol. 4 of *Entretiens Hardt* (Geneva 1958) 39-81, and "L'optimisme de Thucydide," *Revue des études grecques* 78 (1965) 557-575. See also K. von Fritz, *Griechische Geschichtsschreibung* (Berlin 1967) I b 247-250.

beset Thucydidean studies requires an explicit analysis of how the text
works and what responses it elicits. The old questions about Thucydides,
eclipsed to some extent in an earlier period, have come forth again, and,
joined by new and even more insistent ones, demand renewed attention.[14]

An adequate response requires more than a new airing of old scholarly
debates and must not be confounded with the efforts to determine the stages
in which the work was composed. Yet an inquiry into the nature of the
text inevitably shows some resemblances to older movements in scholarship
and has much to learn from them. Unitarian critics have inculcated a respect
for the text as it is, rather than as it might have been at some earlier stage
in the author's career. Separatist critics also have their contribution to
make, for they were often remarkably alert to the work's tensions, contrasts, and changes of viewpoint. They have been much less likely than
Unitarian critics to smooth over the difficult shifts in tone or divergences
in assessment. For the Unitarian there was a single Thucydidean view of
each major figure, topic, and undertaking; we had only to be clever enough,
or vague enough, to recognize and articulate it. All was homogenized.
Separatism, on the other hand, could admit discrepancies, even if it had
a ready-made explanation for every problem—the assumption that all tensions within the work were the result of different periods of composition
(and of a remarkable forgetfulness about what had been written in earlier
drafts).[15] Separatist criticism, moreover, has recognized that whatever the
stages of composition, the work is likely to have taken its present form
amid the disputes and recriminations that followed the Athenian defeat.[16]

---

[14] Historians too have felt they must first be clear about the nature of the text and the ways
in which it is to be approached; cf. G.E.M. de Ste. Croix, *Origins of the Peloponnesian
War* (London 1972) 5.

[15] The strengths and weaknesses of separatist criticism are especially evident in the monograph by Wolfgang Schadewaldt, *Die Geschichtschreibung des Thukydides* (Berlin 1929),
that demonstrates a tension in the work between a strict concentration on exactitude and on
precision in the treatment of event (*Richtigkeit*) and a much broader treatment of the nature
of the war and of historical method (*Wahrheit*). Schadewaldt's attempt to account for this
tension by a hypothesis about the stages of composition is subject to serious objections, as
E. Kapp showed in his review *Gnomon* 6 (1930) 76-100. Schadewaldt's monograph is a
good example both of the perspicacity of the Separatist school at its best, and of the inadequacy
of chronological hypotheses to account for the tensions within the text.

[16] Eduard Schwartz, *Das Geschichtswerk des Thukydides*, 2nd ed. (Bonn 1929) 239-242,
emphasized that Thucydides was reacting to criticism of Pericles (cf. Plato *Gorgias* 515 e);
other Separatists have also tended to concentrate on the question of political leadership. Other
issues, however, may have been more pressing, above all the debates about the advisability
of renewed attempts at empire and, at a more philosophical level, about the relationship
between power and morality. Xenophon *Hellenica* 3.5.2 and 10; Andocides 3 (*On the Peace*)
24f.; *Oxyrhynchus Hellenica* VI 1-3 (V. Bartoletti [Leipzig 1959] 6f.); Isocrates *Panegyricus*
182; Aristotle *Politics* VII 1324 a 36-b 33.

Critics of this school remind us how controversial and radical was Thucydides' treatment of the war and how willing he was to challenge widely held attitudes, including those most cherished by his own social class. They help us recognize that this is revisionist history, albeit of an exceptionally powerful variety.

Whatever the merits of Separatist and Unitarian criticism and indeed of the old "Thuycydidean question" itself, it has become clear that Thucydides' work is not static or homogeneous, either in thought or style. It exploits the potential of the written medium for variation and differentiation. Throughout it are to be found startling juxtapositions, contrasts, abrupt transitions, shattered parallelisms. Stylistically the text varies from crabbed analytical passages, to straightforward, almost formulaic, narrative, to scattered conversational or dialogue portions, to the speeches that, as Macaulay put it, "give to the whole book something of the grotesque character of those Chinese pleasure-grounds in which perpendicular rocks of granite start up in the midst of a soft green plain."[17] The thought and attitudes of the work show similar changes and contrasts. The comments on individuals and forms of government have perennially provoked disagreement among scholars who attempted to formulate clear statements of his views. Different passages suggested different attitudes toward, for example, the reason for the failure of the Sicilian expedition or toward Alcibiades or Brasidas. No one expects total consistency in a work as complex, and written over as long a time, as the *Histories*.[18] But any discussion of the nature of the text has to recognize and account for its complexity and diversity. These have usually been seen as the results of the personality of the author and the subtlety of his mind. The explanation is plausible, for the style and thought of the work show a strong individuality. Whatever our critical principles, we are soon tempted to talk about the author, and his personality, rather than about the work and its complexities. We read the *Histories* but we feel we have met Thucydides. Our journey through the text, alone, isolated, constantly struggling with the difficulties, overpowered by the intensity of the sufferings, changes us.

[17] T. B. Macaulay's essay, "History," originally in the *Edinburgh Review* for 1828, reprinted in F. Stern, ed., *Varieties of History* 77.

[18] We know that Thucydides began his work as soon as the war broke out (1.1.1) and that he lived to see the end of the conflict (5.26.5). Hence he was at work on it for at least twenty-seven years, perhaps a good deal longer. What we know of Thucydides' life is conveniently summarized in J. Finley's *Thucydides* (Cambridge, Mass. 1942) chap. 1, "Life and Political Background," 1-35, and in many of the other standard works on him. My own views are contained in an essay in T. J. Luce, ed. *Ancient Writers: Greece and Rome*, vol. 1 (New York 1982) 267-289.

We come to feel ourselves in the presence of an intensely powerful individuality. Surely then this personality provides the explanation for the tensions and complexities of the work.

Yet, on closer examination, this truism fades into irrelevance. We know, after all, not the author, but the text. We can infer that the text was written by a complex and intense individual, but one who tells us very little about himself.[19]

If we wish to speak more systematically about the complexity of the work, we are forced to concentrate not on the author but on the work itself and on the responses it evokes from its readership. Easier said than done! In studying a twentieth-century work we can obtain almost unlimited information about the audience and its reactions. We know, or can hope to find out, facts about literacy, pattern of readership, attitudes, and expectations. We may be able to pry out figures about sales and circulation. If so minded, we can devise elaborate surveys or in-depth interviews and exploit the techniques of the social sciences to gauge "reader response." In the study of ancient literature nothing comparable is possible. What external evidence do we have about the readership of the *Histories*? Precisely when and how did the work become available? What did it cost? Was it presented through public recitations or was it always approached through individual reading? Who could read in that society? What were the attitudes, values, and assumptions of that readership? If the work was not for a purely Athenian audience, who else read it? Were there Spartan readers? Corinthian? Syracusan? Mytilenean? Almost none of these questions can adequately be answered and although the study of the audience of ancient literature is one of the most pressing items in the agenda of classical studies, it is unlikely that clear-cut answers will soon be obtained, at least for the period in which Thycydides was at work.[20]

But what external information cannot supply, the work itself may provide, perhaps in even more useful form. Henry James' much cited maxim that "the author makes his readers" reminds us that the text itself may provide the most essential clues to the nature of the audience and its

---

[19] The ancient biographical tradition provides more information, not all of it reliable. On the nature and limits of this material see U. von Wilamowitz, "Die Thukydides-Legende," *Hermes* 12 (1877) 326-367.

[20] The readership of the *Histories* is discussed by W.R.M. Lamb, *Clio Enthroned* (Cambridge 1914) and R. T. Ridley, "Exegesis and Audience in Thucydides," *Hermes* 109 (1981) 25-46. For an interesting investigation of the readership of Herodotus' work see S. Flory, "Who Read Herodotus' Histories?" *AJP* 101 (1980) 12-28. A more general discussion of the audience of classical literature is forthcoming in the *Cambridge History of Greek Literature*.

reactions. For what we need to know is not the sociology of the readership of the *Histories* through the centuries, but the ways by which the text elicits responses and shapes its audience. Approaching the problem in this way we can speak at least in general terms about the audience envisioned by the *Histories*. Although the opening chapters, as we shall see, are especially revealing, the work throughout evokes a fiercely intellectual readership, one that is intolerant of cliché and of all that is maudlin or old-fashioned. Its readers, then and now, must be exceptionally willing to struggle with a difficult style, to dispense with the story-telling element, divine interventions and diverting excursuses, to contemplate a radical reinterpretation of the past, to rethink old certainties. They are expected to be tough-minded and unsentimental in their approach to questions of conduct and value. If we cannot be sure of the exact geographical distribution and economic status of this audience, we can at least recognize that the work avoids addressing a mass readership or one that is restricted to the viewpoint of a single city.[21] It leaves as little room for chauvinism as for sentimentality. Both in antiquity and today the readership of the *Histories* has been cosmopolitan, sophisticated, well-educated, and affluent. We can call this text "elitist" in a much stricter sense than we can apply that term to the Homeric poems, Greek tragedy, or indeed to almost any archaic or classical Greek poetry. Nevertheless, all these features are shared in varying degrees with other contemporary writings, especially those associated with the Sophistic movement. Classical scholarship has gradually pieced together a relatively clear picture of the intellectual setting of the *Histories*. The society at large shows signs of impatience with the clichés of political oratory and the self-justifications of the belligerents.[22]

[21] Thucydides emphasizes his Athenian citizenship and chooses Attic rather than Ionic as the dialect. But he explains details (e.g., 2.34; 6.27) that would not need to be mentioned if his intended audience were exclusively Athenian.

[22] The tough-minded and unsentimental tone of diplomacy and foreign policy is to some extent characteristic of Athens in the 430s and 420s and is surely not entirely a Thucydidean fabrication. The stimulating article by H. Strasburger, "Thukydides und die politische Selbst-darstellung der Athener," *Hermes* 86 (1958) 17-46, is insufficiently critical of the fourth-century evidence and underestimates, I believe, the distinctive tone of Greek political life in the time of the Peloponnesian War. Cf. J. R. Grant, "A Note on the Tone of Greek Diplomacy," *CQ* n.s. 15 (1965) 261-266. John Finley's study of the relationship between Euripides and Thucydides, *CP* 49 (1938) 23-68, reprinted in *Three Essays on Thucydides* (Cambridge, Mass. 1967) 1-53, shows how well Thucydides has caught some of the distinctive features of this period. On the other hand, Thucydides' technique is to present these features in high relief and to cut away some of the self-justifying rhetoric of speakers in the Athenian assembly and elsewhere. Distortion is especially likely in his representation of the Athenian motives in the early days of the Delian League and in his omission of its use of the appeal that this alliance would help liberate the Greeks who remained under Persian control. See

We also know of the reassessment of traditional morality that was taking place in Thucydides' day. Some thinkers insisted on the arbitrariness of the conventional restraints on behavior (*nomoi*) and on the importance of the drives and demands of human nature (*physis*) that inevitably would, and perhaps even should, override these restraints. In many quarters the natural right of the stronger to dominate the weaker was vigorously maintained and self-interest asserted as the true guide to conduct. Although these challenges to tradition are most evident in the Sophistic movement, they are surely not restricted to these itinerant teachers and their pupils.[23] The effect of the rethinking of tradition was not always philosophic consistency or logical rigor, but a mood and a disposition in certain quarters—a tendency to view self-interest without alarm, to regard the pursuit of justice as a "noble simplicity" or the respect for oaths as a sign of unmanliness.[24]

Both Thucydides and his audience clearly were influenced by the Sophistic movement, Hippocratic medicine, and the other developments of the time that we group together, somewhat misleadingly, as the Greek Enlightenment. He and his audience have much in common. But just as it is a mistake to confuse the text with the personality of the author, it is dangerous to confuse the writer with his audience, or to identify the attitudes or expectations of the one with those of the other. From time to time we detect signs of a serious tension between them. In the account of the Corcyrean Revolution, for example, Thucydides describes a process of moral disintegration that afflicted Corcyra in the early 420s and was later to disturb virtually all the Greek world. The emphasis on morality, the clarity with which the pernicious effect of unconstrained self-interest are revealed may surprise us when we first encounter this intensely written passage. But even more striking is its abandonment of the pose of sophistication and its devaluation of the claims of intellectuality:

Thus every form of base disposition imposed itself through these *Staseis* on the Hellenic world. And simplicity, of which nobility in no small measure consists,

---

1.96.1 and the illuminating exegesis by H. R. Rawlings, "Thucydides on the Delian League," *Phoenix* 31 (1977) 1-8. Surely this appeal was used in the 470s. Thucydides dismisses it, I believe, because it was so familiar and would seem hackneyed to his audience. Athenians of the time seem to have expected constant innovation. (Cf. Gorgias *VS* 82 B 11 § 5; Plato *Gorgias* 490e 10f.; Xenophon *Memorabilia* 4.4.6; Isocrates *Panegyricus* 8.) See also 2.36.4.

[23] For a lucid introduction to these tendencies see W.K.C. Guthrie's section on the Sophists in his *History of Greek Philosophy*, vol. 3 (Cambridge 1962) 55-134, separately printed as a paperback under the title *The Sophists* (Cambridge 1971).

[24] On justice as "noble simplicity" see Thrasymachus in Plato *Republic* I 348 c; on oaths Meno in Xenophon *Anabasis* 2.6.25.

was laughed off stage and in the absence of mutual trust man's intelligence served to spread conflict far and wide. For discourse lacked the strength and oath the fear to reconcile. All alike when they got the upper hand paid more attention through their contemplation of the impossibility of security to avoiding being attacked than to the exercise of trust. Those who made fewer claims about their intellect for the most part prevailed. For by distrusting their own insufficiency and the cleverness of their opponents, that is by fearing that they would get the worst of discussions and be taken unprepared by the cleverness of other's intellects, they moved boldly to action. But those who held in contempt any plotting which they detected and thought it unnecessary to put into action what they had thought out were less on their guard and more readily destroyed. (3.83)

The tension in passages such as this points to something very important about the text. Thucydides' history is unquestionably aimed at an audience that values cleverness, sophistication, intellect, and self-interest, but it does not simply affirm and reinforce those values. Rather it is prepared, at least from time to time, to exploit uncertainties or inconsistencies in the attitudes of its readers, explore the ambiguities and limits of values, and challenge, perhaps even subvert, expectations and apparent certainties.[25] Ultimately, I believe, the work leads the sympathetic reader—ancient or modern—far beyond the views and values it seems initially to utilize and affirm.

That assessment is, of course, the response of one reader in a society far removed from Thucydides' own world, the reaction of someone whose values are in some respects idiosyncratic and in other respects shaped by the political, intellectual, and social circumstances of the late twentieth century. But I have tried to discipline and test my reactions as rigorously as possible, above all by an investigation of the work's rhetorical strategy and literary technique.

The strategy, as we shall see, is complex, cautious, and implicit, as we might expect if my hypothesis about the progressions of thought and feeling in the work is correct. An occasional outburst such as we have seen in the

---

[25] Cf. W. Iser, *The Implied Reader* (Baltimore 1974) 58 (a translation of *Der Implizite Leser: Kommunikationsformen des Romans von Bunyan bis Beckett* [Munich 1982]):

The critic must also take into consideration the reader's expectations. Through his past experiences, the educated reader expects specific things from prose and poetry; but many works of art play about with those expectations formed by particular periods of literature in past. The expectations can be shattered, altered, surpassed, or deceived, so that the reader is confronted with something unexpected which necessitates a readjustment. If this does happen, the reader gains what Henry James called an "enlargement of experience". However, texts do not necessarily have to be based on expectations formed by the literature of the past. They can themselves awaken false expectations, alternately bringing about surprise and frustration, and this in turn gives rise to an esthetic experience consisting of a continuous interplay between 'deductive' and 'inductive' operations which the reader must carry out for himself. In this way, the experience communicated through the work of art becomes real to the reader.

account of Corcyrean Revolution might be powerful and effective but could not often be repeated. A modest statement of the author's own views, an explicitly argued reinterpretation of the war, or a direct assault on widely held attitudes would at the best be met by respectful expressions of interest, but to convince and to move an audience required a more thorough utilization of the techniques of persuasion. Explicit statements were unlikely to be effective; instead readers had to be led to reexperience the war, to live through it again, seeing it fully, without averting their eyes from the most unpleasant or revealing episodes. An implicit strategy might work when one that depended on explicit affirmations or direct statements might prove inert.

The techniques necessary to implement such a strategy had to a large extent already been developed by ancient orators and rhetoricians and by Thucydides' own great predecessor, Herodotus. They are the familiar ones of author-based criticism—selection of episode and detail, choice of word and phrase, careful determinations of when to draw close to events and characters and depict them with fullness and vividness, and when to draw away and leave them vague or impressionistic. Selection, shaping, shading—all have their place in a proper assessment of Thucydides' work.

The ancient orators, moreover, knew and perfected these techniques. But they applied them to very specific objectives on very defined occasions: voting on a bill at an assembly meeting, the acquittal of a defendant at his trial, the adornment of a festival or ceremonial occasion. The occasion for Thucydides' work is not momentary or specific but recurrent in an undefined future (1.22.4); the subject is a twenty-seven-year war, and the audience not limited to one city or to one time, nor even, as it turns out, to one culture. Nor is his goal a vote, a verdict, a nod of approval or a burst of applause, but something much closer to Henry James' "enlargement of experience." The work thus demands something more than is to be found in ancient oratory or rhetoric.

That "something more" is, I believe, a much greater involvement of the reader in the text. The clearest contrast with ancient oratory is that in the *Histories* we only rarely find a single or explicit evaluation of events, while speeches normally specify and hope to achieve one and only one response. On this basis earlier critics concluded that Thucydides was detached and "objective" and determined to write about the past as it really was, *wie es eigentlich gewesen*, without prejudice or even judgments. A closer examination shows something rather different. If, for example, we study the account in the third book of the Athenian decision to spare Mytilene (3.36-50), the absence of explicit evaluation will not be confused with the avoidance of judgment or feeling. Thucydides does not in his own voice deplore the original Athenian decision to execute the citizenry. But he reports in great detail the reconsideration of the original decision when, on the following day, the Athenians came to feel that their resolution had been "savage and excessive." He then adds:

Immediately another trireme went off, with eagerness, to avoid finding the city destroyed if the previous trireme got there first. It had a lead of approximately a day and a night. The ambassadors of the Mytileneans supplied wine and barley for the crew and promised great rewards if it could beat the other one. And so there was great eagerness of this voyage, so much so that they ate as they rowed, barley mixed with wine and oil. Some took turns sleeping while others rowed. By luck no wind opposed them. The former ship did not sail with eagerness on an errand that might provoke retribution, while this one hastened on in the fashion described. The first trireme had arrived and Paches had time to read the decree and was about to do what had been resolved, when the second ship draws upon the shore, and prevented the destruction. That was the margin of Mitylene's escape from danger. (3.49.2-4)

The race of the two triremes is told with such vividness and involvement and the attitudes of the participants themselves provide such a clear assessment of the situation that the evaluation is inescapable. Here again "objectivity," or the avoidance of explicit judgments, is a technique rather than a goal. But now we can also see that part of the technique is to draw the reader in, to awaken our critical and evaluative faculties, and to make the energy of our own response contribute to the power of the text.

This technique separates Thucydides' work from much of ancient oratory and reminds us of its affinities with the modern novel. One might well adapt to him, for example, Virginia Woolf's description of Jane Austen as "a mistress of much deeper emotion than appears upon the surface. She stimulates us to supply what is not there."[26]

The involvement of the reader in the work is an essential part of its

---

[26] The comment is quoted by Wolgang Iser in an essay called "The Reading Process" in R. Cohen, ed., *New Directions in Literary History* (Baltimore 1974) 126. This essay and Iser's *The Implied Reader* have been very helpful to me in trying to formulate an approach to this aspect of the text, but the essential point had already been made in antiquity by Theophrastus as quoted in Demetrius' treatise *On Style* sec. 222: "These, then, are the main essentials of persuasiveness; to which may be added that indicated by Theophrastus when he says that all possible points should not be punctiliously and tediously elaborated, but some should be left to the comprehension and inference of the hearer, who when he perceives what you have omitted becomes not only your hearer but your witness, and a very friendly witness too. For he thinks himself intelligent because you have afforded him the means of showing his intelligence. It seems like a slur on your hearer to tell him everything as though he were a simpleton" (trans. W. R. Roberts [Cambridge 1902]).

strategy and makes possible an alliance between the author and the reader.
The reader becomes the voluntary participant in the creation of the work,
its co-shaper and fellow craftsman. The tension between the attitude of
the author and those of the audience thus never need turn to confrontation.
Rather by witnessing and assessing the events and characters described by
the author the readers are led to tune their own reactions to those of the
text, and eventually to assimilate their attitudes to those of the author.

This is not to imply that Thucydides' own views were monolithic,
unchanging, or entirely worked out. He himself may have been going
through a similar process—as we all do—of testing his own attitudes and
assumptions against the specifics of experience. But if the involvement of
the reader in the text is as important as we have come to suspect, then it
will repay us to look at the *Histories* very closely to determine Thucydides'
expectations about his reader and the methods by which he shapes and
guides his readers' responses. Although many of the techniques needed in
such an inquiry are the familiar ones of literary study, though directed in
a new way, in one respect a slightly unusual approach is required. If we
suspect a progression in the reader's attitudes, then we should be prepared
to consider the text itself as a progression, that is the first part of the work
may reflect attitudes, assumptions, and ideas that are eventually modified,
restated, subverted or totally contraverted. The text need not be homogeneous to be systematic. The tensions, apparent inconsistencies, and
variations may be part of a progression of thought and feeling. For another
author or another period it might not be necessary even to mention this
possibility. Such progressions are, after all, common in other forms of
literature, especially in imaginative narrative. But Thucydidean scholarship, both Separatist and Unitarian, has regularly proceeded on the assumption that the same attitudes are to be expected throughout. Thucydidean thought is presumed to be constant and unchanging as if by some
classical corollary to the rabbinical principle that "There is no before and
after in Scripture."[27] When discrepancies, or divergences in attitude appear, they have either been denied, interpreted away, or treated as instances
of different stages of the composition of the work. But the basic assumption
must be called into question—and the Thucydidean scholar has to ask if
there are progressions of thought and attitude in the work, and if so, how
they affect the reader.

The following pages try to test such an approach to Thucydides by the
only method that seems to me to be feasible—by looking at the work

---

[27] E. Earle Ellis, *The Gospel of Luke*, Century Bible (London 1966) 7.

sequentially from book 1 to the abrupt break at the end of book 8.[28] My effort has been to recognize tensions and divergences within the *Histories* and yet to treat the Separatist hypothesis as the last refuge of the philologist. Although I have tried to stay close to the text, what follows is not detailed enough to be an explication, nor comprehensive enough to be a "reading," if by reading we mean "relating each element of the text to all the others."[29] My intention has been a modest one—to lead readers through the text as we have received it and prepare the way for their own readings and interpretations. This approach has precedent and sanction in that most sapient advice the King gives to the White Rabbit in the twelfth chapter of *Alice in Wonderland*:

"Read them," said the King.

The White Rabbit put on his spectacles. "Where shall I begin, please your majesty?" he asked.

"Begin at the beginning," the King said, gravely, "and go on until you come to the end: then stop."

[28] My chapter divisions correspond to the book divisions in our manuscripts and printed editions. The arrangement of the work into eight books, however, was not Thucydides' own nor was it universally adopted in antiquity. See W. Schmid, *Geschichte der griechischen Literatur* I, vol. 5 (Munich 1948) 19. In at least one case, the ending of book 5, the division interrupts an important progression within the work.

[29] T. Todorov, *The Poetics of Prose*, trans. R. Howard (Ithaca 1972) 237.

Book 1

THE ARCHAEOLOGY

Hume, echoed by Kant, said the first page of Thucydides was the commencement of real history.[1] But it is a puzzling and difficult beginning—an idiosyncratic introduction to as complex an argument as is to be found anywhere in the eight books of the work or indeed in all the pages of ancient historical writing. After a brief statement of the anticipated greatness of the subject matter, the grand and potentially moving theme of the nature of the Peloponnesian War is abandoned for a digression arguing that early Greek history was all on a small scale. This section, commonly called the "Archaeology," demands a reader of exceptional patience and determination. The ancient critics sometimes deplored its difficult style and peculiar arrangement, explaining how Thucydides should have written the introduction to his work.[2] Modern scholars have been troubled by the difficult language and complexity of arrangement; the greatest of them, Wilamowitz, admitted that "in spite of its deliberate structure" the first book remained to him "a chaos."[3]

The opening repudiates many principles of ancient rhetorical composition. It does nothing to ease the reader into the subject matter or the approach. It abjures blandishments, ingratiations, or promises, except the bald statement that Thucydides, even at the beginning of the war, expected that it would be "great and most worth relating of all previous events." But the nature of this greatness is not specified for many chapters. Initially, there is only the assertion that this was the greatest *kinēsis*, movement or

---

[1] David Hume, "On the Populousness of Ancient Nations" in *Essays: Moral, Politics and Literary* (London 1963) 419. Kant's essay, "Zu allgemeiner Geschichte in weltbürgerlicher Absicht," is cited by E. Täubler, *Die Archäologie des Thukydides* (Leipzig 1927) 119.

[2] See Dionysius of Halicarnassus in *On Thucydides* (Berkeley 1975) ch. 20 and the useful commentary by W. K. Pritchett, esp. 71-73.

[3] U. v. Wilamowitz-Moellendorff, "Thukydides VIII," *Hermes* 43 (1908) 580.

dislocation, for the Greeks or even for most of mankind.[4] The assertion seems excessive: What of the dislocations that followed the Trojan War or the immense movements and destruction of the second Persian invasion? Almost immediately we lose sight of the Peloponnesian War and its effects, "the moral as well as the material loss—the fabric of society nearly broken, both intellect and virtue weakened or abused."[5] Instead the focus turns to a negative point—that the events of early Greek history were never of large scale. Nor are the arguments in support of this position always compelling.[6] The lovers of Herodotus are understandably outraged: "Thucydides magnifies his own subject at the expense of the wars of Hellene and Barbarian, ludicrously missing the oecumenical significance and wantonly compressing the duration and magnitude of the Herodotean theme."[7]

Instead of a rhetorical magnification of the theme of the work we encounter at the outset a polemical essay on the nature of early Greek history, instead of the beginning of the narrative about Thucydides' own time, a revisionist argument about the remote past. The opening sentences set the work apart from the amiable discursiveness of Herodotus and, no doubt,

---

[4] 1.1.2. *Kinēsis* is an unusual word at this point in the development of Greek, clear enough in general meaning but obscure and surprising in this context. It has a neutral, perhaps even technical or scientific tone, as do many of the *-sis* coinages of the late fifth century, cf. H. R. Rawlings, *A Semantic Study of Prophasis to 400 B.C.* (Wiesbaden 1974) 39f., and R. Browning, Greek Abstract Nouns in -sis -tis," *Philologus* 102 (1958) 60-74. Hence it invites speculation both about its precise denotation and about the author's attitude. On its use in the early atomists see L. Edmunds, *Phoenix* 26 (1972) 342-357. "The Arrangement of the Thought in the Proem and in Other Parts of Thucydides I," N.G.L. Hammond, *CQ* n.s. 2 (1952) 130 and 133, n. 1, argued the term *kinēsis* applied not to the war itself but to the emergence of two hostile coalitions in the period before the war, i.e. he relates it to the last part of the preceding sentence rather than to the sentence as a whole. This is based on what I believe to be a mistaken notion of how Thucydidean ring compositions work.

[5] A. W. Gomme, "The Greatest War," in *Essays in Greek History and Literature* (Oxford 1937) 121. Gomme refers to the First World War as an analogy to the Peloponnesian War.

[6] The Trojan War is dismissed by an argument based on the likelihood that the attacking forces had inadequate logistics (ch. 11) and by a calculation derived from the figures in Homer's Catalogue of the Ships (*Iliad* II). Thucydides assumes that Homer mentions the largest and smallest crew sizes (120 and 50) in this catalogue and accepts, provisionally, the Homeric total figure of 1,200 Greek ships against Troy. Taking the mean (85) between the largest and smallest crew sizes (and assuming there were no other warriors aboard) Thucydides concludes that "not many seem to have gone on this expedition considering that they went from all Greece in common" (1.10.5). Thucydides never completes the multiplication of 85 by 1,200. But the total, 102,000 is by Greek standards "a very large number for an overseas expedition . . . and much larger than any that sailed in the Peloponnesian War." (Gomme in *HCT* on 1.10.5 [p. 114]). The Persian expedition is treated no less cavalierly, dismissed as something swiftly completed in a pair of naval and a pair of land battles (23.1), none of which is even named. So much for Salamis and Artemisium, Thermopylae and Plataea!

[7] R. Macan, *Herodotus IV-VI*, vol. 2 (London 1895) 186.

from the inflated rhetorical history of the funeral orations and the display pieces at the Olympic and other festivals. This work, we soon recognize, belongs instead with other examples of a new approach to the past detectable among the fragmentary remains of the prose literature of the late fifth century B.C. The label "Archaeology" widely used in modern discussions of the opening section of the work reflects, albeit obscurely, this connection. Although open to the false inference that Thucydides was trying to unearth whatever information he could about the ill-documented early history of Greece, the term connected this portion of Thucydides' work with other late fifth-century reconstructions of the remote past.[8] The opening chapters are not an attempt at a comprehensive description of early Greece. Thucydides has much more to tell about early Greece than he reports here, as a glance at the beginning of the sixth book shows. He knows—or claims to know—a great deal about the history of Greek colonization, and elsewhere displays detailed knowledge of episodes in the early history of both Athens and Sparta. But in the Archaeology he has constructed an argument, an essay of revisionist history that presents a fresh view of how Greece had once appeared.

Hesiod's idea of a Golden Age is representative of the radically different view of the past held by earlier Greek thinkers. In his view there had once been a happy stage of easy rapport between men and gods and even after that time, ages of heroic accomplishment, blessed in comparison to "contemporary" travail and misery. The myths and legends about early Attica suggested a view similar to that in Hesiod. They reported times full of violence and dissension but set apart by a hero, Theseus, who unified and integrated the state, secured freedom from the domination of King Minos of Crete and established Athens' ancestral ways.[9] Such myths reflect a traditional way of viewing the past and a sense that improvements in man's situation can come only by divine intervention or by recapturing the lost glory of earlier days.

This view persisted through the fifth century and even later, at least in

---

[8] See E. Norden, *Agnostos Theos* (Leipzig 1913) 370ff., and T. Cole, *Democritus and the Sources of Greek Anthropology* (Chapel Hill 1967) 5. In addition to the famous speech of Protagoras in Plato's dialogue of that name (320c-323a), see Plato *Hippias Maior* 285 d (also in *VS* 86 A 11), and the Hippocratic treatise *Ancient Medicine* 3; compare also Diodorus 4.1; 2.46, and the texts cited in W.K.C. Guthrie, *The Sophists* (Cambridge 1971) 79-83.

[9] A chapter of *Quest for Theseus*, ed. A. Ward (London 1970) 143-174 discusses the Greek view of time and of the past as reflected in the Theseus myth and suggests that the myth was steadily adapted for political purposes by the successive leaders of Athens during the sixth and early fifth centuries. See also J. Boardman, "Herakles, Peisistratos and Sons," *Revue Archéologique* (1972) 57-72. For a recent survey of the evidence see M. W. Taylor, *The Tyrant Slayers* (New York 1981) ch. 4.

some quarters. It appealed to various audiences and took various forms, including highly moralizing versions. For the epideictic orator, the patriotic poet, the painter at work on public monuments, history was often the stage for the recurring struggle between bravery and cowardice, greed and restraint, right and wrong. History was the projection of moral qualities and conflicts.

But during the fifth century many thinkers began to repudiate such views of the past. When they imagined the early stages of human life, they found them anything but "golden." Life had been harsh, squalid, brutish, and short. Only gradually, by the accumulation of knowledge and by discoveries and inventions had mankind escaped vulnerability to the wild beasts and the elements. This radically new view of the past can be detected in myth and poetry but often appeared in the prose essays and speeches that can be grouped together as *archaiologiai*. Thucydides' "Archaeology" concerns a later stage of human development than many of these accounts, for it deals not with man's first emergence from savagery, but with the history of Greece and the development of common actions among the Greeks and of a concept of "Greekness." But its view of the past is similar to that of the other archaeologies we know. It is polemical, and quite unsentimental. It has no place for Golden Ages or great heroes. Highly impersonal, it concentrates not on individual qualities or exploits, but on the gradual escape from instability and the accumulation of power in the Greek world.

In the second chapter, which immediately follows the assertion that early Greek history was never on a large scale, Thucydides begins to draw his picture of earliest Greece:

It appears that what is now called Greece was originally not securely settled. In early times there were uprootings and each group readily left its own land when forced by those with a momentary superiority. There was no trade nor were contacts by land or through the sea without fear—each group grazed enough of their land to subsist on, neither accumulating financial reserves nor farming the land, since it was unclear when someone else would descend on them and take everything away. Everything was unwalled. So, thinking that they could seize what they needed for their daily necessities from any other source, they were easily uprooted and for this reason acquired strength neither in size of cities nor in any other resource. (1.2.1-2)

This paragraph—in the Greek two long amorphous sentences—introduces many of the major ideas in Thucydides' reconstruction of early history. It emphasizes the lack of stability,[10] the ease with which settlements were "uprooted"[11] and the absence of capital accumulation.[12] It depicts a pre-agricultural world, without walls, trade, secure communications,[13] or any true unity. Even the name "Hellas" had yet to emerge.[14]

The gradual attainment of greater stability and power comes as a result not of the heroism of Theseus or some other legendary civilizer but is associated with a name that to an Athenian or Ionian Greek would have been one of the most savage in Greek history—Minos of Crete. He becomes a prototype of Aegean imperialism,[15] who uses his navy to rule the islands, wipes out piracy and enjoys the profits. He is one of the few individuals to emerge out of the normally impersonal account of the Archaeology, focussed as it is on process rather than individual qualities or achievements.[16] Although Minos is no benevolent or altruistic ruler, his naval

[10] The word βέβαιος and its cognates are used to mark the gradual growth of security in Greek history. In this passage we are told that Greece was not originally securely settled: οὐ πάλαι βεβαίως οἰκουμένη. Later (1.2.6) Thucydides anticipates himself and indicates that since Attica was more secure than other areas, ὡς βέβαιον ὄν, it attracted so many immigrants that it eventually sent out colonies. After King Minos cleared the seas of piracy, many coastal regions lived in greater security (1.8.3: βεβαιότερον ᾤκουν). The building of walls marked that change (cf. ἀτειχίστων ἅμα ὄντων in 1.2.2; walls are increasingly used in the work as an indicator of security and surplus capital, e.g. 1.7.1). But it is only well after the Trojan War that the process of "uprooting" abates sufficiently for more general security (12.4: μόλις τε ἐν πολλῷ χρόνῳ ἡσυχάσασα ἡ Ἑλλὰς βεβαίως καὶ οὐκέτι ἀνισταμένη).

[11] I use this term for ἀνίστημι and its cognates and compounds, e.g. μεταναστάσεις in 1.2.1, ἀπανίσταντο in 1.2.2; cf. 1.8.2, 12.1, and 12.3. "Migration" or similar words are often used in English translation but these suggest too grand and collective a picture. Part of Thucydides' point is that groups were very small and easily dislocated.

[12] This point is emphasized by recurring concentration on the inadequacy of food supplies, τροφή, especially in the phrase, τροφῆς ἀπορία, in 1.11.1 (twice) and on the eventual accumulation of surplus funds, especially in the phrase, περιουσία χρημάτων (1.2.2 and 7.1). The two phrases coalesce in the discussion of Troy: 1.11.2: περιουσίαν δὲ εἰ ἦλθον ἔχοντες τροφῆς. Cf. also the iteration of ἀχρηματία (lack of funds) in chapter 11, and πρόσοδος (income) 1.4.1; 13.1, 13.5; and 15.1

[13] 1.2.2. Lack of contact is re-emphasized in ἀμειξίαν in 1.3.4. Note also the elaborate echo of 1.2.2 in the discussion of early Corinth in 1.13.5. Trade, ἐμπορία, is again alluded to in 1.7.1.

[14] The argument is hinted at in the phrase, ἡ νῦν Ἑλλὰς καλουμένη, in 1.2.1 and developed in chapter 3.

[15] On Minos (and Polycrates) as forerunners of Athenian imperialism see Herodotus 3.122.

[16] The other individuals include the family of Pelops (ch. 9), Polycrates of Samos (11.6), Cyrus and Croesus (16), Themistocles (14), and Homer (3.3; 9.4; 10.3). Among these Ameinocles of Corinth, the shipbuilder, also takes his place, elsewhere mentioned only in Themistius *Or.* 26 and Pliny *N.H.* 7.207, and in the criticism by Dionysius of Halicarnassus (*On Thucydides*, trans. Pritchett, ch. 19). Although Ameinocles' place is probably due to the fifth century's high regard for inventors (see T. Cole, *Democritus*, 5), it also prepares the way for the theme of naval innovation, so important in the seventh book.

power makes travel over the seas safer and results in an improved situation for many Greeks: "Those who lived near the sea now applied themselves to the acquisition of money and lived more securely. Some even encircled themselves with walls since they were now wealthier than they had been" (1.8.3). Imperialism brings its benefits, not only for the imperialists but even for the subjects. What makes it possible is sea power. Thus it is not surprising that this selective survey of early Greece should turn into a brief essay (13-15.1) on early Greek naval history, for "the ones who acquired strength were not least those who applied themselves to naval power, thanks to the income in money and the domination of others" (1.15.1). These developments anticipate Athens' naval pre-eminence. Near the end of the Archaeology, Thucydides remarks that the Athenians "became nautical,"[17] that is, they abandoned their city and took to the ships at Salamis. But the change was more than a momentary one, for the Athenians became thereby the leader of one of the two great coalitions in the Greek world, a naval empire ranged against the formidable land power of Sparta and her Peloponnesian League (1.18.2).

At a material level, naval supremacy is the primary route to power in Greek history and the Athenian naval empire is the culmination of a process that reaches back to Minos. But there is also a psychological or ethical side to the growth of power. The rhetorical tradition emphasized the boldness and courage of the Athenians in the Persian Wars and the significance of the valor and manliness of their traditional heroes. Thucydides leaves little room for such lofty motives. The cause of the growing prosperity in the time of Minos was not courage or heroism, but something much deplored in the aristocratic literature of early Greece—the profit motive, *kerdos*: "Desiring profits the weaker put up with the 'slavery' imposed by the stronger and the more powerful having surpluses (sc. of capital) subjugated the lesser cities."[18] Here we encounter the dynamic represented as a cause of many phenomena in early Greek history. The developments Thucydides describes are not the result of heroes or heroism but of desires that had often been deplored in early literature. Self-interest, the desire for profit, and even fear lead to the growth of power and security in Greece

[17] 1.18.2: ναυτικοὶ ἐγένοντο. The phrase is repeated in 1.93.3 where its connection with the advancement of Athenian power is explicit.

[18] 1.8.3. On the role of κέρδος, note especially 1.5.1. Thucydides adopts the rhetoric used to criticize the Athenian empire of his day (cf. 1.68.2 and 121.5) and also alludes to the right of the stronger to rule—a topic much discussed by the intellectuals of the late fifth century, e.g. Democritus *VS* 68 B 267; Gorgias *Helen* (*VS* 82 B 11 sec. 6); cf. Plato *Gorgias* 483d. This is the first of a series of uses of this theme in the *Histories*: 1.76.2; 4.61.5; 5.105.2 et al.

and to an escape from the squalor and danger of early times. The analysis of power within the Archaeology is consistent with many of the dominant tendencies in contemporary intellectual life—an unsentimental, unheroic view of the past and an emphasis on the drives for power, self-protection, and self-interest. These are viewed as common to men of the past and to Thucydides' own contemporaries and hence as providing a method of sorting out the reliable information about the past from exaggerations and fabrications. Even more important is the implication that if the nature of man is essentially the same throughout time, then it should be possible both to understand the past and to learn from it. The tone at this point in the work is confident and optimistic, a corollary to the idea of progress that we encounter in the. Archaeology.[19]

In summary, then, the opening chapters of the work are not so much a description of early Greece or a chronicle of events of early times as the establishment of a way of looking at the past. The label "Archaeology" is inappropriate in so far as it suggests the unearthing of whatever remains from the past; Foucault's use of "Archaeology" to mean "the history of that which renders necessary a certain form of thought" comes much closer to making the term appropriate for this section,[20] for it analyzes forces that have long operated in Greek history and that are likely still to be evident in the great war that he has chosen for his subject. It is an anatomy of power based on a view of man's nature.[21] At every level it calls for an

[19] E. R. Dodds' *The Ancient Concept of Progress* (Oxford 1973) 12 argues that "Thucydides saw the past history of Greece as pursuing a gradual upward course" and that he was one of the thinkers who explored the idea of progress in antiquity. Cf. J. de Romilly, "Thucydide et l'idée de progrès," *Annali S. N. Pisa* 35 (1966) 143-191, and *The Rise and Fall of States according to Greek Authors* (Ann Arbor 1977) 4; L. Edelstein *The Idea of Progress in Classical Antiquity* (Baltimore 1967). Dodds' view has been criticized by W. den Boer, *Progress in the Greece of Thucydides* in Mededelingen der K. nederlandse Akademie van Wetenschappen AFD Letterkunde N.R. Deel 40, No. 2 (1977) and in an important review by A. Dihle, *Gnomon* 41 (1969) 435. See also H. Lloyd Jones (*Oxford Magazine* 91 No. 2 [May 18, 1973] 11f.), cited in den Boer, Lloyd Jones' criticism ("These thinkers certainly held that improvement was possible for some people. But did they think it was possible for whole communities, or that it was in the long run automatic and inevitable in the way Victorian sages . . . imagined? Surely the world outlook of a people that had started from such humble beginnings and whose religion was so moderate in its claims for men could be trusted to preserve them from any such delusions.") begs the question. Den Boer's argument that Thucydides represents only material progress fails to take into account the important theme of security in the Archaeology (cf. above Note 10).

[20] M. Foucault, "Monstrosities in Criticism," *Diacritics* 1 (1971) 60.

[21] Cf. J. de Romilly's chapter on "L'Enquête sur le passé" in *Histoire et raison chez Thucydide* (Paris 1956) pp. 240-298 in which she discerns "une théorie assez élaborée de la puissance," p. 261, within the Archaeology. See also J. Finley, *Thucydides* (Cambridge, Mass. 1942) 87-93, and S. Mørch, "Popularité ou impopularité d'Athènes chez Thucydide," *ClMed* (1970) 67.

unsentimental approach to events, emphasizing the significance of self-interest and fear in individual conduct, of naval might and financial reserves in military matters, and of imperialism as a source of power and greatness. Although far removed from the myths and commonplaces of epideictic oratory and popular history, the rejection of conventionality and sentimentality affirms the writer's authority and reliability. Enlightened author and sophisticated audience are in rapport.

The Archaeology is also, however, a demonstration of Thucydides' techniques of historical analysis. At first the emphasis is on the obscurity of the past: "Because of the length of time it was impossible to find out with clarity about the things before these events and even more remote matters" (1.1.3). But as the Archaeology develops, the tone begins to shift; the "impossible" becomes the "difficult": "I found that the past was of this sort, although it was difficult to feel confidence in each indication one encountered" (1.20.1). Later, confidence grows: "A person who concludes, nonetheless, from the above mentioned indications that it was of approximately the sort I have described would not go far wrong. He will put no confidence in the lofty versions told by the poets, who embellish events to make them seem greater, nor in the compositions of the speech writers who choose versions that are entertaining to listen to over more truthful ones, even though much of what they tell has turned implausibly to legend over time and is based on no critical examination" (1.21.1). Finally, as we shall see, the Archaeology promises an exactitude sufficient for useful inferences about the past and the future.

The method upon which this growing confidence is based becomes evident as the Archaeology proceeds. It involves the careful study of details, to be noted also in contemporary Hippocratic medicine and in the techniques of rhetorical instruction developed by the Sophists, who trained their pupils to go through a case point by point assessing what was probable and improbable. Thucydides indicates he used a similar process in investigating reports about the events in the war: "I felt I should record the facts about the actions in the war not as I learned about them from some chance source, nor as I guessed they would have taken place. Instead I went after each one with as much detail work as I could, both events at which I was present and those about which I learned from others."[22] The

---

[22] 1.22.2. The translation and interpretation of the passage are made difficult by the complex and untranslatable verbal ties within it and by the contrast to the preceeding section on the speeches. For a radically different view of the passage see F. Egermann, "Thukydides über die Art seiner Reden und über seine Darstellung der Kriegsgeschehnisse," *Historia* 21 (1972) 597-602. The essential point, however, is clear; Thucydides has used different methods for

crucial word, *epexelthōn*, I have rendered colloquially, as "went after," trying to catch its military overtones (cf. 5. 9.10) and its use for prosecution in the law courts.[23]

A further similarity to the techniques of the law courts is evident in the opening sentences of the work and again in chapter 20 when Thucydides talks about his method of drawing inferences from *tekmēria*. *Tekmēria* are not "proofs" of incontrovertible evidence, but "indications"—facts or observations that point in a certain direction.[24] They do not entail generalizations; rather the leading themes of the Archaeology—the importance of sea power and financial reserves—guide him in the selection of corroborating instances from myth, poetry, archaeology, anthropology, and the like. The consistency and coherence of the picture that emerges help validate the method. If it can produce such plausible results about the remote and ill-attested past, it is likely to be much more convincing when applied to contemporary history, the main subject of the book.

As we recognize the affinity between Thucydides' method in the Archaeology and that used by speakers in the law courts, we also become aware of a further progression. The work begins, as we have seen, with an apparent repudiation of the methods of rhetorical composition. Later the criticism of "speech writers" (*logographoi*) reminds us again of the sharp difference between Thucydides' work and more popular oratory and historiography. The work moreover, initially presents itself as a *treatise*, devoid of rhetorical embellishment, meant for private study rather than public performance but conceived with a very major subject.[25] Gradually

---

reconstructing speeches and events. The second has a smaller degree of guesswork. In reconstructing the speeches it would not pay him to cross-examine witnesses about the detailed arguments and exact wording. But for a battle or the like Thucydides could check each informant's report point by point, testing it by topography, strategic principles, and the reports of other witnesses, etc. See now Dover's comments in *HCT* (vol. 5, pp. 394-397).

[23] E.g. Plato *Euthyphro* 4b-e and 9a and Lysias 23.14. Cf. C. Schneider, *Information und Absicht bei Thukydides* (Göttingen 1974) 141, n. 317.

[24] Σημεῖον in 1.6.2 and 10.1 and μαρτύριον in 1.8.1 are used in a similar way.

[25] Note especially the choice of the verb, ξυνέγραψε, in 1.1.1. Contemporary uses of this verb and its cognates refer for the most part to technical works or those with few literary pretensions. Note especially its application to written diplomatic agreements: Thucydides 5.35.3; 41.3; *IG* i³ 21 line 3; 76 line 47; legal or constitutional documents: Thucydides 8.67; Plato *Gorgias* 451b; contracts: Plato *Laws* 953 e; *IG* i³ 84 lines 7 and 12; treatises or technical works: Plato *Gorgias* 518 b (on cookery); Xenophon *Memorabilia* 4.2.10f. (medicine, architecture, etc.); architectural plans: *IG* ii² 1668 (ca. 340); *IG* i³ 35 lines 8-9, 14-15, 17f.; i³ 45 lines 6ff. (Cf. J. J. Coulton, *Greek Architects at Work* [London 1977] 54); rhetorical treatises; Plato *Phaedrus* 261 b and *Gorgias* 462 b with Dodds' commentary ad loc.; cf. G. Kennedy, "The Earliest Rhetorical Handbooks," *AJP* 80 (1959) 171 and R. Holloway, "Architect and Engineer in Archaic Greece," *HSCP* 73 (1969) 286 and 289. The word was used for historical narrative by Antiochus of Syracuse: *FGrHist* 555 F 2 (cf. T 2 a and b,

it becomes evident that the opening chapters are a demonstration, and a proud and eloquent one, of Thucydides' methods. By the end of the Archaeology we recognize that it is in fact an *epideixis*, a rhetorical display piece, and not a conventional one, but an exhibition of a new technique of analysis and a fully appropriate proemium to the rest of the work, emphasizing in good rhetorical fashion the greatness of its subject matter.[26]

As the tone of confidence grows, the criticism of the poets and speech-writers and the claims of Thucydides' own work become more explicit. The work has transformed itself. It is no longer a mere treatise but a rival to, and ultimately a victor over, the poets. When the theme of the greatness of its subject, announced at the beginning of the work, is reintroduced at the end of chapter 21, the unpretentious prose style slips away and the third person narrator of the opening sentence yields to a new speaker, the war itself: "This war will nevertheless make clear to those who examine the actions themselves that it was greater than all that went before." The language takes on a hexameter cadence:

καὶ ὁ πόλεμος οὗτος . . . δηλώσει ὅμως μείζων γεγενημένος αὐτῶν.

And soon Thucydides is challenging what Martin West has called "the close connection between poetry and prophecy which is widespread in early literature."[27]

The following chapter, although claiming neither divine inspiration nor complete exactitude in the reconstruction of the past, affirms that the work will have a utility for all who wish to know about the past and the recurrence of approximately similar situations in the future.[28] The wording is char-

---

3) and perhaps also by Hellanicus: Thucydides 1.97.2. Although Plato *Phaedrus* 235 c uses the word as a general term for prose, it is an exaggeration to claim that *xyn-* in the compound "bears the sense . . . of artistic composition" as S. Usher, "Lysias and his Clients," *GRBS* 17 (1976) 31, following M. Lavency, *Aspects de la logographie judiciaire attique* (Louvain 1964) 36-45, contends.

Ξύγκειμαι, used at the end of 1.22, is appropriate for works with greater literary pretensions. Cf. Plato *Hippias Maior* 286; and Isocrates IV 168.

Thucydides continues to use ξυγγράφω in his formulae for the end of the years of the war (2.70.4 et saepe) but elsewhere applies this verb to his own narrative only in 4.104.4, preferring γράφω (e.g. 5.20.3), ἔχω εἰπεῖν (6.2.1) μνησθήσομαι (3.90.1) ἐξηγήσομαι (5.26.6) et al.

[26] Cf. Täubler, *Die Archäologie des Thukydides*. Note especially [Aristotle] *Rhetorica ad Alexandrum* xxix 1436 b 7, Isocrates *Panegyricus* 13, and Cicero *de inventione* I xv 20-23 on the appropriateness of "greatness" as a theme for a proemium.

[27] Martin West, *Hesiod's Theogony* (Oxford 1966), commentary on line 32, page 166.

[28] 1.22.4. My translation follows, but I am not entirely convinced by the commonest view among commentators on this troublesome sentence. W. W. Goodwin in the *Proceedings of the American Academy of Arts and Sciences* 6 (1866) 329ff. made a strong case for construing the sentence to mean that the work "will be satisfactory as it is for all who wish not merely

acteristically complex and cautious but in context it makes a strong claim for the utility of the work, one that seems plausible because of the clarity and cogency of the analysis in the Archaeology. The sources of power detected in the opening portion of the work should have a persistent role in history and help illumine the present as well as the past. Thus we are led directly to Thucydides' most famous assertion, that his history "is composed as something to keep forever rather than as a contest piece to listen to for the moment" (1.22.4).

This statement is a dramatic development of the themes in the opening paragraphs of the work. There is, however, an even more important transformation. At the end of the Archaeology, in a carefully constructed ring composition, the theme of the greatness of the war is again stated, and redefined.[29] The greatness of the war is now seen to consist not in the

---

to have a clear view of the past but also to draw useful inferences in regard to events in the future which, human nature being what it is, will again at some point be approximately of the same sort and analogous." Goodwin's interpretation requires that the comma printed in all modern editions after ἔσεσθαι be removed and placed after κρίνειν, and that αὐτὰ be construed as subject of ἕξει. It might be objected that αὐτὰ, if nominative, is gratuitous, but Thucydides is emphasizing the utility of the work "as it is," that is, without the mythological element to which he has just alluded. A more difficult objection is that τῶν μελλόντων et seq. without περὶ is unlikely to mean "in regard to the future." I know of no precise parallel in Thucydides to such a genitive; see, however, 2.65.4, 4.65.4, and 8.86.3. A comparison of the use of ὑποψία in 2.37.2 and 4.27.3 is also instructive. The emphatic parallelism of the infinitive phrases that results from Goodwin's repunctuation does much to alleviate the harshness of the construction. I have greatly benefited from discussions with K. J. Dover on this point.

[29] Scholars have disagreed about the structure of the first book and in particular about the end point of the Archaeology. For varying views on the structure see F. Bizer, *Untersuchungen zur Archaeologie des Thukydides* (Tübingen 1937); de Romilly, *Histoire et raison* 289f.; Täubler, *Die Archäologie des Thukydides*; H. R. Immerwahr, *"Ergon*: History as Monument in Herodotus and Thucydides," *AJP* 81 (1960) 277, n. 48; Gomme in *HCT* on 1.1 (pp. 89 and 154-157).

The excursus is an elaborate ring composition (i.e. pattern A-B-C . . . C-B-A); hence, division at the end of chapter twenty-three is strongly supported. Note how the themes of the opening sentence are reintroduced and expanded at the end of this unit:

A. Greatness: (1.1.1) ἐλπίσας μέγαν τε ἔσεσθαι
   B. Inferential method: τεκμαιρόμενος
      C. Resources in Readiness: παρασκευῇ τῇ πάσῃ
         D. Polarization: τὸ ἄλλο Ἑλληνικὸν . . . ξυνιστάμενον πρὸς ἑκατέρους
         D. Polarization: (1.18.2) διεκρίθησαν πρός τε Ἀθηναίους καὶ Λακεδαιμονίους οἱ . . . Ἕλληνες
      C. Resources in Readiness: (1.18.3) εὖ παρεσκευάσαντο
   B. Inferential method: (1.20.1) παντὶ ἑξῆς τεκμηρίῳ
A. Greatness (redefined as length and *pathēmata*): (1.23) μέγιστον . . . μέγα προύβη

Within this general structure the greatness theme is first restated as *kinēsis* (1.1.2) and then converted into a negative statement about early history (1.1.3): τὰ γὰρ πρὸ αὐτῶν . . . οὐ μεγάλα νομίζω. The negative statement is then corroborated through a three-fold

numbers of men, ships, and talents committed to it, but in its length and the sufferings concentrated in it:

Of former accomplishments the greatest was the Persian War and this had a speedy resolution in a pair of naval battles and a pair of land battles. The length of this war greatly surpassed it, and sufferings for Greece converged in it, unparalleled in any equal time. For neither had there been so many cities captured and left desolate, some by barbarians, some by the rivalry of the inhabitants (and some changed their populations when they were captured), nor so much exile and murder—some in the war itself and some from *stasis* [civil strife]. Things we had heard of in former times, but which were in fact sparsely attested, became credible—stories about earthquakes which both affected large parts of the earth and were very intense, and about eclipses of the sun, which happened more frequently than those reported in former times, droughts, some great, some causing famines, and that which caused not the least harm and no insignificant destruction, the apocalyptic plague. All these joined in the attack along with this war.[30]

The technical treatise investigating the sources of power and success in the early Greek world becomes at the end of the Archaeology a disquisition on the suffering of war. Although it concentrates on the quantifiable sources of power and above all on ships and financial reserves, its claim to report the greatest *kinēsis* is now, we can see, to be judged not by comparisons with the massive operations described by Herodotus, but in the concentration and intensity of human suffering in the long and destructive war. Thus the reader can already anticipate that any foreknowledge made possible by the work is not rational prediction and control but the premonition of recurring misery and loss.

By the end of the Archaeology it is clear that Thucydides intends a new kind of history. His approach is not that of the poets, nor of the speechwriters, nor even of Herodotus. Like his great predecessor he chooses as

---

structure (cf. the scholiast on 1.12.1): ch. 2-8 on Greece before the Trojan War; ch. 9-11 on the Trojan War; ch. 12-18.2 on events following the Trojan War. These three sections in turn contain ring compositions of varying degrees of elaborateness outlined in Appendix One (cf. N.G.L. Hammond, "The Arrangement of Thought in the Proem and in Other Parts of Thucydides I," *CQ* n.s. 2 [1952] 128).

[30] 1.23.1-3. One point of translation requires explanation. Ἡ λοιμώδης νόσος is an unusual and seemingly pleonastic expression that I have rendered "apocalyptic plague," Νόσος is itself a sufficient and appropriate word for the plague. Λοιμός is a more unusual word, often used where there is some suggestion of divine intervention, e.g. Homer *Iliad* 1.61; Hesiod *Works and Days* 242f. Hence a λοιμώδης νόσος is a plague that resembles a divine affliction. Since "plague" in English can be a purely medical term, the translator needs to suggest that the sickness was more than a normal human sickness.

For μέρος τι as an idiom indicating something extensive or large, cf. 7.30.3 and Poppo-Stahl on 4.30.3.

his subject an action, a war, rather than a time period or a geographical
area. But his theme is the suffering of war—what happens to individuals
and cities when events move beyond their control, and when they are
confronted with the greatest dislocations. We can already detect that his
treatment of this war will not fully reproduce the initial austere but confident
approach to the Greek past but will break new ground and grow into a
new form.

THE CORCYREAN ALLIANCE

The tension at the end of the Archaeology between the tough-minded
analysis of power and the presentation of the war as suffering is not
immediately explored or resolved in the following chapters. Instead Thucydides turns to the outbreak of the war and its causes: "The Athenians
and Peloponnesians began the war when they repudiated the Thirty Years
Truce which they had made after the capture of Euboea [in 446 B.C.]. I
have set down first the causes of complaint and the grievances behind the
repudiation so that no one ever has to investigate from what origin such
a great war broke out among the Greeks. The truest reason, although least
evident in the discussion, was, in my opinion, that the Athenians by
growing great caused fear in the Lacedaemonians and drove them into
war. But the openly talked about grievances on each side are these, from
which, having repudiated the truce, they entered into war."[31] This passage
simultaneously presents Thucydides' own view of the cause of the war as
the growth of Athenian power, ties that "truest reason" to the analysis of
the growth of power presented in the Archaeology, and clarifies the organization of the next portion of the book. The rest of the book is arranged
to provide first a discussion of the two principal "causes of complaint and
grievances"—the Corcyrean affair (chs. 24-55) and the trouble at Potidaea
(chs. 56-65)—and then a report of the assembly in which the Spartans
accept the complaints of some of their allies and take the first step to war
(chs. 66-87). Before describing the next step—the Peloponnesian League's

[31] 1.23.4-6. This translation is controversial in one respect: I agree with a large number
of recent scholars who point out that ἀναγκάσαι ἐς τὸ πολεμεῖν is not "made war
inevitable" (Crawley) or the equivalent but something much less deterministic. *Anagkē* is
strong pressure in one direction, not philosophical determinacy or practical inevitability. Cf.
G.E.M. de Ste. Croix, *Origins of the Peloponnesian War* (London 1972) 60-63; K. J. Dover,
appendix 2 to *HCT* 5, p. 419; C. Schneider, *Information und Absicht bei Thukydides* (Göttingen 1974) 101-110; A. W. Gomme, *The Greek Attitude to Poetry and History* (Berkeley
1954) 156f.; Rawlings, *A Semantic Study of Prophasis* 92f. See also Chapter Four, Note 41.

vote to go to war (chs. 118.3-125)—Thucydides discusses the growth of Athenian power during the approximately fifty years between the end of the Persian War and the outbreak of the Peloponnesian War (chs. 88-118.2). This excursus, usually referred to as the Pentecontaetia ("Account of the Fifty Years"), is introduced with a reminder that it contains the background to what in Thucydides' view was the truest cause: "The Spartans voted that the Truce was repudiated and that war was in order, not so much because they were persuaded by the arguments of their allies as because they feared that the Athenians would acquire even greater power. They noted that the greater part of Greece was already under their control" (1.88). Throughout this discussion, attention is focussed on Athens and the growth of her power. The Spartans are vividly presented at a few crucial moments, but even here they are seen primarily as reacting to Athens and her strength.

Thucydides' discussion of increasing Athenian strength follows directly from the analysis of power in the Archaeology, and especially from his emphasis on the importance of naval power. Indeed early Greek history is seen as strongly favorable to the continuing growth of Athenian power and mixed at best for the Spartans:

The ones who acquired strength were not least those who applied themselves to naval power, both by the inflow of money and the domination of others. For they sailed out and subjugated the islands—especially if they did not have sufficient land at home. No coalitions undertook land wars, from which some power is also acquired. As many land wars as took place were individual affairs with their neighbors. The Greeks did not send out armies far from their land to subjugate others. For subjects did not coalesce around the greatest cities, nor did they undertake common expeditions on a basis of equality. Rather individually they battled their neighbors, although in the war long ago between Chalkis and Eretria, the rest of Greece did to some extent take sides. (1.15)

The attitude in the Archaeology, as this passage indicates, deemphasizes land power and stresses the significance of dominating the sea. Since Thucydides never describes Sparta's control of Messenia (except allusively in 10.2) nor the growth of the Peloponnesian league (except to contrast its operation to Athens' treatment of her empire in ch. 19), it rather surprises us when he mentions the Spartans' preeminence in power at the time of the Persian War (1.18.2). The modern reader, especially if he is not thoroughly familiar with Greek history, may overreact to this; Thucydides could assume that his audience would know how formidable Sparta was (cf. 1.102). But at least the modern reader will not miss the thrust of

Thucydides' argument: the early history of Greece shows the importance
of naval and financial power. It points to Athens, not to Sparta.

Indeed, if the Archaeology were our only evidence, we might conclude
that Athens should win the war with Sparta. The view, widespread among
the Greeks at the beginning of the war, that Athens would not be able to
last more than a few years in such a conflict (7.28.3), receives no corroboration from Thucydides' analysis of power. Instead we are led to see
how strong and how well prepared Athens was for the coming conflict
(18.3-19). Every reader knows, of course, that Athens lost the war, but
Thucydides' analysis up to this point has provided no help in explaining
her ultimate defeat. It focuses attention not on the fact of defeat, but on
the potential for victory.

The reader thus leaves the Archaeology aware not only of a tension
between its treatment of power and its anticipation of the sufferings of the
war, but also of a dissonance between the implications of that treatment
of power and the known outcome of the war. Although convinced of the ·
authority and perceptiveness of the narrator, the reader is alert at the same
time to the crucial fact that the author has not yet integrated into his view—
indeed, does not even mention until after the middle of the second book—
that Athens will lose this war. The reader begins the account of the war's
origin with an unanswered question in the back of his mind: What goes
wrong? How does Athens fail?

This question is reinforced by the outcome of the first of the two ''causes
of complaint and grievances,'' the Athenian alliance with Corcyra. The
episode, at one level, is very simple: a dispute with Corinth leads Corcyra
to seek an alliance with Athens. Athens acquiesces, sends a fleet to help
her new ally, and consequently comes into conflict with a member of
Sparta's Peloponnesian League. But beyond this, two other aspects are
developed in the narrative of the episode. The first is the introduction of
what is to be a major theme in the *Histories*—the conflict between right
and advantage;[32] the second is Corcyra's significance as a naval power.
The narrative of her dispute with Corinth rapidly makes clear the size and
skill of Corcyra's navy. She has over 120 ships at her disposal and is able
to defeat the Corinthian fleet in an initial engagement (ch. 29). Her naval
strength proves decisive in her appeal to Athens for an alliance. Although
her ambassadors stress the justice of their case, they are on weak ground
and their arguments are largely tendentious and ultimately irrelevant.[33]

[32] N.B. 1.42.1.

[33] Under traditional Greek values the Corcyreans were in a very weak position. They had
no claim on Athenians either by kinship or by past services. They were Dorians, much more

Their concluding argument, however, has greater effect: "To sum up as succinctly as possible both in general and in particular, one point instructs you not to abandon us, namely: There are three significant naval forces in Greece, ours, your own, and the Corinthians'. If you allow two to combine into one and if the Corinthians beat us, you will have both the Corcyrean and Peloponnesian navy to fight against. But if you ally with us, you will engage them with a larger number of ships—ours" (1.36.3). After hearing the counterarguments of the Corinthians, the Athenians decide to make a purely defensive alliance with Corcyra. Their reasons, as reported in chapter 44, have nothing to do with the justice of the case, but are precisely those practical considerations advanced by the Corcyreans at the end of their speech: "For they thought that the war with the Peloponnesians was going to take place and they did not want to abandon a navy as significant as the Corcyrean to the Corinthians, but to let them collide with each other as much as possible so that they would enter into the war, if it were necessary, with weaker opponents whether Corinthians or any other naval power" (1.44.2). Thucydides then adds a further point, also adduced by the Corcyreans in their speech: "At the same time the island seemed to them well situated for a naval expedition to Italy and Sicily."[34] Such a consideration is fully appropriate in the diplomatic climate of the pre-war years for we know that Athens at this time was concerned with western Greece.[35] But from a post-war perspective the words take on an added

---

closely tied to the Corinthians and the Spartans than to the Athenians. Their conduct, more-over, had been outrageous. They had refused to help their own colony, Epidamnus. The occasion was not minor or routine, but a desperate appeal to help stop civil strife in which one party was aided by barbarians. The Epidamnians had asked for assistance through the most sacred of Greek appeals, the supplication (1.24.7). After being rejected, the Epidamnians consulted the oracle at Delphi to obtain approval for recognizing Corinth, the mother city of Corcyra, as their own mother city (1.25.1). When Delphi sanctioned the request (and thereby implicitly criticized Corcyra's conduct), the Corcyreans haughtily dictated terms to Epidamnus (1.26.3) and then, supported by barbarian Illyrians, attacked and besieged the city (1.26.5). On the arrival of the Corinthians the Corcyreans take a more conciliatory line and offer to arbitrate (1.28.2) but are unwilling to stop their siege. Soon they come into battle with their own mother city, Corinth, and butcher many of the captives taken in the naval battle (1.30.1). With this record they come to Athens to seek aid and represent themselves as the victims (1.33.1, 1.34.1) of injustice!

[34] 1.44.3; cf. 36.2. Ἐν παράπλῳ κεῖσθαι literally refers to a coastline voyage. But since a trading ship bound for Sicily or Italy would not need to cling to the coast, although a warship needed to put into shore each night, the phraseology hints at a military expedition. On the sailing patterns of war ships and merchantmen see de Ste. Croix, *Origins of the Peloponnesian War*, 47f.

[35] The inscriptional evidence, the renewal of the alliances with Rhegion and Leontini (*ML* 63 and 64, also in *IG* i³ 53 and 54) and the alliance with Segesta (*ML* 37 also in *IG* i³ 11) indicates, on the most widely accepted datings, that Athens was already extensively involved in Western Greek affairs by the 450s.

force. Inevitably they bring to mind Corcyra's later role as the marshalling point for the great expedition that then passed along the Italian coast to Sicily and ultimately to defeat at Syracuse. For a second, just in passing, we detect a flicker of irony—what seemed to them an advantage turns out to be a step toward disaster.[36]

And so Athens allies with one of the other three major naval powers in Greece. Her naval superiority should now be decisive and her position in the forthcoming war even stronger.[37] The analysis implicit in Thucydides' narrative still points to sources of Athenian strength and reasons for an expectation of victory, not to the problems and difficulties the city will face. The effect of this section, then, is to intensify the discrepancy between the analysis of power in the text and the reader's knowledge of the outcome of the war.

NATIONAL CHARACTERISTICS

After a comparatively brief treatment of the second of the "causes of complaint and grievances," Corinth's support and encouragement of a revolt in the area around Potidaea,[38] the account turns to Sparta, at one of the most dramatic moments in her history. Sparta has convened her allies in the Peloponnesian League and invited other states that feel Athens has

[36] "Irony is not a characteristic of the Thucydidean narrative" says H. D. Westlake, "Athenian Aims in Sicily," *Historia* 9 (1960) 393 (also in *Essays on the Greek Historians* [Manchester 1969] 101-122). Cf. Dover in *HCT* on 7.86.5 (p. 463). Such assertions have some validity when strictly applied to the rhetorical figure of irony (see E. C. Marchant's introduction to his edition on book 1 [London 1905] p. xlvii; cf., however, Pritchett on Dionysius of Halicarnassus in *On Thucydides*, 122, n. 13). But if the reader wishes to consider irony of viewpoint, then the work as a whole and especially book 1 is surely ironical. The reader knows that ultimately the war is longer and more destructive than most of the speakers recognize and that Athens loses not only the war, but also many of her most valuable characteristics. Thus, inevitably, we read the work from an ironic perspective. Whether Thucydides consciously intended this, can be left to speculation. That this form of irony is a persistent feature of the text is, however, repeatedly evident.

[37] The informed reader would know that Corcyra contributed little to Athens' war effort. The city joins in only one naval expedition (2.25.1ff.) and is soon a source of delay and trouble as her stasis becomes intense (3.80.2). Hermippus' attitude may suggest that Athenians expected more from the alliance than the attrition of the two other largest navies: "Corcyreans, may Poseidon destroy them in their hollow ships, because they are of divided loyalties." (*Phormophoroi*, Fr. 63 Edmonds, *Fragments of Attic Comedy*, vol. 1 [Leiden 1957]). Cf. F. Adcock, "Thucydides in Book I," JHS 71 (1951) 5.

[38] 1.56-66. The Corcyrean episode is developed in considerable detail, especially through the use of an antilogy (paired speeches in direct discourse). Potidaea is treated more succinctly with a fast-moving narrative.

wronged them to come and present their grievances. The issue is whether the Spartan assembly should continue to view itself as bound by the Thirty Years Peace or whether it should convene the Peloponnesian League and recommend a vote of war against Athens.[39] This crucial moment is described in a very brief narrative, which alludes to the Aeginetan grievance that Athens was not allowing them the autonomy guaranteed under the Thirty Years Peace (1.67.2) and to the Megarean complaint that contrary to that peace they were excluded from the harbors in the Athenian empire and from the Athenian agora. But description gives way to direct presentation through a double antilogy, two pairs of speeches in direct discourse. In the first, Corinthians and Athenians argue about what response Sparta should make; in the second two Spartan leaders disagree about the wisdom of going to war at this point. The speeches are vivid and create the illusion that we have stopped talking about events and have become witnesses of one of the most important of them.

Yet even at this moment, narrative and analysis coexist. As we watch Sparta decide that the Athenians have abrogated the Thirty Years Peace and that war is in order,[40] we are also led to a further stage in the assessment of the relative power of the two major contenders in the forthcoming war. For up to this point the analysis has been based almost entirely on the quantifiable factors of—above all, ships and money. These factors, as we have seen, point strongly toward Athenian success. As yet little attention has been devoted to less tangible considerations, the morale and determination of the belligerents. Although the opening of the treatise has insisted upon a tough-minded assessment of power and refused to view events as a conflict of moral or personal qualities, surely some attention must be paid to the factors of mind and will governing the application of power. The Spartans, we know, were intensely proud of their discipline and determination. An investigation of their attitude and those of their allies could do much to balance the emphasis on quantitative factors that has prevailed up to this point.

[39] The procedure is not initially made clear by Thucydides; for the interpretation adopted here see A.H.M. Jones, "The Two Synods of the Delian and Peloponnesian Leagues," *Proceedings of the Cambridge Philological Society* n.s. 2 (1952/53) 43-46, and de Ste. Croix, *Origins of the Peloponnesian War*, 200-210.

[40] The Thirty Years Peace contained an arbitration provision for disputes arising under it (1.78.4; 145). The Athenians repeatedly offer to submit to arbitration (1.71.5; 78.4; 81; 85.2; 123; 140.2; 144.2; 145) but the Spartans reject the offers; their view amounts to the proposition that by the (alleged) violations Athens has abrogated (67.1, σπονδὰς τε λελυκότες εἶεν; cf. 87.2) the treaty. Hence it is no longer binding on them and they need not submit to arbitration. This perverse law and logic Thucydides exposes, without implying that this one issue resolves the wider question of responsibility for the war.

The exchange between Archidamus and Sthenelaidas (chs. 80-86) culminating the conference at Sparta does much to illumine Spartan attitudes.
But by the time Sthenelaidas appears and expresses the bold tenacity of
traditional Sparta, much has been done to encourage a critical examination
of his speech, indeed to let it expose itself as a rhetorical cliché. The
phrasing of the speech brings out its specious sloganeering:

And if they [the Athenians] were *agathoi* [good or courageous] at that time as
regards the Persians but are now *kakoi* [evil or cowardly] as regards us, they
deserve double punishment because from being good [*agathōn*] they have become
evil [*kakoi*]. But we have not changed, and as for our allies, if we are sensible,
we will not let them be mistreated nor will we delay [*mellēsomen*] our retaliation
until they are no longer about to be [*mellousi*] badly treated [*kakōs paschein*].
Others have great wealth and ships and horses; we have good [*agathoi*] allies who
must not be betrayed to the Athenians. Nor is the matter to be resolved by discussions [*logois*] when it is not in name [*logōi*] that they are being harmed. Rather
retaliation is to be undertaken, swiftly and with all strength. (1.86.1-3)

The shallowness is evident in the jingles and equivocations of the language.
But the speciousness of Sthenelaidas' speech is also exposed by its place
in the antilogy. It follows immediately after another Spartan speaker, King
Archidamus, has expounded the reasons for caution and delay (ch. 80-
85.2). He is a wise and experienced statesman, whose arguments are
confirmed by what is already known of the strategic situation and Athenian
resources:

Against men whose land is far off, and who moreover know the sea full well and
have arranged all other matters in excellent fashion, with wealth public and private,
with ships and cavalry and heavy infantry and total population to be found in no
other single Greek city, and who have in addition many allies who pay them
tribute—how should we undertake war against these and in what can we trust when
before we are ready we hasten against them? Is it in our ships? But we are inferior,
and if we practice and make counter preparations it will take time. Or is it in
money? We are even further behind in this respect and our treasury is empty and
we do not readily contribute from our personal funds. Perhaps someone feels
confident because we surpass them in heavy infantry and in numbers, so that we
can ravage their land by repeated invasions. But they have much land in their
empire and can import by sea what they need. And if we try to get their allies to
revolt, we will need ships to help them, since they are for the most part islanders.
What sort of war will we encounter? If we do not have naval superiority and cannot
take away the flow of income from which they support the navy, we will have the
worst of it. (1.80.3-81.4)

Against these words of the wise adviser Archidamus the impetuosity of the advocate of immediate war is swiftly recognized as shallow and deceptive.

The Spartan voters, however, do not share this recognition. By a large majority they vote as Sthenelaidas has urged (87.3). Once again the reader views events ironically, knowing that the war will be far more difficult than the Spartans anticipate. This recognition derives from the form of the debate between Archidamus and Sthenelaidas and from the reader's knowledge of the length and difficulty of the war. But it also has another, and very important, basis: the awareness of some of the characteristics of the Spartans and the Athenians as expounded in an earlier portion of the Conference at Sparta. Thucydides passes over several speeches that made specific complaints about Athenian actions including the denial of autonomy to Aegina, restrictions placed on Megarean travellers and traders.[41] He chooses instead to report the last of these speeches by foreign critics of Athens. The address of the Corinthian delegates is fresh and surprising in its strategy and introduces a theme of recurring importance in the *Histories*, the contrast between Athenian and Spartan character. The Corinthian delegates are represented as concerned less with attacking the Athenians than with chastising the Spartans for their slowness to act and reluctance to take firm measures against the expansion of Athenian power. The point is driven home in an elaborate contrast between Athenian and Spartan character:

They are innovators and sharp at forming a plan and at completing in action whatever they resolve, while you try to save what you already have and make no further resolutions, and in practice do not even follow through on what is essential. Or again, they are bold even beyond their power and risk takers even when reason says no and full of hopes in the midst of trouble. But your pattern is to do less than your power allows, not even to trust in secure plans and to think that you will never get out of trouble. They do not hesitate; you delay; they strike out abroad while you are stay-at-homes, for they think that by their absence they will

---

[41] 1.67.3-4. The most notorious omission is the Megarean complaint. Thucydides' contemporaries attached great importance to the Megarean decree as a cause of the war; they were followed in the fourth century B.C. by Ephorus (*FGrHist* 70 F 196) whose account influenced many writers of later antiquity (e.g. Diodorus Siculus 12.38-41.1) and of modern times. A strong case can be made that the Megarean decree had an important role in the growth of hostility and tension in the pre-war years, and that Thucydides' account attaches too little significance to it. The reason for Thucydides' de-emphasis of the Megarean affair is more difficult to assess. My own suspicion is that he saw his account as a corrective to a simplistic view that the war resulted from the passage of this decree and Pericles' resistance to its repeal. Amid the immense scholarly literature on this problem de Ste. Croix's *Origins of the Peloponnesian War* provides a controversial but illuminating starting point.

acquire something and you believe that aggressiveness will damage what you already have. When they defeat an enemy, they push the advantage as far as they can; if defeated, they retreat as little as they must. And they expend their bodies for their city as if they were not their own, but they use their intelligence as if helping her were strengthening their own home. When they form a plan and it does not succeed, they think they have been deprived of their own property, but when their aggression results in gain, they think they have accomplished little in comparison to what will happen in the future. If they fail in some attempt, they fill the gap with new hopes. They alone simultaneously attain and hope for whatever they plan thanks to the swift application of their resolutions. . . . Thus if someone summed them up by saying that their nature was neither to enjoy tranquillity themselves nor allow it to other human beings, he would speak correctly.[42]

The rhetorical strategy is daring and ingenious. The Corinthians avoid rehearsing their grievances and making moralistic criticisms of Spartan conduct. They might have tried to provoke the Spartans by pointing out that delay would be considered *anandria*, or cowardice.[43] This injects the element we have expected into the analysis of power—the nonquantifiables of disposition and character. But the specific characteristics are as surprising as the rhetorical strategy of the speech. The Sparta we meet through this speech is not the conventional disciplined military state, the Sparta of Leonidas, prepared to march out against overwhelming odds in defense of freedom and honor but a city slow to plan and reluctant to act.[44] The Athenians by contrast have qualities that might be deplored in some circumstances but that are presented as effective and likely to bring success against the old-fashioned ways of the Spartans: "Your dispositions are old-fashioned by comparison to theirs. As in the crafts, innovation is destined to prevail. For a tranquil city undisturbed customs are best, but those who are compelled to respond to many situations have need of many innovations" (1.71.2). Thus in his first consideration of the less tangible factors in the war Thucydides contrasts the Athenians and the Spartans and again points toward Athenian success. The Sparta presented by the Corinthians is an obsolescent power, lacking the innovative and aggressive

---

[42] 1.70.2-9. Two features of the passage are especially difficult to bring over in English: the iteration of γνώμη and related words (six times in the passage) and the repetition of words with the prefix, ἐπι-, usually with a hostile sense (nine times in the passage). Γνώμη is not associated exclusively with the Athenians in this passage, but the ἐπι- prefixes are used to suggest their aggressiveness.

[43] Archidamus rebuts this unmade argument in 1.83.1f. But to use it would be trite and might be thought old-fashioned, and this any sophisticated speaker would wish to avoid; cf. 7.69.2. The Corinthians are represented instead as advancing quite unconventional arguments about Sparta.

[44] N.B. 1.69.5.

daring of the Athenians. The implication is clear: in a war with Sparta Athens should be able to prevail.

To the reader this presents in intensified form the recurring paradox of the first book. The analysis of events seems to compel the conclusion that Athens has both the power and the qualities that should prevail in a war with Sparta and her allies. The known outcome of the war is, however, Athenian defeat. But while the reader cannot escape the conflict between analysis and fact, the author can retain his distance and remain taciturn. The contrast between Athenian and Spartan characters, for example, is not presented as the author's own view but as a persuasive device adopted by Corinthian diplomats. Thucydides ultimately makes explicit his agreement with much of the Corinthians' analysis. But his statement comes only in the eighth book after a Spartan failure to follow up on a victory is described. "But not on this occasion alone did the Lacedaemonians prove to be the most convenient of all possible opponents for the Athenians. There were many other instances, for being most at variance in their dispositions— the one group sharp, the other slow; the one aggressive, the other lacking boldness—the Spartans were very helpful, especially in the case of a naval empire. The Syracusans demonstrate this: since they were in disposition most like the Athenians, they were their most effective opponents."[45] In the meantime, readers have been able to assess, and to qualify, the characterization of the Athenians and the Spartans presented in the Corinthian speech. We have seen the counterexamples of individual leaders such as Pausanias and the campaigns of Brasidas, all of which serve to give shading and tone to the initial contrast. On the Athenian side as well, the narrative eventually imposes qualifications and nuance. The case of Nicias makes it clear how much an individual leader can vary from the characteristics of his country and show resemblances to those of the opposing power. It is not long until the events reported in the *Histories* remind us of how many adjustments must be made in the Corinthians' useful but incomplete generalizations. It has already been revealed that the Spartan authorities have promised the Potidaeans that they would come to their aid by invading Attica.[46] In addition, as we have seen, the outcome of the Conference at Sparta is that the critics of hesitation and compromise carry the day. To

---

[45] 8.96.5. There are, to be sure, signs of authorial agreement earlier in the *Histories*, e.g. 6.93.1; but this is the most explicit statement.

[46] 1.58.1. This is one of Thucydides' most sensational revelations about Spartan policy in the pre-war years, similar to his report that earlier in the century the Spartans had promised the Thasians they would assist them by invading Attica (1.101). In each case the assertion is introduced succinctly, almost in passing, without clarifying precisely who made the promise, how they thought they could deliver on it, and above all how Thucydides knew.

the stereotype of Spartans must be added the qualities that let Sthenelaidas persuade his fellow citizens.

By the completion of the account of the Conference at Sparta the reader is confronted with several unresolved issues. The largest, and most difficult, is what went wrong and where precisely are to be found the causes of Athens' defeat. More immediate, however, is the question of national characteristics and the extent to which the Corinthians' characterization can be accepted. Hence we approach the next section of the work with a new set of questions in mind. This consideration may help explain the unusual arrangement of material in the book. Logically and chronologically this first assembly at Sparta should be followed by the convention of the allies and the vote of the Peloponnesian League to go to war, that is by chapters 118-126.1. Instead Thucydides digresses on the events in the approximately fifty years between the Persian and the Peloponnesian Wars. This account, the "Pentecontaetia," has often been thought to be peculiarly placed. Should it not directly have followed the Archaeology?

But, as we have seen, Thucydides' narrative often performs many tasks simultaneoulsy. The Pentecontaetia, like the Archaeology, is not a simple story of events in a given time period. It is again highly selective and focused on themes and ideas rather than on comprehensive coverage.[47] Its placement comes at the point the reader is ready to contemplate these themes and ideas. After an initial section devoted to the building of the Athenian walls and the acquisition of the leadership of the war against the Persians (chs. 88-96) Thucydides briefly comments on the principles of his treatment of the fifty-year period. He indicates he wishes to provide an account of a period that had been neglected by other historians, except for Hellanicus whose treatment was brief and chronologically imprecise. He indicates it contains a demonstration of the way by which the empire of Athens was established" (1.97.2). He indicates he will particularly discuss the Athenians' relations with the Persians, the revolts of their allies, and contacts with the Peloponnesians (1.97.1). Even within these categories, however, the account of the Pentecontaetia is selective and omits significant episodes in each category.[48]

[47] Cf. P. K. Walker, "Purpose and Method of the Pentekontaetia in Thucydides, Book I," *CQ* n.s. 7 (1957) 27-39.

[48] (1) Relations with Persians: Even if the much disputed Peace of Callias did not exist, there certainly must have been some diplomatic contacts with the Persians during the fifty years. One is implied by Herodotus 7.151. See J. Walsh's important discussion, "The Peace of Callias and the Congress Decree," *Chiron* 11 (1981) 31-63.

(2) Revolts of the allies not mentioned by Thucydides seem likely in several cases on the basis of epigraphical evidence, e.g. Miletus (see J. Barron "Milesian Politics and Propa-

When the digression is complete Thucydides restates the leading ideas in language reminiscent of the earlier passage. There is, however, a new emphasis:

All these events among the Greeks and between them and the Persians took place in approximately fifty years between the withdrawal of Xerxes and the beginning of this war. During this time the Athenians strengthened their control over the empire and made great strides forward in power. The Lacedaemonians, though they saw what was happening, did not try to stop it in any significant way, but remained tranquil for the better part of the period. Even before this they were not swift to go to war unless forced to it. They were also inhibited by domestic battles. But finally the power of the Athenians had advanced so unmistakably and their own alliance was so threatened, that they decided it could no longer be tolerated. They resolved that every effort was to be made and Athenian strength was, if possible, to be destroyed by the undertaking of this war. (1.118.2)

This restatement, as so often in Thucydides, brings out the themes that have been implicit in the preceding narrative. It can be seen that the growth of Athenian power, the truest cause of the war, is the underlying topic of the Pentecontaetia[49] and that this growth of power is explained in part by the characteristics and dispositions of the two great powers. The Athenians continue the growth of power that was evident in the Archaeology; the Spartans illustrate the slowness and hesitation of which the Corinthians have accused them.

In addition to its other functions, the Pentecontaetia provides an opportunity to test the ideas and generalizations that were adduced in the first debate at Sparta. In that debate the Athenians, for example, had explained in general terms how it was that they acquired their leadership of the naval confederacy of the Greeks: ''We received this not by force but when you

---

ganda,'' *JHS* 82 [1962] 1-6, and cf. *ML* p. 106); Erythrae (*ML* No. 40 also in *IG* i³14); and Colophon (*ML* No. 47, also in *IG* i³37).

(3) Relations with the Peloponnesians are very inadequately treated, especially for the period of the so-called ''First Peloponnesian War.'' The background to the truce mentioned in chapter 112, for example, is not explained. Nor is the Spartan treaty with Argos noted (cf.5.14). These omissions suggest that the Pentecontaetia is incomplete and would have received further revision if Thucydides had lived. The same is suggested by the juxtaposition of the criticism of Hellanicus as chronologically imprecise with a narrative that is itself open to similar criticism. Thus it would be a mistake to put much emphasis on omissions from the Pentecontaetia, but we are still left with the question why even a first draft would include this selection of episodes. It is to this question that the comments in the text are directed.

[49] Cf. H. D. Westlake, ''Thucydides and the Pentekontaetia,'' *CQ* n.s. 5 (1955) 66: ''It is beyond doubt that the purpose of the excursus of the Pentecontaetia is very largely, if not wholly, to substantiate the view of Thucydides on the *alēthestatē prophasis* of the Peloponnesian war.''

Spartans were unwilling to see the remainder of the operations against the
Persians through to a conclusion, the allies came to us and of their own
accord asked us to become their leaders'' (1.75.1). In the Pentecontaetia
the story of the Spartan regent Pausanias (chs. 94 and 95) helps the reader
to assess the Athenian claim. Pausanias' arrogant behavior and evident
treasonous collaboration with the Persians provoke great ill-feeling and he
is eventually recalled to Sparta: "They no longer sent him out as an official,
but in his place instead Dorkis and some others with him, in charge of a
small force. To these the allies no longer granted the position of leadership.
They saw what was happening and withdrew. The Spartans no longer sent
out others, for they feared that those who left Sparta turned bad—which
the case of Pausanias could be seen to confirm. And they got out of the
Persian war this way and thought the Athenians were accommodating
enough as leaders, at least for the moment.''[50]

The account in the Pentecontaetia not only corroborates the main assertion of the Athenians in the debate at Sparta but obliquely justifies their
subsequent twists of the Spartan tail: "If you pulled us down and took
over the empire, you would swiftly turn in the good will which you have
acquired thanks to fear of us—if your present policies were similar to those
you showed in the short period when you were the leader against the
Persians. Your customs do not mix with those of others and each person
who is sent out from Sparta observes neither these nor what is customary
in the rest of Greece'' (1.77.6). The narrative of the Pentecontaetia, in
other words, functions in part as a confirmation of ideas and claims introduced in the debate at Sparta.[51] It further illustrates the energy of the
Athenians and helps corroborate the Corinthian characterization of the
contrast between the Spartans and the Athenians. As in that passage the
Athenians are the center of attention. The narrative shows them in action
in every quarter of the eastern Mediterranean, sailing around the Peloponnese (108.5), establishing control of the narrows of the Corinthian Gulf
(103.3), and engaged in northern Greece (100.2), Asia Minor (100.1),
Cyprus (112.4), and Egypt (104). From time to time episodes not only
help confirm the determination and vigor of the Athenians, but seem to
be shaped to illustrate it:

[50] 1.95.6-7. A significantly different version is presented in Aristotelian *Athenaion Politeia*
25.2; cf. Herodotus 9.106. These indicate immediate hostility on the part of Sparta to Athenian
leadership.

[51] For the use of narrative as confirmation in ancient rhetoric, see [Aristotle] *Rhetorica ad
Alexandrum* chs. 30-32.

When a battle took place at Tanagra in Boeotia the Lacedaemonians and their allies won and there were heavy casualties on both sides. The Lacedaemonians moved into the Megarid, cut down some trees, and went home via Mt. Geraneia and the Corinthian Isthmus. But the Athenians on the sixty-second day after the battle made an expedition into Boeotia, under the command of Myronides. In a battle at Oenophyta they defeated the Boeotians, won control of the territory of Boeotia and Phocis, pulled down the walls of the Tanagrans, took the hundred wealthiest men of the Opuntian Locrians as prisoners and completed their own long walls. (1.108.2-3)

In a succinct narrative such as the Pentecontaetia, there is no need to report the number of days between the two battles nor the details of Athenian operations after Oenophyta. Allusion to Athenian domination of central Greece would suffice. But the contrast between the Athenian conduct and the Spartan illustrates the Corinthian claim that the Spartans do less than their power allows while when the Athenians "defeat an enemy, they push the advantage as far as they can; if defeated, they retreat as little as they must" (ch. 70). Another episode refutes a Peloponnesian expectation about the Athenians: Since the Peloponnesians wanted to help the Aeginetans [in their struggle with Athens], they landed three hundred Corinthian and Epidaurian hoplites as auxiliaries [on Aegina]. Then the Corinthians and their allies seized the passes through Mt. Geraneia and moved down to the Megarid, thinking that the Athenians would be unable to assist the Megareans when they had a large force operating in Aegina and another in Egypt. Or if they did assist them, they would withdraw from Aegina" (1.105.3). But the Peloponnesians badly misassess their opponent. The Athenians "did not move the expedition at Aegina, but the oldest and youngest draft classifications, who had been left at Athens, come to Megara under command of Myronides" (1.105.4).[52] The result is an Athenian victory.

The impression that emerges from the Pentecontaetia is of the restless energy of the Athenians, their refusal to be stymied, their ability to come out of every setback with even greater vigor than before. At a civic level they display precisely what Themistocles represents as an individual: boldness, decisiveness, cleverness, a willingness to take risks. The Spartans,

---

[52] A similar pattern appears in chapter 114: While Euboea is in revolt, Megara, with the assistance of Corinth and others, breaks away from Athens. Under Spartan leadership the Peloponnesians then invade Attica. But Pericles quickly withdraws from Euboea, the Peloponnesians withdraw from Attica, and Pericles then returns to Euboea and reduces it. The narrative emphasizes the speed and decisiveness of Athenian action. It says nothing about the widespread rumor that Pericles had bribed King Pleistoanax of Sparta to withdraw his army from Attica. See 2.21.1 and Gomme in *HCT* on 1.114.2 (p. 341).

by contrast, seem to have indecisive leadership and to be without a clear direction for growth. They distrust boldness and innovation.[53] What impedes them, however, is not always lethargy or failure of will; sometimes very practical considerations prevent them from acting. At the time of the revolt of Thasos from Athens, for example, the Spartans were, according to Thucydides, willing to help the Thasians, but they were incapacitated by "domestic wars," that is, by the revolt of disaffected groups within their society:

When the Thasians had been defeated in battle [by the Athenians] and were besieged, they called upon the Lacedaemonians and urged them to come to their aid by invading Attica. The Lacedaemonians made a secret promise that they would, and were about to, but were prevented by the earthquake during which the Helots and the Thouriatai and Aithaeans of the perioikic class broke away to Mt. Ithome. (The Helots for the most part were the descendants of the old Messenians who had been enslaved. For this reason they were all called "Messenians.") So the Spartans had a war with the rebels on Ithome and the Thasians after two years of siege came to terms with the Athenians. (1.101)

Thus we move beyond the generalizations of the Corinthians to an understanding of some of the mechanisms of power and the patterns that contribute to or detract from the effectiveness of the two major states. The Spartans are not unaware of the growth of Athenian power, nor unwilling to act, but are prevented from effective action, especially by the Helot problem.[54] The Athenians at the same time benefit from the procedures of the empire and the natural reluctance of the subject cities to do military service: "Because of this avoidance of military expeditions the majority of them arranged to pay in cash rather than in ships the due expense so that they did not have to leave home. The naval power of Athens was increased by the expenditures which they contributed, while they were unprepared when they broke away and lacked skill in warfare" (1.99.3).

The Pentecontaetia thus forges a link between the quantitative analysis of power in the Archaeology and the emphasis on national characteristics in the Corinthian speech at Sparta. Moreover, it lets the reader see how these rather abstract and general considerations apply in specific historical

[53] N.B. 1.102.3 "fearing the boldness and innovation of the Athenians" δείσαντες τῶν Ἀθηναίων τὸ τολμηρὸν καὶ τὴν νεωτεροποιίαν, though in 102.3 the Spartan fear of innovation is quite specific: the fear that the rebels on Mt. Ithome will persuade the Athenians to try revolutionary activity: μή τι . . . νεωτερίσωσι.

[54] There were certainly many other problems affecting Spartan effectiveness, including the rivalry between the two royal houses and the built-in conflicts between ephors and kings, but Thucydides feels the Helot problem was the crucial one: αἰεὶ γὰρ τὰ πολλὰ Λακεδαιμονίοις πρὸς τοὺς Εἵλωτας τῆς φυλακῆς πέρι μάλιστα καθειστήκει (4.80.3).

circumstances. As we watch, the dynamic of Greek history seems again to be working in the Athenians' favor. Her power, readiness, and experience grow, her opponents are so far unable to take effective action to stop her. At the outbreak of the war, with Samos subjugated and Corcyra in alliance, it appears almost too late to stop her.[55]

WINNING THE WAR

At the end of the Pentecontaetia (ch. 118) the narrative returns to the Spartan decision to make war. The themes and some of the language evoke chapters 88 and 89. In addition we once again witness an assembly at Sparta and hear another polemical speech by the Corinthians (chs. 120-124). On this occasion, however, the audience is composed of representatives of the states of the Peloponnesian League. They vote to support Sparta and to go to war. Their decision, although unequivocal, does not lead to immediate hostilities. The end of the summer of 432 and the opening months of 431 B.C. are spent in preparations for an attack on the Athenians and in the sending of ambassadors to make charges against the Athenians "so that they might have the greatest justification for war, if the Athenians did not make concessions."[56]

If Thucydides is right in presenting the Peloponnesian vote as an unqualified decision to make war and the diplomatic activity as propaganda, then the reader is forced to accept the cogency and reasonableness of Periclean policy. Although willing, even eager, for the arbitration provisions of the Thirty Years Peace to be invoked, Pericles rejected concessions to the Peloponnesians, on the grounds that they would lead the enemy to conclude the Athenians were afraid and thus result in further and greater demands (1.140.5). He was, moreover, confident of Athens' ability to sustain a war with the Peloponnesians, emphasizing in his analysis the importance of precisely the naval power and financial reserve that operated so strongly in the Archaeology.

[55] 1.118.2 is mildly sarcastic: The Spartans did little or nothing until the power of Athens had greatly increased; *then* they thought it was intolerable and that all zeal (*prothymia*) had to be used in destroying it. The iteration of expressions for necessity in *-tea* echoes Sthenelaidas in 86.3.

[56] 1.126.1. Since Thucydides reports no conditions or restrictions in the decision to make war (125.1), the final phrase in 126.1, ἢν μή τι ἐσακούωσιν, is puzzling. What if the Athenians made a concession, such as the repeal of the Megarean decree? Could there then have been a process of negotiation that might have avoided the war? The last group of Spartan ambassadors to go to Athens before the war say so. More significantly, perhaps, Archidamus seems to act on this notion, immediately before the first invasion (2.12.1 and 12.4; cf. 18.5).

Pericles' confidence is the culmination of the analysis of the first book. The factors that have shaped Greek history in the past are the ones upon which Pericles builds his strategy. We know that if the innovative and energetic spirit of the Athenians endures, Pericles has good reason for his assurance. In addition, a third consideration encourages confidence in Athenian success. The new factor is leadership. Throughout much of the first book political leadership is a rather peripheral issue. The Archaeology, as we have seen, concentrates on process rather than personality or alludes to individuals largely to illustrate processes and sources of power. The characteristics discussed by the Corinthians and clarified by the narrative of the Pentecontaetia and other sections are national rather than personal ones. But in the final portion of the book attention moves away from collective and abstract considerations toward a consideration of individuals and the ways in which they shape events. We can already glimpse this shift in the conflict between King Archidamus and the ephor Sthenelaidas at Sparta. Thucydides' purpose here is not so much to clarify the nature of political factions and tensions within Sparta as to alert the reader to an important contrast between pre-war Sparta and Athens. As the first book draws to a close the full significance of that contrast becomes clear. While Sparta is divided in its counsels and subject to the persuasive manipulations of a Sthenelaidas, Athens seems unified behind the leadership of Pericles.

Pericles comes into focus only gradually and late. Apart from a few allusions to him in the Pentecontaetia, his importance first becomes clear when the Spartan embassy demands that the Athenians drive out the descendants of a group of Athenians who two hundred years earlier had committed a religious crime. With a hint of sarcasm Thucydides affirms the sincerity of the Spartan concern about the gods, but goes on to observe that the Spartans knew that Pericles was related to the guilty ones on his mother's side and thought that if he were removed Athenian affairs might make easier progress.[57] They thought in any event that the charge might weaken his standing with the Athenians.

The Athenian rejection of this embassy's demands leads to a digression on the two most brilliant Greeks of their day, Themistocles of Athens and Pausanias of Sparta. The excursus (chs. 128-138) sustains the new attention to individual leaders and at the same time adds new depth and complexity to the contrast of national characters introduced earlier in the book. But it is also a reminder that, for all their brilliance, both men were rejected by

---

[57] 1.127.1. On δῆθεν to indicate sarcasm see Classen-Steup ad loc. and G. Denniston, *The Greek Particles*, 2nd ed. (Oxford 1954) p. 264.

their cities and strongly suspected of treason. Each turns to the King of Persia and ends his life despised by his countrymen.

Against this background the narrative turns to Pericles and to the first of a series of his speeches reported in the first and second books. His purpose in this oration is to dissuade the Athenians from any concession and to convince them that Athens can overcome in a war with the Peloponnesians. This brilliant and compelling speech is not balanced against the words of a rival politician in a typical Thucydidean antilogy. It is rather an antilogy at a distance, answering, almost point by point, the arguments of the Corinthians in their last speech at Sparta.[58] The answer is built in large part upon the analysis of power in the Archaeology, but also restates and reinforces Archidamus' arguments about the difficulties that confront the Peloponnesians and the opportunities for the Athenians:

And if they march with their infantry against our territory, we will sail against theirs. It will not be an even trade to ravage part of the Peloponnese and all of Attica, for they will not acquire other territory without a fight, while we have abundant land on the islands and on the mainland. The command of the sea is a great thing. Consider this: if we were islanders, who would be less vulnerable? In our present circumstances we should develop a strategy that approximates this situation, by letting our land and houses go, while guarding our city and the sea. We must never get angry over them and join battle with the Peloponnesians who far outnumber us, for if we win, we will battle again with no fewer opponents, while if we blunder, we lose in addition the source of our strength—the control of our allies. They will not stay tranquil if we cannot mount an expedition against them. (1.143.4-5)

[58] The similarities to chapters 121 and 122 of the Corinthian speech are evident throughout chapters 141-143 but the verbal connections are especially clear in Pericles' comments in 143.1:

1.121.3, ἐξαρτυσόμεθα καὶ ἀπὸ τῶν ἐν Δελφοῖς καὶ Ὀλυμπίᾳ χρημάτων· δάνεισμα γὰρ ποιησάμενοι ὑπολαβεῖν οἷοί τ' ἐσμὲν μισθῷ μείζονι τοὺς ξένους αὐτῶν ναυβάτας.

1.143.1 Εἴ τε καὶ κινήσαντες τῶν Ὀλυμπίασιν ἢ Δελφοῖς χρημάτων μισθῷ μείζονι πειρῷντο ἡμῶν ὑπολαβεῖν τοὺς ξένους τῶν ναυτῶν.

The similarities are so close that some critics have argued that Thucydides in effect illustrates Mencken's definition of a historian as a "failed novelist"; i.e. he composed the two speeches to advance his own presentation of the war, with little regard for what was actually said by the speakers. Surely Thucydides wants to emphasize the counterpoint of ideas but we must be cautious before assuming that Pericles never knew of or responded to the Corinthian analysis. The Corinthian speech was given before delegates from a large number of cities and the vote was by no means unanimous (1.125.1). Secrecy would not easily be maintained. Reports of their arguments would eagerly have been sought in Athens and much discussed. Hence Pericles would have had a strong incentive to respond to the Corinthians' claims. Thucydides task would then have been to select this speech out of others given in this period and to shape it in a way that brought out its relationship to the themes and ideas of the rest of the *Histories*.

The arguments of the second Corinthian speech are easily dispatched. The Peloponnesians, Pericles shows, will not find it easy to hire away the rowers on the Athenian fleet, since higher pay will not outbalance the greater danger (ch. 143). Nor can they swiftly acquire the naval skill that the Athenians have been developing since the Persian Wars (142.6f.); nor will any enemy fortification in Attic territory prove effective. Whatever damages it inflicts will be outweighed by Athenian naval attacks on their territory (142.2-4).[59] While refuting these arguments, Pericles can drive home the importance of finances and of naval power which emerges from the analysis of the Archaeology and has been affirmed by Archidamus.[60]

Pericles' speech then is the culmination of the analysis of the book and carries us with it by the rigor and intelligence of its analysis.[61] His strategy derives from the Themistoclean transformation of Athens into a walled naval power and from the analysis of power that seems so amply confirmed by the narrative of the first book. He sees what needs to be done and convinces the assembly that his advice is best (*arista* 1.145.1). Decisive, unchallenged, he seems properly described by Thucydides' introduction, with its epic ring: "a man who was at that time the first of the Athenians, most powerful in word and action."[62] But the undercurrent of doubt and tension that we have felt in other passages persists even now. The course of the war will not be as simple as Pericles seems to imply; with it will come loss and sufferings, as yet only alluded to, but of great intensity and significance. The war as projected through the speeches of the first book is a chess game, logical and remote, a testing ground of ideas and strategies.

[59] The references to an *epiteichismos* in Attica have provoked much scholarly discussion, because they so obviously call to mind the fortification of Deceleia in 413. As so often the composition question has obscured the problem, with advocates of a late dating for this section of the work arguing that the references to such fortifications must belong after Deceleia and advocates of earlier composition point out that such ideas were discussed long before the actual operations began. See Gomme in *HCT* on 1.124.3 (p. 418). Nothing can be proved about the date of original composition, but as he read through these passages a post-war reader would certainly be reminded, as the scholiast in 1.122.1 was, of Deceleia. Since Thucydides surely revised his work in the post-war period, he must have been willing to let the remainder of Deceleia stand, even though it might easily have been suppressed in a narrative as succinct as this.

[60] The first is emphasized by the repetition of the word, χρήματα, throughout the speech: 1.141.3, 1.141.5; 1.142.1; 1.143.1. The second is expresed in more varied language but is no less prominent: 1.141.4; 1.142.2, 1.142.4-9; 1.143 passim.

[61] The speaker's self-characterization in the opening sentence of his first speech is often an important clue to the way Thucydides wishes us to view him. Thus Archidamus' *empeiria* (80.1), Sthenelaidas' "know-nothingism" (86.1), Cleon's egotism and anti-democratic disposition (3.37.1), are all significant. Pericles' opening underlines the constancy of his *gnōmē*.

[62] 139.4. Cf. Homer *Iliad* 9.443, Thucydides' own description of Pericles in 127.3 (ὢν γὰρ δυνατώτατος τῶν καθ᾽ ἑαυτὸν, and Protagoras in Plato *Protagoras* 318 d.

Pericles is clearly a superb player but what will the effect be when the game moves to the battlefields? There are signs already of problems. When, for example, Pericles points out that the war may prove to be a long one he adds "for them," the enemy (1.141.5). But the reader knows it is not just "for them" that the war turns out to be longer than expected. Its unexpected length affects all participants, not least the Athenians. And although in the short run the Peloponnesian arguments are flawed, over a longer period they can prove correct. It is not easy for them to hire the crews away from the Athenian navy nor to develop comparable naval skill of their own, but ultimately they manage to do both. An effective Peloponnesian base of operation in Attica is not established in the opening years of the war, but eventually the fort at Deceleia reduces Athens itself to a virtual garrison.[63] When Pericles in the phraseology current at the time of the outbreak of the war[64] says, "if we were islanders, who would be less vulnerable," he makes a telling point about the ability of Athens to resist a Peloponnesian invasion. But the reader knows that there is a potential irony in the question. Athens is not an island and will find it difficult to pretend to be one. A strategy of self-confinement behind the walls may not be as easy as it appears. Pericles' comment that he has a greater fear of Athenian errors than of Peloponnesian planning hints not only at the well-known Athenian mistakes during the course of the war but at the possibility that even Pericles' brilliant analysis may yet contain a flaw.

The effect of his speech then is, as often in Thucydides, complex. We are carried along by its logic and force, but remain aware simultaneously of ironic possibilities. Knowing the outcome of the war, we recognize the discrepancy between his confidence and the difficulties that await both sides. The tension that we have detected under the surface throughout the first book persists, then, even at the very end. Only the war itself can provide a resolution.

[63] In 142.4 Pericles refers to such a fortification as a *phrourion*. In 7.28.1 Athens itself is described as reduced to a *phrourion* by the occupation of Deceleia. The language of 142.4 is also adapted in 7.27.4f.

[64] The same idea is expressed in pseudo-Xenophon *Athenaion Politeia* 2.14. The dating of this treatise continues to be disputed though the case for a date early in the Peloponnesian War seems to me to be overwhelmingly strong. See now E. Lévy, *Athènes devant la défaite de 404* (Bibliothèque des Écoles Françaises d'Athènes et de Rome, fasc. 225, Paris 1976) 273-275.

Book 2

THE OUTBREAK OF THE WAR

O N A RAINY night in the spring of 431 B.C. during a month set aside by their fellow citizens for sacred observances, a group of wealthy but disaffected Plataeans opened the gates of their city to troops from Thebes. The Theban force, a little more than three hundred, moved swiftly, took the town by surprise and seemed to be in command. But later that night the other inhabitants recognized their superior numbers, counterattacked and forced the Thebans to withdraw. Some were killed; some captured and later put to death. When Thebes sent a larger force against the city, the Plataeans asked for help from their ally, Athens, and prepared for a siege. The Peloponnesian War had begun.[1]

The beginning is as surprising to the reader as to the unwary Plataeans. Throughout the first book we have heard little of them or their opponents, the Thebans. Plataea has been mentioned only as the site of the famous battle in the second Persian invasion, where the Spartans under Pausanias' command turned back the Persian land forces (1.130.1). But Plataea's alliance with Athens and the close ties that bound the cities together are not mentioned. Nor do the Thebans appear with any prominence in the first book, despite their strategic location just north of Attica and their

---

[1] Throughout the Plataean episode Thucydides shows a tendency to postpone the introduction of important material until very late in the narrative. Thus although the rain is important for the setting, and would almost certainly be mentioned by a modern writer at the opening of the story, Thucydides does not allude to it until its relevance is inescapable (2.4.2); the fact that the attack came during a sacred month and the composition of the Plataean fifth column are clarified only in the third book (3.56.2, cf. 65). This technique of "postponed information" is also used in the narrative of the Pylos operations in book 4 and contrasts sharply with that commonly used elsewhere, e.g., in book 6. When using this technique Thucydides does little to set the stage or provide background or mood. He plunges his reader into events and only gradually makes available the information needed for an assessment. The result is a swift narrative that conveys the surprise of the immediate moment, and postpones or leaves open other questions, e.g. the strategic significance or justification for the operation.

military potential. Thebes is not even alluded to in the account of the Pentecontaetia, though some Athenian operations in Boeotia (e.g. 1.108.3) were almost surely aimed at preventing her domination of the other cities of Boeotia. Nor is her value as an ally alluded to by the Corinthian speakers in the debates at Sparta, nor by Sthenelaidas.[2]

Thus the Theban attack on Plataea is a double surprise. A sudden night offensive at a place to which little attention has been paid encourages the reader to react like a contemporary with surprise at the unexpected form taken by the outbreak of the war. But this reaction gives way to more serious reflections. In the analysis of the first book, we have not been prepared for the significant factor of Theban intervention in the conflict between Athens and the Peloponnesians. The attack on Plataea is the first major indication of an omission in the elaborate calculus of power that was developed in the first book; it is moreover, the first of a series of indicators in the second book that the Athenian situation is more complex than we have as yet been led to contemplate.

The episode at Plataea illustrates the warning delivered by Athenian speakers to the first Conference at Sparta reported in book 1: "recognize before you enter into it, how much there is in war that cannot be predicted."[3] But it applies to the Athenian as well as to the Spartan situation.

The element of the unexpected remains prominent among features of the second book, especially in the account of the Great Plague, which began to afflict Athens in the second year of the war. We shall return in subsequent sections to the plague and the famous Periclean Funeral Oration. But it is necessary first to examine the structure and major themes of these two episodes. Chapters 7 through 65 of the book focus increasingly on Pericles and his leadership of Athens during the opening years of the war and indirectly on more general problems of political leadership. These

---

[2] Thebes' great strength as a land power in the fourth century may tempt us to exaggerate her significance in the fifth century. She was then still far from acquiring the power she later enjoyed under Epaminondas, and moreover, was reluctant fully to apply what force she had. Her policy was at first not to join in operations outside of Boeotia (4.92), and she seems not to have taken the obvious step of helping supply the Peloponnesian armies during their invasions of Attica; if 2.23.2 is indicative, the Peloponnesians brought their supplies with them and withdrew when they were depleted. Nor did the Thebans prevent the Thessalian cavalry (2.22f.) from reaching Attica. We might also have expected them to have moved more vigorously against Oropos (cf. 2.23.3), which was not brought over to their control until 412/11 (see Gomme in *HCT* on 2.23.2 [p. 80f.]). Thus Thebes seems to have had quite limited objectives in the war, and to have been willing at first to make only a modest commitment to the Peloponnesian side. Nonetheless we would expect a clearer delineation of her hostility to Athens, an important strategic factor in the outbreak of the war.

[3] 1.78.1: τοῦ δὲ πολέμου τὸν παράλογον, ὅσος ἐστί, πρὶν ἐν αὐτῷ γενέσθαι προδιάγνωτε.

topics are explored amid and through the development of the major themes
of this section of the *Histories*: the conflicts between reason and passion,
the predictable and the unpredictable, public interests and private. This
portion of the second book also draws attention to several factors that have
not previously been clarified. For example, it reports, with some irony,
the wide enthusiasm for the Peloponnesian cause,[4] lists the allies on each
side,[5] and summarizes Athenian financial and military resources.[6] But the
second book chiefly battles out once and for all the paramount question
of strategy in the war. The Athenians, as we know from Pericles' analysis
in book 1, can use their walls, sea power, and financial reserves to develop
an unprecedented strategy against the Peloponnesians. They can let the
enemy ravage their land, outwait them, and retaliate by naval attacks on
the Peloponnese. But they cannot meet the Peloponnesians in a pitched
land battle and hope to win. Hence, from Pericles' point of view all depends
upon Athenian willingness to implement and adhere to this strategy. From
the point of view of the Spartan command the best hope of victory is
somehow to draw the Athenians into a land battle.

We find out whether the Spartans can achieve this goal by watching the
conflict between two of the major figures of the first book, Pericles of
Athens and King Archidamus of Sparta. The narrative moves in a recurring
pattern in the *Histories* from the collective discussion of Athenians and
Spartans to what we will call "commander narrative," that is to a story
dominated by a few leading individuals, usually military leaders. The

[4] 2.8.4f.: "Most people directed their support much more toward the Lacedaemonians,
especially because they proclaimed [*proeipontōn*] that they would bring freedom to Greece."
Cf. 2.11.2, Gomme in *HCT* on 2.8.4 (p. 9f.) points out that the narrative does not confirm
Thucydides' generalization. Thucydides himself later makes it clear that the Spartans felt
uneasy about their own conduct in beginning the war (7.18.2); cf. also 1.81.5. Thucydides
is so vague about the groups that held this favorable attitude toward Sparta that it seems
likely that he is primarily concerned with developing a contrast between Greek attitudes
toward Sparta at the beginning of the war and those at the end, when Spartan imperialism
replaced Athenian imperialism and the claims of "liberation" could be seen to be specious.
A postwar reader would see in this sentence an ironic comment about Spartan policy rather
than an attempt to make a precise statement about the varied attitudes of different cities and
classes in Greece.

[5] Chapter 9, D. J. Smart, "Catalogues in Thucydides and Ephorus," *GRBS* 18 (1977) 33-
42, argues for the deletion of the passage on the grounds that it was interpolated from Ephorus
(cf. Diodorus Siculus 12.42.4-5). Some peculiarities of fact and phrasing are indeed evident
in the passage, but Smart's amputation is needlessly severe and posits an interpolator of more
than average incompetence.

[6] 2.13.3-8. The financial picture in this chapter is not easily reconciled with the evidence
from the tribute *stēlai* etc., but the inscriptions, despite much brilliant work, are still obscure
at many crucial points. The best introduction to the problem is R. Meiggs, *The Athenian
Empire* (Oxford 1972) ch. 13, pp. 234-254 and app., pp. 11-14.

introduction of this type of narration often marks a change to greater detail both in the reporting of events and in the exploration of the strategy or motives behind them.[7] In this case the commander narrative uses two leaders, one on each side, and presents the outcome as the result of the struggles between their ideas and leadership. Archidamus at first has the initiative and appears with greater prominence.[8] Before the first invasion of Attica he calls the leaders of the various Peloponnesian allies together and gives a speech modeled after the addresses made by commanders to their troops before pitched battle. The speech reiterates the respect Archidamus showed in the first book for good military order and preparation and his recognition of how formidable the Athenians are as a foe. He is again the wise and sound adviser, but his estimation of the Athenians is in one crucial respect mistaken: "We should certainly hope that they will join battle, if they are not hastening out even now before we have arrived, then when they see us in their land ravaging and destroyed their possessions. For passion [*orgē*] afflicts everyone in the eyes, that is, when they suddenly see themselves suffering something unexpected. Those who least use calculation, most often act under anger. It is to be expected that the Athenians will do this to a greater extent than others, for they think they deserve to rule others and to attack and ravage other people's land rather than see it happen to themselves" (2.11.6-8). Archidamus' strategy is to overcome the Athenians' *gnōmē*, that untranslatable combination of intelligence, planning, and resolve,[9] and his chief weapon is the eyesight of the Athenians.[10] His plan becomes more explicit when the actual invasion begins;

[7] Note for example the change from civic to commander narrative in 4.2.4., when the account of Pylos' campaign begins.

[8] On Archidamus in this section see J. de Romilly, "Les intentions d'Archidamos et le livre II de Thucydide," *REA* 64 (1962) 287-299, and cf. V. Hunter, *Thucydides the Artful Reporter* (Toronto 1973) ch. 1, pp. 11-21.

[9] *Gnōmē* is an extremely important concept in the *Histories* and is a component of two of the fundamental antitheses in the work. In the sense of "reason and intelligence" it often contrasts with *orgē*, "passion and anger"; in the sense of "planning and rational control" it contrasts with *tychē*, "change and indeterminacy." Useful discussions and bibliographies on the term can be found in H. Herter, "Thukydides und Demokrit über Tyche," *WS* N.F. 10 (1976) 106-128 esp. 109, n. 8, and L. Edmunds, *Chance and Intelligence in Thucydides* (Cambridge, Mass. 1975) esp. 5, n. 10, and P. Huart, *Le Vocabulaire de l'analyse psychologique dans l'oeuvre de Thucydide* (Paris 1968) 304-313.

[10] On the effects of vision on the emotions see E. M. Cope's note on Aristotle *Rhetoric* (Cambridge 1877) vol. 2, sec. 18f. In Gorgias *Helen* (*VS* 82 B 11, esp.15ff.) sight is the means by which *erōs* affects the *psychē*. K. R. Jackson of the University of Melbourne has pointed out to me how striking the parallels are between this fragment of Gorgias and the second book of Thucydides. There are, for example, similarities between the psychological role of sight in the *Helen* and the notion in the Funeral Oration (2.43.1) that the vision of the greatness of the city can produce a love that results in self-sacrifice. The vision theme

for instead of moving directly against Athens and surrounding the plain, he leads the invaders to Acharnae, a populous township in northern Attica, and remains there for some time ravaging land:

With some such *gnōmē* as this is Archidamus reported to have remained near Acharnae ready for battle and not to have come down into the plain during this invasion. He hoped that the Athenians with their large number of young people and their unprecedented preparations for war would perhaps come out against him and not allow their land to be ravaged. And when they did not meet him when he was at Eleusis and the Thriasian plain, he made a probe by remaining at Acharnae seeing if they would come out against him. The location also seemed to him well suited for a camp and at the same time the Acharnians were a large percentage of the population—3,000 citizens.[11] They were not likely to allow their holdings to be destroyed but would drive all the others into battle. And if the Athenians did not come out against him on this invasion, he could on subsequent invasions proceed more confidently to ravage the plain and approach the city itself. For once the Acharnians were deprived of their holdings, they would not be equally enthusiastic to take risks for the rest of the citizens. *Stasis*[12] would be present in their resolution. With such intentions Archidamus remained near Acharnae. (2.20)

At first Archidamus' analysis seems to be correct. Athenian sentiment, especially among the youth is for immediate action (21.3f.). But Archidamus has left Periclean leadership out of his calculation. From the first book the reader has gained a clear impression of Pericles' power and intelligence; a telling example of his foresight has recently confirmed this impression. Anticipating that the Spartans might leave his farm unravaged, while destroying those of other citizens, Pericles has told the Athenian assembly that he would, under those circumstances, give his farm to the state so that there would be no basis for suspicion against him.[13] Thus the

---

is also prominent in 2.18.5, 20, 21.2, and perhaps in 49.8. It recurs in book 6, esp. 24.3 and 31.1.

[11] The manuscript reference to 3,000 hoplites (heavy armed infantry) in 20.4 poses difficulties for the analysis of the Athenian military forces, especially since Thucydides has just said that the total number of active hoplites was 13,000 (13.6). See Gomme in *HCT* on 2.20.4 (pp. 73f.). It seems impossible for one deme to account for 23 percent of the city's heavy infantry. Hence, Dow's emendation, "Thucydides and the Number of Acharnian Hoplitai, *TAPA* 92 (1961) 66-80, is attractive; he would reverse the first two letters of the noun and read *politai*, "citizens," instead of *hoplitai*, "hoplites." This, not implausibly, posits that Thucydides' source was a deme register rather than a conscription list. See also M. H. Hansen, *Symbolae Osloenses* 56 (1981) 19.32.

[12] *Stasis* is properly the term for the division of a city into factions and the turning of the factions to violence against one another. "Discord," "faction," "civil strife," "revolution," "class warfare" are all used from time to time to render the term into English.

[13] 2.13.1. Earlier, a *gnōmē* (here a proposal in the assembly) of Pericles had been passed, specifying that no herald would be received from the Lacedaemonians during their expedition against Athens (12.2). This provides another reminder of Periclean planning and control.

reader approaches Archidamus' plan knowing that Pericles is likely to anticipate it and take counter measures. This Pericles does despite hostility directed against him:

The city was thoroughly chafed and they were passionate in their annoyance at Pericles and remembered nothing of what he had said before but accused him of cowardice because, though a commander, he would not lead them out to battle. They thought he was responsible for everything they suffered. But Pericles saw that they were provoked under the present circumstance and were not assessing things well. Trusting he was right in his resolution [*gignōskein*] not to go out against the enemy, he convened no assembly or other gathering of them lest they come together under the influence of passion rather than reason, and blunder out. He kept watch on the city and kept it tranquil, as best he could.[14]

The Periclean response is successful. The Athenians do not join battle. The Peloponnesians ravage Acharnae and some villages in the area between Mt. Parnes and Mt. Pentelicus and then return to the Peloponnese. Not until Mantinea do we hear of an Athenian plan to meet the main force of the Peloponnesians in a hoplite battle.[15]

Archidamus has, in effect, been defeated; he never again appears in commander narrative in the *Histories*.[16] Pericles has overcome Archidamus' threat. Yet, although he now dominates the narrative until the valedictory comments in chapter 65, the challenge to his leadership is not

[14] 2.21.3-22.1. By what means did Pericles, whose position was only that of one of ten *stratēgoi*, keep the Athenians from convening in the assembly? A *stratēgos*, or at least the board of *stratēgoi*, had the right to convene the assembly when deemed necessary. But despite P. Brunt, "Spartan Policy and Strategy in the Archidamian War," *Phoenix* 19 (1967) 265, n. 37, it is not clear they had the converse power, to prevent a regularly scheduled meeting. Such an action would run against the whole direction of Athenian political development in Pericles' lifetime—a development in which Pericles played no insignificant part—though the absence of precedents might let it fall into an area where there were no clear rules. Whatever the precise legal status of Pericles' act, it is not likely to have been meekly tolerated by the Athenians; indeed some of the criticism of Pericles as a tyrant in Attic comedy of these years may have been based on animosity against this action.

On the position of *stratēgoi*, see especially K. J. Dover, "Dekatos Autos," *JHS* 80 (1960) 74f.; and P. J. Rhodes, *The Athenian Boule* (Oxford 1972) 43-47. Note also Theramenes in Lysias 12.71. A new discussion of the problem by M. H. Hansen is forthcoming in *ClMed* 34 (1983).

[15] Since Thucydides will often present one episode as typical of a number, there may have been other debates on whether to engage. But it seems more likely that the temptation to meet the Peloponnesians was never as strong as it was in the first year of the war. In the second year the plague broke out and thereafter Athenian military resources were much reduced.

[16] There is one interesting exchange with the Plataeans in 2.72, but otherwise Archidamus is mentioned only in the formula marking the annual invasions: 2.47.2; 71.1; 3.1.1. Since in 3.26.1 (427 B.C.) Cleomenes, from the other Spartan royal house, commands for the young Pausanias and in 3.89.1 (426 B.C.) Archidamus' son commands, it is often inferred that he was ill in 427 and died by 426.

over. After the Great Plague breaks out during the second year of the war, the Athenians again find it difficult to maintain the course that Pericles has urged.[17] Their changing mood poses a new problem for Periclean leadership. Their present impulse is just the opposite of the previous year's: now they want peace negotiations with the Spartans.[18] And Pericles' response is the opposite of his earlier one; he now convenes an assembly to deal with the mood of his fellow citizens who,

underwent a transition in their *gnōmai* and were annoyed, holding Pericles responsible for persuading them to make war. Because of him they had fallen on misfortunes. They pushed ahead to make a settlement with the Lacedaemonians. They sent out some embassies to them who came back unsuccessful. Not knowing where to turn in their resolution, they directed their hostility to Pericles. But he saw that they were provoked under present circumstances and were doing just what he expected. Convening an assembly (he was still a commander) he wanted to put some spine in them, and by drawing off the empassionment of their resolution, to turn them to more gentleness and confidence.[19]

[17] Immense scholarly efforts have gone into identifying the plague with a known disease but no agreement has resulted. For a sophisticated view of the problem and what seems to me the most plausible solution see J.C.F. Poole and A. J. Holladay, "Thucydides and the Plague of Athens," *CQ* n.s. 29 (1979) 282-300. They argue that the plague is not to be identified with any known disease but is an illness that has since become extinct or dormant.

[18] More accurately, they want to continue peace negotiations after one or more embassies had returned unsuccessful (ch. 59.1). Since it is unlikely that Pericles has approved of the sending of ambassadors, we can infer that he was not in continuous or easy control of the assembly and its moods. Cf. below on 2.65.9. Thucydides passes over the earlier discussion of negotiations to concentrate on this occasion; he is more interested in the relationship between Pericles and his audience than in the proposed approach to Sparta. Thus we are not sure whether his speech was part of a general discussion of foreign policy or directed to a specific proposal for further negotiations. There may, however, be a clue in 2.64.6 when Pericles urges the Athenians μήτε ἐπικηρυκεύεσθε. This is an unusual way to say "don't send another embassy." Literally it means not to make use of *kēryx*, a herald. On the use of this word see W. R. Connor, "Tyrannis Polis," in *Ancient and Modern: Essays in Honor of G. F. Else*, ed. J. H. D'Arms and J. W. Eadie (Ann Arbor 1977).

[19] 2.59. This passage exploits, I believe, medical terminology. Adam Parry's article, "The Language of Thucydides' Description of the Plague," *BISCL* 16 (1969) 106-118, showed that Thucydides' language in the account of the Great Plague can only rarely be called distinctly or technically medical and that a physician of the period was likely to use language very similar to that of his patients, even when writing a technical treatise for other specialists. Thus "medical terminology" of this period is by its very nature difficult to separate from ordinary Greek. But there are occasional signs of a Thucydidean utilization of the more unusual parts of medical vocabulary. In this passage ἠλλοίωντο τὰς γνώμας seems to me to be more than just a peculiar way to say "a change came over the spirit of the Athenians" (Crawley). The verb has a striking medical parallel in the Hippocratic *Praecepta* 9. Thucydides used it, I believe, to suggest some affliction of their judgment, an extension as it were, of the psychological effects of the plague described in chapter 53. The metaphor is then continued, though in less technical language, at the end of the chapter in ἀπαγαγὼν τὸ ὀργιζόμενον τῆς γνώμης ("drawing off the empassionment of their resolution"). Cf. 7.68.1.

In ἀνηρέθιστο in 2.21.3 another medical metaphor is used to bring out the parallelism between the two challenges to Pericles' leadership; cf. the Hippocratic *Humors* vi.

The underlying parallelism of the two episodes is brought out both by the phraseology of this introduction and by its restatement of the theme of the conflict between passion and reason, *orgē* and *gnōmē*.[20] In the next speech a further theme, briefly suggested earlier in the book, appears with new clarity: the relationship between public (*dēmosia*) and private (*idia*) concerns. The theme has already been hinted at in Pericles' offer to turn his farm over to the state if Archidamus spared it. His gesture showed a willingness to subordinate immediate personal advantage to maintain his public role. The outcome of Pericles' speech against the proposed negotiations with Sparta further shows a new aspect of this theme and extends the parallel between Pericles' actions in the first year and those in the second year of the war. After reporting Pericles' speech, Thucydides sums up its effect:

Speaking in this fashion Pericles tried to relieve the Athenians of their passion [*orgēs*] against him and to draw away their thoughts [*gnōmēn*] from the present troubles. At the public level [*dēmosiai*] they were persuaded by his words and sent no further embassies to Sparta. Rather they pushed ahead into the war. But at a private level [*idiai*] they were grieved by what they were suffering, the common people because having started with little they were deprived of even this; the powerful because their splendid estates in the countryside with their buildings and expensive furnishings were lost—but most of all because they had war instead of peace. In fact they did not stop holding Pericles in anger until they fined him. A little later, however, as a crowd often does, they re-elected him general and entrusted him with all affairs. (2.65.1-4)

The outcome is success for Pericles at the level of public policy and failure at the private level. He is fined and removed from office, although only temporarily.[21]

In summary, after the Plataean episode the second book explores two major challenges to the Periclean strategy for winning the war.[22] The first is the temptation, encouraged by Archidamus, to join in a land battle. The second is the desire to seek an early negotiated settlement. Our attention

[20] Note the following parallels between 21.3, καὶ τὸν Περικλέα ἐν ὀργῇ εἶχον, and 59.2, καὶ τὸν μὲν Περικλέα ἐν αἰτίᾳ εἶχον; between 21.3, στρατηγὸς ὤν, and 59.3, ἔτι δ' ἐστρατήγει; between 22.1, Περικλῆς δὲ ὁρῶν μὲν αὐτοὺς πρὸς τὸ παρὸν χαλεπαίνοντας, and 59.3, ὁ δὲ ὁρῶν αὐτοὺς πρὸς τὰ παρόντα χαλεπαίνοντας; between 22.1, ἐκκλησίαν τε οὐκ ἐποίει αὐτῶν οὐδὲ ξύλλογον, and 59.3, ξύλλογον ποιήσας; and between 22.1, τοῦ μὴ ὀργῇ τι μᾶλλον ἢ γνώμῃ, and 59.3, ἀπαγαγὼν τὸ ὀργιζόμενον τῆς γνώμης.
[21] Fined for what? Gomme in *HCT* on 2.65.3 (p. 182f.) lays out the possible charges. The possibility should be added that he was fined for illegally preventing the assembly from meeting the previous year.
[22] The organization of material in this portion of the book is schematized in Appendix Two.

is focused increasingly on Pericles; he stops both threats and embodies thereby the leadership that is so essential for Athenian success in the war. This parallel structure leads directly to a discussion of the nature of Periclean leadership introduced through a valedictory on Pericles (ch. 65). The distinction between Pericles and his successors drawn by this passage is especially important, for it ties together the two major themes of this portion of the narrative, the contrasts between public and private[23] and reason and passion:

But they [Pericles' successors] did the opposite in all these matters and in other affairs that seemed unrelated to the war. They acted in accordance with their private ambitions and private profits. Their policies were pernicious for themselves and for their allies. If they were successful they brought honor and advantage to private citizens; if they went wrong, they meant damage to the city's war effort. The cause was that by his standing, his resolution [gnōmē], and his patent incorruptibility he was able to hold back the majority in a free manner.[24] He was not so much led by it as he was himself the leader, since he did not speak to please as someone does who tries to get power from inappropriate sources. Rather he had the standing to speak up against their passion.[25] When he saw them exulting in their boldness at an inappropriate moment, he spoke and struck fear into them, and when they were frightened without reason, he turned them back to boldness. What emerged was called a democracy but was in fact domination by the pre-eminent man.[26]

[23] On the public/private antithesis see J. de Romilly, "The *Phoenician Women* of Euripides," *Bucknell Review* 15 (1967) esp. 119. Earlier Greek literature prepares us to expect pernicious public effects such as *stasis*, murders, tyrannies etc., from excessive devotion to private interests: See, e.g., Theognis 39-52 and Herodotus 3.82.3.

[24] Ἐλευθέρως is ambiguous. It could refer to the freedom of the Athenians under Periclean leadership or to Pericles' own freedom, especially in his manner of speaking to the assembly. Κατεῖχε strongly reinforces the second sense. See L. Edmunds and R. Martin, "Thucydides 2.65.8," *HSCP* 81 (1977) 187-193.

[25] The Greek sharply contrasts Pericles' ability πρὸς ὀργήν τι ἀντειπεῖν, to the tendency of others πρὸς ἡδονήν τι λέγειν. It is difficult to convey the assonance in English, but the similarity in sound helps clarify the interpretation of the passage. By itself πρὸς ὀργήν might mean, as many editors suggest, "in anger," but the contrast with the preceding phrase shows that the point is not that Pericles was angry but that his speaking bore some relation to his audience's anger. The verb, moreover, is now ἀντειπεῖν hence he spoke not "so as to provoke their anger" (Gomme in *HCT* ad loc. [p. 193]) but "in response to their passion." This is of course precisely what he has done in the speech that immediately precedes this valedictory.

[26] 2.65.7-9. The last sentence has often been taken out of context and overinterpreted. "Perhaps the most quoted of Thucydides' opinions, it withstands analysis least," as M. McGregor notes in "The Politics of the Historian Thucydides," *Phoenix* 10 (1956) 97. The context is vital: Pericles has just been fined and removed from the generalship. His power was always dependent upon his ability to persuade the leaders of the city and the assembly. He could always be outvoted or repudiated. In a constitutional sense his powers were very limited, though his influence was great.

The passage traces Pericles' success as a leader not only to his reason and incorruptibility but to the standing he enjoyed. The nature of that standing becomes clear by the contrast to his successors,[27] whose obsession with private advancement and gain drove them to flattery of the masses and made them followers rather than leaders. They thus dealt ineffectively with the variable moods of the Athenians, while Pericles could implement his *gnōmē* by an oratory that challenged the extremes of popular feelings, raised despair to confidence, and checked arrogance with fear.

Periclean leadership is thus an essential factor in the implementation of the Athenian strategy for winning the war. Although it has been another of the factors omitted or sketchily examined in the first book, only in description of the war itself in book 2 does its full significance emerge. Ostensibly it is a further factor favorable to the Athenian side in the calculus of power, for the possession of a leader of Pericles' skill is an immense advantage to the Athenians; but at a deeper level Periclean leadership reflects two paradoxes, each of which has negative implications for Athenian success in the war. The first of these is that successful leadership such as Pericles' depends on a willingness to subordinate personal interests to civic ones. It must repudiate a purely individualist calculation of advantage. Pericles is willing without apparent hesitation to subordinate his own interests to those of the city, but such conduct is exceptional, almost unnatural. The tendency of *physis* is to self-gratification and self-aggrandizement. The full implications of this aspect of Periclean leadership are not immediately developed. They become apparent in the contrasting situation at the outbreak of the second major phase of the war—the Sicilian Expedition. Athens is then under quite different leadership, with no preeminent man to provide clear and balanced direction. None of its leaders

[27] The successors are twice alluded to in the passage, both times by a vague οἱ δέ (sec. 7 and sec. 10). Discussions of the passage usually assume that both refer to politicians and that Thucydides is tacitly exempting one or more politicians of whom he approves; for example, G.E.M. de Ste. Croix, "The Character of the Athenian Empire," *Historia* 3 (1954/55) 34, n. 2, says "Prima facie, all the post-Periclean political leaders are included . . . but Nicias must certainly be left out." In fact the indictment is very general and at least initially is directed as much against the Athenians as a whole as against the politicians. The concern with private ambitions and profits gradually takes more specific form in the passage, as Thucydides concentrates on the desire to gain political pre-eminence (secs. 10 and 11). Here he surely has the politically ambitious in mind, but even so ἐπιγιγνώσκοντες and ἐκπέμψαντες hint at the Athenian assembly generally. If he makes an exception for some "good politicians," the text is remarkably devoid of language to make this clear. As we shall see in subsequent chapters, all the latter politicians are shown as falling short of the independence and strength of Periclean leadership. Cleon, Nicias, Alcibiades, all come to be included in Thucydides' criticism. See also W. Thompson, "Thucydides II 65.11," *Historia* 20 (1971) 141-151.

has the standing or the will to stop the Athenian desire to conquer Sicily. Each in varying ways substitutes personal considerations for public ones.

The second paradox reflected by Periclean leadership is the relationship between the leaders and the citizenry. The Pericles of book 1 represented qualities that had already been ascribed to the Athenians—their boldness, determination, swiftness to act, etc.—as well as a clearness of mind and purpose. Like Themistocles he seemed to embody his city. In the second book, however, a further aspect emerges as we see the leader in tension with his society. Periclean leadership is effective not only because it represents tendencies in Athens, but also because it is able to check those tendencies when they become unbalanced. The effective leader now appears as one capable of reacting against the tendencies and dispositions of this city. Pericles, for example, has to try to keep tranquil (22.1) a city whose citizens, as the Corinthians say in book 1, "neither . . . enjoy tranquillity themselves nor allow it to other human beings."[28] The leader is thus always vulnerable and his advice must often run counter to the tendencies of his fellow citizens, and when Pericles urges the Athenians "to pursue tranquillity, and tend to their navy and not seek to acquire additional empire during the war nor put the city at risk" (2.65.7).

The implications of this paradox for Athenian success in the war are complex. If Thucydides' analysis is correct, then Athens could win the war, as suggested in book 1 and as Athens' ability to hold out for so long seems to confirm: "They took a fall in Sicily both with the rest of their force and with the greater part of their navy, and they were now in *stasis*. Yet despite their attrition, they still held out against their former enemies, and against the reinforcements that came from Sicily, and as well against the majority of their allies who now revolted, and later in addition against Cyrus, the son of the Great King, who supplied funds to the Peloponnesians for their navy; they did not give in until by entangling themselves in domestic disagreements, they took a fall."[29] This explanation arises out of the analysis in book 1, yet moves beyond it. It reaffirms the importance of naval power and finances, especially through the allusion to Cyrus' provision of funds for the Peloponnesian navy, but points as well to the significance of the Athenians' own choices, and above all to the conflict

---

[28] 1.70.9. Cf. L. Edmunds, *Chance and Intelligence in Thucydides* (Cambridge, Mass. 1975) 92f.

[29] 2.65.12. My translation is based on the emendation ὅμως τετρυχομένοι ἔτι ἀν-τεῖχον, in line 28 of the Oxford text as proposed in "Thucydides 2.65.12," *Arktouros: Hellenic Studies Presented to B.M.W. Knox*, ed. G. Bowersock, W. Burkert, and M.J.C. Putnam (Berlin 1979) 269-271.

between private interests and public policy. Although Athens could win, the practical difficulties confronting her now become apparent, just at the moment Pericles disappears from view. We wonder how such a leader is to be replaced and if any other leader can respond with equal power and forthrightness to the varying moods of the Athenians. One crucial ingredient in the formula for Athenian victory—the right leadership—will not easily be obtained. Our sense of the prospect for Athenian success, and hence our assessment of Periclean policy, have thus become complex and ambivalent.[30]

THE PLAGUE AND TWO SPEECHES
BY PERICLES

In our investigation of book 2 we have to this point concentrated on a structure that the reader gradually detects in the account of the first years of war. On a first reading, however, attention is more likely to focus on a sequence of three famous passages: the Periclean Funeral Oration, the account of the Great Plague, and Pericles' last speech to the Athenian assembly. These are powerfully written passages and occur in rapid sequence, with only minor episodes between them. And they are of great importance for the understanding of the second book.

The relationship between two of the three has often been noted. The picture of the carefully arranged state funeral for those Athenians who died in the first year's campaigns,[31] which provides the setting for the Periclean

[30] This is the tone, I believe, of the last sentence in chapter 65, usually construed as unambiguous praise of the great man. Thus Crawley: "So superfluously abundant were the resources from which the genius of Pericles foresaw an easy triumph in the war over the unaided forces of the Peloponnesians." But the phrasing is ambiguous and repeatedly provokes demurral. The first word, τοσοῦτον, is left undefined and interpreters differ radically on what should be understood: *LSJ*, following the scholiast's gloss of φρονήσεως understands it as "reason"; Classen-Steup and Crawley more plausibly suggest "things/resources." The sentence unquestionably affirms the power and resilience of the Athenians, and yet does not make an explicit statement of their *dynamis*; it uses the ambiguous potential construction with ἄν, which can emphasize the false belief that Athens "would" win, as well as the current belief Athens "could" have won. The main verb, moreover, ἐπερίσσευσε (it occurs only here in Thucydides), suggests not only abundance but also something extreme and excessive, an idea also hinted at by the iteration of *peri-* in Περικλεῖ ἐπερίσσευσε . . . περιγενέσθαι. Furthermore, πάνυ ἄν ῥαδίως suggests a Periclean disregard of the cost, sufferings, and *kinēsis* of even a short war.

[31] 2.34. It is unlikely that there were many Athenian casualties during the first year of the war; those were probably most cavalry, especially from the engagements at Rheitoi (19.2) and at Phrygia (22.2). For a possible sculptural fragment from the monument in honor of these dead and an introduction to some of the current interpretive disputes about the oration

Funeral Oration, contrasts with the disruption and disintegration of burial customs during the Great Plague. Two radically different images of Athens are presented in adjoining episodes: in the one a city ordered by and deriving much of its strength from generally accepted civic customs and procedures; in the other a place of increasing self-gratification and anomie. The willingness to endure sufferings for the common good, so central to the Periclean Funeral Oration, is eroded by the plague (53.3). The two episodes thus constitute one of Thucydides' dramatic juxtapositions; their effect is as much derived from the contrast between the two situations as from the individual components.

The relationship between the plague and the Periclean last speech is less dramatic but no less significant. After describing the symptoms of the plague, Thucydides turns to describe some of its wider effects, especially the breakdown of the customs and restraints of society, its *nomoi*. Although the implications for society are great, the emphasis initially is on individual conduct and attitudes (ch. 53). There is, however, a further effect of the plague, one that becomes obvious only after the apparent closure in 54.5. The further allusion to the plague in Pericles' last speech serves to re-open the episode; Pericles tells the Athenians that they are unwarrantedly changing course: "and in the debilitation of your resolution [*gnōmē*] my argument seems not to be correct. That is because grief has a hold on your individual perceptions while the clarification of the communal benefits is still at a distance. When a great change takes place without advance warning, the disposition to persevere in what you have resolved gives way. What happens suddenly, unexpectedly and in the highest degree against reason reduces one's determination to that of a slave. This is what has happened to you, especially in the plague.''[32] This passage points to a further effect of the plague, the weakening of civic resolve.[33]

---

see G. P. Landmann, "Das Lob Athens in der Grabrede des Perikles, Thukydides II, 34-41," *MH* 31 (1974) 65-95. His criticisms are largely directed against the important study of the Funeral Oration by H. Flashar, *Der Epitaphios des Perikles* (Heidelberg 1968).

[32] 2.61.2f. The very complex ideas in this passage make translation difficult. A Greek citizen would normally have a high sense of self-esteem, φϱόνημα (cf. 43.6 and 62.3f.), and this would inhibit light or rapid changes in any matter on which he has made up his mind. But sudden or unexpected events (cf. 6.49.2) make things *seem* different—one may see only the distressing side of a situation or may panic (cf. 2.91.3; 4.96.5; 7.3.1). Under such circumstances one's willingness to persevere gives way and hence one resembles persons of lower status who must adapt to others' whims and orders. Hence one's διάνοια, "intention," becomes "humble/low status," ταπεινή, and one's φϱόνημα is no greater than that of a slave. In the context of the passage, δουλοῖ involves both loss of status and loss of self-direction. Cf. 7.71.3 and especially the attitude of the light-armed troops (*psiloi*) when first confronted with Spartan hoplites, 4.34.1.

[33] Cf. 2.59.1; the public/private contrast that marks the movement from chapter 53 (private

These connections among three episodes, Pericles' Funeral Oration, the Great Plague, and Pericles' last speech, remind us that we are dealing with a carefully developed structure. The two Periclean speeches surround a central episode, the Great Plague, and at the same time evoke and contrast sharply with one another.[34] In such a structure seemingly minor details can be significant and revealing. The Funeral Oration, for example, is almost entirely an address in the first person plural—as we would expect in this genre. Pericles is the spokesman for civic values and attitudes. But in his last speech, the form of address alternates between the first singular and the second plural. "We" disappears: "I" and "you" become the means of discourse: "I am the same and don't shift; you are the ones who change" (61.2). Pericles speaks of himself more directly and more frequently and with unabashed self-praise.[35] He contrasts himself with his audience, and hence naturally has need of the second plural.[36] The language reflects the tension between Pericles and the Athenians, a tension that becomes fully evident at the end of the debate when Pericles is fined and removed from command. By the end of the sequence, the valedictory on Pericles (ch. 65), the leader appears in a new light. His effectiveness derives not so much from his ability to express the characteristics and attitudes of his people as from his ability to counterbalance some of their tendencies. The structure, in other words, helps lead to a more subtle understanding of the nature of Athenian political leadership.

The relationship between the citizen and his city is also explored and developed in this structure. This is most evident in the contrast between the Funeral Oration and Pericles' last speech. The Funeral Oration provides

effects) to chapters 59-64 (public effects) is recapitulated in chapter 65, when Thucydides stresses the contrast between the Athenians' public (*dēmosiai*) acceptance of Pericles' recommendations and their private (*idiai*) grief at their losses that impels them to fine Pericles and remove him from the generalship. The antithesis is then expanded to help analyze the differences between Pericles' leadership and that of his successors.

[34] Cf. Flashar, *Epitaphios*, 38 and Note 22 above.

[35] A good example of the self-praise is 2.60.5: "And you are in a passion against me, a man of a sort that can claim to be second to none in recognizing what is appropriate, and in communicating it, and at the same time a lover of the city and incorruptible." The tone is self-confident, and perhaps close to arrogance, even in an age in which politicians were allowed to speak with fewer pretensions to humility than in our day. The claim of incorruptibility, moreover, defies the suspicion of Periclean malfeasance that was widespread in his last years; cf. Plutarch *Pericles* 32f. The wording is so provocative that Plutarch seems to have concluded that Pericles was attempting to bring the anger of the citizenry on himself and thereby remove it from the public realm (Plutarch *Pericles* 33).

[36] Some of this, to be sure, is inevitable in a symbouleutic speech. But compare the last speech in book 1. Here Pericles uses the second person plural, e.g. 1.140.5 and especially in 143.5-144.1, but the language always returns to the first person plural, and Pericles to his role as spokesman for a civic unity. N.B. the sharp contrast between 1.144.2 and 2.64.6.

an ideal setting for the development of the commonplaces about the need
for individual sacrifice for the common good. Such topics are inevitable
in the genre and not surprising in their context. More remarkable is another
aspect of the relationship between the citizen and his city: Pericles' emphasis on the relaxed quality of Athenian life. While paying tribute to
former generations of Athenians who, among their other accomplishments,
turned back the Persian invasion and won the Athenian empire (36.2-4),
the speech emphasizes the confident amateurism of Athenian life. This
point is developed by a rhetorical strategy unparalleled in other extant
funeral orations. Pericles passes over the customary survey of Athenian
history, real and mythic, and concentrates instead on those habits, civic
arrangements, and dispositions that stand behind Athens' growth to greatness:[37]

Since you know them so well, I will avoid long-winded reiteration of the accomplishments in war by which our dominance was progressively acquired or of the
various successes our fathers and we have had in our determination to ward off
Greek and Persian aggression. Instead I will first make clear from what patterns
of conduct we attained this level and with what civic structure and from what
dispositions such greatness derives. Then I will proceed to the praise of the fallen
with the view that these observations would be far from inappropriate in our present
situation and that this entire gathering, both citizens and visitors, would benefit
from hearing them. (2.36.4)

This substitution of a discussion of patterns of Athenian life for the traditional material of funeral oratory opens the way for a discussion of the
difference between Athenian ways and those of other Greek cities: "We
enjoy a style of civic life that does not copy the *nomoi* of our neighbors
and is more a model to some than an imitation of others." (2.37.1). The
contrast between Athens and the unnamed "others" gradually concentrates
on her differences from the disciplined and regimented life of Sparta, so
much admired, though only rarely imitated, by other Greeks:

    [37] 2.36.4. Cf. Aristotle's *Rhetoric* 2.22, 1396af. and J. Ziolkowski, *Thucydides and the
Tradition of Funeral Speeches at Athens* (New York 1981). Thucydides apparently deplored
the mythologized treatments of the past, especially those presented in epideictic oratory, and
did not want such a version of Athens' past to have any prominent place in his work. N.B.
his comment in book 1 that work was not written "as the speech-writers compose, to maximize
pleasure in listening rather than truth" (1.21.1). I take *logographoi* here to be a sneer at
speech writers and orators (cf. K. J. Dover, *Lysias and the Corpus Lysiacum* [Berkeley 1968]
155f.) rather than a technical term for Thucydides' predecessors in the writing of history or
an allusion to Herodotus or to "Prose writers in general" (Gomme in *HCT* on 1.21.1 [p.
138f.]).

We also differ in our war preparations from our opponents, in these respects: We allow our city to be accessible to all and there is never an occasion when we use *xenēlasiai* [expulsions of foreigners] to keep someone from learning something or seeing something, even if by our failing to preserve secrecy, some enemy might derive some advantage. Our reliance is not so much in preparations and deceptions as in that courageous readiness for action which we derive from our own selves. In their education others from earliest youth chase after manliness by an effortful discipline; but though we live in a relaxed style we march out no less than they to fair and square contests.[38]

This picture of the spontaneous bravery and commitment of the Athenians carries on the contrast between them and the Spartans that the Corinthians drew in the first book (esp. 1.70), but new contrasts and a further function emerge. Athenian society is now viewed according to its contribution to the individuals who comprise it: "To sum up I say that this city taken collectively is an education for Greece and that at an individual level a citizen among us, it seems to me, dexterously attains in the largest number of respects and with all graciousness full self-sufficiency."[39]

Epideictic oratory, despised in the first book, finds a new function in

---

[38] 2.39.1. Of course Athenian troops were not at this point marching out to contests with the Spartans and Pericles was not advocating that they engage. "Fair and square" is restrictive or conditional ("if contests are fair and square," i.e., "if the Spartans didn't have land superiority"). The argument is specious; is the reader then to conclude that Pericles is fraudulent and Thucydides implicitly critical of him? Variations of this problem arise repeatedly in the Funeral Oration. Much can be made of the discrepancy between the Funeral Oration and the reality of contemporary Athens, even the reality described elsewhere by Thucydides himself. Freedom was neither so universal nor so unqualified, Athenian soldiers neither so lacking in drill and training nor so unequivocal in their courage, boldness, and calculation or such congenial companions as the oration implies. (And if we look outside the Thucydidean text we discover that the outspoken advocate of self-effacement for women [45.2] returned home to the embraces of the anything-but-self-effacing Aspasia!) The instances can be multiplied, but the interpretive question is constant; do these discrepancies constitute, as Flashar and others have thought, an "exposure" of Pericles and his Machtdenken? (Flashar, *Epitaphios*, 33; cf. H. Strasburger, "Thukydides und die politische Selbstdarstellung der Athener," *Hermes* 86 [1958], 29 n. 5). I am not persuaded; as soon as we enter into an epideictic setting the mode of discourse changes (cf. 42.2) ἃ γὰρ τὴν πόλιν ὕμνησα) and with it the critical techniques that are appropriate. We can allow in a Funeral Oration a tension with reality that in other settings would surely appear as ironic.

[39] 2.41.1. Τὸ σῶμα αὔταρκες ("full self-sufficiency") may be a colloquialism of the period; cf. Xenophon *Memorabilia* 4.7.1, which in any event helps clarify it. In the *Memorabilia* the phrase refers to the skills a man needs to get along without dependence on specialists, e.g. geometry, a little astronomy, an understanding of diet and exercise. In the Funeral Oration the sense is extended almost to "self-realization, self-fulfillment." The idiom recurs in 2.51.3 to point to the inability of human beings to resist the plague and by implication to the loss of this potentiality of Athenian life during the long war. On the claim to be the "School of Greece" see Flashar, *Epitaphios*, 25 n. 48, who plausibly suggests it is a counter to a similar claim by Sparta.

the second book. Its task is not to project a glorified image of the past
history but to explore a potentiality in Athenian life. No Greek listening
to an epideictic speech would have expected it to be a mirror held up to
the world. We need not detain ourselves over the argument of whether the
oration is a description or an idealization of Athens. The genre implies,
demands and exalts idealization and encomiastic selection. But Thucydides
uses the form not to look back into the past but forward toward what
Athens might become. It establishes the idea of a festival society in which
the individual is not subdued to the good of the herd, but becomes a
concelebrator renewed in his efforts by his participation in society: "And
further we have devised for our resolution [*gnōmē*] the largest number of
relaxations; we observe contests and sacrifices throughout the year and
private elegance from which the pleasure we take each day drives away
whatever is grievous."[40] The speech repeatedly conveys an image of the
freedom of Athenian life: "We conduct our public business with a respect
for freedom. When it comes to suspicion about the patterns of daily life
adopted by our fellow citizens our way is not to be passionate in annoyance
at a neighbor if he tries to please himself a bit, nor to retaliate on one
another in ways which, however unofficial, still cause grief when observed."[41]

In passages such as these the Funeral Oration develops an image of a
society that sustains individual freedom and fulfillment and is in turn
sustained by its citizens' willingness to fight and die for it. That willingness
emerges not from compulsion but from the relationship of the citizen to
his city, a bond described by the metaphor of falling in love: "Beholding
day by day the power of the city and becoming her lovers, and when you
recognize her greatness, bear in mind that the men who entitled her to that

---

[40] 2.38.1. The Corinthians (1.70-78) by contrast claim that the Athenians never take a
vacation. Within the *Histories* the image of Athens presented in the Funeral Oration contrasts
most sharply with the perverted festival of the Corcyrean revolution. But there is a further
implication—Athens progressively loses many of the qualities and potentialities we glimpse
in the Funeral Oration. Does the city in the end become anti-Athens?

[41] 2.37.2. Most commentators and translators take the last portion of the sentence to mean
"indulge in those injurious looks which cannot fail to be offensive, although they inflict no
positive penalty" (Crawley). The point, I believe, is rather different. A society in which
minor self indulgences provoke a mean or vindictive response (cf. *di' achthēdona* in 4.40.2)
increases *to lupēron*. This, like *orgē*, just mentioned in the sentence, is a threat to a society
and especially to its capacity for making sound judgments. This idea, after a discussion of
the persistence of a beneficial form of fear in Athens, leads to the reinterpretation of Athenian
festival life in chapter 38. The benefit of the festivals and games is not pleasure for its own
sake, but a banishment of *to lupēron*. The implication of this becomes clear in 61.2 when
Pericles discusses the effects of decision making when afflicted by grief. See also Chapter
Six, Note 58 below.

greatness knew and dared what had to be done and in action would not be disgraced. If in some undertaking they met failure, they did not think that they should refuse to offer their valour to their city. They brought their contribution to the fairest of love feasts. Their communal gift of their bodies won for each individual the praise that grows not old" (2.43.1-2). In this speech the public and private realms are momentarily united, as individual self-realization and the sacrifices necessary for the common good feed one another. Swept along by the eloquence of epideictic oratory we glimpse a reconciliation of contraries and a balance of counter tendencies: "We pursue elegance with economy and wisdom without effeminacy. . . . We differ from others in this additional respect, that we, although a single people, act with boldness, yet reason out what we are about to attempt. In this regard other people find that ignorance is the source of bravery, and reason of hesitation."[42]

But such a mixture is a delicate balance, and easily destroyed. The swiftness of change is brought out both in the account of the plague and in the next speech of Pericles (chs. 60-64). In this speech we detect a series of contrasts to the Funeral Oration. For example, the Athenians are now shown to be in the state of passionate annoyance that Pericles said (2.37.2) was uncharacteristic of them.[43] The ease and relaxation of Athenian life is no longer mentioned; instead the call for sustained efforts and sacrifice drowns out any other note.[44] Individuals fail to recognize the way to collective safety (2.60.4). At the same time the relationship to the empire appears in a new light: "You now hold this as a tyranny—to have seized it seems wrong, but to give it up dangerous."[45] The empire is no longer

[42] 2.40.1 and 40.3. Cf. J. T. Kakridis, *Der thukydideische Epitaphios* (Munich 1961) 31, who notes that the Athenian citizen "eine Reihe von sich widersprechende Eigenschaften verkörpert," and Edmunds, *Chance and Intelligence*, on the combination of *gnōmē* and *tolma*. See 1.144.4 and 2.43.1.

[43] *Orgēs* in 2.37.2 is echoed in 59.3, 60.1 and 60.5 and 65.1. Chapter 37, to be sure, is restricted to private issues; the following speech concerns public policy.

[44] "Efforts," (*ponoi*) are mentioned in 62.1 and 62.3, 63.1, 64.3, and 64.6. The Funeral Oration did not deny the importance of *ponoi*, e.g. 2.36.2, but stressed the significance of pauses in these efforts (38.1) and the contrast between Athens and Sparta in this regard (39.4). The importance of the theme of *ponoi* in this section is evident even statistically: 12 of the 40 occurrences of words of this stem (excluding *ponēros* and relatives) are to be found between chapters 35 and 64 of the second book, i.e. 30 percent of the occurences are found in approximately 3 percent of the text.

[45] 2.63.2. It is often thought that 2.40.4f. alludes to the Athenian empire and to a claim that Athens treated it relatively benignly. If so, the contrast between the Funeral Oration and the last speech is even sharper than I have suggested. Caution is needed, however, since the phraseology of 2.40.4 is so general that it could equally well apply to personal relationships within the city.

a possession acquired by generations past and increased in more recent
times (36.2f.), but an active power, confronting its possessor with the
grim alternatives of risking its abandonment or of accepting the hostility
it engenders.

With this shift comes another: the amenities of Athenian life, confidently
recognized as refreshments for the mind (2.38.1) in the Funeral Oration,
are now to be cast overboard in the effort to maintain Athens' power: "The
power of the city bears no comparison to your use of your homes and
land, which you consider so important. You are mistaken to be angry at
their loss. Consider them instead the flower garden or embellishment of
your wealth and de-emphasize them in comparison to your power" (62.3).

In the discussion of the power of the city, however, the two speeches
draw closer together. In fact, the second speech develops the conceit
alluded to in the Funeral Oration that Athens has by its boldness subor-
dinated both land and sea under the feet of its citizens (40.4). Now the
idea is expanded as if it were totally new: "I will emphasize this point
too, one which neither you nor I in my previous speeches have taken
seriously, although it demonstrates the greatness of your dominion. I would
not use it now, boastful and pretentious as it is, if I did not see you
unreasonably despondent. You think you rule only your allies. But I say
there are two divisions of the world for man's use—land and sea. Of all
of one of these you are the total rulers, both what you now control and,
if you ever want, even more. There is no one—not the Great King, not
any nation of this period—who will stop you if you sail out with your
present naval resources."[46] But at the moment of the greatest emphasis
on Athenian power there also comes the first explicit indication of her
eventual decline. Her defeat, long in the back of the reader's mind, now
comes to the surface in an extraordinary sentence that drives home the
greatness of Athens and the uniqueness of her accomplishment in a series
of no less than seven superlatives, in the midst of which comes an allusion
(in a brief parenthesis) to the inevitability of her decline:

Bear in mind that Athens has the greatest fame among all men because she does

---

[46] 2.62.1f. Since the conceit is already introduced in 41.4, some critics have assumed an
inconsistency in thought or a different period of composition. But the problem is specious.
In this passage Thucydides does not claim that the idea has never before been heard but that
no one has taken the idea seriously: ὅ μοι δοκεῖτε οὔτ' αὐτοὶ πώποτε ἐνθυμηθῆναι
. . . οὔτ' ἐγὼ ἐν τοῖς πρὶν λόγοις. He then proceeds to develop the conceit much more
elaborately than in the earlier passage. An audience familiar with Herodotus 7.49 might
notice an ominous echo of Artabanus' advice to Xerxes.

not yield to misfortunes, because she has expended[47] the greatest casualties and efforts in the war, and because she possesses the greatest power yet acquired, the memory of which will endure through subsequent generations unto eternity, even if at this late point we should give way (since all things by their nature undergo diminution)—namely, that of the Greeks we, being Greeks ourselves, ruled the largest number, that we held out against the greatest enemies, singly and collectively, and that we dwelt in a city with the highest level of general prosperity and the one that was the greatest. (2.64.3f.)

This is perhaps the greatest contrast between this speech and the Funeral Oration. The Funeral Oration looks forward to a potentiality in Athens for a new pattern of civic life; the last speech looks forward, albeit briefly, to Athens' decline. The first speech transforms epideictic to a new role and function; the second sounds, if only in passing, an elegiac note on the imagined passing of the city.[48] It writes Athens' epitaph.

At the same time the language evokes Thucydides' own opening chapters. Greatness is the subject matter; "greatest" occurs four times in this sentence, and greatness ensures the everlasting remembrance of Athens, come what may. Thucydides affirmed at the beginning of his work the greatness of this war and claimed that it would be remembered to eternity, *es aiei*, through the intermediary of his work (1.22.4). As the beginning of the *Histories* has opened a great vista back to the earliest days of Greece, the allusion to the decline of Athens leads the reader to a glimpse of the future. We are brought to a great height and invited to view the war *sub specie aeternitatis*. This perspective is an ironic one, because the reader knows what Pericles and his audience do not, not only the fact but something of the cost of Athens' defeat. The Great Plague, "the one phenomenon of all that has proved stronger than our expectation" (2.64.1), has raised questions not only in the Athenian assembly but also in the reader's mind about the wisdom of Periclean policy. The assembly reacts in anger

[47] Thucydides has Pericles use as his verb, ἀνηλωκέναι, a word that is properly applied to financial transactions, not to losses of human life. The financial uses are common, e.g. 1.109.3; 117.3; 2.24.1; 6.31.5 etc. Application of the word and its cognates to human "losses" is usually restricted in Thucydides to passages of high emotional content, e.g. 4.48.3, 7.30.3. Tragedy uses the word for human casualties, Aeschylus *Agamemnon* 570 et alibi. In 3.81.3 the word is used of those who were put to death for financial reasons. An elaborate interplay between words for financial and human losses is developed in 7.29-30. For Thucydides, financial and human "losses" are two distinct categories with their own language. In the *kinēsis* of the war these categories, like so many others, become confounded.

[48] Note the parallels in 26.4 to the texts in W. Peek, *Griechische Grabgedichte* (Berlin 1960) e.g. ἐν ἅπασιν ἀνθρώποις no 10, βροτοῖσι δὲ πᾶσι, and see A. Cameron, "An Epigram of the Fifth Century B.C.," *Harvard Theological Review* 33 (1940) 115-117; Greeks fighting Greeks, no. 9; and especially emphasis on lasting fame, nos. 10, 13, 16, and 88.

and dismay at the loss of possessions. The reader contemplates the related question of whether Pericles has overestimated the predictability of the war and underestimated its cost. At a more general level, as Adam Parry has said, "the plague offers the most violent challenge to the Periclean attempt to exert some kind of rational control over the historical process. Thucydides ultimately leaves it undecided whether Periclean will and fore-thought—*gnōmē*—in fact is able to meet this challenge."[49] We share the Athenians' doubts and hesitations, although at a different level. Pericles' speech is thus double edged, and deals with a double audience: the imagined assembly of 430 B.C. and the responses of subsequent readers to Periclean policy. The doubts are real ones, and more intense for the second audience, which knows something about the ending of the war, than for the first. We know, or have been compelled to suppose, that there is no middle ground, no happy compromise whereby Athens can continue to enjoy her empire and yet reach accommodation with the Peloponnesians. We know too that Athens will eventually be defeated. Under those conditions, the question "Should Athens seek a negotiated settlement?" raises inescapable problems. But any answer raises problems. If our impulse is to say "yes," we are reminded that to yield entails the loss of Athens' heroic status. And we have grounds for suspecting that no such accommodation can be attained unless Athens is willing to give up her empire and, contrary to all her national characteristics, become a quiescent city. If we advocate that, we must be prepared to encounter Pericles' scornful words in the next sentence of his speech: "The do-nothing would find fault with our actions but the person who himself wishes to accomplish something will envy them."[50]

The reader is caught in this dilemma and finds no easy way out of it. Since the eventual defeat of Athens is in view, the temptation is strong to repudiate Pericles and his policies, and to insist upon the folly of the war. The passage as a whole, however, seems to be constructed to block such an easy conclusion. The setting of the last speech, the branding of the Athenian disposition to negotiate as an affliction of their intelligence or resolution (*gnōmē*), and the comments in chapter 65 all prevent a simple acceptance of the view that the war was a miscalculation and that Athens' best course was to extricate herself from it as swiftly as possible. At one

---

[49] A. Parry, "The Language of Thucydides' Description of the Plague," *Bulletin of the Institute of Classical Studies London* 16 (1969) 116.

[50] 2.64.4. Gomme in *HCT* on 2.40.2 (p. 121) and 2.63.3 (p. 175) insisted that *apragmōn*, here translated as "do-nothing," was a complimentary term, but this argument does not convince me. That a quality is the opposite of a vice (*polypragmosynē*) does not make it into a virtue; it is indeed an opposite extreme.

level at least the text affirms the fact that Pericles was right in objecting
to concessions and that despite the terrible losses from the plague, Athens
still had the strength to resist the Peloponnesians and eventually wrest from
them a satisfactory peace settlement. Thus the conclusion of chapter 65
argues, albeit in contorted language, that Pericles' analysis was quite correct: "Such an overabundance influenced Pericles at that time from which
he knew in advance that the Peloponnesians unaided would quite easily
be overcome in the war."[51]

Many readers, among them some of the most brilliant Thucydidean
scholars, have found in this chapter, and above all in its final sentence,
the essence of Thucydides' thought about the war. In these words they
hear the voice of the defender of Pericles and his policies against critics
who fail to recognize that if only his advice had been followed, Athens
could have won. This is an attractive interpretation but, if our analysis is
correct, oversimplified. It ignores several important factors. The failure to
follow Periclean leadership, for example, is not a simple mistake or moral
deficiency on the part of the Athenians but the result of a conflict between
the Periclean demand for restraint and tranquility and the innately restless
character of the Athenians. Since Athenian national character is to a large
extent responsible for the city's power, Athens' ultimate failure in the war
is closely connected to her greatness.

Even more significant, perhaps, is another factor rarely considered in
the analysis of Periclean policy. That Athens could have won the war is
plausible. But at what cost? We have already seen the erosion of some of
the most valuable features of Athenian civic life in the short interval
between the Funeral Oration and Pericles' last speech. Much more, we
know, is to come for in a war of attrition not only the enemy is ground
down. When chapter 65 concludes with the assertion that the "Peloponnesians would quite easily be overcome in the war," the tension and dissonance behind much of this chapter is intensified. However correct the
assessment about the defeat of the Peloponnesians might be, the Athenians,
uprooted from the countryside, tormented by the plague, confronted with
destruction of their land and the erosion of their patterns of life, have
found the war anything but easy. Success, it is clear, will have a high
price.

In Pericles' view the compensation for the losses of the war is, as we
have seen in chapter 64, fame. The same consideration makes the hostilities
engendered by the empire worth enduring: "To be hated and to be thought

---

[51] 2.65.13. On the translation and interpretation see Note 30 above.

grievous is the immediate lot of all those who aspire to dominate others. But whoever risks such hostility for the greatest gain, judges well. Hate does not prevail for long but immediate splendor glows on into the future, eternally remembered."[52] This view, though deeply rooted in Greek culture, in the context of the *Histories* is not fully persuasive for the sense of loss is so vivid, the emphasis on the suffering of the war so intense, and the implications of the words for Athens so ironic.[53] Its ultimate basis, moreover, is the view that greatness is self-justifying, not dependent upon its social or human effects or its conformity to justice or any other moral standard.[54] As the work progresses, this view of greatness is explored, subverted, and finally repudiated.

Pericles' last speech and the valedictory comments on him, then, do not provide an encapsulation of Thucydides' views about the war or a resolution to the interpretive problem of the text. They maintain, even intensify, the conflict between the reader's foreknowledge of the cost and outcome of the war and his appreciation of the analysis of power presented in the work. The ironic perspective continues. The force of the apparent defense

---

[52] 2.64.5. The theme of "splendor" (*lamprotēs*) is an important one in the *Histories*, especially in the sixth and seventh books. The brilliance of Pausanias and Themistocles is long remembered (1.138.3), though the endings of their careers were far removed from the heights of power. The Athenian expedition against Sicily was splendid at its start (7.75.6, cf. 6.31.6) but ended in humiliation (7.75.6), though the Syracusans achieve a splendid success (7.87.5), and acquire the "name," i.e., fame, which the Athenians have lost. Splendor, in other words, turns out to be not a permanent possession to be obtained, as Pericles here suggests, by a momentary attainment, but a shifting and ambiguous assessment of events, the possession of the most recent victor.

[53] At the end of the war the victors debate what punishment should be inflicted upon the city, which escapes destruction by the narrowest of margins, Xenophon *Hellenica* 2.2.17.

[54] The amoral strain in Pericles' thought comes out clearly in his last speech, but is already hinted at in the Funeral Oration when he argues that Athens' greatness is demonstrated by her accomplishments, above all by her subjection of both land and sea under the feet of her citizens. He then adds "since we have everywhere established ageless monuments of good and of bad" (2.41.4). We ask ourselves for a second whether we have heard correctly. The text critics echo our surprise. Can it really be, they ask, "of the good and of the *bad*?" A little change, a lambda for a kappa, will tame the phrase into a cliché, "monuments of the fair and the fine." Shall we amend, as F. Müller argued in "Die blonde Bestie und Thukydides," *HSCP* 63 (1958) 171ff.? Or, recognizing that the manuscript support for such an emendation is weak and that Müller has failed to show why a more humdrum expression should have been corrupted into a less familiar one, shall we leave the text but interpret the difficulty away by understanding "monuments of success and failure," rigorously repressing any evaluative tone in the words? The latter course has often been followed but surely it too depletes and avoids the richness of the Greek, and leaves us with a puzzle of what sort of monuments the Athenians have established of their own failures! None of these treatments of the offending κακῶν satisfies; all are evasions. The phrase must be recognized as a sign of Pericles' refusal to contaminate his idea of greatness with any other considerations, and of its consequent amorality.

of Pericles in chapter 65 is, then, not to develop a theory about the war but to prevent premature and facile judgments about it. It shows that it is too simple to dismiss Pericles or to conclude that Athens should simply have yielded to Peloponnesian demands or engaged in a quest for peace based on a diplomacy of unilateral concessions. But at the same time we cannot escape the growing recognition of the vulnerability of Athens and the immensity of her ultimate loss.

ATHENS LEADERLESS

Pericles delivered what I have called his last speech in the summer of 430 B.C. Although this is his last appearance in the *Histories*, we cannot be sure that it was in fact his last address to the Athenians, for he lived until the autumn of 429 B.C.[55] During some of this time at least he once again held office as a commander and the Athenians "entrusted all their affairs to him" (2.65.4). Although in the year or so between the last speech and his death the Athenians made several major decisions, Pericles' role in them is quite obscure.[56] Thucydides' valedictory to Pericles in chapter 65 of the second book is in effect a premature burial, an obituary pronounced a year or more before his actual demise. The comments are not so much a general assessment of Pericles and his policies,[57] as the explication of what has been implicit in much of the first part of the second book, the importance of proper leadership for Athenian success in the war and the difficulties that leadership encountered. While emphasizing the strength and independence of Pericles' leadership, they draw a sharp, perhaps exaggerated, contrast between his leadership and the conduct of Athenian policy after his death.[58] The comments thereby constitute an abrupt division

[55] So Diodorus 12.46.1 and Athenaeus 271 e; cf. Plutarch *Pericles* 38, although it is by no means an unchallengeable interpretation of the Greek of 2.65.6. "He lived on for two and a half years" could mean two and a half years after the speech just reported rather than two and a half years after the start of the war.

[56] Among the decisions in this period were: to assure the Plataeans of full Athenian support if the Peloponnesians besieged them (72.3), not to attempt to prevent or later to relieve the siege, to post Phormio at Naupactus in order to control traffic in the Corinthian Gulf (2.69). On the decision to allow the reinforcements for Phormio to go first to Crete see below, Note 62. It is not clear whether this comes before or after Pericles' death.

[57] Cf. H. D. Westlake, *Individuals in Thucydides* (London 1968) 40.

[58] Chapter 65 is commonly interpreted as contrasting Pericles and some demagogic politicians who enjoyed power after his death. This, I believe, distorts and needlessly narrows the passage. The attack is not restricted to demagogues or even to politicians. Section 10, it is true, alludes to politicians and to the characteristic charge against the demagogues that they said what people want to hear. But the language is very general and does not seem to

within the *Histories* and impose over the natural time-scheme of the year-to-year narrative a further chronological division based on the end of Periclean leadership.[59] We are led to view events as before or after Pericles and, since Pericles has been portrayed as the one significant Athenian leader of this period, to picture Athens as a city without strong leadership. When Pericles abruptly, prematurely, disappears from the narrative, no one immediately emerges to take his place.[60] Not until 427, when Cleon is first mentioned (3.36.6), or even until 425, when Cleon achieves his coup at Pylos, does Thucydides again depict a dominant leader in Athens. We are surprised by the suddenness of Pericles' disappearance and, as so often in Thucydides, unexpectedly find ourselves replicating some of the attitudes of the Athenian citizenry during the war. We have felt the doubts about the course Pericles had set, realized the difficulties of the alternatives, and are now astonished to find him gone. We knew, of course, that sooner or later Pericles would be lost, but before we are quite prepared for it, we have come upon a divide and entered new territory.[61]

Amid this surprise we note a change in narrative technique. In the first

---

be drawing a distinction between good (nondemagogic) politicians and bad politicians, *dē-magōgoi*. The criticism is rather that all the successors failed to provide the kind of leadership Pericles had given. The condemnation thus includes Nicias and Alcibiades as well as politicians more commonly classed as demagogues such as Cleon and Hyperbolus. Indeed, it is by no means clear that the criticisms in section seven of the chapter are directed specifically at politicians. Rather they are phrased in very general terms and apply to the Athenians as a whole. Only later in the passage (especially sections 10 and 11) does Thucydides focus on the struggle for first place in the city and the complications and miscalculations it engendered.

[59] The basic time system of the *Histories* is the natural year, the alternations of summer and winter (2.1.1.), with subdivisions based largely on the crop cycle, especially the growth of grain: 2.19.1; 2.79.1; 3.1.1; 4.1.1; 4.2.1; 4.6.1. In adopting this system Thucydides rejected the use of the civic calendar of any major Greek state (cf 5.20), although at the beginning of the second book he provided a correlation between his system and three of the civic calendars. The division based on Pericles' career has an important literary function to perform in the work, but has often led an unproductive search for continuities, e.g. for true successors' to Pericles and into the effort to assess strategies and actions by whether they were "Periclean" or not. The purpose of Thucydides' division is not to transform Pericles into some touchstone of what was desirable or undesirable in the conduct of the war but to lead the reader to a better understanding of the problems of political leadership in Athens.

[60] Other sources (e.g. Plutarch *Pericles* 24) allude to various successors, such as Lysicles; fourth-century schematizations of politics viewed Cleon's primacy as the immediate sequel to Pericles. The schematizations are arbitrary and overdrawn (cf. W. R. Connor, *Theopompus and Fifth Century Athens* [Washington 1968] 124-128) but there are indications both in comedy and in Plutarch's life of Pericles that Cleon was already politically active, and attacking Pericles, in Pericles' last years. Thucydides, in other words, may have exaggerated the lack of strong political leadership in Athens in the years immediately following 430.

[61] On Pericles' date of birth, see J. Davies, *Athenian Propertied Families* (Oxford 1971) 457. If born between 498 and 493, he would be in his sixties when the war broke out. One could reasonably have expected another decade of political leadership.

part of the book much attention has been paid to the process by which Athens makes major decisions concerning the war. We see the factors that are involved in the policy of avoiding major land engagements and of resisting premature negotiations. We sense the mood of the Athenian citizenry and glimpse the assembly in action. After chapter 65 the narrative reports the major decisions but has little to say about the processes by which they were reached. The assembly disappears and along with it, the individuals who aspired to lead it. There is no glimpse of the political maneuvering induced by Pericles' removal from office, sickness, and death. Eventually, to be sure, Thucydides will return to the operation of the assembly and to the problems of political leadership. The Pylos episode in the third and fourth books receives a full and dramatic development and makes possible an assessment of the leadership that Cleon offers his city. But for the rest of book 2 and the opening of book 3 decisions are reported succinctly, and their authors and advocates are at best passing names.[62] Athenian military policy, moreover, lacks decisive leadership. Perhaps the best example is the mishandling of relations with King Sitalces of Thrace. Athens had long been seeking ways of persuading this powerful ruler to help her bring back into the empire the rebellious cities of northeastern Greece. An alliance had been arranged in 431 (2.29) but he apparently did not assist the Athenian operations mentioned in chapters 58 and 79. Now, in 429 (ch. 95ff.) Athenian ambassadors achieve what must have been a considerable diplomatic coup: Sitalces agrees to use the immense resources of his land to form a huge expedition part of whose objective will be to subdue Athens' rebellious subjects in Chalcidice. Athens, of course, must do its part by sending "ships and as large a land force as possible."[63] But the Athenians fail to send the ships (the land force is not even mentioned), "doubting that he [Sitalces] would come, though they did send gifts and ambassadors to him" (2.101.1). Sitalces ravages Chalcidice for eight days, but does not bring over any of Athens' allies. He then returns home. Athens gains nothing of significance from the great

---

[62] The most tantalizing of these is "Nicias" in 2.85.4ff. My argument ("Nicias the Cretan?" *AJAH* 1 [1976] 61-64) for a slight emendation in the text and the identification of this Nicias with the famous son of Niceratus has been criticized by G. Daux, "Thucydide et l'événement," in the *Comptes Rendus de l'Académie des Inscriptions et Belles Lettres* Jan.-Mar. 1979, 89-103, and by P. Karavites in *Klio* 62 (1980) 307-310. Κρὴς Γορτύνιος is a legitimate double ethnic. The rest of the original argument seems to me still to hold and I believe we must allow the possibility that this episode is Nicias's first appearance in Thucydides' work.

[63] 2.95.3. The language echoes 92.7 and 82.1, perhaps thereby hinting at the comparison between this expedition and the operations in the Corinthian Gulf.

expedition. This episode points to a serious problem in Athens' conduct of the war and a deficiency in her leadership. Meantime the conflict spreads and the narrative responds as if shaped by the centrifugal force that draws the action of the war toward the edges of the Greek world, to Thrace and Macedon, Acarnania and Amphilochia (chs. 68, 79, 82, 102). As the fighting broadens, we see less and less of Athens. But one glimpse is revealing. After a surprise Peloponnesian raid on the island of Salamis, the fire signals sending news of the raid induce a panic (*ekplēxis*) "second to none in this war. The Athenians in the city thought that the enemy had already sailed into the Piraeus while those in the Piraeus thought that Salamis had been captured and that the enemy was almost upon them— which could in fact easily have come about if the Peloponnesians had been willing not to hesitate, for no wind would have prevented them."[64]

This one glimpse of Athens is not, I believe, without a wider significance. It confirms and makes vivid the impression of a city that has lost the foresight and balanced judgment that Periclean leadership often provided. It has become a city adrift, leaderless, and, it will appear, vulnerable not only to outside incursions but also to adventurism and self-seeking leadership.

[64] 2.94.1. Similar language is found in 8.96.3f. describing the danger of a Peloponnesian seizure of the Piraeus in 411 B.C.

Book 3

CLEON AND DIODOTUS

FROM A CITY adrift and leaderless to one driven by demagogues is but a small transition. The concern with the absence of effective leadership in Athens in the years following Pericles' pre-eminence naturally draws attention to the false leader, Cleon. The contrast is conspicuous because verbal echoes link Cleon to Pericles.[1] Cleon dominates Thucydides' narrative through much of the third, fourth, and fifth books.

But his emergence is gradual. Thucydides does not move directly from analysis of the lack of leadership in Athens to an examination of Cleon and his significance. Instead he pauses to develop a theme already present in the second book, one that now becomes the basis for our assessment of the new leadership of Athens. Much of the third book can be viewed as an exploration of the role of *logos* in the war, a term that signifies both speech and reason. Only when this theme is fully developed is attention concentrated on Cleon and the nature of his leadership.

---

[1] Note the following echoes of Pericles in Cleon's speech on the Mytilenean question: 3.37.2 of 2.37.2 and 63.2; 3.37.4 of 2.40.2 and 42.4; 3.38.1 of 2.61.2, cf. also 1.140.1; 3.39.2 of 2.62.4; 3.39.5 of 2.64.3; and 3.40.4 of 2.63.2. The sharp contrast between the speaker and his audience recalls Pericles' last speech; see Chapter Two, Note 36. And the introduction of Cleon in 3.36.6 is a virtual parody of the introduction of Pericles in 1.139.4. The purpose of these similarities is much disputed. See H. Lloyd-Jones, *The Justice of Zeus* (Berkeley 1971) 139f.; J. Finley, *Thucydides* (Cambridge, Mass. 1942) 139ff.; A. W. Gomme, *Essays in Greek History and Literature* (Oxford 1937) 186; J. de Romilly, *Thucydides and Athenian Imperialism* trans. P. Thody (Oxford 1963) 160; H. Herter, "Pylos and Melos," *RhMus* 97 (1954) 341, esp. n. 67; and J. T. Hooker, "Charis and Aretē in Thucydides," *Hermes* 102 (1974) 166. It may be, as Lloyd-Jones suggests, that the similarity in language was "meant to suggest that the policy of Pericles was likely to lead in different circumstances to the policy of Cleon," but this is an inference that a cautious reader would accept only after seeing a good deal more of Cleon and his policies. The immediate effect is surely to establish a contrast between Cleon's superficial resemblance to Pericles and his advocacy of a policy whose *orgē* (passion) (N.B. 3.38.1) contrasts sharply with the *gnōmē* of Pericles (cf. 2.21.3-22.1; 2.60.5; 2.64.1; 2.65.8). See now F. Cairns, "Cleon and Pericles," *JHS* 102 (1982) 203f.

The new theme has already been sounded in episodes such as the execution of Aristeus of Corinth and the other Peloponnesian ambassadors
who, in 430 B.C. while en route to the King of Persia, were captured and
turned over to the Athenians by Sadokos of Thrace (2.67). The Athenians,
recollecting the trouble that Aristeus had caused by encouraging the revolt
of Potidaea and fearing what might happen if he escaped, put him and his
fellow captives to death before they had a chance to complete their defense.[2]
A worse atrocity followed: their bodies were denied proper burial and
thrown into a ravine. The Athenians "considered themselves justified in
treating them in the same way the Spartans were already acting. Whenever
they captured merchants of Athens or her allies sailing around the Peloponnese in merchant vessels they killed them and threw their bodies into
ravines. Indeed all those the Spartans captured on the seas at the beginning
of the war were treated as belligerents and destroyed, both those on the
Athenian side and neutrals" (2.67.4). This is one of the passages where
Thucydides moves beyond conventional narrative about military planning
and operations to let us see some of the brutality of the war. War, he later
remarks, is a "teacher of violence" (3.82.2); its story is therefore one of
many atrocities. Our attention first focuses on Athenian conduct; the realization of a Spartan atrocity, however, comes casually, almost acciden-
tally, not through reporting in the normal sequential order, but as a flashback to earlier events. These, moreover, are reported not for their own
sake but for their role in the Athenians' rationalization of their violation
of the Greek conventions that before condemnation, an accused man should
be able to say what he wants in his defense, and that even enemies receive
proper burial, unless they are guilty of especially heinous crimes. Many
such conventions give way in the course of the war and Thucydides frequently reports the effects of their collapse. He concentrates attention on
the frame of mind and the rationalizations whereby the perpetrators justify
their actions. His concern is not only with the deeds (*erga*) but also with
logos.

Often, to be sure, the theme of the violence of war is carried on without
an effort to explain the motives of the actors. But even in those cases *logos*
often has an important role. The actions of the Athenian commander Paches
while conducting operations at the town of Notium in Asia Minor provide
a good example. The town has been divided by civil strife (*stasis*), and
Paches has been called in by one of the factions. He makes an agreement

---

[2] 2.67.4. Cf. 1.60.2f. The proverb cited in Plato *Phaedrus* 272c, "Even a wolf deserves
to be heard," is indicative of conventional attitudes toward such situations.

with Hippias, the commander of the mercenary force that is supporting the other faction. Let Hippias come and discuss matters; Paches will offer him terms; if the terms are not satisfactory, he will guarantee his return, safe and sound, to the fortification (3.34.3). Hippias agrees and Paches takes advantage of his absence to make a surprise attack, seize the fortification, and slay the garrison. Thucydides concludes the story: "And later, bringing Hippias back in, just as he promised, when he was inside, he ties him up and has him shot down by archers."[3] The shift to present tense makes the murder of Hippias especially vivid, and the phrase "just as he promised" underlines Paches' convenient literalism.

This episode does not explore Paches' self-justifications. It is told largely as a clever stratagem that turns upon Paches' careful manipulation of language. But by its place both in a larger structure and in a major thematic development, it acquires greater significance. The thematic development is the role of *logos* (language and thought) in the intensifying violence of the war. The structure, through which this and related themes are explored, is an elaborately interconnected series of episodes that begins and ends with instances of *stasis*, one here at Notium, another at Corcyra (3.70-85). Within this frame two principal stories alternate, one the Athenian suppression of a revolt at Mytilene, the other the siege of Athens' ally, Plataea. This structure, as we shall see, brings out the similarities between two disparate actions, and emphasizes the manipulation of *logos* in each of them. The final episode in the arrangement, the discussion of the *stasis* at Corcyra, turns into a meditation on the role of language in that brutal and paradeigmatic revolution. Paches' literalist treachery is thus a very appropriate introduction to a long section in which Thucydides draws attention to the role of *logos* in the war.

But Paches' connection with the action is not immediately perceived at this more general level. His role is much more specific. As the Athenian commander when the Mytilenean revolt is suppressed, he sends back to Athens both the Spartan Salaithos who had encouraged the Mytileneans in their revolt (3.25.1) and those leaders of the Mytileneans whom he considers most to blame for the revolt. Since Salaithos' death is reported

---

[3] 3.34.3. In this case the atrocity results from an excessively narrow adherence to the words of the promise. It evokes the literalism and the barbarian treachery in episodes such as Herodotus 4.201 and the Plataeans' understandable but nonetheless deceptive literalism in their execution of the Theban captives early in book 2. Cf. C. W. Macleod, "Thucydides' Plataean Debate," *GRBS* 18 (1977) 233. Another form of literalism is evident at the end of the Plataean episode as the Spartans conduct their role as judges of the Plataeans by asking if the captives had done any service in the war to the Spartans and their allies (3.51.4, cf. 54.2 and 68.1).

in language that evokes the Athenians' execution of Aristeus of Corinth,[4] we are again reminded how swift and severe Athenian action can be. Once Paches' character is well established, we know what to expect when the Athenians decide that all Mytilenean males over the age of puberty should be executed and all women and children sold into slavery (3.36.2). A trireme is dispatched to convey the decision to Paches; when it arrives we know he will promptly and decisively carry out his orders.

With this background established, Thucydides stops to report in considerable detail the debate that took place in Athens on the day after the decision to execute the Mytileneans. Even though the trireme is on its way, the Athenians decide to reconsider their decision. They had initially made up their minds under the influence of passion (3.36.2). Now second thoughts suggest the decision was "uncivilized and excessive."[5] Thucydides has stylized this debate into his familiar antilogistic form. He omits any report of other speakers while representing in direct discourse the speeches of Cleon and an otherwise unknown speaker, Diodotus, the son of Eucrates.[6]

Cleon, who speaks first, begins with an attack not only on speakers who urge reconsideration of the decision, but also on his audience, singling out the Athenians' tendency to be misled by rhetorical skill. A surprising amount of this debate is devoted to argument not about the punishment of the islanders but about the role of discussion in Athenian decision making. Cleon, the most persuasive of the citizens at this time (3.36.6), and a speaker who is represented as having mastered the very techniques of

---

[4] 3.36.1. Cf. esp. εὐθὺς ἀπέκτειναν, ἔστιν ἃ παρεχόμενον with βουλομένους ἔστιν ἃ εἰπεῖν αὐθημερὸν ἀπέκτειναν in 2.67.4.

[5] 3.36.4. The Greek, ὠμὸν τὸ βούλευμα καὶ μέγα, is literally "raw and big." Each of the adjectives links this passage to important themes within the work as a whole. The emphasis on greatness is prominent throughout the work. This passage is part of the transition from the view of greatness as something benign and self-justifying to a recognition of it as the measure of the suffering of the war. To call the action "raw" is more remarkable. The adjective is unusual in Thucydides, occuring only here and in 3.82.1 (cf. 84.1). The connotations of savagery and barbarism (3.94.5) are important in the development of the presentation of the Athenians in the work; in effect a food code signifying the barbarization of Greece. The adjective also links the passage to a wider pattern in the culture, the use of food as a metaphorical system for justice. This is already evident in Hesiod's allusions to "bribe eating" barons and in his contrast between the cannibalism of wild animals and the justice of man (*Works and Days* 277-280). In the *Rhetorica ad Alexandrum* 1420 a 30ff. the raw is contrasted to action in accord with *logos* and compared to animal-like actions. In Thucydides the feasting and festival world depicted in the Funeral Oration (esp. 2.38) is progressively destroyed as the war turns Greece to cannibalism (2.70.1), savagery (here and 3.82), and starvation in sieges and the quarries at Syracuse (7.87.2). See also Notes 45 and 61 below.

[6] See M. Ostwald, "Diodotus," *GRBS* 20 (1979) 5-13.

contemporary rhetoric that he denounces,[7] deplores the reconsideration of the decision: "I am unchanging in my resolve and I am amazed at those who propose a second discussion concerning Mytileneans and who make us waste time. This is more in the interest of those who have wronged us" (3.38.1). Indeed, almost two of the five pages of his speech are devoted to an attack on re-opening the question and on the motives of those who speak on the side to which he is opposed. Often in Thucydides the speakers reveal, apparently inadvertantly, their true colors.[8] Cleon, the professed protector of the common people, is no friend of democratic discussion, doubts the ability of a democracy to hold on to an empire (3.37.1), and advocates that the common people of Mytilene, not just the oligarchs, be put to death: "Punish them now as their wrongs deserve; and do not let the blame fall on the few while letting off the common people. All of them alike made the attack on you—though they had the chance to turn to your side and now be back in their city" (3.39.6).

Diodotus, on the other hand, no very active politician, it would seem, spends the long first portion of his speech rebutting Cleon's charges and affirms the importance of full and free discussion.[9] This emphasis on the role of argument is not simply rhetorical sparring between the two opponents. Rather, as we study the debate, it becomes clear that its issue is as much the role of *logos* as the fate of the Mytileneans. Hence the debate functions simultaneously on two levels: that of immediate practical decision and that of more general political discourse. These levels emerge with some clarity as the rhetorical strategy of the debate unfolds. Cleon's position emphasizes the wrongs that all Mytileneans have committed against the Athenians. Under Greek ethics he has a strong case. They have revolted without specific provocation, abandoned their oaths of loyalty to the Athenians and sought aid from Athens' worst enemy. The Athenians themselves recognize that punishment directed against the whole population would be a very severe measure, but it would not be without justification. Cleon argues that it would be both right and advantageous to make an example out of Mytilene: "Summing up I say: do what I say and you will simultaneously achieve both justice as regards the Mytileneans and self-interest. If you decide in any other way, you will have no gratitude from them and you will condemn yourselves [to the loss of empire]" (3.40.4).

[7] C. W. Macleod, "Reason and Necessity," *JHS* 98 (1978) 64-78.

[8] Euripides *Philoctetes* (*TGrF*[2] 797) apud *Rhetorica ad Alexandrum* 1433 b 11ff.

[9] Two useful recent discussions of Diodotus' speech are M. Cogan, "Mytilene, Plataea and Corcyra," *Phoenix* 35 (1981) 1-21, and B. Manuwald, "Der Trug des Diodotus," *Hermes* 107 (1979) 407-422.

Against this highly effective speech Diodotus devises a remarkable strategy.[10] After affirming the appropriateness of reconsideration, he turns the discussion in a new direction: "I did not come forward either to make excuses for the Mytileneans nor to make denunciations. For our contest is not about their wrongs—if we are sane—but about our own proper decision making. And if I should affirm that the Mytileneans have surely wronged us, I will not on that basis urge you to kill them, unless it is advantageous. And if they have some basis for being forgiven—well, let it be, if this forgiveness is not clearly a good thing for the city."[11] His strategy is not to deny the justice of punishing the Mytileneans, but to deny the relevance of Cleon's approach and to transform the argument from one primarily about right and wrong (*to dikaion*) to one about advantage (*to xympheron*). His point concerns both practicality and the canons of ancient rhetoric. At a practical level Diodotus urges the advantages of a policy of moderation, against Cleon's severity. He points out that to condemn the common people of Mytilene would be to encourage longer and stiffer resistance in other cities when they revolt. As it is now, he claims, "the common people in all the subject cities are well disposed to you and either they do not join in revolts with the oligarchs or if they are forced to, they swiftly turn hostile to the leaders of the revolt, and you have the mass of the opposing city as your ally when you move into war" (3.47.2).

This practical approach coincides with a more subtle argument deriving from the categories of ancient rhetoric. Ancient rhetoric classified speeches by the type of occasion on which they were delivered. Thus, courtroom oratory was sharply distinguished from that intended for a deliberative assembly or for a celebratory or festival occasion. Diodotus' arguments exploit the distinction. This is not, he implies, a courtroom (dicanic) situation but a deliberative one in which considerations of right and wrong should yield to considerations of advantage: "And I do not think it proper that you should be driven away from the advantage which I offer by the speciousness of his speech [*logos*]. Since his speech is more just [*dikaioteros ōn*] in the light of your present passion toward the Mytileneans, it may perhaps be followed. But we are not trying a law case [*dikazometha*]

---

[10] A useful analysis of the relationship between the speech and ancient rhetorical theory is to be found in Macleod, *JHS* 98 (1978) esp. 72-77.

[11] 3.44.1f. The translation of the last sentence assumes that εἶεν in the manuscripts is correct, and idiomatic. Cf. Classen-Steup ad loc. Diodotus means, but does not say, "I'd kill them if they were innocent if it were in Athens' best interest"; hence he breaks in mid-sentence, interjects a colloquial expression "let it be" (εἶεν) and phrases the criterion with the more persuasive term, ἀγαθόν ("a good thing"), rather than with a repetition of ξυμφέρον, "advantageous." I assume that τι ξυγγνώμης is the subject of φαίνοιτο.

concerning them, so that we need arguments from justice [*tōn dikaiōn*], but we are deliberating [*bouleuometha*] about them, so that they will serve our advantage" (3.44.4). Diodotus thereby gains an advantage over Cleon who has chastised the Athenians for viewing each occasion as one for display (epideictic) oratory or the showmanship of the sophists.[12] Under this attack Cleon's assumption that justice and advantage can simultaneously be attained seems naive (3.47.5) and his advocacy of what Diodotus terms the "laws of terror" (3.46.4) strangely unsophisticated and ill-considered.

Diodotus, on the other hand, presents himself as the clear-thinking, tough-minded realist. Many readers have suspected that for all his insistence on advantage he is nonetheless secretly in sympathy with the claims of justice, not Cleon's justice of revenge, but a justice that seeks a punishment proportionate to the offense and would thereby spare the average citizens of Mytilene.[13] When he says the present climate compels the advocate of severity to use deception to lead the majority, and while the advocate of the better course wins confidence by lying (3.43.2), he is perhaps signaling to the advocates of mercy, pity, and leniency that the arguments he presents do not necessarily reflect his own true sentiments. The rhetorician Teisias is said in Plato's *Phaedrus* (273aff.) to have urged that in some situations each party should lie in order to construct a case more convincing than the plain truth; Diodotus has perhaps learned this lesson.[14]

In any event his speech is a magnificent *tour de force*. It reaffirms the ability of *logos* to shape policy and skillfully urges the repeal of a decision that we know was adopted in passion (3.36.2) and whose inappropriateness was soon recognized by many Athenians (36.4-5). It reaffirms the Periclean notion that intellect and practical policy can coexist. Cleon, whose speech amply confirms Thucydides' introduction of him as the most violent of citizens (3.36.6), is beaten at his own game.[15] He has crawled out on the

---

[12] 3.38.4-7. Diodotus' τῷ εὐπρεπεῖ τοῦ ἐκείνου λόγου (3.44.4) is an especially pointed response to Cleon's own barb in 38.2.

[13] Cf. D. Kagan, "The Speeches in Thucydides and the Mytilene Debate," *YCS* 24 (1975) 85, and B. Manuwald, *Hermes* 107 (1979) 407-422.

[14] The lesson is repudiated by Isocrates 3.5-9; cf. 15.253-57 and see Macleod, *JHS* 98 (1978) 73-74.

[15] Much has been said about the apparent prejudice in introducing Cleon in this way. That Thucydides disliked Cleon is perfectly clear; that the historical Cleon, when viewed from other perspectives, is not a totally depraved character can readily be maintained. Thucydides is not "objective" in his treatment of Cleon. But it is a mistake, I believe, to think that "introductions" of this sort are intended as a comprehensive judgment of the character or that they are intended to substitute the historian's evaluation for the reader's. Rather they

long pious limb of Right and found himself cut off by a few deft strokes
of Advantage. Diodotus has saved the day; a second trireme sets off with
the reprieve, and as we have seen in the Introduction, the reader shares
in the eagerness for it to arrive in time:

They ate as they rowed, barley mixed with wine and oil. Some took turns sleeping
while others rowed. By luck no wind opposed them. The former ship did not sail
with eagerness on an errand that might provoke retribution,[16] while this one hastened
on in the fashion just described. The first had arrived and Paches had time to read
the decree and was about to do what had been resolved, when the second ship
draws up on the shore and prevented the destruction. That was the margin of
Mytilene's escape from danger. (3.49.3-4)

The race of the two ships, the vivid narration, the hair-breadth escape,
the sudden change to the present tense, draw us into the action and direct
our responses. We want the Mytileneans to be spared and are relieved
when the second trireme brings the reprieve. The successful outcome
reinforces the initial reaction to Diodotus' speech. He has achieved the
goal we so earnestly desire.

But the sequel to this brilliant scene creates a more complex reaction.
The outcome is not quite what we expected. In the very next sentence it
turns out that Cleon has not been so completely defeated as we thought.
A resolution moved by him turns out to have passed the assembly, and as
a result the men sent by Paches to Athens are put to death.[17] They number
a little more than one thousand.[18] In the next sentence of the severity of
the Athenian punishment of Mytilene becomes even clearer, as we learn
what Diodotus' proposal meant by "letting others keep their homes"

---

evoke reactions already likely to be present in Thucydides' audience and alert the reader to
qualities likely to be significant in the ensuing debate. Thus they are not final authorial
assessments, but initial assumptions that, as we shall see, can from time to time be modified
as new situations are investigated.

[16] "That might provoke retribution" is a cumbersome phrase and not very satisfactory as
a translation of ἀλλόκοτον. But "horrid" (Crawley), "distasteful" (Warner), and "unwelcome" (*LSJ*) are all inadequate. The word derives from the Homeric and archaic word,
κότος, "wrath," especially divine wrath. It does not imply, of course, that Thucydides or
even the sailors thought that Poseidon or Zeus might destroy them, but it evokes the uneasiness
of those who cannot fully believe in a cosmic indifference to an act of excessive severity.

[17] 3.50.1, Κλέωνος γνώμη. The word, γνώμη, is totally appropriate for a proposal in the
assembly, but it is also ironic and carries on the theme of the contrast between reason and
orgē, passion.

[18] Some commentators have been shocked by the number. Surely Thucydides could not
have meant "more than 50-100 individuals, whereas 1,000 and more would mean the oligarchs
in general, the governing class" (Gomme, *HCT* ad loc. [p. 325]). Yet the manuscripts are
unanimous and no palaeographically convincing emendation is at hand. Cf. R. Meiggs, *The
Athenian Empire* (Oxford 1972) 316. The number, I believe, is sound—and meant to shock.

(3.48.1): All the agricultural land on the island (with the exception of the territory of the loyal Methymnaeans) is divided into 3,000 units. The residents of Lesbos are to work the land, each paying 200 drachmas per year to an Athenian, chosen in a lottery. The Lesbians are reduced thereby virtually to the status of serfs; the Athenians, whether permanently resident on the island or not, become a rentier class benefiting from contributions exacted from the native inhabitants of the island.[19]

The account that seemed to draw to a happy ending with the rounding-off sentence, "That was the margin of Mytilene's escape from danger" (3.49.4), turns out, after all, to have not quite so happy an ending. After false closure, the narrative reopens and we see that the punishment of the Mytileneans is still severe even if not as "uncivilized and excessive" as originally proposed. There is something very disquieting in the outcome and in retrospect underneath the surface brilliance of Diodotus' speech. His remarkable and welcome success is partially based, after all, on deception. Thucydides, for example, by no means encourages the notion that the common people were universally well disposed to Athens. On the contrary, he often gives voice to the view that the price of empire is inevitable hostility and ill will.[20] Diodotus (3.47.2) has misrepresented the subjects' attitude toward the empire. And he has even more flagrantly misstated the facts of the Mytilenean situation. It is not accurate to say, as he does (3.47.3), that the common people had no part in the revolt and willingly turned the city over to Athens once they acquired arms. The facts, as Thucydides reports them in chapter 27, contradict Diodotus. Once armed, the common people responded by demanding that the remaining

[19] On the arrangements see P. Gauthier, *REG* 79 (1966) 83-85. The parliamentary situation in Athens can now also be stated rather more clearly. The assembly convened to reconsider the previous decision to execute all the adult males etc. As the sentiment for reconsideration grew, the council would first have convened to discuss the matter. Most likely the council drafted a new *probouleuma*, and Diodotus was the councilor who introduced it in the assembly. (If so, the allusion to Diodotus' official responsibility in 3.45.4 may be explained without recourse to Ostwald's hypothesis; see Note 6 above). The new proposal was to substitute a clerouchy for the execution of those males still on Lesbos. It would be an attractive proposition, holding out the prospect of profit to several thousand Athenian voters. The motion was carried; but a proposal of Cleon (probably voted on the preceding day) to execute those males whom Paches had sent to Athens remained in force. What is surprising in this process is that in Thucydides Diodotus does not point out the financial advantages of a clerouchy and the impracticality of working the Lesbian land if all the males are put to death. These would surely be arguments one would include among *ta deonta* in this situation. Thucydides' failure to report them seems to me best explained by his tendency to withhold important information until late in his story. Here he perhaps wishes us to reconsider Diodotus and his proposal after the "false" conclusion to the story at the end of chapter 50.

[20] E.g.1.76.1, 2.64.5; cf. pseudo-Xenophon *Athenaiōn Politeia* 1-14.

grain be accounted for and divided among all citizens. If that were not done, they threatened to make an agreement with the Athenians to hand over the city. (Presumably if the grain were divided, they would have supported the revolt.) The oligarchs, then, turned to Paches and it was they, not the common people, who decided to call in the Athenians.[21]

Diodotus has seriously misrepresented the facts of the case. A reader who shares Thucydides' professed regard for exact detail is likely to recognize and deplore the distortion. Other features in the speech are also disquieting. We are reminded, for example, of the contrast between Diodotus' approach to an assembly under the influence of passion (*orgē*) and that which Pericles used in his speech after the plague.[22] The speech illustrates what Thucydides described as Pericles' ability to "hold back the majority in a free manner. He was not so much led by it as he was himself the leader, since he did not speak to please as someone does who tries to get power from inappropriate sources. Rather he had the standing to speak up against their passion" (2.65.8). Pericles directly challenged the Athenian passion and dealt with it forthrightly. The state benefited thereby, even if Pericles was fined and temporarily removed from power. Diodotus' approach is totally different. Although he does not flatter the Athenians, he manipulates them in a sophisticated and disingenuous fashion. The bold Periclean directness has been replaced by a new deceptiveness of language and argument.

Diodotus' strategy is based, moreover, as we have seen, on a manipulation of rhetorical categories. Cleon had argued that what a rhetorician would call "the right" (*to dikaion*), that is, the considerations deriving from justice in the rhetorical situation, coincided with "the advantageous" (*to xympheron*). Diodotus detects in this a weakness and severs the connection. He enunciates a doctrine that restricts considerations of right (*to dikaion*) to courtroom situations and allows only considerations of advantage to operate in deliberative oratory. The paradox is evident: Diodotus urges a policy that we feel is right (*dikaion*) but advances his case by denying the right a place in deliberative oratory. This is a departure from the canons of ancient rhetorical theory. Aristotle in the *Rhetoric* (1.3.4, 1358 b) emphasizes that the goal of deliberative oratory is the analysis of

[21] Cf. P. Gauthier, "Les clérouques de Lesbos," *REG* 79 (1966) 80. And Macleod (above, Note 7). Macleod, p. 76, was wrong, I believe, in suggesting that Diodotus felt his policy would prevent revolts. Diodotus' argument is that revolts are likely to occur but they will be more easily suppressed if his policy is followed.

[22] Note the emphasis on *orgē* in 2.59.3 and 60.2 and again in 2.65.1 and esp. 65.8. The theme is less emphatic in book 3 but clear enough in 3.36.2

what is beneficial or harmful, and the goal of courtroom oratory is what is right or wrong (*to dikaion* or *to adikon*), but he makes clear that the latter considerations also apply in speeches delivered during political deliberations.[23] The so-called *Rhetorica ad Alexandrum* is even more explicit in including the right (*to dikaion*) and the conventional (*to nomimon*) along with the advantageous (*to xympheron*) in the list of "topics" to be used in deliberative oratory (1421 b 24. When Diodotus' speech is viewed in the context of ancient rhetorical theory, its distortions of historical fact can be seen to parallel distortions in rhetorical method. Its brillance is achieved not through the methods of ancient oratory, but by distorting and exaggerating them and by imposing a rigid antithesis between the right and the expedient.

These are considerations that in the early parts of the *Histories* seemed to be somehow reconcilable, even in an empire. In the first book the Athenians, in justifying the empire, stress the dominance of fear, interest and advantage but claim for themselves some residual justification: "Those who follow human nature and rule over others but are yet more fair than their realized power obliges them to be, deserve praise. We think that if others took over our position, they would supply a good indication of the moderation" (1.76.3f). Pericles, too, in the Funereal Oration describes Athens as benefiting others not through some "calculation of advantage but through the confidence of freedom" (2.40.5).

As the war continues we have seen a growing tension between advantage and right. The empire, Pericles said, can be compared to a tyranny that it seems was wrong (*adikon*) to pursue but is dangerous to let go (2.63.2). Cleon echoes Pericles, but eliminates a slight ambiguity in the phrasing ascribed to Pericles. Thucydides has Pericles say that the Athenians hold their empire *hōs tyrannida*, words that can mean either that the empire is like a tyranny (but not really one) or that the empire is the virtual equivalent of a tyranny. In Cleon's phrasing (3.37.2) the qualifying word, *hōs*, disappears and the identity of empire and tyranny is unhesitatingly accepted.[24]

[23] *Rhetoric* I 3.5; cf. Quintilian 3.4.16.

[24] This is a small shift and many critics, especially those who contended that Thucydides does not show a significant development in Athenian attitudes toward the empire, might contend it is an insignificant one. Yet, almost infinitesimal changes in the role of self-interest, self-restraint, fear, and many other topics in the *Histories* lead ultimately to a radically different attitude toward power and the conduct of foreign policy. No individual shift is decisive, but the cumulative result is still a major change. Cf. M. Cogan, *Phoenix* 35 (1981) 7f., esp. n. 13, "Moderation has disappeared not because Cleon has substituted new principles, but because war has eroded that confidence and decency on which moderation depends."

· Nor is it in Cleon's speech alone that the tension between advantage and right is evident. In Diodotus' words, too, all pretense of the reconciliation of the two is abandoned.

Diodotus' speech is thus part of a progressive disassociation of advantage and justice in the early part of the *Histories*. Its clever rhetorical strategy is, moreover, grounded in a view of man and nature that proves to be of great significance in the work.[25] The bedrock upon which Diodotus builds is a belief that laws, conventions, and punishments are ineffective: "It is quite impossible, and a sign of much naiveté, if someone thinks that one can find in the strength of laws or any other terror some bulwark against human nature when it sets out eagerly to do something" (3.45.7). Human nature drives individuals and states toward mistaken courses of action, and restraints or laws will never prevent this (3.45.3). Punishments of ascending severity have, Diodotus argues, already been tried and found ineffective. The forces that work against them are much stronger:

Poverty inexorably supplies boldness; prosperity through over-reaching and planning supply self-aggrandizement; all other circumstances that affect men by passion, as each one of those circumstances is brought into place by a *force maieure*, lead into dangers. And there is expectation [*elpis*] and eros in each situation; the second leading; the first following. The one plans an attack; the other supports it with the resources that derive from chance. These two do the greatest harm by their invisibility and are more powerful than visible terrors. And chance [*tychē*] also, no less than they, contributes to raising false confidence. (3.45.4-6)

Such passages seem to break out of the careful rational limits of the *Histories* and to reveal a world of shadowy powers, who, momentarily personified, swiftly retreat into darkness and gloom. This is the world of pure *physis*, of nature without limitation or restraint, uncontrolled by *nomoi*, unmoved by punishments. Against such force justice and punishment can have little hope of success.

Diodotus' rhetorical strategy is the natural extension of such a view of man. Since men, by their nature, are driven to self-aggrandizement, to risk, to danger, to false confidence and over-reaching, nothing can stop this process except the prospect of greater disadvantage. Right is ineffective and unpersuasive. Men act as advantage dictates. Persuasion, then, must neglect arguments from convention or from justice, and proceed through

---

[25] The theme is a major one, which continues in portions of the work, e.g. in Euphemus' comment (6.85.1) that for tyrant or imperial city nothing is irrational (*alogon*) that is advantageous (*xympheron*). This is perhaps the most explicit statement of the subordination of *logos* to the calculation of self-interest.

reliance on what is advantageous and expedient. There is no place for right.

We are left then with unresolved and complex reactions. We have wanted Diodotus to win and acclaimed him. Yet his victory, not only at the practical but also at the theoretical level, is unsatisfying. We sense that the price is too high; Mytilene has achieved some alleviation of the suffering it might have experienced, but a greater pain is inflicted, the recognition of the possibility that ultimately justice or restraint must give way before self-interest. The bleakness of that prospect outweighs any gain Diodotus has achieved.

THE PUNISHMENT OF PLATAEA

The Mytilenean episode, however, is not to be viewed in isolation. The first part of the third book develops a parallelism between the events on Lesbos and the continuing siege of Plataea. To be sure, at the beginning of the book when we first hear of the intended revolt of Mytilene, no similarity to the operations at Plataea described in the second book is immediately evident. Indeed, the contrasts between the two are dominant: Book 2 began with a surprise Theban attack on a small ally of Athens; book 3 begins with the carefully planned revolt of one of Athens' last independent confederates. The Plataeans, at least at first, are an innocent party; the Mytileneans violate, without any immediate or specific provocation, their oaths of loyalty and widely held Greek attitudes about the proper behavior of allies.[26] Gradually, however, attention is drawn to the similarities between the two situations. Each campaign turns into a siege, by one of the great powers, while the other major power is unable or unwilling to render any significant aid to its ally. Athens is no more effective in helping Plataea than Sparta is in bringing aid to Mytilene. The sieges stretch on; the grain supplies run out.[27] When capitulation finally occurs, the major power must decide what punishment to impose. The issue is analyzed through an antilogy in direct discourse; the decision in each instance coincides with the immediate interest of the major power.

[26] Cf. G.E.M. de Ste. Croix, *Origins of the Peloponnesian War* (London 1972) 305f. and C. W. Macleod, *JHS* 98 (1978) 64ff.

[27] Thucydides' descriptions underline the similarities in the events. The start of the siege of Mytilene in 3.18 recalls the language of the Plataean siege in 2.78.1; the exhaustion of the grain supply at Plataea in 3.20.1 is described in terms that are echoed in the Mytilene narrative, 3.27.1.

By the time the siege of Plataea is over and the punishment has been imposed, the narrative has closely assimilated itself to that developed for the revolt of Mytilene.[28] The casualties are listed; the disposition of the land is announced—with foreigners controlling it in each case. A religious dedication is reported[29] and finally the "rounding-off" sentence used in the Mytilene affair (3.50.3) is expanded and applied to the Plataean episode: "And such was the ending of the Plataean affair in the 93rd year after their alliance with the Athenians" (3.68.4).[30]

Within this structure themes such as supplication, benefaction, and betrayal serve further to bind together the Plataean and Mytilenean episodes without obscuring the contrasts between them.[31] Hence as we read on in

[28] The relationship of the Plataean episode to other episodes in the center of book 3 is schematized in Appendix Three.

[29] At Mytilene (3.50.2) 300 lots set aside for the gods as a tithe; at Plataea (3.68.3) an inn (καταγώγιον) and temple for Hera are established. In the midst of the desolation, religious celebrations will continue. For religious dedications as a sign of hypocrisy, see 3.57.1.

[30] The sentences are typical of Thucydides' frequent practice of marking the end of a major section or of a digression with τὰ μέν, a prepositional phrase, οὕτως, and a verb in the past tense (cf. 1.139.6). In the Plataean case the "rounding off" formula is expanded with a note of pathos. But the technique is not quite what the reader expects. An indication of the length of Plataea's existence as an independent town or the number of years from the great victory against the Persians would be the obvious strategy. Instead Thucydides calls attention to its long-standing alliance with Athens and implicitly thereby to the Athenians' ineffectiveness in aiding Plataea, or even to their unwillingness at one point (3.36.1) to explore a possible way of saving the Plataeans. The emphasis on Athens moves the reader beyond the obvious pathos of Plataea's fate and the cynicism of Sparta's action and hints at a theme that will prove of importance in the Corcyrean episode later in the book, the tendency for alliances with great powers to increase destruction, rather than prevent it.

[31] *Supplication*: The Mytileneans appeal to the Spartans by claiming to be "the equivalent of suppliants" of Olympian Zeus (3.14, cf. 3.28.2). Later the Plataeans appeal to the Spartans by representing themselves as suppliants of the graves of the Spartans' ancestors buried in their town (3.59.2 and 59.4, cf. 58.3). For the Theban response see 66.2. On the practice see J. Gould, "Hiketeia," *JHS* 93 (1973) 74-103.

Benefaction: Diodotus claims the members of the Mytilene *dēmos* are benefactors (*euergetai*) of the Athenians and hence it would be wrong to kill them. The Plataeans repeatedly urge that they are *euergetai* of Greece (3.57.1, 58.3, 59.1; cf. 55.3f.). The Theban response: 63.3 and 67.3. For the central role in popular Greek ethics of the proper treatment of benefactors, see *Rhetorica ad Alexandrum* 1421b 37ff.

Betrayal: The Mytileneans in their appeal for Spartan assistance express their fear that they will be despised as betrayers of their friends (3.9.1). The Plataeans refuse to betray their old ally Athens (3.55.3); the Thebans accuse them of betraying all the Greeks by their support of Athens (3.63.3); Cleon urges the Athenians not to be betrayers of themselves (3.40.7).

Note in addition the theme of the paradigm or example: The Mytileneans revolt because they anticipate Athenian aggression, based on past examples (3.10.6 and 11.8); Cleon says they did not use past examples properly (3.39.3) and wants to make them an example to others (40.7). The Plataeans and Thebans both use the term in their appeals to the Spartans (57.1 and 67.6). There are important continuations of this theme in the Melian Dialogue (5.90 and 5.95).

the third book, our impression of the Mytilenean affair continues to be shaped by comparison to the Plataean episode. And conversely our reactions to the debate on the treatment of the Plataean captives are formed in part by our recollection of the Mytilenean episode and by our increasing awareness that in the world Thucydides describes advantage and not right decides the outcome of discussions. The reader, of course, already knows that the Plataeans' appeal will be unsuccessful, for every Greek was aware of the fate of Plataea. Hence appeals based on their past services, or on the promises made at the time of the Persian Wars are recognized immediately as ineffective. There is no suspense in the Plataean debate, for the outcome is well known. Yet the Plataean speech, although quite incapable of persuading the Spartans, has a powerful effect. It increases and emphasizes the discrepancy between the real world and an ideal world in which such appeals would be effective.

It also implicitly contrasts this war with the Persian War. The significance of this contrast is at first easily overlooked. Thucydides himself in the first book omits any continuous account of the Persian War, indeed passes over it with the observation that "of former actions the greatest was the Persian affair and this had nonetheless a swift resolution in a pair of naval battles and a pair of land battles. But the great length of this war [the Peloponnesian War] surpassed it, and in it sufferings converged on Greece unequalled in any comparable period" (1.23.1). The speakers in Thucydides pass over the Persian War or treat it as a topic too hackneyed to develop.[32] But Thucydides' narrative hints at or alludes to that war and its immediate sequel at some of the crucial moments in the Peloponnesian War—at its outbreak (1.128-138), at the Pylos battle (4.36.3), and throughout the account of the final days of the Athenian expedition in Sicily. It becomes, as the work goes on, the standard by which the "greatness" of the Peloponnesian War is measured, and by which individual episodes can be assessed.

The comparison of the Plataean episode to the Persian Wars, and specifically to the promises made to Plataea after the great battle on its territory, underlines the ineffectiveness of promises, of oaths, of obligations to friends and benefactors, indeed of anything except triumphant, dominant self-interest and advantage. Neither the Plataean speech nor the Theban arguments for their condemnation determine the outcome. Advantage decides. The Spartans need Theban support and know how to secure it: "And

---

[32] Pericles himself avoids it in the Funeral Oration where the reader would most expect it (2.36.4). Others apologize for its introduction (1.73.2) or avoid it as "rhetorical embroidery" (οὐ καλλιεπούμεθα: 6.83.1; cf. 5.89).

it was almost entirely on account of the Thebans that the Lacedaemonians turned their back in this fashion on the Plataeans, for they thought that the Thebans would be useful in the war that was just beginning" (3.68.4). The reminder that we are still close to the beginning of a long war hints at greater changes, and perhaps greater severity in the future. At the same time it calls to mind Athens' decision shortly before the outbreak of the war to accept the Corcyrean alliance. There too a major power made a crucial decision not on the basis of the elaborate arguments presented in debate but on an assessment of what would prove useful in the war.[33] In both the Corcyrean and Plataean decisions *logos* loses its expected relevance. But it is a more complex relationship between speech and action, *logos* and *ergon*, which runs through this portion of the text. The pressures of the war do not simply limit the range or effectiveness of *logos*; they shape speech and reason into instruments of violence. This development is fully evident only in the report of the Corcyrean revolution, to which we shall soon turn. But the distortion of language and argument can already be detected in the speeches of Cleon and Diodotus on the punishment of Mytilene. The course of reason and restraint was maintained by distortions that excluded considerations of right and wrong, alleging that they applied only to dicanic or law-court oratory.

In the Plataean episode the distortions are of a different sort. Neither speech excludes considerations of right and wrong, indeed both are filled with the language of justice and piety. But the two long speeches neutralize each other. The techniques of contemporary rhetoric are used to cover up the weaknesses in each case and ultimately to obscure the fundamental moral issue. The Plataeans try their best to draw attention away from their execution of Theban prisoners (2.5.7) and to their services in the Persian Wars when the Thebans had gone over to the side of the invaders.[34] Their obfuscation, however, is nothing compared to the inversion of Greek values and language in the Theban speech.[35] A masterpiece of deception, this address seeks to exculpate Thebes from her past medism and accuses Plataea of an equally heinous-sounding offense, "atticism."[36] In effect,

---

[33] 1.44.2. In fact the Corcyreans did not contribute very much to the Athenian war effort, nor was the fact that the island provided a convenient staging area for operations in Sicily an advantage to Athens.

[34] For a perceptive analysis of the Plataean speech see C. W. Macleod, *GRBS* 18 (1977) 227.

[35] The Greeks did not condone the killing of captives who surrendered; see P. Ducrey, *Le traitement des prisonniers de guerre* (Paris 1968) ch. 9.

[36] 3.62.2; cf. 64.1. This word is a coinage designed to parallel and deflect the Plataean charge of "medism," i.e. their support of the Persians in the Persian invasion. The word "atticism" is first attested here, but Aristophanes' *Babylonians*, probably produced in 426

the two long speeches cancel each other out and the way is opened for
another form of speech—the "short question" directed to the Plataean
captives—which asks if they had done any good service to the Lacedaemonians and their allies in the war.[37]

Once again Thucydides is working in the categories of contemporary
rhetoric, which distinguished between a short question and answer exchange (*brachylogia*) and a longer and more formal speech (*makrologia*).[38]
Some fifth-century thinkers, notably Socrates, considered the short question
and answer exchange a more reliable way of getting at the truth. But here
the question is framed in such a way as to make the condition of acquittal
a confession of treason. The short question leads not to a Socratic cross-
examination and clarification but to the destruction of one of the most
famous towns of Greece, the extermination of the men, and the sale of
the women into slavery.

CORCYRA

Immediately after the conclusion of the Plataean affair, Thucydides turns
back, momentarily, to Lesbos and follows the return of the fleet that the
Peloponnesians had sent to assist the Mytileneans. Thirteen ships and an
adviser, Brasidas, join the returning fleet near Cyllene with orders to sail
directly for Corcyra and to anticipate Athenian naval movements in that
theater (3.69).

"For *stasis* has broken out among the Corcyreans," Thucydides explains
(3.70.1), and a faction determined to draw Corcyra away from an alliance
with Athens toward alignment with Corinth had come into conflict with

---

B.C., uses the word, λακεδαιμονιάζω, "to support the Lacedaemonians," a parallel coinage
indicative of Thucydides' perceptiveness about a pattern of linguistic change that was occuring
at this time. See also C. W. Macleod, *GRBS* 18 (1977) 240.

[37] The question is repeated in almost identical words three times, first in Thucydides'
narration (52.4), then by the Plataeans in their speech (54.2), and finally at the end of the
narrative just before the execution (68.1).

[38] J. Finley, "Euripides and Thucydides," *HSCP* 49 (1938) 56 (also in *Three Essays on
Thucydides* [Cambridge, Mass. 1967] 1-54), and H. L. Hudson-Williams, "Conventional
Forms of Debate and the Melian Dialogue," *AJP* 71 (1950) 150-169. And note Plato *Protagoras* 329b, 334c-335b; Hudson-Williams distinguishes the types very clearly, but I am
not persuaded by his argument that the short question and answer exchange was restricted
to private intellectual discussions. Surely it would have been of use in debate in the assembly,
in cross-examining witnesses in court, and in conferences and negotiating sessions. Our
documentation about fifth-century rhetoric is grievously deficient and we must be very careful
not to be misled by silence. But it is odd that later Greek theory devotes very little attention
to this important part of oratory.

Athenian supporters; fighting had broken out; the Athenian citizen-repre-
sentative (*proxenos*), Peithias, had been murdered along with sixty citizens
who shared his pro-Athenian views. The factions were not simply advocates
of different foreign policies. Thucydides calls the pro-Athenian group the
dēmos, "the commons"; and the pro-Peloponnesian faction, *hoi oligoi*
"the few," that is, the more well-to-do citizens. Thus a foreign policy
dispute was superimposed upon a division along socioeconomic lines.
Tension between the few and the commons was not unusual in Greek cities;
when it broke into violence, as at Corcyra, the Greeks termed it *stasis*
(literally "a standing") and recognized it as the bitterest and most destructive form of strife.[39]

Thucydides departs from his usual annalistic form to provide a summary
of events between his last discussion of Corcyra, at the outbreak of the
war, and the events of 427 B.C. that he will soon analyze.[40] The account
is at first swift and summary but gradually the detail increases and calls
attention to the underlying significance of the episode.[41]

The structure of the book points in the same direction. Another episode
of class warfare—this one at Notium in Asia Minor—had preceded the
account of the fall and punishment of Mytilene (3.34), and the conduct of
the Paches, the Athenian commander there, and drawn attention to the
distortion and abuse of language that is such a prominent theme in the
third book. The Corcyrean account neatly balances the episode at Notium
and forms with it a ring encompassing the Mytilenean and Plataean debates.
But as we read, it becomes clear that this is no mere ornament but one of
the most crucial episodes in the entire work. As often, what seems minor
or of passing interest in the first element in a ring-composition, returns in
the last element with renewed significance. Paches' betrayal of the commander at Notium through a promise whose words were literally fulfilled
but whose intention was totally violated, might seem, when first encountered, little more than a clever but appalling stratagem. But the themes in
that episode—the distortion of language, the violation of widely accepted
restraints—are precisely the subject of much of the narrative of the Corcyrean *stasis*. The Corcyrean story is told, for example, as a series of

[39] Since English "factionalism" is too tame and "civic strife," "civil war," "revolution,"
"class warfare" have the wrong connotations, I simply retain the Greek term, *stasis*, as a
convenient label for this phenomenon.
[40] The episodes are connected by a verbal link between 1.55.1: ὅπως αὐτοῖς τὴν Κέρκυραν . . . προσποιήσειαν and 3.70.1; πεπεισμένοι Κορινθίοις Κέρκυραν προσ-
ποιῆσαι.
[41] Note the movement toward personal narrative in the story of Peithias (3.70.3-6), followed
by a shift to day-by-day narrative in 72.3ff.

attempts at persuasion. The captives persuade the Corinthians to release them on the grounds that they will bring Corcyra over to the Corinthian side (3.60.1). Peithias resists them by a counterstrategy and persuades the Corcyreans to apply the law against five leaders of the opposite faction.[42] When he seems about to persuade (3.70.6) the citizenry to form a defensive and offensive alliance with Athens, his opponents murder him, move the city toward a policy of neutrality, and send ambassadors to Athens to instruct the Athenians about the events and to persuade (3.71.2) the Corcyrean exiles there to avoid any improper action. The Athenians arrest the ambassadors and confine on Aegina any exiles who were persuaded by them (3.72.1). Meanwhile, in Corcyra the strife breaks out again, until the Athenian commander Nikostratos persuades the parties to make an agreement with each other and the defensive and offensive alliance with Athens (3.75.1). The leaders of the democratic forces persuade (3.75.2) him to leave five ships and some Messenian troops. They then urge the opposing faction to man five Corcyrean ships and sail off with Nikostratos and his fleet. But this group fears to go off with the Athenians and takes refuge in a shrine. When Nikostratos fails to persuade them to withdraw, he gives weapons to the pro-Athenian faction. Soon there are more suppliants at the shrines, then further attempts at persuasion (3.80.1) until the democratic faction ''made those disembark whom they had persuaded to go on board the ships and then dispatched them. They entered in the shrine of Hera and persuaded up to fifty of the suppliants to stand trial. All were condemned to death. But the majority of the suppliants, the ones who were not persuaded, when they saw what was happening, destroyed one another right there in the shrine—some hanged themselves from trees, others expended themselves as they could individually arrange it'' (3.81.2f.).

This is one of the longest and most complex of what can be called ''persuasion narratives'' in Thucydides—episodes, that is, in which the action is traced by the attempts of one party to persuade another to adopt a certain course of action. There are over a dozen occurences of the verb ''to persuade'' and its compounds in half as many pages of text. But the

---

[42] 3.70.5. Is it possible that there is a play on the name Peithias in the phrase ὁ Πειθίας . . . πείθει? Thucydides is certainly not beyond echoing or playing with the etymology of a proper name; cf. for example 8.97.1f. and 1.110.2; 3.30.2; 3.101.2 ad fin.; 3.104.5; 4.42.2. Note also that in the Plataean debate (3.52.5) Thucydides names two Plataean speakers while referring to the other side only as ''the Thebans.'' Is the introduction of the Plataeans' names designed to emphasize the irony of one of them—Lakōn, son of Aeimnēstou (Laconian, son of Ne'r-forget? On Aeimnēstos see G. R. Huxley, ''Two Notes on Herodotus,'' *GRBS* 4 (1963) 5-7.

theme is ironic: discussion, argument, persuasion produce no conciliation, only growing horror and violence.[43]

Language, as we have come to expect in this book, is unable to impede violence. Even an apparent success, as when Nikostratos persuades the factions to make an agreement, is only temporary, a pause in a passage to greater destruction, as further decisions are made, and fear leads to harsher actions.[44] The Corcyrean episode thus carries on a theme of major importance in the third book, and parallels the story of Paches at Notium, not only in subject matter (*stasis*) but in its continued exploration of the relationship between language and violence. At the same time another closely related theme is introduced: the inability of the traditional Greek restraints and conventions to operate under the pressures of war. One of the strongest of these, the taboo that sacred places should be kept free from bloodshed and death, is violated when the Corcyrean "few" who have taken refuge in the shrine of Hera are driven to suicide. In the perverted festival of Corcyra,[45] there is even worse to report: "Every form of death took place, the sort of thing that is likely to happen in such a situation; there was nothing that did not take place—yes, even things more out of bounds.[46] For example a father killed his child and some were dragged

[43] There is an earlier "persuasion narrative" in 2.67, the mission of Aristeus of Corinth and his colleagues and their capture and execution by the Athenians. Here a series of efforts at persuasion comes to an end when the Athenians refuse to allow the ambassadors to speak. The episode, as we have seen at the beginning of this chapter, anticipates some of the themes of book 3.

[44] Note the emphasis on fear, often conveyed by the reiterated nominative participle, δείσας or δείσαντες, "fearing," in 3.74.2; 3.75.3; 3.75.5; 3.78.2; 3.79.1; cf. 3.80.1. Fear escalates and dominates; persuasion is effective only as its agent. The other prominent Greek root for fear, *phob*, is used in this narrative only in relating the naval operations (3.77.1; 78.1; 79.3), never to describe the civic strife. On the role of fear and the distinction between the two roots see J. de Romilly, "La crainte dans l'oeuvre de Thucydide," *ClMed* 17 (1956) 119-127, who contrasts the intellectual aspects of *deos* against the more irrational connotations of *phobos*.

[45] 3.81.3; cf. 81.5. What shoud go on in the shrine is the worship of Hera through festivals in her honor. The festivals are themselves a form of *nomos* and their social function includes extending and reinforcing the bonds that unite *philoi* within a society. Instead we witness the undoing of these bonds until father kills son (81.5; cf. 82.6). Part of a true festival was often a series of contests. In Corcyra the contest theme is prominent (82.7 line 6; 82.8 line 14 and line 22), but the contests are destructive; for example, the rivalry between the factions is presented as a race (note the emphasis on "getting there first," φθάσας, in 82.5 and 82.7). The desire to win (*philonikia*) contributes to the destruction of fair judgment (82.8). The gatherings at Corcyra are thus not conducted with the help of the existing *nomoi* but oppose and destroy them for self-aggrandizement (82.6). At the end of a festival one expects sacrifices and the roasting of meat for the honor of the goddess and the enjoyment of the participants. In Corcyra the stasis is "raw," ὠμή (82.1). Cf. Note 5, above, and the pleasure (ἡδονή) of a true festival is perverted into joy at the destruction of one's enemy (81.6).

[46] I am not proposing to emend καί in 3.81.5 (*OCT* 1. 17) to ναί. But since καί ἔτι

away from the shrines and killed nearby; some others were walled up and died in the shrine of Dionysus" (3.81.5). The horror is clear enough, but the full significance may not immediately be evident. The basic ethical principle of the Greeks is to help one's own *philoi*, families and friends.[47] Thus for a father to kill a son is not, as it might seem in some cultures, a terrible misfortune, nor the occasional result of social tensions. It is rather the dissolution of the human basis for morality. If this tie cannot hold, no fellow citizen, no other Greek, no other human being can be brought within the bounds of human morality. And if in addition divine sanctions fail to operate, then no morality is possible; the only principle is the calculation of self-interest.

Corcyra's political anarchy readily symbolizes a moral anarchy. Now all the conventions of Greek life—promises, oaths, supplication, obligations to kin and benefactor and even that ultimate convention, language itself—give way.[48] It is Hobbes' *bellum omnium contra omnes*.

The *stasis* at Corcyra is one of those extreme moments in the war upon which Thucydides concentrates so intensely, even if they are not strategically of major consequence or the "greatest" by any quantitative measure. Melos is another such episode, disproportionately developed, whose significance lies not in the greatness of the event but in what it tells about the nature of the war and the mind of the participants. Extreme moments provide the chance to penetrate the repetitive and routine and let us glimpse a deeper reality.

The description of the Corcyrean *stasis*, it has often been noted, resembles the analysis of another extreme moment, the Great Plague in book 2.[49] Each begins with a precise description of what actually happened, with careful attention to the day-by-day sequence of events (2.49.6). The

---

περαιτέρω abruptly breaks the chain of thought after οὐδὲν ὅτι οὐ ξυνέβη, one needs some stylistic equivalent in English; at least a dash. I prefer the interjection as a device to deal with the translation problem.

[47] See W. R. Connor, *New Politicians of Fifth-Century Athens* (Princeton 1971) 41-53.

[48] There was considerable interest in the fifth century in the nature of language. Some Greeks believed in an inherent connection between names and things; another school of thought, of which Thucydides, I suspect, was an adherent, held that language was conventional and that names were associated with things not by nature or divine dispensation but by human use and habit. Cf. W.K.C. Guthrie, *The Sophists* (Cambridge 1971) 204ff., who cites the Hippocratic *de arte* 2 that (as emended) treats names as *nomothetēmata* while *eidea*, "appearances," are the outgrowths of nature. Under this view language would readily be grouped with *nomoi*. See also L. Woodbury, "Strepsiades' Understanding," *Phoenix* 34 (1980) esp. 116.

[49] Cf. C. N. Cochrane, *Thucydides and the Science of History* (London 1929) 133f. and L. A. Losada, "Megara and Athens," *ClMed* 30 (1969) 157, n. 31.

detail gives way to an increasingly impressionistic presentation[50] while the language becomes more complicated and the syntax more convoluted. Eventually the accounts turn to generalization and seem to be drawing to a close (2.51.1 and 3.81.5), but then even greater horrors are reported. Finally, description gives way to meditation on the psychological and moral implications of the events. The plague marked the beginning of a lawlessness that affected Athens in many ways (2.53.1); similarly the violence in Corcyra occurred near the beginning of a process that affected many other cities (3.82.1 and 82.3). Each of these afflictions strengthens and exaggerates the boldness (*tolma*) of actions within the cities (2.53.4; 3.82.6 and 82.8) and in each case conventions and restraints, whether human or divine, cease to function (2.53.4; 3.83.2; cf. 84.2). Indeed, we can think of these two parallel episodes as forming a boundary within the work, the one introducing, the other bringing to its culmination a unit exploring the inability of any of the conventional restraints to control the powerful drives of nature.

There is, however, an additional, and much less discussed similarity between the accounts of the plague and of the Corcyrean *stasis*. In each case *logos* is overpowered. Thucydides makes this explicit in 2.50.1 although the crucial phrase is often reduced to blandness in our translations. Thucydides asserts that the appearance of the plague was "stronger than *logos*." The translators catch one aspect of the phrase when they render it, "the nature of the distemper was such as to baffle all description" vel sim.[51] But other resonances are equally important. The plague defied the skill of all doctors (2.51.2) just as it defies the narrative techniques of the historian. The other aspect of *logos*, rational analysis of events, in this case the Hippocratic premise that all diseases are derived from understandable causes gives way to a suspicion that the plague was "something other than one of the home-grown variety."[52]

These hints that the plague surpasses the human faculty for rational discourse are developed in the following chapters. Passion (*orgē*) dominates the Athenians' minds and resolution (2.59.3 and 65.1); memory is distorted

---

[50] 2.50.1 and 51.1; cf. 3.81.5.

[51] Κρεῖσσον λόγου may be an idiom of the late fifth century for what surpasses description. Note Socrates' amused manipulation of the phrase when applied to the beauty of Theodote, Xenophon *Memorabilia* 3.11.1.

[52] 2.50.1. The phrasing is rather coy; *LSJ* does not do it justice by suggesting "everyday evils." Thucydides does not assert the plague was a divine visitation but uses a phrasing that leaves that possibility open. (For *xyntrophon* as a term for local produce then metaphorically extended, see Herodotus 7.120).

under the pressure of the suffering.[53] And the phraseology of the text itself responds to the same pressures, turning first to wordplay and then, very briefly, to an investigation of the transvaluation of moral terms during and after the plague.[54] In Book 2 attention to this change of language is fleeting and easily dismissed as a stylistic affectation in the manner of the rhetorician Gorgias: "What was pleasant at the present and whatever contributed to it from whatever source was found fully fair and functional."[55] But much more than wordplay is involved. In the meditation on the Corcyrean revolution the topics of moral analysis and linguistic usage unite into a single concern:

And they modified at their discretion the customary valences of names for actions. For example, irrational boldness was considered "bravery in the cause of the party"; cautious delay was "a smokescreen for cowardice"; moderation, "an excuse for the timid"; assessment of every issue, "sloth on every front." To strike out sharply was "acting like a man"; to plan with and for security was "a nice-sounding excuse for desertion." The advocate of atrocity was always reliable; his opponent was a man to be suspected. If you succeeded in a plot, you were shrewd; if you anticipated someone else's plot, you were even cleverer. But anyone who tried to arrange it so that no one of these actions would be necessary was a "destroyer of the party and scared out of his wits by the other side."[56]

This passage draws together the theme of the distortion of discourse already present in the discussion of the plague and throughout much of book 3. Language has now become an agent of violence, intensifying rather than alleviating the *kinēsis* and the destruction. Revolutionary New-speak makes violence seem simple and appropriate. War, as Thucydides points out, becomes a teacher of violence and hence depends, as any teacher

[53] 2.54.1-4 is usually taken as Thucydidean sarcasm about oracles. In fact, it says very little about the validity of oracles and a great deal about the way oracles are remembered, transmitted, and interpreted. Its point is the vulnerability of human memory, a crucial concern for the historian (cf. 1.22.1), and a sign of Thucydides' awareness of the limits of his own art.

[54] In 2.53.1 Thucydides chooses *nosēma* instead of *nosos* and juxtaposes it at the end of the sentence with *anomias*. The effect is a jingle and a reminder of the possibility of the manipulation of language.

[55] 2.53.3. The similarity of ἤδη and ἡδύ and the alliteration of "k" sounds in κερδαλέον. Τοῦτο καὶ καλὸν καὶ χρήσιμον κατέστη is not easily rendered in English. In book 1 language is a key to historical reconstruction (cf. 1.3; 1.9.2; 1.13.5): increasingly we become aware of the ease of its manipulation.

[56] 3.82.4f. I follow the Oxford text except that I am unable to accept the ἐπι- prefix in ἐπιβουλεύσασθαι in line 15; See Gome's criticism in *HCT* on 3.82.4 (pp. 375f.). I have borrowed some phrases from Crawley and Gomme and retained quotation marks despite the subtle comments of J. Wilson, "Thucydides 3.82.4," *CR* 32 (1982) 18-20.

must, on words and arguments to achieve the desired results.[57] Thucydides
continues to explore the pathology of language, the inability even of oaths
(3.82.7) to resist the effects of the revolution. Only at the end does he do
what he studiously refused to do in the account of the plague, namely
make some statement about cause. His words (3.82.8), however, are unusual and obscure, so much so that some critics have wished to emend
them.[58] Whatever conclusion one reaches about the text, it is clear that
Thucydides traces the origin of the *stasis* back to psychological factors
such as self-aggrandizement (*pleonexia*) and ambition (*philotimia*). Just as
the Athenian dominance (*archē*) is deeply rooted in human nature,[59] the
stasis at Corcyra is a manifestation of a tendency within human beings
that can take especially pernicious forms. The progression we have noted
in the accounts of the plague and of the *stasis* thus leads from the observed
surface of events to a contemplation of their underlying psychological and
moral implications and, in Corcyra's case, to a consideration of what is
responsible for the process. Gradually we realize that the ineffectiveness
of conventional restraints and the change of language and ethical evaluations are symptoms of something much deeper. The drive for dominance,
self-aggrandizement, and ambition, are all manifestations of something in
the very nature of man.[60] They are not passing moods or externally imposed

[57] 3.82.2. Βίαιος διδάσκαλος is ambiguous, a violent teacher and a teacher of violence.
I believe both are intended. War is a strict headmaster, ever ready to use the whip, and the
lesson that is taught is violence. See Gomme *HCT* ad loc. (p. 373), and P. Pouncey's cautious
remarks, *Necessities of Power* (New York 1980) 182, n. 5.

[58] At first glance αἴτιον and ἀρχή in 3.82.8 are redundant. But ἀρχή is protected by
ἡ διὰ πλεονεξίαν and the deletion of αἴτιον still leaves a very peculiar phraseology.
If, however, the manuscript text is retained and ἀρχή extended to a new range—to refer
not to empire or origin or political office but to the dominance which stands behind these
manifestations—the sentence is a powerful statement of an idea thoroughly consistent with
other aspects of the text. To be sure, ἀρχή in this sense becomes almost a psychological
term, "the desire for power." Cf. the scholiast ad loc. I know of no precise parallel to this
use of the word, but such an extension of its range seems to me not uncharacteristic of
Thucydides.

[59] 1.76.3; cf. 1.75.3. See also de Romilly, *Thucydides and Athenian Imperialism*, esp.
16-57.

[60] This conclusion is secure enough from 3.82.2 but is more emphatic in 3.84.2. But is
that chapter authentic? The doubts are ancient and have been widely shared by modern
scholars. Many of the objections, however, could apply to other sections in Thucydides, not
least to the two preceding chapters. And, one wonders *cui bono*? Who except Thucydides
would write such a piece and why? Would even the most fervent imitator create a sentence
such as the first one in this chapter? And how would such an imitation come to be included
in the text? It seems much more likely, as E. Schwartz suggested, that chapter 84 is an
earlier version of chapters 82-83, inadvertently included in the text. For recent discussions
see C. Scheider, *Information und Absicht bei Thukydides* (Göttingen 1974) 35, n. 67;
E. Wenzel, "Zur Echtheitsfrage von Thuk., 3.84," *WS* N. F. 11 (1968) 18-27; and for a
skeptical view, A. Fuks, "Thucydides and the Stasis in Corcyra," *AJP* 92 (1971) 48-55.

seizures or afflictions, like the physical plague, that suddenly beset man
from some unknown origin or cause. They emerge from within. Corcyra
thereby becomes a manifestation of one aspect of human nature just as the
imaginary society Plato sketched in the *Republic* manifested the soul of
man.

"Thus savage *stasis* progressed," says Thucydides (3.82.1), combining
the verb he used for the "progress" of early Ionian civilization and the
adjective used for the decision to destroy the Mytileneans, "and it was all
the more conspicuous because it was among the first since later all the
Hellenic world, so to speak, was disrupted."[61] In this sentence, at the
moment of transition from description to contemplation, Thucydides evokes
the opening of his history and at the same time the ending of the war. The
stasis in Corcyra, intensified by the Athenian presence, eventually comes
home to Athens in the city's own internal struggles during the last decade
of the war and through the rule of the Thirty Tyrants. By using the word
"disrupted" he brings us back to the first chapter of the work and helps
clarify the opaque claims made there (1.1.2) that this war was "the greatest
disruption (*kinēsis*) for the Greeks, and for some portion of the barbarians,
and, so to speak, among the largest portion of mankind."[62] Now we can
begin to understand that peculiar phrase. The allusion is not simply to the
physical disruptions of the war: the deaths, exiles, the migrations of populations and even the attendant earthquakes and plagues.[63] After Corcyra,

---

[61] Προυχώρησε; cf. 1.16.1. Cf. C. W. Macleod, "Thucydides on Faction," *Proceedings
of the Cambridge Philological Society* 205 (1979) 52-68. It is a paradox to say that *stasis*
(a "standing") progressed, and an equal paradox to combine a word with connotations of
"progress" with the adjective, ὠμή, "raw or savage." See also Notes 5 and 45 above.

The phrase διότι ἐν τοῖς πρώτῃ ἐγένετο is often translated to mean that the *stasis* at
Corcyra was the first in the war. Cf. Gomme in *HCT* ad loc. (p. 372); H. W. Smyth, *Greek
Grammar* rev. G. Messing (Cambridge, Mass. 1959) sec. 1089; Andrewes in *HCT* on 8.89.2
(p. 296). But what is the reader then to make of the *stasis* at Notium (3.34), an earlier episode
of *stasis* connected to the Corcyrean situation both by the structure (see Note 28, above) and
by verbal echoes, e.g. ἐπάγεσθαι and cognates in each passage. The idiom is by no means
easily interpreted. The relevant Thucydidean examples were gathered by L. Herbst in the
Jahresbericht in *Philologus* 16 (1860) 345ff. He made a strong case that Thucydides uses
such expressions to mean "among the first" vel sim. Or it may mean "in the first rank
among the examples of *stasis*." This avoids the necessity of emendation in 3.17.1 and if
extended to 8.68.4, allows Thucydides simply and plausibly to say that Theramenes was in
the first rank among the conspirators of the Four Hundred. I am not persuaded by Andrewes'
assertion that 7.19.3 is "decisive" against this view. I have greatly benefited from discussing
this problem with George Gellie.

[62] The root *kin-* in a metaphorical sense is quite unusual in Thucydides. (The most recent
occurence is 3.75.2.) The connection between 3.82.1 and 1.1.2 is further emphasized by
the reference to Greeks or the Greek world and by the qualification, ὡς εἰπεῖν, in each
passage.

[63] 1.23.1. Note the progression from war to *stasis*. On *kinēsis* see A. W. Gomme, "The

the disruption is seen to exist at a much deeper level as well. Along with the physical circumstances of life are disrupted language, values, and the view of the past, the future, and of history. The optimistic view of the Archaeology with its presentation of man's progress toward ever greater accomplishment collides with the implications of the Corcyrean *stasis*.[64] The illusion of progress is shattered. The constancy of human nature, the premise upon which much of the analysis of the Archaeology is based, remains, but its implications are deeply pessimistic: "Many atrocities afflicted the cities in stasis, things that continue to happen and will keep happening as long as there is the same physis for human beings, though more intense or more tranquil, or more adapted in their manifestations as individual changes of circumstances appear" (3.82.2). No longer is there a suggestion that knowing the recurrence of events will enable us to draw useful inferences about the future (1.22.4). The past will recur, but that recurrence has become a threat, not a promise. Gone is the optimism of the early part of the *Histories*, which binds the reader to Pericles in a common confidence about the possibility of seeing far enough into the future to be able to adapt to it or even direct it. The plague was the first and a surmountable challenge to that confidence. The events of book 3, in which all the conventions of Greek civilization, and eventually language itself, give way before and become part of the intensifying violence of war, pose a much more serious challenge.[65] We are left at the end of the Corcyrean narrative with an awesome prospect. The facile confidence of an earlier generation, indeed of some of Thucydides' contemporaries, is gone.[66] But we are not allowed to retreat, as some critics have thought, to the old "archaic pessimism." An inexorable, impersonal regularity prevails, quite unlike anything in the archaic thought. We have left that

---

Greatest War in Greek History," in *Essays in Greek History and Literature* 116ff., who seems to me to be on the right track in contrast to N.G.L. Hammond, "The Arrangement of Thought in the Proem and in Other Parts of Thucydides I," *CQ* n.s. 2 (1952) 133, n. 1.

[64] Greatness in the Archaeology (1.3.1 and 1.17) depends on common action. *Stasis* prevents common action, even within a single city.

[65] Note the role of *logismos*, "calculation," in 3.83.2.

[66] Xenophon *Memorabilia* 2.6.18ff. reports that Socrates in conversation with Critoboulos held that while the *ponēroi* can never form friendships with other *ponēroi*, the *chrēstoi* are able to cooperate: "For those who desire to win honour and to bear rule in their cities that they may have power to embezzle, to reward others with violence, to live in luxury, are bound to be unjust, unscrupulous, incapable of unity" (sec. 24, trans. E. C. Marchant in the Loeb Classical Library). Could anyone who had understood Thucydides' depiction of Corcyra speak in such terms and so grievously underestimate the ability of evil to combine and, at least temporarily, cooperate in cruelty and violence? On the same fallacy in later Greek thought see Diodorus' account of Charondas (12.12.3), and H. C. Baldry, "Zeno's Ideal State," *JHS* 79 (1959) 7.

melancholy but blessed age and its theology far behind us, passed through and absorbed the Greek enlightenment and entered a world where neither the traditional assurances of an ultimate kosmos nor the promises of pragmatic rationalism offer consolation or hope.

DELOS

The strained, breaking language of the Corcyrean meditation now gives way to familiar, almost formulaic patterns that lead the reader swiftly through the rest of the year 427 and the campaigns of 426. The narrative moves swiftly and for the most part impersonally. Only the Athenian commander Demosthenes briefly emerges with any prominence. More conspicuous are the descriptions of the warlike and primitive tribes of northeast Greece as the war expands into their region.

There is a rhythm to the account of the campaign year 426. Sicilian affairs alternate with those of mainland Greece, while both at the beginning and at the end of the year Thucydides pauses to recount natural disasters and in one case to speculate about the cause (89.5 and 89.116, esp. 2). Within this frame is a further balancing of episodes. Demosthenes' unexpected defeat in the Aetolian campaign is described in chapters 94-98 and 100 in language that recurs in the account of his victory in the Ambraciot campaign of chapters 105-114.[67] These in turn surround an excursus on the ritual purification of the island of Delos in response to "a certain oracle" (ch. 104).

The arrangement is neat, attractive, manageable. It may be a mistake to look for any elaborate development of theme or any deep analysis. The general who wrote these pages knew the routine of war, and it, no less than the underlying questions of cause and nature, interested him. But historian and general can never be totally separated. The military significance of the campaigns in the northwest—that light-armed troops can prove effective against the more "developed" hoplite system—hints at one of the historian's themes. The war is simultaneously a culmination of the growth of power of earlier Greek history and a reversion to a more primitive existence. This theme had already been sounded in the Corcyrean account. The Corcyreans, having regressed toward savagery, turn to piratical raids, an activity characteristic of an early stage in Greek civilization

[67] The language reflects, of course, a similarity in situation, especially the use of light-armed troops to rout hoplites. The convergence between 3.98.1-3 and 3.112.6 and 112.7 is especially close.

(cf. 1.5). Now the best Athenian forces are operating in a backward region of Greece, where the stage of walled civic life has not yet arrived,[68] and where some tribes are reputed to be savages who eat their food uncooked (3.94.5). Demosthenes is persuaded that it would not be difficult to subdue men "who dwelt in unwalled villages and these widely scattered, a tribe that used light armor" (3.94.4) before any common defense could be arranged. But when the operation is over, the crack, heavy-armed troops of the Athenians have perished (3.98.4). In later operations against the Ambraciots Demosthenes adopts and develops the tactics that have been used so successfully against him.

Between Demosthenes' defeat at the hands of the Aetolians and his victory over the Ambraciots Thucydides relates the Athenian purification of the island of Delos. The story stands out from the surrounding narrative not only by the symmetrical arrangement pointed out above but by its unusual structure and its utilization of the Homeric *Hymn to Apollo*. The citations from the hymn, thirteen lines in all, are the longest quotation from poetic texts in the *Histories* and paint a vivid picture of the ancient festival of the Ionians on Delos: "But when, Phoebus, you delighted your heart with Delos, there the Ionians with their long robes gather with their wives and children in your assembly; they turn their thoughts to delight you with boxing, dancing and song, whenever they convene the contest."[69] Thucydides also quotes verses from the ending of the same hymn that imply Homer himself participated in this festival.

In this episode Thucydides alternates between succinct sentences relating the events of 426 and a series of digressions on the past. The initial mention of the purification calls to mind an earlier purification by Pisistratos. The sentence reporting the removal of the graves to the nearby island of Rheneia introduces another excursus that repeats and expands upon information already provided (1.13.6) about Polycrates of Samos and his activities on these islands when he dominated the Aegean. Thucydides then returns to the present to report the establishment of a festival called the Delia. But this immediately leads into the long excursus on the earlier festival and to the citations from Homer. In the last sentence Thucydides returns to the present with the note that the new festival added horse races.

The antiquarianism, the unusual alternation between narrative of the present and reminiscence about remote times, and above all the extensive quotation, without deprecatory remarks, of Homeric poetry make this a

---

[68] 3.94.4; note the similarity to 1.5.1.

[69] 3.104.4.-5; quoted from the Homeric *Hymn to Apollo* lines 146-150, with textual variations.

most unusual passage. Historian and epic poet are temporarily in accord as an early age of Greece returns to life. The elegant leaders of the Ionians gather, their wives and children with them, for a celebration of Apollo in which both god and man delight. We are led back to an age of fabled tranquility and beauty, of poetry and order. We enter a festival of families bound together in common observances, contests of simple physical joy. How complete a contrast to the perverted festival we have just witnessed in Corcyra![70] For a moment we stand on a little island of calm equipoised amid the expanding and intensifying war. Delicate and deft, the episode provides the contrast that lets us assess the events of Thucydides' day. At the same time it subverts and refutes all facile notions of progress, not least the assurance that in Greek history there was a dynamic at work that led gradually to growing material greatness and thereby to higher levels of civilization. There is perhaps no more eloquent refutation of the clichés of progress than this unpretentious chapter.[71]

[70] Cf. Note 45 above.

[71] It is also a link in a chain of increasing bleakness and horror. In 5.1.1 we learn that in 422 B.C. the Athenians drove the Delians out of Delos because of "some old charge." Later (5.32.1) the Athenians repent, after military reverses (esp. Amphipolis 5.7ff. but probably not Delium as well, as suggested by Classen-Steup ad loc.). Not all the Delians return. Some remain in Asia Minor where they had been given refuge by Pharnakes (5.1.1). Still later the best troops among these are betrayed and butchered by Arsakes' treachery, just at the end of book 8 (ch. 108).

Book 4

PYLOS

To THE HISTORIAN, the fourth book of the *Histories* is perhaps the least convincing of the entire work. In it Thucydides relates two highly innovative, and risky, undertakings, one by the Athenians and one by the Spartans. The strategy of each of these is based on premises that up to this point had been rejected in the war. Each results in a movement toward peace, although the respective leaders, Cleon in Athens and Brasidas of Sparta, both resist a settlement. And, most important for our purposes, Thucydides' treatment of each strategy is complex and controversial.

The narrative of the first of these operations, the Athenian occupation of Pylos in 425 B.C. poses an especially large number of historical problems. Thucydides says that while the Athenian expedition of forty ships en route to Sicily (3.115.4) was sailing around the Peloponnese, Demosthenes, on board as a private citizen (4.2.4), urged the fleet to put in at Pylos, in the southwestern Peloponnese, and "to do what is necessary" (4.3.1). Although Demosthenes had received authorization from the assembly to use the fleet (4.2.4), the generals were reluctant to do as he requested. But a storm forced the fleet to take refuge in the bay. Demosthenes thereupon immediately urged that they fortify the spot, for that had been his purpose in sailing with them: "He listed its assets—a great surplus of wood and stones; it was naturally strong and deserted, both the spot itself and much of the surrounding country."[1] The generals, understandably, were not persuaded by such arguments and replied with a sarcastic adaptation of Demosthenes' financial language: "They said that there were many deserted headlands in the Peloponnese if he wanted to run up a bill for the city by seizing one" (4.3.3).[2] Demosthenes was not easily put off: "But this spot seemed to him unique—there was the harbor and the Messenians, who had dwelt there of old and who spoke the same dialect as

[1] 4.3.2. Note the financial terminology in ἀπέφαινε and εὐπορίαν.
[2] 4.3.3. Ἢν βούληται . . . τὴν πόλιν δαπανᾶν.

the Lacedaemonians, would do extreme harm by making their attacks from there and at the same time would be reliable guards of the place" (4.3.3). At first Demosthenes was unable to persuade the generals or the troops. But in the boredom of the delay, a sudden impulse afflicted[3] the soldiers (4.4.1) and they began to construct the walls, even though the proper equipment was lacking (ch. 4). After six days a rudimentary fort was complete; the Athenian fleet then sailed off to Corcyra leaving Demosthenes five ships and presumably about one thousand crew members at Pylos.

To a historian's eye the implausibilities in this account are obvious.[4] If, for example, we ask how Demosthenes persuaded the assembly to allow him to use the force that was to sail around the Peloponnese, the answer must be that he convinced his fellow citizens that he had a plan for its effective use. He need not have revealed every feature, but he could scarcely have expected carte blanche from the Athenians. What, then, was this plan? And how did he convince the Athenians it was sound? Thucydides so completely avoids discussing these issues that many critics have accused him of pretending the entire operation was a series of lucky improvisations and coincidences. By emphasizing the Athenians' lack of proper equipment for fortifying and defending the spot, he seems to imply that the Athenians had not properly prepared for the attack. Even more troublesome is his report of the arrival of Messenian reinforcements without any discussion of the coordination of their role with that of the Athenians: "For it was not possible to procure heavy armor in a deserted spot, instead even these things were acquired from the privateering triaconter of the Messenians who arrived at that time and a yawl. There were also around forty Messenian hoplites whom he used along with the others."[5]

---

[3] The word for "afflicted" is ἐσέπεσε, or ἐνέπεσε (Poppo's emendation), words normally reserved for physical attacks and grievious physical or psychological states. Note 2.48.2 (emended to ἐσέπεσε by Herwerden); 49.4; 53.4; 61.2. In 6.24.3 ἐνέπεσε is used with *erōs* as subject; in the passage relating to Pylos it hints at something irrational or potentially destructive in the soldiers' activity. We see them through the eyes of Eurymedon and Sophocles, engaged in what seems a frenzy of work on an ill-conceived project. See also V. Hunter, *Thucydides, the Artful Reporter* (Toronto 1973) 63.

[4] The principal critiques of Thucydides' account of the Pylos operation are F. M. Cornford, *Thucydides Mythistoricus* (London 1907) 82-109 and E. C. Woodcock, "Demosthenes, Son of Alcisthenes," *HSCP* 39 (1928) 93-108 and Symphonien Van de Maele, "Démosthène et Cléon à Pylos," *Mélanges d'études anciennes offerts à Maurice Lebel* (St.-Jean-Chrysostôme. Quebec 1980) 119-124. I have benefited from discussing these articles with Hunter R. Rawlings III.

[5] 4.9.1. Cornford, *Thucydides Mythistoricus* 82f. (but note page 88, n.2), contended that by using ἔτυχον that the arrival of the Messenians was an accident. *Tychē*, personified chance, was thereby presented as the real agent in this episode. But as Gomme has shown (*HCT* on 4.41.4 [p. 488f.]; cf. C. Schneider, *Information und Absicht bei Thukydides* [Göttingen 1974] 97, n. 189, and L. Edmunds, *Chance and Intelligence in Thucydides* [Cambridge,

A historian, confronted with this narrative, is likely to conclude that Thucydides has left out vital information or needlessly belittled Demosthenes' strategic skill.[6] That Demosthenes had a plan, and a clever one, is undeniable. Surely his previous experience in the Acarnanian campaign (3.106-114) and his close contacts with the Messenian refugees at Naupactus had led him to the conclusion that these inveterate opponents of the Spartans could be used to good advantage if they were provided with a base on the Peloponnese coastline and naval and logistic support. Thucydides hints at such a plan in 4.3.3 but does not stop to explain it.

His lack of attention to the element of planning in the campaign demands explanation. If, as has often been conjectured, Cleon and Demosthenes were working closely together on the Pylos project, a reason for his reticence is at hand: he was biased against Cleon and disliked anyone associated with him.[7] Alternatively we can follow Cornford in his suggestion that Thucydides was constructing an elaborate mythic drama in which one of the personified actors was Chance, Tyche.[8]

Attention to Thucydides' literary techniques, however, leads to a more cautious assessment. Although some Thucydidean narratives, as Madame de Romilly has so clearly pointed out in *Histoire et raison chez Thucydide*, present at the outset a plan or strategy and proceed to show how events confirm or modify initial expectations, other portions of the work are written in quite the opposite fashion. In these the plan only gradually unfolds, or vital information is provided only late in the story. The account of the Theban attack on Plataea is a good example. This attack, as we have noted in the discussion of the second book, comes as a surprise since Boeotian affairs have been accorded only minimal attention in book 1. Crucial information, moreover, is provided only late in the narrative, for example, the fact that the attack took place during a month of sacred truce emerges only in the third book during the debate after the capitulation of the city (3.56.2).

Mass. 1974] 5, n. 10) the verb indicates mere simultaneity. Nonetheless the root *-tych-* is prominent and important in its tie to the *eutychia* theme.

[6] Demosthenes' speech (4.10) transforms the traditional appeal for a military force to be εὔελπις (cf. 1.70.3) by adding the neologism ἀπερισκέπτως (for ἀφρόνως) "uncontemplatively." The speech suggests a repudiation of *xynesis* and *logismos* (cf. Edmunds, *Chance and Intelligence*, 9, n. 6) and reverses Pericles' approach and advice (cf. 2.62.5), even though behind Demosthenes' actions is a plan of considerable thoughtfulness and even brilliance.

[7] Cf. Woodcock *HSCP* 39 (1928) 93-108.

[8] See Cornford, *Thucydides Mythistoricus*, esp. 88ff., followed by Hunter, *Artful Reporter*, esp. 103f. Cf. J. de Romilly, *Thucydides and Athenian Imperialism*, trans. P. Thody (Oxford 1963), p. 175ff. For further bibliography see Schneider, *Information und Absicht*, 97, n. 189, and Edmunds, *Chance and Intelligence*, 5, n. 10.

In the case of the Theban attack on Plataea, we might conclude that the postponement of important information indicates negligence or some other weakness in Thucydides' technique. But in the Pylos episode, there is more reason to suspect a deliberate and artful purpose. Paradox and surprise are emphasized and elaborated at every turn: "Luck had turned about to this extent—Athenians from land, indeed from Laconian land, were repelling Spartans who were attacking from the sea. And the Spartans from ships were attempting to make a landing against Athenians on their own land which had come into enemy hands. This caused a great sensation at that time for they were very much a continental power and very strong in infantry while the Athenians were a sea power and preeminent in their navy" (4.12.3). Paradox has an important role in the account, and a fully appropriate one. The Pylos operation marks a major turning point in the *Histories*. It is the first sign of the grand reversal in which the war culminates—the Athenians, at the outset Greece's major naval power, ultimately lose their fleet; the Spartans, traditionally a land power, acquire an empire and develop the navy to control it. Pylos is our first glimpse of the larger pattern.

At a more detailed level the same concern with paradox and surprise shapes the narrative. At the beginning of the account, the reader's attention is on Sicily. This is the ultimate objective of the Athenian expedition; indeed, at first (3.115.4 and 4.2.2) we are not even aware that Demosthenes is himself on board or that there is any thought of an operation along the shores of the Peloponnese. And when he appears (4.2.4), we have no glimpse of his plan or intentions and scarcely any awareness that this is indeed the beginning of the famous Pylos campaign. Our view is very similar to that of the commanders—so eager to get on to Corcyra and Sicily that Pylos seems a distraction. Demosthenes' rationale for occupying the headland, moreover, is at first obscure and ill-presented. It seems an absurd waste of time and money, as the commanders point out (4.3.3). Gradually, however, a plan unfolds. Demosthenes, we learn, intends to use Messenians, that is the refugees at Naupactus, to guard the place and to make raids from it (4.3.3). After a while the troops voluntarily undertake the fortification, although their decision is viewed, as we have noted, from the critical and hostile perspective of the commanders (4.4.1), and hence seems an irrational impulse.

The significance of the Pylos operation becomes clear as the reader watches the Spartans' response. Initially the Spartan authorities make little of the occupation (4.5.1). But the force invading Attica reacts more strongly, withdraws to the Peloponnese and prepares for a large-scale operation

against the fortification (4.8.1f.). The reader is now alerted to the importance of Demosthenes' undertaking, even if we have not yet been told
precisely how the ultimate success will be won. Since, however, even at
the beginning of the narrative the outcome is well known, the reader readily
views the events ironically. The Spartan confidence that they "will easily
capture a construction rapidly built and with only a few creatures inside"
is, we know, mistaken, however reasonable it may have seemed at that
moment.[9] The irony is again evident in the description of the Spartan
decision to move troops on to the island of Sphacteria (4.8.7-9), a decision
plausible enough at the time but ultimately of the gravest consequence for
their city.

In the opening chapters of the fourth book, then, the reader is gradually
led from a very casual, almost disdainful, attitude toward the operation to
an increasing awareness of the details of Demosthenes' plan and to an
intensifying concentration on its potential and significance. Sicily, Corcyra,
and other operations fade into the background; the narrative becomes more
vivid and dramatic; we recognize one of the most significant campaigns
in the war.

But the initial engagement provides only a hint of greater developments
soon to follow. When the crack Spartiate troops placed on the island of
Sphacteria are blockaded by the Athenian fleet, the Spartans decide to send
a delegation to Athens to negotiate a settlement to the war. The seemingly
casual decision to fortify that deserted headland has produced the most
substantial opportunity for peace yet encountered. And a further surprise
follows. The Athenians, who up to this point had been the party more
eager for a settlement (4.21.1), accept Cleon's advice and reject the terms
offered by the Spartans.[10]

---

[9] 4.8.4. Ἀνθρώπων is contemptuous; the word is often used for nonhoplite forces. Cf.
3.98.1 and 98.2; 4.33.2. Ἐλπίζοντες (or νομίζοντες) and ῥαδίως (or ῥᾷον) are often
used ironically: 2.2.4; 2.3.2; 2.80.8; 3.94.2; 4.2.3; 8.25.5.

[10] Both the forms and the substance of this section are unusual. The Spartan ambassadors
deliver a major speech reported in direct discourse (4.17-20). In normal Thucydidean practice
the speech would have been followed by a parallel address presenting the reasons for rejecting
the Spartan offer. But the expected antilogy never appears. Instead we are immediately told
that the Athenians rejected the offer "and reached out for more" (4.21.2). The account then
continues with a report of Cleon's role and his insistence that the Spartans restore the status
quo ante the Thirty Years Peace.

By so swiftly passing over Cleon's main speech, Thucydides obscures the most extraordinary feature of the debate. The Spartans propose not just peace but *alliance* (4.19.1), a
dramatic reversal after so many years of hostility and after the Spartan claims to be the
liberator of Greece from Athenian enslavement. Now the belligerents are to march together
as "allies, friends, and intimates" (4.19.1). It is hinted that together Athens and Sparta can
dominate Greece (4.20.4; cf. Aristophanes *Peace* 1082).

Once we recognize that the narrative technique of this portion of the work recreates some of the surprise and sense of paradox produced by the events of 425, we can approach the most difficult portion of the story from a fresh perspective. Athens' ultimate success in the Pylos episode derived from a decision to force the issue and to attempt a landing on the island of Sphacteria. In such an operation Athenian troops would have to defeat crack Spartan hoplites. The reluctance of the Athenian commanders to attempt such an operation is easy to understand: Athenian land forces were thought to be no match for the famed Spartiates. But the attack is eventually undertaken and results in one of the most astounding victories of the war. Thucydides' account of this episode has again been widely criticized and he has been accused of being so biased against the leaders of the assault, Cleon and Demosthenes, that he obscured the true background of the events. His account, as we shall see, is far removed from any ideal of detached, objective reporting, but it is shaped not so much by animosity as by an elaborate strategy of replicating some of the emotions and reactions experienced at the time of the events.

In summary, Thucydides' account (4.27ff.) is this: The Spartans manage to smuggle in supplies to their force blockaded on the island of Sphacteria; the Athenian garrison on the mainland, on the other hand, suffers from lack of adequate provisions. No capitulation of the Spartans seems imminent; the prospect of trying to maintain the blockade through the winter is most unwelcome. The Athenians are now sorry that they did not accept the Spartans' offer of a peace treaty and direct their animosity against the principal opponent of the peace treaty, Cleon. At first he reacts by denying the distressing reports that arrive from Pylos. But when the messengers invite the assembly to send its own fact-finding mission, and when Cleon

---

From an Athenian point of view such an alliance would have to be viewed very skeptically. Spartan land power was not likely to be of much use to Athens in dealing with recalcitrant members of the naval empire, but Athens might find itself drawn into helping Sparta suppress another Helot revolt (cf. 1.102). Or, in four years when Sparta's treaty with Argos expired, Athens might be called upon to join in military operations against democratic Argos.

There was a great deal to discuss, then, in the Spartan proposal and strong arguments to bring against it. Cleon could well have distrusted Sparta's intentions and felt that there was no need for an immediate response. It was not unreasonable that the first stage in the negotiations should be an Athenian demand for generous territorial concessions. But Thucydides' account pays little attention to the question of an alliance and thereby invites the conclusion that the Athenians were rash and greedy in rejecting the Spartan offer. (Gomme in *HCT* on 4.20.4 [p. 460] rejects de Romilly's conclusion that Thucydides approved of the Spartan arguments. Gomme's criticisms of the Spartan offer are well taken and, I believe, he is correct in contending that the Athenians were well advised to reject these proposals. But we must distinguish our judgment about the wisdom of Athenian action from an assessment of how Thucydides presented the issue and how he expected his readers to react.)

is made one of the members, he tries a new maneuver. Thucydides leads
us to view the events from Cleon's point of view and thereby makes us
very aware of his discomfiture:

And recognizing that he would be forced either to agree with those whom he had
slandered or to be exposed as a liar if he disagreed, he advised the Athenians,
seeing that they were more ready to make a military expedition, that there was no
point in sending a fact-finding mission nor to lose by delay a good opportunity.
If they thought the reports were true, they should sail against the men. Then pointing
to Nicias, the son of Niceratus, a general and an old enemy, and criticizing him
he said that it would be easy to sail with a force and capture the troops on the
island, provided the commanders were real men. At any rate he would do that, if
he had that office. (4.27.4-5)

Nicias, stung by Cleon's taunt, urges Cleon to take whatever force he
wishes and see if he can do any better. At this point Thucydides again
represents Cleon's inner thoughts. At first he thinks Nicias is only pretending to let the command go over to him, but when he recognizes that
Nicias is serious, he backs off and "said that *he* was not general, Nicias
was. Cleon was now frightened but did not think that Nicias would be so
bold as to withdraw in his favor. But again Nicias urged him and withdrew
from his command of the Pylos operation and made the Athenians his
witnesses. As a crowd naturally does, the more Cleon sought to avoid the
expedition and back down from what he said, the more they urged Nicias
to hand over his command and shouted at Cleon "sail!" (4.28.2f.).

It is a delicious scene, all the more welcome to the reader by the memory
of Cleon's persuasive violence in the Mytilene affair. But almost immediately a shift begins. In one extraordinary sentence Cleon is forced to
yield to the shouts of the assembly, in apparent total discomfiture, and
responds with astonishing confidence: "Thus having no way to untangle
himself from what he had said, he accepted command of the expedition
and came forward to say that he was not afraid of the Lacedaemonians
and he would sail taking no one from the city except the Lemnians and
Imbrians who were present and the peltasts who had come as auxiliaries
from Ainos and four hundred archers from other places; with these forces
and the troops already at Pylos he said he would bring the Spartans back
alive or kill them on the spot" (4.28.4). No longer are we provided with
reports of what is going on in Cleon's mind. We hear only his denial of
the assertion that he was frightened,[11] and his compounding of his own
difficulties by promising to clear up the Pylos problem in the astonishingly

---

[11] 4.28.2: δεδιὼς ἤδη; 28.4 οὔτε φοβεῖσθαι . . . Λακεδαιμονίους.

short time of twenty days, without the use of citizen troops. We are invited, in effect, to shift our perspective from Cleon's feelings of entrapment and dismay to those of an outside observer who is enjoying his distress and the apparently impossible position into which he has worked himself: "Some laughter afflicted the Athenians at his empty talk; there was pleasure nonetheless among the saner elements of humanity who calculated that one of two things would be achieved—either they would get rid of Cleon, which they rather expected, or if they were mistaken in their estimate, the Lacedaemonians would become their captives."[12] Cleon now chooses as his colleague Demosthenes (4.29.1) who in turn develops a plan exploiting both a chance fire that had cleared out much of the underbrush on the island and his experience in the use of light-armed troops against hoplites.[13] The result of the vividly reported battle is the encirclement of the Spartans by Messenian troops under the command of Comon,[14] and the surrender of the Spartan force, a total of 292 men, including about 120 Spartan citizen hoplites (4.38.5). Finally the focus returns to Cleon: "The Athenians and the Peloponnesians withdrew from Pylos with their forces to their several homes and the promise of Cleon, although it had seemed

[12] 4.28.5. The language is rich and evocative. Thucydides does not say "The Athenians could not help laughing at his fatuity" (Crawley) vel sim. but chooses the same word, ἐνέπεσε, for sudden, normally destructive, physical or emotional stress that he used for the decision of the troops on Pylos to begin fortifications (4.4.1): ὁρμὴ ἐνέπεσε (emended by Poppo). Cf. Note 3 above. The choice of words underlines the irony of the situation; the reader knows that Cleon will succeed and that this laughter is unwarranted. In a similar way Thucydides does not say "sensible men comforted themselves with the reflection" (Crawley) but expands the simple τοῖς σώφροσι with τῶν ἀνθρώπων. The parallels in Classen-Steup on 3.47.3 show the effect of the expansion—a condescending or compassionate attitude is adopted. We are reminded that the so-called "saner elements" are mistaken in their confidence. Cleon will not fail; and his success will not make the Lacedaemonians their captives. Cleon's power will be strengthened and a "sensible" national policy will be more difficult to achieve. On *kouphologia* see Plutarch *de Herodoti mal.*, *Moralia* 855b.

[13] The plan is conveyed in a quasi-stream-of-consciousness narrative in 4.29.3f.; cf. 32.3f. We know Demosthenes' thinking but very little of Cleon's ideas until 37.1. There the participle γνούς is applied for the fourth time to Cleon in the Pylos account, 4.37.1; cf. 27.3; 27.4; 28.2.

[14] Thucydides' habit was whenever possible to name the individual whose advice or stratagem was decisive in a campaign or battle, even if the individual is otherwise obscure or insignificant. Cf. 2.33.1; 2.85.5; 2.101.5; 3.29.2f.; 4.91f.; 7.39.2. (The suppression of the name in 6.60.2 occurs in a discreditable domestic incident and is not analogous. On 2.91.3 see Gomme in *HCT* ad loc. and H. D. Westlake, *Individuals in Thucydides* [Cambridge 1968] 51.) We would expect, then, that Thucydides would provide the commander's name in 4.36.1, if he knew it. Thucydides was well informed on Messenian affairs (3.98.1; 3.107.1; 3.112.4; 4.9.1), and Comon was famous and attested on an accessible document (Pausanias 4.26.2; cf. 5.26.1). Hence the name may originally have been supplied in 4.36.1. Haplography of -ων can account for its disappearance.

quite crazy, came true. For within twenty days he brought back the men, just as he had promised.''[15]

Many historical objections can be brought against this account, and especially against the assembly scene with which it begins. Cleon, whatever his faults, was clearly a clever and skillful politician whose career was based on his ability to read the moods of the Athenian assembly. It is hard to believe that he was unaware of Nicias' probable reaction to the taunt that if the commanders were real men they would already have captured Sphacteria. Almost any Greek male would be outraged by such an insult and challenge his critic to do better. It has often been suspected that Cleon deliberately provoked Nicias in order to implement the more innovative strategy advocated by Demosthenes. This suspicion is strengthened by the sequel. Why does Cleon needlessly compound his difficulty by promising to take no citizen troops and to accomplish his objectives within such a short time? Would someone who has just been forced into an unwelcome command act in this way? Would he not rather ask for the largest possible force and the longest period to plan and complete his operation?

Questions such as these have led many critics to suspect Thucydides' account of Pylos. In particular some coordination between Demosthenes and Cleon seems likely. Collaboration with a leader of the assembly was the obvious technique for an innovative tactician such as Demosthenes. The continuing coolness of the board of commanders to his plan, even after its initial success, and their understandable reluctance to try to force a landing against the famed Spartan hoplites, would pose a serious problem for the advocates of the Pylos operation. Unless decisive action were soon taken, the winter storms would force a withdrawal of the Athenian force and permit the escape of the Spartan force. At this point Cleon's support could prove vital for the success of Demosthenes' plan. Cleon's skill in manipulating the assembly could make it possible to circumvent the board of commanders and give Demosthenes the authorization and the additional forces that he needed.[16] The opposition of the commanders and the rep-

---

[15] 4.39.3. Most translations make the comment into a simple statement of Thucydides' opinion that the promise was insane: "and crazy as Cleon's promise was" (Crawley): "however mad he may have been to have made it" (Warner). But adjectives with the -*ōdēs* suffix (e.g. *loimōdēs* in 1.23.2) are often ambiguous, "denoting either fullness or similarity"; see H. W. Smyth, *Greek Grammar* (Cambridge, Mass. 1950) sec. 858.16; cf. 833 a; cf. Schneider, *Information und Absicht*, 21, n. 29. The translation should preserve the ambiguity, for the statement is not a simple affirmation about the promise but also a reminder of the reaction that had been provoked by its apparent madness. We are reminded of the contrast between Cleon's craziness and the miscalculation of his "sensible minded" opponents (4.28.5).

[16] Not the ambiguity in 4.30.4: Κλέων δὲ ἐκείνῳ τε προπέμψας ἄγγελον ὡς ἥξων καὶ ἔχων στρατιὰν ἣν ᾐτήσατο, ἀφικνεῖται ἐς Πύλον. Does this mean that Cleon sent

utation of the Spartan hoplite force (4.40) would make it difficult to get such a bill through the assembly. But clever maneuvering might provoke Nicias to a rash move. If this is correct, Cleon knew all along how Nicias and the assembly were likely to react and was deliberately goading him into a resignation. In other words, all goes precisely according to Cleon's plan. Nicias resigns; the assembly insists that Cleon take over the command and he then jauntily makes his promise that he will succeed in Pylos without using citizen hoplites and within twenty days.[17]

Given the lack of other sources for the period such a reconstruction must remain speculative,[18] but it reminds us that Thucydides is interpreting events and that his interpretation is not the only possible one. Before hastening on to generalizations about Thucydides' objectivity, we would do well to look more closely at his interpretation and the techniques by which it is presented. As often in Thucydides much depends on changes of viewpoint. At the beginning of the assembly's debate on Pylos the reader's position is close to that of the general citizenry, who now regret turning down the earlier peace offer. As the debate progresses, however, we begin to learn Cleon's worries about the shift in public opinion. The viewpoint alternates between the assembly's merriment and Cleon's own

---

word that he was coming with the additional force that he himself had requested or that he was coming with the forces which *Demosthenes* had requested? F. Solmsen, *Intellectual Experiments of the Greek Englightenment* (Princeton 1975) 199, n. 47, remarks "The grammatical subject . . . is, we tend to assume, Demosthenes." Gomme in *HCT* ad loc. (p. 473) believed it is Cleon but inferred from 27.4 that Demosthenes had indeed requested additional troops.

[17] Why twenty days? A. Thibaudet, *La campagne avec Thucydide* (Paris 1922) 37f., and others have suggested that the Pylos campaign took place so late in the year that winter storms would prevent operations after approximately twenty days. Cf. Schneider, *Information und Absicht*, 21, nn. 29 and 50. This view, however, is untenable if Gomme's chronology is correct; see especially his note in *HCT* on 4.39.1 (p. 478). In his view the final battle on Pylos should have taken place between August 5 and 10, leaving another six weeks in the campaigning season. Other explanations of the twenty-day period are possible. Some crucial part of the force, for example, the archers (4.28.4, possibly Cretans 6.25.2), may have been committed for only part of the campaigning season. Correspondence with Daniel Tompkins has been especially helpful on this point, as on so many others in the manuscript.

[18] One objection to this hypothesis is that Aristophanes' *Knights* emphasizes the hostility between Paphlagon (Cleon) and the servant commonly identified with Demosthenes. The second of the two ancient prefaces to the play, however, indicates that the texts available to its author did not identify the two servants with Nicias and Demosthenes. Clearly the identifications result from an ancient interpretation of the play, not from Aristophanes' explicit indications. Even if the interpretation is a legitimate one, the reader should not overestimate the historical significance of the jokes about "Cleon's" theft of Pylos from "Demosthenes." Aristophanes himself may have wished to minimize the credit due to Cleon; relations between Cleon and Demosthenes may have deteriorated once the victory had been achieved.

thoughts as he attempts to extricate himself from his ever increasing difficulties. We share the amusement when he is forced into the command
and smile at his apparent bluster in promising to resolve the matter in
twenty days. As the assembly ends, the attitude of the "saner elements of
humanity" seems the best assessment of the situation—either Cleon will
discredit himself or Athens will benefit from a victory at Pylos.

An ironic perspective, however, also prevails throughout this episode.
The reader knows that Cleon will succeed, remain powerful, and use his
influence against an early and peaceful settlement of the conflict. Thus the
reader simultaneously recreates the emotions of one part of the citizenry
and yet separates himself from these reactions by his knowledge of what
is to come. The tension between these two aspects of the narrative is only
resolved at the very end, when Cleon returns to Athens. At this point his
promise is reassessed: "and Cleon's promise, although it had seemed quite
crazy, came true" (4.39.3). The irony is now complete. The "saner elements of humanity" were quite unwarranted in their pleasure at the outcome
of the assembly. And what had seemed mad turns out to succeed.

Paradox and reversal are the predominant features of this narrative. Its
goal is not to make judgments about Cleon, Nicias, or Demosthenes, nor
to characterize in greater depth any of the participants in the action. All
are known quantities; Cleon in particular is already sufficiently evaluated
at the very outset. Nor is the concern primarily directed to the precise
nature of the strategy and its implementation. On any interpretation of the
passage much of the military planning is neglected or very lightly treated.
Rather the narrative is shaped by the progression of thoughts and feelings
and by a sense of participation in the attitudes of the moment. Thus it
logically culminates not in a discussion of the strategic or political aspects
of the affair but in an explicit statement of the astonishment created by
the Pylos victory: "This was the event most contrary to expectation in the
entire war among the Greeks. For they thought that the Spartans ought
never to hand over their arms, not if they were starving or under the most
intense pressure. They should keep their arms and fight as best they could
until death."[19]

---

[19] 4.40.1. This is the third in a series of paradox or reversal markers in the Pylos story
(cf. 4.12.3 and 14.3). An expectation that Spartans would resist as they had at Thermopylae
underlies the surprise at their surrender on Sphacteria. The comparison to Thermopylae is
first injected in a purely tactical comparison (4.36.3) and then implicitly reintroduced in 40.1
and in the anecdote that follows. From here to the end of the seventh book, the Persian War
provides an important counterpoint to Thucydides' narrative.

HERMOCRATES' SPEECH AT GELA

The second major strategic innovation reported in the fourth book is the account of Brasidas' operations in northern Greece. It is a counterpart to the Pylos operation, both in significance and in narrative technique. But between the Pylos narrative and the story of Brasidas' expedition various other matters are reported. Of these Sicilian affairs are prominent, a natural sequel to the Pylos adventure since, as we are reminded (4.48.6), the expedition on which Demosthenes had sailed had Sicily as its objective.[20]

The balancing of Cleon's success at Pylos and Brasidas' victories in the north gives a clear form to this portion of the narrative and directs attention to Sicilian affairs as to a centerpiece in a panel and especially to the conference at Gela in Sicily that brings about a temporary cessation of hostilities on the island. Although the settlement worked out during this conference at Gela was short-lived and its direct effect on subsequent events limited, Thucydides accords it seemingly disproportionate attention. The negotiations might swiftly have been passed over or presented as a ruse or temporary pause in Syracusan imperialism. Two years later the settlement proved ineffective when Syracuse expelled the lower classes from Leontini (5.4.3), an act that shattered the appearance of pan-Sicilian unity, so much discussed at Gela, and that impelled the Athenians to take action in support of their long-standing ally, the democratic government of Leontini.[21]

Thucydides, however, concentrates on another aspect of the story. The use of "commander narrative" directs attention to one individual, Hermocrates; his views are given full expression in direct discourse. Again, as in the debate in Athens at the time of the Spartan peace proposal (4.17-20) and in the discussion at Acanthus of Brasidas' demands (4.85-87) a single speech is given where we might have expected an antilogy. Everything contributes to the prominence of the Syracusan Hermocrates, now first introduced into the work.

His speech and the events that follow make it easy to conjecture why Thucydides has chosen this pattern for his narration. In the midst of a concentration on mainland Greece, we look away and view events for the

---

[20] Corcyra is the first stage of the expedition's journey. Its mention provides the opportunity for another chapter in the long story of its *stasis* (4.47). By contrast other episodes in this period are related in succinct fashion and there is one major omission: the reassessment of tribute known to us from the decree of Thoudippus (*ML* 69; also in *IG* i³ 71). See Gomme in *HCT* on 4.51 (pp. 500-504).

[21] The alliance of Athens and Leotini is epigraphically attested (*ML* 64; also in *IG* i³ 54).

first time through the eyes of a Sicilian. In the gradual progress toward
the Peace of Nicias we are reminded of the eventual outbreak of war in a
new theater. More important, subsequent Sicilian history will now be
viewed with the awareness that this great and diverse island has the potential
to resolve its own differences and take a common stand, even if only
temporarily, against outside intervention. These are important functions,
but they do not exhaust the significance of this episode. For it is also the
pivot about which book 4, and to some extent, the whole first portion of
the *Histories* turns. It marks the transition from Athenian success at Pylos
to the setbacks that are related in the later portions of the book. Thucydides
eventually turns the episode into a further exploration of the psychology
of the Athenians and their response to the good fortune (*eutychia*) of
Pylos.[22] The importance of the theme of good fortune in this portion of
the *Histories* is evident if we recollect the great prominence given to it in
the speech of the Spartan ambassadors (4.17-20). The Athenians reject
their advice to make secure their good fortune; instead they reach out for
more (4.21.2). The Spartans take an opposite course; they are eager to
recover their prisoners "while Brasidas was still enjoying good fortune."[23]
Thucydides' comment on the Athenian reaction to the conference in Sicily
reemphasizes the Athenians' confidence that these successes will continue.
The Athenian generals, we are told, having given their approval to the
settlement reached at Gela are penalized on their return by the Athenians
who conclude that they accepted bribes to withdraw when they could have
"subjugated Sicilian affairs for them."[24]

Athens' treatment of the commanders is presented as a reflection of
Athenian *pleonexia*, their "grasping for more": "So using their then pres-

---

[22] 4.65.4. The concern with *eutychia* is evident in the statistics. Of twenty-eight examples
of *eutychia* and cognates in von Essen's index, seven occur in book 4 and four in the first
twenty-five chapters of book 5, i.e. over a third of the instances in approximately one-sixth
of the text.

[23] 4.117.2. The theme also links the events of book 4 with the Sicilian Expedition. Nicias
is represented in both undertakings as being anxious to preserve his good fortune: 5.16.1;
cf. 6.17.1; 6.23.3 (also 5.46.1). The culmination of the theme is in 7.77.2.

[24] 4.65.3. The phrasing (τὰ ἐν Σικελίᾳ for τὴν Σικελίαν) suggests and perhaps
implicitly deplores the assembly's fuzzy thinking. It was absurd to think that the commanders
could have subjugated Sicily. The assembly recognized this, but apparently wished for a
settlement that would have provided for a dominant Athenian voice in Sicilian affairs. This
would, obviously, have been difficult for the commanders to achieve. Hence Thucydides'
criticism of the Athenians. But is he entirely fair to the assembly? The commanders have
given their approval to a settlement that totally excluded Athenian influence in Sicilian affairs
and that provided no secure restraints on Syracusan imperialism. There were legitimate
grounds for deploring such a weak policy. If bribery could be shown, exile or a fine was
not an unwarranted penalty by Greek standards.

ent good luck they felt that nothing should stand in their way, but that they could accomplish both the possible and the less feasible, either with a grand or equally well with a more deficient force. The cause was success on many counts beyond expectation which gave them the underpinning of Hope.''[25] This passage links the account of the Conference at Gela to the theme of good fortune, so prominent in the fourth book. That theme, however, is not developed in the main portion of the episode—Hermocrates' speech. The effect of Hermocrates' words is rather to introduce new issues and a fresh view of events and even of power itself. At the center of his speech is the idea of Sicily as a unit, a notion obvious to us, but by no means evident to a contemporary. At this point in Greek history the western Greeks had given no greater evidence of unity and cooperation than their relatives in the east. They had been torn and divided by the conflict between Ionian and Dorian, by regional tensions, and by class struggles within their cities. But Hermocrates invokes, and is able temporarily to create, a sense of Sicilian identity. The opening words of his speech appeal to Sicilian interests rather than those of any individual city: "Sicilians, I will speak as a representative of a city that is far from the smallest, and that has not had the worst of it in this war; but the advice I render is what seems to me to be best for all Sicily" (4.59.1). Hermocrates frequently returns to the idea that there is a common Sicilian advantage and unity.[26] The inhabitants of the island are, he notes, called by a single name, "Sicilians."[27] There are several implications of their common identity. First, when viewed from a pan-Sicilian perspective the interests of any single city are individual or private matters, *idia*.[28] If the cities are in the status of individuals, then war among them is like war within or among the household units (*oikiai*) that make up any individual city. It is *oikeios polemos* "domestic warfare" (64.5) or *stasis* "civil strife" (61.1). This provides Hermocrates with a strong rhetorical position from which to condemn the continuation of interstate warfare. By identifying it with *stasis* he is able to urge his audience "to consider that it is *stasis* above all which destroys our cities and Sicily" (61.1). By contrast, he can represent his own policy as a way toward collective safety: "It is proper that we should recognize this and be reconciled individual to individual, city to city, and

[25] 4.65.4. I have accepted Bekker's emendation of τε to τότε.

[26] N.B. 4.60.1; 61.2: τὴν πᾶσαν Σικελίαν; Σικελία without πᾶσα: 61.1; 61.3; 64.5. Ξύμπαντες has a similar use in 61.1 and 64.4.

[27] 4.64.3. The name is, of course, the one used at the beginning of Hermocrates' speech to address the gathering, 4.59.1.

[28] 4.60.1: οὐ περὶ τῶν ἰδίων μόνον, . . . ἡ ξύνοδος ἔσται, ἀλλ' εἰ . . . τὴν πᾶσαν Σικελίαν . . . δυνησόμεθα ἔτι διασῶσαι.

try in common to save all Sicily.''²⁹ The same conception of war between cities as "domestic warfare" makes this reconciliation easier: "For there is nothing shameful if members of a household give way to other members, either Dorian to Dorian or Chalcidian to their kin—or at a more general level, since we are neighbors and fellow members of a single land, surrounded by the same sea, and called by a single name, 'Sicilians' " (4.64.3).

Hermocrates' appeal could be represented as a cynical cover for Syracusan ambitions. A speech from the opposing viewpoint could easily point out that once the Sicilians had agreed to deny the Athenians a base in their land and witnessed the withdrawal of the Athenian force, Syracuse or other aggressive powers could move against weaker and now unprotected states. What guarantees would Syracuse offer? What basis was there for accepting Syracusan promises at face value? Such a response is easy to imagine, and surely some representatives at the conference had misgivings about some parts of the proposed settlement. But of these the Thucydidean text provides no hint. Thucydides has again chosen not to use antilogistic form.³⁰ Instead he concentrates on a single speaker, Hermocrates, who dominates the scene. Nor is sympathy encouraged for the natural Athenian demurrer to a settlement that left Ionian Greeks vulnerable to Dorian attack and denied Athens continuing influence in Sicilian affairs. Instead, as we have seen, the comments on the penalties inflicted on the Athenian commanders suggest that Athens was caught up in delusions of expansion and self-aggrandizement.

A historian analyzing this account will again feel many doubts and hesitations. At the very least there are many other ways in which the same events could be viewed. But from a literary approach Thucydides' shaping of his material makes an important contribution to the development of the themes of the *Histories*. This is especially clear in one portion of Hermocrates' speech. He avoids many easy criticisms of the Athenians—that they have abused their preeminence and perverted the league against Persia into a device for subjugating the Greeks—and other arguments that the enemies of Athens are known to have used. Instead, like many of the Athenian speakers, he attempts to ground his arguments on what is real

---

²⁹ 4.61.2. Other references to Hermocrates' policy as a form of σωτηρία are in 60.1 and 62.2 (bis). The repeated use of the phrase εἰ σωφρονοῦμεν in 60.1 and 61.1 (cf. 64.4) also suggests Hermocrates' policy of "saving-mindedness."

³⁰ Cf. H. D. Westlake, "Hermocrates The Syracusan," *Bulletin of the John Rylands Library* 41 (1958) 243: "Had an Athenian speaker taken part in the debate . . . it would have been easy for him to have argued that the motive of the Syracusans . . . was to give themselves a free hand to coerce their Chalcidian neighbors when the Athenians had withdrawn."

or natural: "There are ample grounds for excusing the Athenians for such planning and such self-aggrandizement. My criticism is directed not against those who wish to dominate but against those who are more disposed to yield. For it is the nature of what is human to dominate everywhere anyone who gives way, and to ward off the attacker."[31] This passage begins as a commonplace: one does not condemn anyone for doing what is natural and it is natural to want to dominate. The Athenians have themselves used this argument in their speech at Sparta in the first book: "We have done nothing astonishing nor out of the human pattern if, when domination was offered, we took it, and then did not give it up" (1.76.2). The idea seems widespread in the late fifth century;[32] it is grounded in the Greek idea that ruling others is an expression of true freedom.[33] But Hermocrates after stating the commonplace goes one step further. He transforms the proposition by looking at its other side. If it is natural to want to dominate, it is also natural to want to resist domination. One may not blame aggressors, but one can condemn those who submit to aggression: "We all make a bad mistake if we understand these things but fail to take proper measures in advance, or if one of us has come here not considering it of highest priority for us to restore to good order what threatens us all" (4.61.6).

This is an innovative and highly effective inversion of a familiar commonplace. Its significance, however, transcends the immediate rhetorical situation. What Hermocrates adduces is not a mere oratorical device, but, as later becomes increasingly evident, a way of approaching the future. Hermocrates' stance is grounded in a perception of the role of fear in human events. His speech exploits fear of Athens but it is also based on a recognition of the uncertainty of the future. Rhetorically he must deal not only with his audience's diverse assessments of the present situation but also with their hopes of future advantage. Thus he argues:

And if someone thinks that by fair means or foul he will surely achieve something, he had best watch out that he does not have a fall when his hopes are disappointed! He should recognize that by now many have tried to avenge themselves on wrong doers and others have hoped that they had some power to aggrandize themselves. Some of these did not just come short of their hopes—they were not even saved; others lost what was theirs while failing to gain what belonged to others. Vengeance

[31] 4.61.5. Alcibiades echoes the idea in 6.18.2 but, characteristically, concludes from it that one must use every opportunity for expansion.

[32] Cf. Gomme in *HCT* on 1.76.2 (p. 236).

[33] On this idea see de Romilly, *Thucydides and Athenian Imperialism*, 72ff., and J.A.O. Larsen, "Freedom and Its Obstacles in Ancient Greece," *CP* 57 (1962) 231.

does not succeed, however just it may be, because someone has wronged you; nor is strength secure just because you have fine hopes. (4.62.3-4)

Against hope, Hermocrates invokes fear. The fear is grounded in generalizations about the past; but the real point concerns the future: "The unpredictability of the future exercises the greatest control and although it is hazardous, it nevertheless can be seen to be most useful. For if we share equal fear, we are more inclined to approach each other with forethought."[34] This argument, so far removed from the confidence Pericles showed at the time of the outbreak of the war, reintroduces an element of constraint into a system in which the analysis of human nature has justified or even exalted the unlimited use of power for self-aggrandizement. The speech then goes on to a further inversion of conventional wisdom. Hermocrates urges his audience to accept the uncertainty of the future and to be "struck out of their wits" (*ekplagentes*) by it. The state (*ekplēxis*) to which the speaker alludes is normally in Thucydides a prelude to panic and disaster—something which a speaker urges his listeners to avoid.[35] Here Hermocrates encourages it, because it is likely to restrain agression and war: "Let us conclude then that the deficiency of analysis through which we have each thought to gain something is sufficiently inhibited by these constraints and send away the intruding enemies from the land" (4.63.1).

Hermocrates turns upside down many of the assumptions and clichés of contemporary political analysis. The so-called Law of the Stronger becomes an injunction for the weaker to unite, much as Socrates turned a similar argument against Callicles by pointing out the collective power of those who are individually weak.[36] War becomes either *stasis* or a household squabble; astonishment (*ekplēxis*) becomes a virtue; the careful calculation of the likelihood of success "the insufficiency of analysis." In the transformation of terms and expectations Hermocrates' speech evokes the comments on Corcyra in book 3. But the implications are radically different. In his view the surest means of security is not ingenuity and speed in plotting nor a rational means of prediction, but a recognition of the limits of knowledge in a world that cannot totally be predicted or controlled. His

---

[34] 4.62.4. Προμηθία is a crucial word, unusual in Thucydides but used again by Hermocrates in 6.80.1. Like *pronoia* it refers to contemplation of the future, but the emphasis is not on what can be known about the future and hence on prediction, but on what cannot be known—the element of unpredictability or immeasurability, here τὸ ἀστάθμητον (cf. 3.59.1).

[35] E.g. Hermocrates' speech 6.33, esp. section 4; cf. 2.91.3f.

[36] Plato *Gorgias* 488 c-e.

message is the exact opposite of the divisive violence of the revolutionaries on Corcyra. He urges settlement, accomodation, and common action based on restraint and *promēthia*.[37]

These are striking and original ideas, perhaps manipulated by Hermocrates to the advantage of Syracuse in the circumstances of Sicily in 424 B.C., but provocative and highly significant in the context of the work as a whole. They stand in tension with the confidence in prediction that characterizes both the Archaeology and the Periclean analysis of the war. But the view of the future expressed by this speech is very close, we shall see, to that implicit in much of the *Histories*. The reason for this is not to be found so much in the author's admiration for Hermocrates as in a recognition that his words at Gela clarify a process underlying many events reported in the work. Repeatedly in the *Histories* an individual or state gains some power and grows to greatness or prominence. The good fortune (*eutychia*) encourages hope (*elpis*) on the part of the successful party.[38] But when it is recognized by others, they feel threatened.[39] Fear in turn leads to innovation, preventive action, or to the formation of alliances or confederations against the rising power.[40] A good illustration has already been provided by the Syracusan attack on Sicilian Messene, "seeing that the place provided a base of operations against Sicily and fearing that the Athenians might at some point set off from that place with a greater force against them" (4.1.2). But the outbreak of the Peloponnesian War itself can be considered the most important instance. Thucydides' famous comment about the "cause" of the war should be viewed as the application of this process to the events leading up to the outbreak of hostilities: "The truest reason, although least evident in the discussion, was, in my opinion,

---

[37] Of the examples of *promēthia* in earlier Greek literature note especially Herodotus 3.36.1: ῏Ω βασιλεῦ, μὴ πάντα ἡλικίῃ καὶ θυμῷ ἐπίτρεπε, ἀλλ' ἴσχε καὶ καταλάμβανε σεαυτόν· ἀγαθόν τοι πρόνοον εἶναι, σοφὸν δὲ ἡ προμηθίη. In this passage it is parallel to, but may even surpass, *pronoia* (πρόνοον εἶναι) and is closely linked to the idea of self-restraint.

[38] Athens' response to Pylos is the best example; n.b. 4.65.4.

[39] This is often conveyed by sequences such as γνόντες/ὁρῶντες followed by words for fear, e.g.: 3.78.2: γνόντες δὲ οἱ πρὸς τοῖς Κερκυραίοις καὶ δείσαντες; 4.1.2: οἱ μὲν Συρακόσιοι ὁρῶντες . . . καὶ φοβούμενοι; 4.55.1: Οἱ δὲ Λακεδαιμόνιοι ἰδόντες . . . φοβούμενοι; 4.66.3: γνόντες δὲ οἱ τοῦ δήμου προστάται . . . δείσαντες.

[40] *Innovation*, e.g. 4.55. The Spartans develop naval and cavalry strength after the Athenian occupation of Cythera.

Preventative action, e.g. 4.79.2. Perdiccas and Athens' allies in the Thraceward region.

Cooperative action, above all, Sicily versus the great Athenian expedition. N.B. 7.15.1. Cf. 6.21.1; 6.33.5; 6.34.2; 6.37.2; and J. de Romilly, "La crainte dans l'oeuvre de Thucydide," *ClMed* 17 (1956) 121f.

that the Athenians by growing great caused fear in the Lacedaemonians and drove them into war.[41]"

This process, long implicit in the events of the war, is made clear by Hermocrates' comments and confirmed by the outcome of the conference. The Sicilians block Athenian intervention. On a very small scale we recognize in this a process of great significance—although Athens' expansion was natural, there are also in nature countervailing tendencies that in the long run can check or perhaps even destroy unrestrained growth. The Athenians in their present mood are quite oblivious to these constraints, but Hermocrates' speech alerts the reader to their potential significance. His words have both an immediate and a longer range application. In the immediate context they remind us how swiftly hopes and calculations about the future can prove false. Hermocrates' speech marks a pivotal moment in Athenian affairs, just after the success at Pylos and just before the reverses inflicted by Brasidas. But it has a wider application as well, for by calling attention to Sicily, it invites the reader to anticipate the great invasion of that island and its awesome implications for Athens and for the understanding of power.[42]

TOWARD PEACE AND ALLIANCE

Inevitably the long course of the war leads both belligerents to attempt innovative and risky strategies. The Athenians have supported Demosthenes' bold plan of a fortification along the Peloponnese; the Spartans are now persuaded to send Brasidas north to operate against Athenian holdings in the region adjoining Macedon. The surprising success of the Pylos operation is matched by Brasidas' victories in the north. Peace initiatives result in both cases, but Brasidas proves no more eager than Cleon for an early settlement. The peace ending the first phase of the war comes about

---

[41] 1.23.6. Perhaps the most discussed passage in Thucydides and still poorly understood. On the usual view Thucydides contradicts himself since his own speeches show that the growth of Athenian power was quite evident in the discussions (cf. 1.86.5). His point, however, is not that the pre-war discussions failed to note the growth of Athens' power, but that the *pattern* (growth in power provokes counteraction, quite independently of the rights and wrongs of the case) was not widely remarked. See also Chapter One, Note 31.

[42] Is there an even wider implication? When Hermocrates argues that the Sicilians are a single people designated by a single name (ὄνομα ἕν κεκλημένους, 4.64.3) and hence that warfare among them is to be deplored and settled as swiftly as possible, the reader thinks naturally of the other people who were distinguished by a single name, albeit late in time, the Greeks (cf.1.3.3f.). By implication Hermocrates' argument applies as well to Greece as a whole as to Sicily as a whole. All war among Greeks is a kind of *stasis*.

only after Cleon and Brasidas both die in the same battle outside Amphipolis.

Although the parallelism is in large part imposed by events, Thucydides seems to welcome its potential for comparisons and contrasts, which he emphasizes by adopting in each case a similar narrative technique. The action of the Spartan campaign is presented largely through commander narrative and is centered on Brasidas, just as Demosthenes and Cleon were the center of attention in the Pylos campaign. Individual episodes in the two campaigns are linked together by similarities in language.[43] As at Pylos, the full import of the commander's plan is only made clear as it gradually unfolds. No advance explanation is given of the strategy that Brasidas proposes. Indeed, his expedition is first introduced obliquely, almost casually, as background to his appearance outside of Megara: "Brasidas, the son of Tellis, a Lacedaemonian, was at this time near Sicyon and Corinth, preparing an expedition against Thrace" (4.70.1). The allusion to Thrace is not immediately explained, instead we focus on his characteristically decisive intervention at Megara. He gathers 3,700 troops from allied cities to supplement his own force and prevents an Athenian takeover of the city. His strategy is clever and sound: he will not begin an engagement but will show his willingness to defend Megara if it is attacked. The Athenians decide that an engagement is not worth the risk. When the Athenians withdraw, the pro-Peloponnesian faction in Megara gets the upper hand and exterminates many of its opponents through a carefully contrived plot. A narrow and long-lasting pro-Spartan oligarchy is established (4.73-74).

So far the focus has been on Megara. Brasidas returns to his preparations for a campaign "to Thrace."[44] But there is still no clarification of what

[43] The description of Brasidas' capture of Torone, for example, emphasizes elements similar to the Athenian attack on Pylos. Both are dawn operations (cf. 4.110 and 4.31.1 and 32.2), in which light-armed troops (4.111.1, cf. 4.32.4) play an important role, and involve a charge (δϱόμῳ) 4.112.1, cf. 4.31.1) and the overrunning of an outpost (φυλακτηϱίου, 4.111.2, cf. 4.31.1). The strategy is to take the enemy from the rear (κατὰ νώτου, 4.110.2, cf. 4.32.4 and 33.1, 4.36.1 and 36.2) and then attack them from two sides (ἀμφοτέϱωθεν, 4.111.2, cf. 4.36.3) thereby inducing panic (ἔκπληξιν, 4.112.1, cf. 4.34.2). See also the valuable discussion by D. Babut, "Interprétation historique et structure littéraire chez Thucydide," *Bulletin assoc. G. Budé* 40 (1981) 417-439.

[44] 4.74.1 repeats the language of 70.1. In 4.78.1 (cf. 79.2 and 3.92.f.) the phrasing changes to ἐς τὰ ἐπὶ Θϱάκης, good fifth-century chancery language for the region of the Athenian empire that included Macedon and adjoining areas. We would expect ⟨ἐς τὰ⟩ ἐπὶ Θϱάκης in 70.1 and 74.1 but the repetition makes emendation implausible. The ultimate objective of Brasidas' campaign may have been the Thracian Chersonese and hence the Athenian grain supply; see D. W. Knight, "Thucydides and the War Strategy of Perikles," *Mnemosyne* ser. 4, 23 (1970) 150-161, esp. 154 and 157. Discussions with Fordyce Mitchell have been helpful to me on this point.

he has in mind. Nothing more is heard of him until chapter 78 when he and 1,700 hoplites attempt to move through Thessaly into northern Greece. Even then the composition of his force and the nature of his plan are obscure. These considerations, to be sure, would be irrelevant if Brasidas could not find a way to move across Thessaly, an area that has been well-disposed to Athens and that is likely to discourage any Spartan attempt to use it as staging area for northern operations. As Brasidas' force enters that region, it is met by a Thessalian delegation that says he does wrong (*adikein* 4.78.3) to pass through without authorization. His escorts assure their fellow Thessalians that they will not lead him through their country; Brasidas himself tells them he comes as a friend and intends to conduct military operations not against them but against the Athenians, with whom he is at war. He knows of no enmity between Thessalians and Lacedae-monians such as to prevent them from crossing each other's land, and if they are now unwilling he will not proceed, nor could he, even though he does not think it fair for him to be turned away (4.78.4). The answer satisfies the Thessalian delegates, who withdraw, but Brasidas, "at the urging of his escorts, before any great opposition gathered, went forward, not stopping, on the run."[45] Only after he has passed through Thessaly does the text provide essential information about the operation, for example, the fact that King Perdiccas of Macedon and the Greek cities of Chalcidike had promised support.[46]

The technique is very similar to that used at the opening of the Pylos campaign. Only gradually does the plan become clear; in retrospect we can derive that the preparations must have been elaborate and time-consuming. In particular we recollect that the Spartan colonization of Heraclea in Trachis in 426 B.C. had been in part intended to assist an expedition similar to Brasidas'.[47] In contrast to the suspicions concerning the Pylos

---

[45] 4.78.5. In a surprising number of passages Thucydides uses forms of τρέχω (to run), of its compounds, or of the noun, δρόμος (running), when referring to Brasidas. He is often presented as a man of rapid motion: 2.25.2, διαδραμών and ἐν τῇ ἐσδρομῇ; cf. 2.94.3, καταδραμόντες (of the Peloponnesians generally); 4.78.5 δρόμῳ; 4.79.1, διέδραμε; 4.104.3, ἐπέδραμε; 4.112.1, δρόμῳ; 5.9.6, δρόμῳ; 5.10.6, δρόμῳ. The characterization is all the more striking when the reader remembers the repeated criticism of the Spartans for their slowness (βραδυτής): 1.71.4 (Corinthian criticism); 1.84.1 (Archidamus' answer); 5.75.3 (change of Greek assessment of the Spartans after Mantineia); and 8.96.5 (Thucydides' own observation).

[46] 4.79.1: "and he made his way to Perdiccas and into Chalcidice." The following section clarifies first the Chalcidian attitude and then that of Perdiccas. Chapter 80 then sketches Spartan attitudes. In 80.5 we are told that Brasidas has 700 Helot hoplites with him. From this and 78.1 we can derive that the other 1,000 in his force were hired troops from the Peloponnese.

[47] 3.92. N.B. section 4: τῆς τε ἐπὶ Θρᾴκης παρόδου χρησίμως ἕξειν.

campaign, however, no one accuses Thucydides of maligning Brasidas or of suggesting that he lacked a plan or relied purely on chance.[48]

One other important difference separates the story of Brasidas from that at Pylos. There the Athenian operations provoked an immediate Spartan response, one at first contemptuous but rapidly turning into intense alarm. Brasidas' expedition, however, at first leaves the Athenians unconcerned. Apart from their renunciation of friendship with Perdiccas and unspecified security measures (4.82), the Athenians are not seen as reacting strongly to Brasidas. Their concern seems almost exclusively directed to an elaborate Boeotian campaign led by Hippocrates and Demosthenes (4.77 and 89-101). Only when this plan fails at the Battle of Delium, and when Brasidas captures Amphipolis, are the Athenians said to experience real fear (4.108.1) and to recognize the possibility of widespread losses in the Thraceward region.[49]

By this point the underlying strategic similarity to the Pylos campaign is obvious, and the narrative technique invites us to draw comparisons and contrasts between the two expeditions and their leaders. Cleon and Brasidas are sharply defined opposites: the one a military man never presented in a political role, the other a politician who seems to stumble into military command; one the advocate of violence and terror, the other an example of the practical advantages of moderation and gentleness.[50] The text, so far at least, evokes radically different responses to Cleon and to Brasidas. Cleon's actions have done little to refute the initial characterization of him as "most violent and most persuasive"; Brasidas' conduct throughout the first part of the *Histories* is consistently courageous and admirable.[51] While Cleon carries to an extreme the restless vigor of the Athenians, Brasidas, in his vigor, persuasiveness, decisiveness, and boldness, is a most untypical Spartan and seems to possess the qualities badly needed if his city is to succeed against Athens. So far he has the potential for heroic stature, to

[48] Note, however, the continued use of words related to *tychē*: 4.70.1, ἐτύγχανε; 4.70.2, ἔτυχε; 4.73.3, ἐν τύχῃ, and κἂν τυχεῖν; 4.86.6, ἡ τύχη; 4.104.5, ἔτυχον; 4.111.2, ἔτυχον; 4.112.2, ἔτυχον; 4.113.2, ἔτυχον. Cf. Note 5 above.

[49] Woodcock, *HSCP* 39 (1928) 93-108, suggests that Thucydides may have felt that Athenian obsession with Demosthenes' Boeotian project denied him the resources he needed to hold Amphipolis.

[50] Cf. J. de Romilly, "Fairness and Kindness in Thucydides," *Phoenix* 28 (1974) 95-100.

[51] N.B. 2.25.2, his bravery in the defense of the Laconian Methone; 2.85-87, advice to the Peloponnesian fleet in the Corinthian Gulf; 2.93: bold attack on Salamis; 4.11: determination and courage in the assault on the Athenian position at Pylos. The one blemish is his deception of the Thessalians in 4.78, but the effect is somewhat neutralized by Thucydides' emphasis on the insistence of the guides—κελευόντων τῶν ἀγωγῶν—in section 5.

be an Achilles among men, as Alcibiades speaks of him in Plato's *Symposium* (221 c).

This highly favorable view of Brasidas, and the implicit contrast between him and Cleon, is continued in the comments about him at the beginning of the narration of his operations in the northern region:

The Lacedaemonians sent out Brasidas who himself very much wanted to go; the Chalcidians were also eager for him, a man who at Sparta had the reputation in all matters of getting things done and when he went out was of the greatest value to the Lacedaemonians. At the immediate moment he presented himself as just and moderate to the cities and induced a large portion of them to revolt; some of the places he captured when they were betrayed to him. Thus when the Spartans wanted to make a treaty—as indeed they did—they had something to exchange and restore and thereby an alleviation of the war from the Peloponnese. As for the later war, after the Sicilian expedition, the excellence [*aretē*] and comprehension [*xynesis*] which Brasidas had shown at that time—some experienced them first hand, others through reports—were especially effective in creating pro-Spartan desires among Athens' allies. For since he was the first to go out from Sparta and have the reputation for being excellent in all respects, he left a secure hope that the others too would be like him.[52]

These remarks surely reinforce a positive response to Brasidas and have been widely taken as expressing Thucydides' own assessment of Brasidas. Brunt, for example, refers to them as "Thucydides' eulogy on his justice."[53] Critical concern thereby has been directed to the suspicion that

[52] 4.81. The passage is an elaborate development of one device used by Thucydides to herald the importance of an individual or an action: the name is expanded with a form of ἀνήρ ("a man who . . .") and by adjectives, especially superlatives. Further *megalōsis* can be achieved through sentences appended with or other connectives. The last significant use of this formula was in 4.21.3 when Cleon was described as ἀνὴρ δημαγωγὸς κατ' ἐκεῖνον τὸν χρόνον ὢν καὶ τῷ πλήθει πιθανώτατος. The comments on Brasidas also echo language used for Pericles; e.g. πλείστου ἄξιον in section 1 parallels 2.65.4. Indeed the structure of the section is similar to that used in the discussion of Pericles in 2.65. In each case the assessment is divided into two chronological periods, closely coordinated by the use of τε . . . τε: 2.65.5, ὅσον τε γὰρ χρόνον προύστη τῆς πόλεως ἐν τῇ εἰρήνῃ . . . ἐπειδή τε ὁ πόλεμος κατέστη; 4.81.2, line 13, τό τε γὰρ παραυτίκα, line 18, ἔς τε τὸν χρόνῳ ὕστερον . . . πόλεμον.

The passage also implicitly draws a contrast between Brasidas and another Spartan commander, Pausanias the regent; compare ἑαυτὸν παρασχὼν δίκαιον καὶ μέτριον to the similar construction used for Pausanias in 1.130.2—δυσπρόσοδόν τε αὐτὸν παρεῖχε. Brasidas appears in this passage as an apparent refutation of the generalization that when Spartans go abroad they observe neither their own *nomima* nor those of the rest of Greece (1.77.6).

[53] P. Brunt, "Spartan Policy and Strategy in the Archidamian War," *Phoenix* 19 (1965) 276.

Thucydides may have drawn "perhaps too roseate a picture of Brasidas."[54] But in fact there is relatively little in the passage that indicates the author's own view and a great deal concerning contemporary reaction to him. The focus is on how he appeared to observers at the time.[55] Thucydides avoids implying that Brasidas' reputation is undeserved but his own viewpoint is largely detached and noncommittal, except for his statement that Brasidas' services were of great value to Sparta and that he indeed had excellence and comprehension—*aretē kai xynesis*—qualities of undeniable impor- tance in the *Histories*.[56] But even here the point is not to affirm Brasidas' virtues but to lead the reader from a recognition of these qualities to an appreciation of their long-run importance; the creation among Athens' allies of a climate of opinion favorable to the Spartans.

The comment in chapter 81 is thus neither the author's own encomium of Brasidas nor a criticism of him. Rather it emphasizes the importance of Brasidas and draws our attention to the reactions he inspired among the Greek cities of the north. These are the issue, not the author's views or those of the Athenians. They are set, moreover, not in the immediate context of Brasidas' operations but in the more remote perspective estab- lished by the allusions to "the later war, after the Sicilian expedition" (4.81.2). The perspective is crucial. From Thucydides' comment that the Greeks of the area had "the secure hope that other [Spartans] too are like him," "we are surely meant to understand that they were not."[57] Indeed we have just learned in this chapter and the preceding one the real objectives of the Spartan authorities: to diminish the threat of insurrection among the Helots by sending some of them away (4.80.2) and to strengthen the Spartans' position in peace negotiations. Whatever we feel about Brasidas, the mention of the Helots reminds the reader how deceptive Spartans can be. For Thucydides takes this opportunity to recount an episode of uncertain date when the Spartans promised freedom to some Helots "but not much

[54] A. W. Gomme, *The Greek Attitude To Poetry and History* (Berkeley 1954) 158.

[55] Δοϰοῦντα in section 1 and δόξας in section 3 need not imply that the appearance contradicted the reality; they are Thucydides' way of indicating "the reputation enjoyed by an individual . . . without stating whether or not he subscribed to it," Westlake, *Individuals in Thucydides*, 6. Cf. 1.79.2 and 3.10.1.

[56] Compare the comment on the Pisistratids, 6.54.5.

[57] D. M. Lewis, *Sparta and Persia* (Leiden 1977) 29. *Elpis* in Thucydides is psychologically important (e.g. 7.41.4), but never truly "secure," βέβαιος. It is a consolation in danger (5.103.1); it builds one up with the "prosperity that comes from luck" (3.45.5), but it often swiftly changes and can mislead and destroy. Cf. 2.62.5; 4.65.4; 4.108.4. Here it is "secure" only in the sense of persistent or long-lasting. Εἰσιν is surprising in a setting where we might expect an optative or indicative with ἄν, or a future; cf. 5.9.7 and 1.81.6. But the phrasing vividly conveys the attitude of the Greek cities at the time of Brasidas' operations.

later they made them disappear and no one knew in what manner each had been destroyed'' (4.80.4). With this story in mind, we approach Spartan promises of liberation with caution and skepticism.

Although the reader is aware of the hazards of accepting at face value Brasidas' claims and promises, the successes continue and Brasidas enjoys undiminished popularity. King Perdiccas of Macedon, to be sure, abandons his favorable view of Brasidas. When Brasidas wants to arbitrate between him and Arrabaios, he points out that he did not bring Brasidas as a judge (*dikastēn*) but as a destroyer (*kathairetēn*) and that Brasidas would do wrong (*adikēsein*) if he supported Arrabaios (83.5). Brasidas abandons his plan to arbitrate, but the damage is done; no military operations take place. Perdiccas continues to feel he has been wronged (*adikeisthai*).[58] With the Greek cities Brasidas is more successful. At Acanthus he achieves his first major success. He addresses the assembly, assures them of generous treatment and autonomy, misrepresents the recent operations outside Megara to magnify his own effectiveness and to suggest temerity on the part of the Athenians,[59] and restates the old Spartan claim that they are waging the war to liberate Greece.[60] The Acanthians are cautious but find what he says attractive.[61] At the same time they are worried about the damage Brasidas can inflict on their harvest and are persuaded by the solemn oath that he says he has imposed upon the authorities at Sparta, compelling them to respect the autonomy of the cities he brings over.[62] Acanthus decides to accept Brasidas' proposals; Stagirus soon follows (4.88.2).

The attentive reader recognizes the need for caution. He knows that the facts of the Megarean campaign do not match Brasidas' report and rec-

---

[58] The convergence δικαστήν . . . ἀδικήσειν and ἀδικεῖσθαι is especially striking after the statement in 4.81.2 that Brasidas presented himself as just (δίκαιον) and moderate toward the Greek cities in that region. Note also the justice theme in the Thessalians' comment 4.78.3, and in 4.106.1.

[59] 4.85.7. His argument depends on two misrepresentations: first that his force at Megara was the same as the 1,700 troops he now has with him. In fact his army was then approximately 3,700 troops. Second, it is misleading to suggest that the Athenians were not willing to fight at Nisaea. Both parties were willing to go into battle but neither wished to begin the engagement. His argument is weak and it is hazardous for his listeners to conclude that Athens will not effectively respond.

[60] 4.85.1-5. The claim was much emphasized in the first book and said to have been well received by the Greeks in 2.8.4. Subsequent Spartan actions have done little to back up these pretensions, as the Samian ambassadors point out in 3.32.2. The reader also has in mind that the Spartans have recently proposed peace and alliance with the alleged enslaver, Athens.

[61] 4.88.1, ἐπαγωγά. His comments are later (4.108.5) described as ἐφολκὰ καὶ οὐ τὰ ὄντα.

[62] 4.88.1 echoing 86.1. On the reliability of Spartan oaths cf. the Plataeans' appeal in 3.59.2 and its outcome.

ollects that the outcome at Megara was the establishment of a very narrow oligarchy (4.77.4). Especially when viewed from a post-war perspective, when Spartan support of oligarchies and imposition of garrisons were in the foreground, Brasidas' comments to the Acanthians demand a skeptical response:

I do not come to join a faction, nor would I feel that I was offering a secure freedom if, in violation of our ancestral practice, I enslaved the many to the few or some portion to the whole. That would be harsher than foreign oppression and for us Spartans would result not in gratitude in response to our efforts but in recrimination in place of glory and honor. The very charges which we use in our war against the Athenians would apply to us—indeed more bitterly than to someone whose acquisitions were obtained without profession of virtue. (4.86.4-5)

We think, of course, of post-war Spartan imperialism. It may be objected that those words should not be projected forward, that is, interpreted with Sparta's later record in mind; the next sentence in Brasidas' speech, however, produces a similarly ironic effect while looking backward to his trickery in crossing Thessaly: "For on someone who is well regarded aggrandizement by fine-sounding deception brings more disgrace than open force. The latter proceeds by the justification of power, which is a gift of circumstance [*tychē*]; the former by the plotting of an unjust mind" (4.86.6). The idea that these words could be applied to Brasidas' own conduct or the policy of Sparta[63] passes swiftly away in the concentration on the immediate situation, on the campaigns in Boeotia, and on Thucydides' own unsuccessful attempt to save Amphipolis from Brasidas.[64]

But after the capture of Amphipolis the narrative again temporarily halts and introduces a further comment on Brasidas, similar in subject and vocabulary to chapter 81, and similar in setting as well, since each passage is set in a ring by discussions of Athenian and Spartan attitudes.[65] The

---

[63] Thucydides sometimes has speakers make comments that inadvertently apply to and implicitly criticize their own conduct e.g. Cleon in 3.38.5, Diodotus in 3.43.2, etc. Cf. C. W. Macleod, "Thucydides on Faction," *Proceedings of the Cambridge Philological Society* 205 (1979) 53f.

[64] Thucydides' account of his own campaign has been so extensively treated elsewhere that I see no need to go into it in detail. There is a particularly important analysis by Schneider in *Information und Absicht*, 11-28, which sets the passage in a new light. Among earlier discussions, see especially H. D. Westlake, "Thucydides and the Fall of Amphipolis," *Hermes* 90 (1962) 276-287, reprinted in Westlake's *Essays on the Greek Historians and Greek History* (New York 1969) and in the Wege der Forschung volume *Thukydides*, ed. Hans Herter (Darmstadt 1968).

[65] 4.80, Spartan attitudes; 4.82.1, Athenian attitude; 4.108.1, Athenian attitude (cf. 4.108.6); 4.108.7, Spartan attitude.
The balance is further emphasized by the recurrence of forms of βούλομαι used to convey

passage is, indeed, so reminiscent of chapter 81 that many critics have been troubled, suspecting its presence is due to differing stages of composition, careless revision, or some peculiarity of technique.[66] Another possibility, however, is that the similarities are designed to return us to the ideas and themes of the earlier passage and to renewed awareness of the rashness of the hopes of the Athenian allies in the north. Having heard Brasidas at Acanthus and seen him in action,[67] the reader is now prepared for a more explicit and more critical analysis of Brasidas' claims.

For Brasidas not only presented himself as moderate in other matters, he also everywhere made it clear in his words that he had been sent out to liberate Greece. And the cities which were subject to Athens, when they learned of the capture of Amphipolis and the terms he offered and his gentleness, were mightily lifted up to revolt and conducted secret negotiations with him, urging him to come to their assistance, each one wanting to be the first to break away. For they thought they had a grant of immunity, although they were deceived about Athens' power to an extent that later became evident. But even more, they judged with a wishing that is unsure rather than with planning that is secure—men usually entrust what they desire to hope that sees no obstacles; but they rationalize away what they do not crave by giving calculation free rein. At the same time, with Athens recently routed in Boeotia and with Brasidas saying seductive but untrue things, namely that the Athenians had not wanted to engage at Nisaea with his unreinforced army, they were encouraged and trusted that no one would bring aid against them. But the greatest factor was that by taking pleasure in the immediate situation and in the fact that they were for the first time about to have experience of Spartans who were bursting with energy, they were ready in every way to take the risk. (4.108.2-6)

Although this chapter is more explicit than chapter 81—and more hostile to Brasidas—the focus is still only secondarily on him. Its main function is the continued examination of the theme introduced in the earlier chapter:

the intention of the Spartan authorities: βουλομένοις in 4.80.2 and 4.81.2; βουλόμενοι in 4.108.7. Initially the authorities' desires coincide with Brasidas' wishes (αὐτόν τε Βρασίδαν βουλόμενον, 4.81.1) but eventually their objectives diverge as Brasidas becomes a strong opponent to the Spartan movement toward peace (cf. 5.16.1).

[66] J. de Romilly, for example, in *Thucydides and Athenian Imperialism*, trans. P. Thody (Oxford 1963) 47 suggests that Thucydides changed his view of Brasidas.

[67] His speech at Acanthus is effective and sophisticated oratory and served as a model for his other addresses in the north. See L. Bodin, "Thucydide et la campagne de Brasidas en Thrace," *Mélanges Navarre* (Toulouse 1935) 47-55. It is, however, deceptive and quite contrary to fifth-century stereotypes of the simple, direct truthfulness of Spartans, e.g. Stesimbrotus *FGrHist* 107 F 4. Thucydides calls these stereotypes to mind when he introduces the speech at Acanthus by remarking that Brasidas was not an ineffective speaker "for a Lacedaemonian" (4.84.2). Brasidas shows traits normally associated with Athenians, e.g. boldness, *tolma*, and is thereby very effective against the Athenians. Cf. 8.96.5.

the rashness of the northern allies in accepting Brasidas' inducement to revolt. The point is made, moreover, by the use of the same ironic perspective adopted in chapter 81. The reader knows that Athens will take strong measures against revolts in this area. And the language of the passage reminds us how badly mistaken was the allies' confidence. They were "mightily lifted up to revolt," he says, using a verb that regularly conveys not mere excitement but the exaltation that precedes a disaster.[68] Thucydides is quite explicit about their mistake. They feel they have a grant of immunity from prosecution (*adeia*) and they are deceived about the nature of Athenian power. To reinforce this point Thucydides again changes the time perspective in which the actions are viewed, by alluding to what appeared "later."[69] This shift makes it easy to point out how hope misleads, a topic already implicit at the end of chapter 81.

The belief, moreover, that "no one would bring aid against them" is easily recognized as mistaken. Soon, as contemporary readers would well know, Cleon, the most violent of contemporary Athenian politicians, would lead the expedition against the rebels. There is, however, a more imminent threat to the cities that have chosen to side with Brasidas. In the midst of Brasidas' successes, without warning, background, or explanation, Athens and Sparta achieve a truce. Suddenly the question is upon us: What will happen to the liberty of these cities if the ultimate peace settlement gives Athens a free hand in northern Greece? The sincerity of Sparta's concern for the liberation of Greece, we know, must not be overestimated; what if she chooses to use these cities, as chapter 81 indicated she might, as "something to exchange and restore" for other places? And how will Brasidas react to this problem? Two small cities in the region—Scione and Mende—provide the opportunity to study the situation, and the man. Scione revolted from Athens two days after the armistice had been agreed upon, but before word reached that region. Brasidas, ignorant, in so far as we can tell, of the negotiations between Athens and Sparta, encourages the

---

[68] Ἐπήρθησαν 4.108.3; cf. 4.121.1. For the fatal connotations note especially 3.45.1 and 8.2.1 and 5.14.2. The verb has the manuscript authority only of B in 7.51.1. See also H. C. Avery, "A Poetic Word in Herodotus," *Hermes* 107 (1979) 1-9, whose useful article seems to me to underestimate the extent to which Thucydides uses this word in a "pregnant" sense. The use of νεωτερίζειν rather than ἀφίστασθαι may hint that a change to the Spartan side was often accompanied by a change in type of government, presumably from democracy to oligarchy.

[69] To what period precisely does Thucydides allude? H. D. Westlake, "Thucydides IV, 108, 4," *Proceedings of the Cambridge Philological Society* n.s. 7 (1961) 63-67, contends that the reference is to 423-421 and not to the period after the Sicilian Expedition as one would conclude from the comparison to 4.81.2.

revolt and assures them of his support.[70] The reader knows that the political situation in Sparta will in the long run make it very difficult for Brasidas to assist his new ally. Indeed, the ultimate destruction of Scione was one of the most notorious events in the war, and almost any Greek reader would know of its fate.[71]

But the residents are quite oblivious to the danger that confronts them: "The citizens of Scione were lifted up by his words and took courage— all of them alike, even those who formerly did not like what was going on. And they made up their minds to wage the war eagerly and they received Brasidas splendidly in all respects and they crowned him with an officially voted gold crown as the liberator of Greece. Individual citizens put ribbons around his head and set out ritual offerings as they would to an athlete."[72] Some commentators assure us that the passage is simply a way of emphasizing "the enthusiasm and unanimity with which Brasidas was welcomed at Scione."[73] Surely it is that. But why is it so important to stress this enthusiasm? We immediately recognize that the passage again emphasizes the mistaken assessments made by the Greek cities of the area. When, one page later, Thucydides reports the Athenian anger at the revolt of Scione and their adoption of Cleon's proposal "to expel and to kill the citizens of the town," the reader knows that their enthusiasm at their freedom was as ill-founded as that of the Helots in Sparta (ch. 80.3) who mysteriously disappeared after crowning themselves and went about the shrines "like ones who were being liberated." It is on the folly of Scione, not on praise of Brasidas, that the passage turns.

Brasidas himself has no illusions about the security of the area. He knows, contrary to what he had claimed, that the Athenians will "bring aid"[74] and is anxious to move swiftly against both Mende and Potidaea. The arrival of news of the armistice does not change his opinion or strategy. Indeed he is perfectly willing to accept Mende's revolt even though it was

---

[70] 4.120.3. His speech in indirect discourse reflects his confidence, while at the same time reminding the reader of the vulnerability of Scione. For example he praises the zeal the Scionaeans show despite the fact they are "nothing other than islanders" (120.3). Athens, of course, both can and will act especially severely against islanders (122.4) as Brasidas well knows (121.2).

[71] E.g. Isocrates *Panegyricus* (4) 100; cf. Chapter Five, Note 19.

[72] 4.121.1. The verb "were lifted up" is ἐπήρθησαν. See above, Note 68. Προσήρχοντο is ambiguous and might be translated "crowded around," but see C. Meyer, *Die Urkunden im Geschichtswerk des Thukydides*, 2nd ed., *Zetemata* 10 (Munich 1970) 16f.

[73] George Grote quoted in Gomme's note on the passage in *HCT* (p. 610). Gomme is impelled to add, "And, I believe, there is no satire here in Thucydides."

[74] Βοηθῆσαι in 4.121.2 contrasts with the expectation in 4.108.5 that "no one would bring aid (βοηθῆσαι) against them."

clearly after the armistice (ch. 124). His refusal to let Scione go is readily understood, though Thucydides makes clear that in fact this secession took place two days after the armistice (122.6). But why does Brasidas receive Mende? Thucydides gives a reason: he did not think "that he did wrong [*adikein*] because they came over quite clearly in the time of armistice. For there were certain complaints of violations which he too had against the Athenians" (4.123.1). The rationale is far from satisfactory, for the treaty included an arbitration clause for such disputes.[75] Legally there is little justification for Brasidas' action. Its practical effects are equally troublesome. To receive Mende under these circumstances is to pretend that the armistice is not legally binding and to invite its repudiation, an action that can only impede the progress toward a lasting peace. Does Brasidas not know, or not care, about this?

A further question is raised by the immediate sequel. Brasidas recognizes the danger that faces Scione and Mende. The Athenians will surely move to recover them and they will not be gentle if they succeed. Brasidas has given Mende strong assurances. Yet as the danger approaches, he joins Perdiccas in the long-promised expedition against Arrabaeus of Lyncestis (4.124), leaving a small force to protect the two cities and transferring the women and children to Olynthus for safe keeping. By the time his expedition is over, Mende has fallen to the Athenians (4.129). Brasidas' support of Perdiccas has prevented any effective aid to Mende; the Athenians plunder the city and only with difficulty are the troops restrained from killing the remaining inhabitants.[76]

Readers may differ in the extent to which they feel Brasidas' actions make him responsible for the fate of these cities. One related issue, however, is clarified in an oblique but telling fashion. Late in the campaigning

[75] 4.118.8. The Athenians also disregard this clause: 4.122.5. Compare the Spartan neglect of the similar clause in the Thirty Years Peace: 1.71.5; 78.4; 85.2; 123.2; 140.2; 144.2; 145.1.

[76] 4.123.2 and 130.4ff. A faction in Mende opposed Brasidas and favored Athens. To what extent is the enthusiasm for Brasidas in other cities less broadly based than we would conclude from Thucydides? Is it primarily the advocates of a restricted franchise who welcome him and who expect that under Spartan control it will be easier to change from democracies to oligarchies? Cf. on νεωτερίζειν in 4.108.3, Note 68 above. The issue has been much discussed in recent historical scholarship. See especially G.E.M. de Ste. Croix, *Origins of the Peloponnesian War* (London 1972) 34-45 from which one can derive the earlier bibliography. We need not conclude that Thucydides was blinded by class prejudice or oligarchic sympathies even if we recognize that many citizens in Chalcidice resisted Brasidas' liberation. Other considerations may have shaped his narrative, especially a desire to emphasize how mistaken was the enthusiasm for Brasidas. This may have led him into deemphasizing those groups that had early reservations about his promises. The effect would still be a distortion, but it would not be caused by the political bias that has often been ascribed to Thucydides.

season of 423 the Spartans attempt to send reinforcements to Brasidas, but are blocked in Thessaly: "However Ischagoras and Ameinias and Aristeus came to Brasidas, sent out by the Spartans to oversee matters. They also brought out from Sparta some citizens of military age, contrary to normal practice [*paranomōs*], to be in charge of the cities so as not to entrust them to just anyone. And they set up Clearidas, the son of Cleonymus in Amphipolis and Pasitelidas, the son of Hegesander in Torone" (4.132.3). This routine-sounding, factually over-burdened account is easily passed over in a casual reading. But to anyone who recollects the last years of the war and the period of Spartan domination that followed, they are powerful and ominous sentences. As the commentators note, the episode is the first sign of the later Spartan harmost system.[77] It also emphasizes the emptiness of the Spartan oath that they would preserve the autonomy of the cities Brasidas liberated. Brasidas' reaction to this imposition of archons is not reported.

Thus as book 4 comes to a close it is evident that of the three major points that Brasidas made in his speech at Acanthus and elsewhere, none can sustain scrutiny. First the Athenians have shown themselves willing and determined to act in the region and the argument from their conduct at Megara has been exposed and labelled as "seductive but untrue." Second, the Spartan promise to respect the autonomy of the cities has been broken. Finally, whatever Brasidas' personal intentions, the Spartans have shown little serious commitment to the freedom of Greece. Their interest has been much more pragmatic: above all they wish to achieve a favorable peace settlement.

These actions inevitably raise doubts and questions about Brasidas. But the narrative does not pause to make them explicit or to encourage any condemnation.[78] The issue is Spartan "liberation" and the reactions of the

[77] See E. Schwartz, *Das Geschichtswerk des Thukydides*, 2nd ed. (Bonn 1929) 227; Gomme in *HCT* on 4.132.3 (p. 623f.) and A. Andrewes, in *Imperialism in the Ancient World*, ed. P.D.A. Garnsey and C. R. Whittaker (Cambridge 1978) 305, n. 19. A. B. West, *History of the Chalcidic League* (Madison, Wisc. 1918) 93-96 contended that decarchies, harmosts, and the other instruments of Spartan imperial control were not imposed upon this area following the Spartan victory in the war. The evidence is not decisive, but certainly many cities in the nearby regions came to feel the harshness of Spartan rule: Xenophon *Hellenica* 3.4.2 and G. E. Underhill's commentary ad loc. (p. 103f.); Diodorus 14.10; Plutarch *Lysander* chapters 19-22; *Agesilaus* 6 especially Isocrates' criticism of Spartan leadership in *Panegyricus* 55: "They so far outdid all those who lived before their time in lawlessness and greed that they not only ruined themselves and their friends and their own countries but also brought the Lacedaemonians into evil repute with their allies and plunged them into misfortunes so many and so grave as no one could have dreamed would ever be visited upon them" (Trans. G. Norlin in the Loeb Classical Library).

[78] In later antiquity (Plutarch *Moralia* 219 d) the account was read as favorable to Brasidas.

northern Greeks. Many of the best features of Brasidas are again evident in his penultimate appearance in the *Histories*, the battle with the Athenians outside Amphipolis. His military good sense, courage, and decisiveness can all once again be seen. The battle develops just as he expects and the victory is all the sweeter because of the death of Cleon. Brasidas too is mortally wounded but lives long enough to see the victory.[79] Amphipolis, like Scione, accords him elaborate honors—public burial in a site of special prominence, games in his honor, sacrifices, hero cult, treatment as a savior and as the founder of the city (5.11.1)—a lavish and extravagant accumulation, eloquently attesting the gratitude and relief of the local population. Then Thucydides adds, "Clearidas and his staff took care of matters at Amphipolis" (5.11.3), reminding us of the new Spartan administrative arrangements in the area and the end of the autonomy that Brasidas had promised.[80]

As the account of the northern campaign progresses, the responses to Brasidas from the citizens of the region grow progressively more enthusiastic and lavish. The reader, however, moves in the other direction, to a greater awareness of the ambiguity of Brasidas' actions and of the danger in his appeals. His heroization at Amphipolis comes when we are most sharply aware of a double threat to the cities of the area—the resurgent Athenian power and a new Spartan tendency toward imperialism.

From that point it is an easy step to Thucydides' last significant comment about Brasidas. The armistice is ultimately replaced by a more permanent treaty, the so-called Peace of Nicias. The attainment of this long-desired peace is in large part due, Thucydides says, to the change of leadership

[79] Just before his death they convey him, ἔτι ἔμπνουν, into Amphipolis (5.10.11). The phrase is used in only one other passage—the removal of Pausanias from the temple of Athena in Sparta (1.134.3). It completes a circle begun in 4.81.2, which echoes the description of Pausanias in 1.130.2. Cf. also the honors granted to Brasidas in Amphipolis (5.11.1) with the posthumous honors of Pausanias in Sparta (1.134.3).

[80] H. R. Rawlings III, *The Structure of Thucydides' History* (Princeton 1981) 236-243 argues that Thucydides wrote this account with Lysander in mind. Can we go further and suggest that Brasidas is initially seen as a refreshing and effective change from normal Spartan *tropoi*? Gradually the reader recognizes affinities between him and another aggressive Spartan commander, Pausanias, and is thereby prepared for the Spartan who differs most radically from traditional Spartan ways and restraints, Lysander, described by hostile sources as "unscrupulous and subtle, a man who tricked out most of what he did in war with the varied hues of deceit, extolling justice if it was at the same time profitable, but if not, adopting the advantageous as the honourable course, and not considering trust as inherently better than falsehood, but bounding his estimate of either by the needs of the hour." (Plutarch *Lysander* 7, trans. B. Perrin in the Loeb Classical Library). Cf. the Athenians' attack on the Spartans in 5.105.4. Lysander, if Thucydides had adopted such a view of him, would embody many of the themes of the *Histories*: the triumph of advantage over justice, the distortions of language, and the changes of national *tropoi* under the influence of war.

after the battle around Amphipolis; for in that battle "Cleon died, and Brasidas, who were the ones on both sides especially opposed to the Peace; the one because he had success and honor through the war; the other believing that if tranquillity were achieved, he would be more readily seen as a trouble maker and would be less credible as a slanderer" (5.16.1). This is no more a final assessment, a full and balanced judgment of Brasidas, than any of the other passages concerning him. But his pairing with Cleon is the last of many ironies in this account. It is a harsh and bitter ending for a story that centers on the Achilles among men, the man who did most for Sparta. But whatever the differences in their background and personal qualities, both Brasidas and Cleon had come to oppose the movement toward peace and for personal and self-interested motives had encouraged the continuation of war.[81] We have come full circle—the story that began by implicitly contrasting the two men ends by bringing them together.

[81] Compare P. Brunt, *Phoenix* 19 (1965) 277, n. 78.

Book 5

THE INSECURE INTERLUDE

THE DEATHS of Brasidas and of Cleon make peace possible. After the battle outside Amphipolis we move swiftly toward the Peace of Nicias and to an apparent conclusion of the hostilities. We return, in effect, to the opportunity that had been missed after the initial success at Pylos. At that point a temporary truce had been arranged while Spartan ambassadors traveled to Athens and appealed to the assembly to preserve their current good fortune by agreeing to peace and alliance (4.16-20). Now the one-year armistice arranged in 424 B.C. (4.117) leads to negotiations and to treaties of peace (5.18-19) and alliance (5.23-24) between Sparta and Athens. No Cleon intervenes to sabotage the negotiations. His death has brought new leadership to Athens, Nicias the son of Niceratus, whose aim is to do precisely what the Spartan ambassadors had urged when they first brought the offer of peace to Athens. He wishes to preserve the good fortune (*eutychia*) of his city while entrusting himself as little as possible to the risks of chance (*tyche*).[1] Athens seems willing to follow his lead and to avoid the self-aggrandizement (*pleonexia*) of her earlier conduct. She once again repents her refusal after Pylos to make peace.[2]

Sparta, too, seems to have moved back from the innovative and aggressive policies of Brasidas to the frame of mind that prevailed after the Pylos defeat—a recognition of the unexpected course the war was taking[3] and of her vulnerability to attacks from Pylos, the desertion of Helots, and even revolution.[4]

In this climate of opinion peace seems at hand. The elaborate treaty quoted in chapters 18 and 19 seems to cover all the possible issues and

[1] 5.16.1. Cf. the Spartan ambassadors in 4.17.4-18.5.
[2] 5.13.2. Cf. 4.27.2.
[3] N.B. παρὰ γνώμην in 5.14.3 that applies to Sparta the more general Hellenic astonishment alluded to by παρὰ γνώμην in 4.40.1.
[4] These factors, mentioned in 5.14.3, are the same as those noted in 4.41.3.

contingencies and is ratified by an impressive delegation from each city.
All moves nicely toward closure, precisely ten years after the outbreak of
the war.[5] Despite the refusal of the Boeotians, Corinthians, Elians, and
Megareans to join in the peace settlement (5.16.1) and Clearidas' reluctance
to turn Amphipolis over to the Athenians (5.21), Sparta and Athens draw
closer to one another through a treaty of alliance, fully quoted in chapters
23 and 24. The original Spartan peace offer has now, after so many
surprising developments on both sides, been brought to fulfillment. As the
summer begins the Athenians return the captives from Pylos (5.24.2).

But confidence in the settlement is underminded just at the moment of
closure: "The sequence of events of the first war over these ten years has
now been reported" (5.24.2). A "first war" implies a second. The *kinēsis*
of war, we are warned, has not been eliminated and the peace between
the two major powers is not secure, nor does it prevent Corinth and some
other Peloponnesian cities from trying to disturb (*diekinoun*) the arrangement (5.25.1). We see continuing suspicion between Athens and Sparta,
six years and ten months of ill-disguised hostilities, and the eventual repudiation of the treaties and the resumption of open warfare:

> For those who accepted the treaty there was peace, but the Corinthians and some
> of the Peloponnesian cities kept disturbing what had been arranged and further
> disorder immediately followed in the relationship of the allies to Sparta. And
> likewise as time went on, the Spartans became suspect in the eyes of the Athenians,
> especially since they did not do what was stated in the agreements. For six years
> and ten months they avoided expeditions against each other's territory, although
> in other areas during this insecure interlude they harmed one another as much as
> they could. Then, finally forced to abandon the treaty they had made after the ten
> years of war, they again entered into open hostilities. (5.25.1f.)

As we look ahead to the renewal of war, the language reminds us of the
outbreak of hostilities in 431 and to the pressures which led to the abandonment of the Thirty Years Peace between the two powers.[6]

With the movement toward closure so decisively interrupted Thucydides
makes a new beginning: "The same Thucydides of Athens has also written
these events, in the sequence in which they occurred, by summers and

---

[5] 5.20.1. On the chronology and its important implications for the structure of the *Histories*
see Hunter R. Rawlings III, *The Structure of Thucydides' History* (Princeton 1981) esp. ch.
1.

[6] The language at the end of 5.25.3 is especially close to that used in 1.23.6 to give what
Thucydides thought was the truest cause of the war: 5.25.3, καὶ ἀναγκασθέντες λῦσαι
τὰς μετὰ τὰ δέκα ἔτη σπονδὰς αὖθις ἐς πόλεμον φανερὸν κατέστησαν and 1.23.6,
ἀναγκάσαι ἐς τὸ πολεμεῖν· αἱ δ' ἐς τὸ φανερὸν λεγόμεναι αἰτίαι αἵδ' ἦσαν
ἑκατέρων, ἀφ' ὧν λύσαντες τὰς σπονδὰς ἐς τὸν πόλεμον κατέστησαν.

winters, up to the point at which the Spartans and their allies brought to an end the empire of the Athenians, and seized the long walls and the Piraeus. The total number of years in the war was twenty-seven. And anyone who does not think it correct to consider the accommodation in the middle as war, makes an unwarranted assessment'' (5.26.1-2). This is the so-called "Second Preface," widely assumed to imply "an earlier work," a history of the first ten years of the war, which Thucydides is supposed to have completed, perhaps even to have published, during this insecure interval of apparent peace.[7] According to this view, when he later came to recognize that the Sicilian Expedition and the renewed hostilities in continental Greece were parts of the same conflict as the ten-year war, he revised his earlier work, incorporated it into the present *Histories*, adding the "Second Preface" to mark the transition to the new material. On this passage, then, hangs much of the Separatist criticism of Thucydides.

Nowhere is the domination of Thucydidean studies by "the Thucydidean question," the problem of the composition of the work, more evident or more pernicious. Separatist approaches to the work tend to divert attention from the literary effects of the work to alleged changes and modifications of the author's views. But if our analysis is correct, the issue is not the history of Thucydides' own thinking about the war, but the way in which the reader's understanding is directed and deepened. From this point of view, the Second Preface has an important function to perform. It is a vigorous and unmistakable denial of a facile and perhaps widespread approach to the history of the period. We know that some of Thucydides' contemporaries saw not a single twenty-seven-year war, but a series of shorter conflicts.[8] The "Second Preface" rejects the notion that the Peace of Nicias introduced a true cessation of hostilities. In Thucydides' treatment this "peace," far from being the end of the war, marked the opening of a new phase in the conflict. Hence Thucydides made use of the literary form, the preface, that most dramatically reflected the substance of his argument. A preface destroys any illusion that the war is about to come to a conclusion, just as the allusion to the oracles which asserted that the war would last thrice nine years (5.26.4) affirms the length and unity of the whole war.[9]

[7] Cf. a recent Separatist critic, V. Hunter, "The Composition of Thucydides' *History*: A New Answer to the Problem," *Historia* 26 (1977) 269.

[8] Andocides 3 (*On the Peace*) 8f.

[9] The passage does not show that Thucydides believed or disbelieved in oracles in general or in this particular oracle. It is part of a pattern of using phenomena commonly thought to have a supernatural origin to underline the structure and interpretation of his work. Cf. 1.23.3.

The same point is reinforced later in the fifth book by the account of the battle of Mantinea in which the Lacedaemonians and some of their allies defeated the Athenians and various Athenian allies. Thucydides' account provides what is perhaps our most vivid picture of a classical hoplite battle and one of our best glimpses into the organization of the Spartan army. No other battle in the *Histories* approaches this one in the detail with which it is presented. We can calculate the number of Peloponnesian troops (5.68.3), observe their disposition on the battlefield and the structure of command (5.66.3); we can even hear the flutes as the troops march to battle (5.70.1). As often when Thucydides pauses to report in detail, the account is so vivid that modern readers have conjectured that he himself must have been present.[10] A more compelling reason for this detailed treatment, however, lies readily at hand. Mantinea is Thucydides' paradigmatic hoplite battle—as Plataea was among sieges, or Corcyra among revolutions. Thucydides often adopts the technique of presenting one instance of a phenomenon in rich detail, while leaving other examples relatively undeveloped. It admirably suits this pattern of writing, Thucydides' love of paradox, and his argumentative purpose to present his paradigmatic battle in the midst of a period of ostensible peace. The reader is thereby again reminded that the war continues through this "insecure interlude" (5.25.3).

THE DOCUMENTS

The battle of Mantinea is described with a fullness and richness of detail that contrast sharply with the succinctness and compression of most of the fifth book.[11] The other major expansion in this part of the narrative is found in the series of treaties and other documents that had already begun with the armistice (4.118-119) and includes the so-called Peace of Nicias (5.18-19), the alliance between Athens and Sparta (5.23 and 24), an alliance between Argos and Athens (5.47), a treaty between Sparta and Argos

---

[10] C. Thirlwall in his *History of Greece*, vol. 3 (new ed., New York 1845) 338, n. 1 suggested that Thucydides was present. See W. J. Woodhouse, *King Agis of Sparta* (Oxford 1933), 17f. in refutation. Cf. Gomme in *HCT* on 5.74.1 (pp. 101f. and 125).

[11] H. D. Westlake, "Thucydides and the Uneasy Peace," *CQ* n.s. 21 (1971) 315 denied that this portion of the work was written "on a small scale." He is surely justified insofar as the events leading up to and including the Battle of Mantinea are concerned. But much of the rest of the account is highly compressed as C. J. Dewald has shown in a useful dissertation, "Taxis: The Origin of Thucydides' *Histories* II-VIII" (University of California at Berkeley diss. 1975) 102ff. and esp. table 21.

(5.77), and finally an alliance between them (5.79). Both in content and in style the series is exceptional. The last two documents are even quoted in the Doric dialect. The legalistic phrasing and sing-song diplomatic jargon also make the treaties stand out from their surroundings and shatter any illusion of homogeneous style. Wilamowitz and other excellent scholars have propounded the rule that Thucydides aimed at unity of style throughout the work and hence have concluded that these documents could not have been intended to stand in the final version of his work.[12] From this, and from other considerations such as the avoidance of direct discourse, it has often been thought that the fifth book is unfinished and might have been extensively revised if Thucydides had lived on.[13]

Once again "the Thucydidean question" has obscured other aspects of the text. The concern with the composition of the *Histories* has impeded attention to the literary role of the documents. They are, in effect, not present because the Separatist critic assumes it was Thucydides' intention to delete them or blend them into a homogeneous narrative. The premises upon which this confidence is based are, however, quite insecure. It is by no means evident, for example, that Thucydides felt bound by the rule of unity of style. Elsewhere he allows great variation, including in his work quotations from the Homeric hymns (3.104), epigrams (1.132.2; 6.54.7, and 59.3), and letters using the phraseology of the Persian court (1.129.3). From time to time he delights in the idiom of oracular discourse (2.54.2 and 5.16.2).[14] Nor do the other arguments which have been adduced compel the conclusion that the book is incomplete. The avoidance of direct discourse and variations in some formulae can be explained by the desire to limit the overall length of the account. Before we dismiss the documents, then, it would be wise to investigate whether they have a literary function to perform, and in particular whether they carry their own weight in a section that in many other respects aims at succinctness.[15]

[12] U. v. Wilamowitz, "Die Thukydideslegende," *Hermes* 12 (1877) 338, n. 21. Wila-mowitz conceded, however, that even in paraphrased documents (e.g., 2.24 and 4.16) the style of the original document could sometimes still be detected.

[13] Cf. most recently Hunter, *Historia* 26 (1977) 270. Note, however, E. Meyer, *Forschungen zur Alten Geschichte*, vol. 2 (Halle 1899) 364f., whose argument that the subject matter of the period demanded a different approach has been developed by C. Dewald in the thesis cited in Note 11 above.

[14] Cf. A. W. Gomme, *Greek Attitude to Poetry and History* (Berkeley 1954) 118, n. 3, and O. Luschnat, "Thukydides," in *RE*, supplemental vol. 12 (Stuttgart 1971) 1122ff., and K. von Fritz, *Die Griechische Geschichtsschreibung* (Berlin 1967), Ib, 308f.

[15] The literary role of the documents is stressed by H. Erbse, "Argos und Melos im 5ten Buch des Thukydides," *Würzburger Jahrbücher für die Altertumswissenschaft*, N.F. 1 (1975) 59-70, who, however, argues that the disproportionate attention paid to the Argive-Spartan

When approached in this way these documents can be seen to have a dual role. First, they help mark out the stages in an otherwise complex and amorphous diplomatic narrative. Their placement emphasizes the major stages in the rapidly changing patterns of Greek diplomacy. They serve as stopping points in the often perplexing progression of events.[16] The armistice in 4.118-119 follows swiftly after the setbacks at Delium and Amphipolis. As a sequel to the battle of Amphipolis two documents, the treaty and the alliance between Athens and Sparta, proclaim cooperation between the two rivals. As a sequel to the battle of Mantinea two documents, the treaty and the alliance between Argos and Sparta, proclaim cooperation between other inveterate opponents. Although in each case the cooperation is short-lived, the documents mark out the major developments in the diplomacy of these years and provide a clearer structure for the narrative.

When the reader stops to examine the documents and their setting more closely, a further function becomes evident. In each case there is a vast discrepancy between what the document proclaims and what actually occurs. The Peace of Nicias, for example, begins with a guarantee of access to the common sanctuaries of the Greeks—Delphi, Olympia, and the Isthmus. But the ineffectiveness of the treaty soon becomes evident in the exclusion of Spartan contestants from the Olympic games (5.49.1). The next section of the treaty specifies that it is to last fifty years. Within the same year mutual suspicion and distrust lead to the refusal to return Amphipolis to Athens or Pylos to Sparta (5.35.3ff).[17] The one-hundred-year treaty between Athens and Argos (5.47.1) is even less enduring. The provisions for nonaggression in the Peace of Nicias and for mutual assistance in the ensuing alliance between Athens and Sparta become a mockery when Athens and Argos ally and when open hostilities break out (esp. 5.47). The effect of the documents, then, is ironic for they emphasize the discrepancy between professions of enduring stability and the rapidly shifting reality of events.

This also helps explain the great attention paid to oaths and the pro-

---

treaty is paralleled by the Melian episode in an effort to illustrate two analogous episodes of Machtpolitik. Since the publication in 1955 of the first edition of C. Meyer's book *Die Urkunden im Geschichtswerk des Thukydides* , Zetemata 10 (2nd ed., Munich 1970), scholars have increasingly tended to accept the documents as part of the design of the book.

[16] The schematization in Appendix Four is designed to bring out the role of the documents in marking the major stages of the action in this portion of the narrative.

[17] "Fifty years" is used to designate the treaty in 5.27.1, thereby calling further attention to the discrepancy between the documents and the reality of events.

cedures for ratifying the agreements.[18] Although these details have nothing to do with the matters of substance ostensibly resolved by the documents, they underline the ironic disparity between the solemn rituals of interstate relationships and the instability of the settlements. At the same time they carry one step further the theme of the breakdown of oaths and of other religiously sanctioned restraints on human nature. Similarly we can better understand why the one alliance that endures for a significant period of time, the Athenian rapprochement with Argos after the restoration of Argive democracy (5.82), is not cited.[19] If the documents are cited largely for their ironic effect, nothing would be gained by quoting this document.

MELOS

The compression that is evident in much of the fifth book extends to Thucydides' treatment of the fate of several small cities destroyed by the major belligerents. One of the most notorious of these episodes was the Athenian punishment of Scione for accepting Brasidas' invitation to revolt (4.120). Scione had broken away from Athens after the armistice had been signed; Cleon had then successfully proposed a motion to put its citizens to death (4.122.6). The Peace of Nicias explicitly allowed the Athenians to do to this city whatever they wished (5.18.8). A vivid presentation of the Athenian punishment of the city would have provided a powerful and appropriate culmination for Thucydides' treatment of events in northern Greece. Instead it receives only brief mention: "About the same time in this summer the Athenians captured the Scioneans by siege and killed all the males over the age of puberty, enslaved the women and children and gave the land to the Plataeans to settle in."[20] Later a Spartan atrocity at Hysiae is given similarly succinct and formulaic treatment: "Seizing Hysiae, a region of Argos, and killing all the free citizens they could capture, they withdrew and disbanded, each to his own city" (5.83.2). The contrast with the exposition of the Plataean and Mytilenean episodes is remarkable. Now there seems to be no place for the drama, the vivid detail, and the

[18] Oaths and oath-taking procedures are mentioned in 5.18.9 and 18.10; 19.2; 23.4; 24.1; 47.8.10; 77.4; cf. 30; 38; 42.1; 46.4; 56.3; and 80.2.

[19] The text of the agreement is partially preserved on stone, *IG* i³ 86.

[20] 5.32.1. On Scione's prominence in fourth-century views of the Athenian empire see Xenophon, *Hellenica* 2.2.3 and 2.10; Isocrates, *Panegyricus* (4) 100f.; and *Panathenaicus* (12) 63-107. Cf. also Diodorus Siculus 13.30.4-6, and Arrian, *Anabasis* 1.9.3-6. For an interesting interpretation of Thucydides' comments on Scione, emphasizing the *pathos* of the narrative, see D. Lateiner, "Pathos in Thucydides," *Antichthon* 11 (1977) 41.

involvement of the reader in the fate of the victims. All is matter of fact, swiftly reported, and equally swiftly passed by. There is neither emotional nor moral hesitation.

The account of the most notorious of the atrocities in the war, the Athenian extermination of Melos, begins in the same routine way, as another in a series of minor operations, introduced almost casually with an "and": "And the Athenians made an expedition against the island Melos" (5.84.1). Almost immediately, however, appear signs of a more elaborate development—the ships in the expedition are identified with more than customary precision: "with thirty ships of their own, six of the Chians, a pair from Lesbos"; the exact, and overwhelming, composition of the land forces is recounted; and crucial background information is provided: "The Melians are colonists of the Lacedaemonians; unlike the other islanders, they were unwilling to submit to the Athenians."[21] The treatment continues to become more detailed; finally, for the first time since the battle of Amphipolis, direct discourse reappears.[22] The speeches delivered at Melos are not, however, long addresses before a popular assembly but *brachylogies*, short, blunt thrusts in a closed conference room (5.84.3). The result is a dialogue, a form which has been absent in the *Histories* since the negotiations between King Archidamus of Sparta and the Plataeans in book 2 (chs. 71-74).[23] The siege of Plataea and its parallel in book 3, Mytilene, are inevitably much in our mind as we read the story of Melos. It too is the account of a siege, and the destruction of a smaller state by a larger one; the fate of the conquered city depends upon a discussion in which considerations of advantage eclipse arguments from

[21] 5.84.2 echoing the earlier Melian episode in 3.91.2, and introducing the colonization theme, which recurs at 5.89, 96, 106, and in 116.4. This theme continues in book 6, e.g. chapter 6.62. See H. C. Avery, "Themes in Thucydides' Account of the Sicilian Expedition," *Hermes* 101 (1973) 1-13.

[22] The avoidance of direct discourse through much of the fifth book may be motivated primarily by a desire for compression, but it has the incidental effect of making the reappearance of direct speech in the Melian Dialogue all the more dramatic.

[23] Dionysius of Halicarnassus, in *On Thucydides* trans. W. K. Pritchett (Berkeley 1975) ch. 37, describes this exchange as a *dialogos*. Cf. G. Deininger, "Der Melier Dialog" (Erlangen University diss. 1939) 139f., and R. Hirzel, *Der Dialog* (Leipzig 1895) 1.44f. The other short exchanges in the *Histories* are either conversations (3.113) or are kept in indirect discourse (4.97-99). On dialogue form in the fifth century see J. Finley, "Euripides and Thucydides," *HSCP* 49 (1938) 56 and H. L. Hudson-Williams, "Conventional Forms of Debate and the Melian Dialogue," *AJP* 71 (1950) 156-69. In attempting to understand the form it is important to distinguish the historical question of whether the Athenians and Melians would use such conference-room diplomacy from the literary question of why Thucydides chose to represent the negotiations through this most enlightened and sophisticated literary form. See also Chapter Three, Note 38 above.

justice and in which the short question and answer (3.52.4 and 68.1) displaces continuous discourse. Melos is also the culmination of the theme of the relationship between great powers and small that recurs throughout the first part of the *Histories*.

The similarities to Plataea and other siege narratives are, however, of a very unusual sort. The fully developed Thucydidean siege, of which Plataea is the best example, often begins with an offer from the attacking side designed to achieve a settlement without the expense and delay of encirclement. If this is rejected, the military operations commence, siege-works are constructed and a long period of waiting ensues, in which the crucial issue is whether the grain supply and the loyalty and the endurance of the defenders can outlast the determination of the besiegers. If the city capitulates, a debate ensues about the punishment. This commonly consists of two lengthy and antithetical speeches. A decision is rendered; its implementation is described, and some note of pathos or compassion for the victims is often sounded. The episode is usually completed with a rounding-off sentence. Not all these elements need be present in an individual siege narrative; as we have seen, the accounts can be very compressed. Thus to find the siege of Scione reported in half a sentence is not especially remarkable. In the Melian episode, however, most of the elements are present, but in a surprising fashion.[24]

Unlike Archidamus' discussion with the Plataeans, the initial negotiations between the Athenians and the Melians require more than a brief exchange. They become the center of the story and subsume many of the typical elements of a siege narrative. The principal debate thus precedes rather than follows the main account of the military operations. The outcome of the siege is resolved within the debate itself, for the only serious question is whether the Melians will agree to capitulate. The Athenian strength is overwhelming and their assertion—"the Athenians have never withdrawn from a single siege through fear of other powers" (5.111.1)— is amply corroborated by the earlier history of Athens. The reader knows that Athens can and will conquer. He witnesses not the elaborate series of military measures and countermeasures observed at Plataea, but the gradual destruction of the intellectual bases for Melian resistance. Neither neutrality (94-98) nor hope (102f.), nor divine assistance, nor the Spartans[25] are likely to save the Melians. There is no possibility of preservation except

[24] The relationship between the Melian narrative and those of the Plataean and Mytilenean operations is schematized in Appendix Five.

[25] 5.101-104. Cf. the Plataeans in 3.57.4 who regard the Lacedaemonians as their one hope and the Mytileneans (3.8-15) who counted on effective support from them.

through submission; yet as the Athenian arguments become stronger, the Melian resistance intensifies.[26] Within the speech itself the outcome is foretold: the Melians will resist; the Athenians will conquer; the city will be destroyed.

In the Melian Dialogue speeches eclipse events. Little space is provided for background material, qualifications, explanations, or details.[27] Not the siege, not the suffering of the Melians, but the dialogue itself and the patterns of thought it represents are the subject and center of attention. Even the few explicit elements of *pathos* that are present in this episode are subsumed in the dialogue. The enormity of the destruction of Plataea and the ambiguities of Athens' role in the siege are brought out, as we have seen, in the transformation of the typical rounding-off sentence: "Such was the end of the Plataean affair in the ninety-third year after their alliance with the Athenians."[28] The Melian account lacks a rounding-off sentence; it confronts us directly with Sicily. The elegiac note struck by the allusion to the length of the Plataean alliance with Athens, has its counterpart in a comment of the Melians who, after withdrawing from the conference and reconsidering the Athenian demands, reaffirm their determination to resist: "We will not take away the independence of a city which has existed for seven hundred years. Trusting both in the *tychē* that comes from the divine and has until now kept us safe and in the protection of mankind and especially of the Lacedaemonians, we will try to maintain our safety" (5.112). The Melians thereby write their own epitaph. Their speech becomes their destiny.

The Melian episode is one of the most important, and controversial,

---

[26] This is especially true after chapter 99, the central speech of the dialogue. Cf. M. Treu, "Athen und Melos und der Melier Dialog des Thukydides," *Historia* 2 (1953/54) 264-70; H.-P. Stahl, *Thukydides: Die Stellung des Menschen im geschichtlichen Prozess* (Munich 1966) 163; A. Andrewes, "The Melian Dialogue and Perikles' Last Speech," *Proceedings of the Cambridge Philological Society*, n.s. 6 (1960) 1ff.

[27] The debate about the historical circumstances of the siege of Melos is a continuing reminder of the cost of this narrative strategy. Many historians would agree with Andrewes in *HCT* on 5.84.2 (p. 157) that "On balance . . . it seems unlikely that the attack in 416 was due solely to an Athenian whim, without any immediately antecedent quarrel." Athens may have been considerably provoked by Melian actions, but Thucydides' narrative, perhaps more for literary than for partisan reasons, fails to provide the information needed to make a full historical assessment. See also *ML* 67, pp. 181-84. Again, at the end of the book, his account implies that there were virtually no survivors. Surely this is an exaggeration. The traitors (5.116.3) were no doubt spared and Lysander later found some Melians to resettle on the island, Xenophon, *Hellenica* 2.2.9 and Plutarch, *Lysander* 14.4; cf. Isocrates (4) *Panegyricus* 100.

[28] 3.68.5 transforming and expanding the formula used in 3.50.3. Cf. Chapter Three, Note 30.

portions of the *Histories*, but despite Thucydides' great attention to this
episode, so disproportionate to its military significance, there is virtually
no overt sympathy for the Melians, few elements of the usual pathos
narrative, no direct sign even at the moment of their destruction of compassion or involvement. The end of the Melian episode returns to the
pattern of Scione and Hysiae with stark, factual reporting and formulaic
language: "They killed all the Melians over the age of puberty whom they
could capture, and enslaved the women and children. They settled the
territory themselves, later sending out five hundred colonists" (5.116.4).
The passage seems to offer the perfect confirmation of the textbook portrait
of the *Histories* as "severe in its detachment, written from a purely intellectual point of view, unencumbered with platitudes and moral judge-
ments, cold and critical,"[29] and of Thucydides himself as "a complete
and ruthless realist."[30] As Russell Meiggs says, "there is strangely little
emphasis on the final penalty, the killing of the men and the enslavement
of the women and children. Thucydides' interest seems to be concentrated
on the analysis of power and the logical implications of the natural law
that the strong rule the weak.[31]

Meiggs is surely correct in stressing the connection between this passage
and others in the *Histories* that emphasize the law of the stronger: that the
strong will rule wherever they can and the weak must accommodate to
them.[32] Thucydides, indeed, seems to be wrenching the Melian episode
away from a group of episodes that emphasize the horror and destruction
of the war and placing it among the passages that expound the nature of
power. Although it has obvious affinities with the debates in book 3 on
the fate of Mytilene and Plataea, and with the antithesis between justice

[29] J. B. Bury, *History of Greece*, 4th ed., rev. by R. Meiggs (New York 1975) 252.
[30] G.E.M. de Ste. Croix, *Origins of the Peloponnesian War* (London 1972) 11f.
[31] R. Meiggs, *The Athenian Empire* (Oxford 1972) 388.
[32] The notion that the domination of the weaker by the stronger is a long-established
principle is not, to be sure, a purely Thucydidean idea. Cf. Callicles in Plato's *Gorgias* 483
c-e; Gorgias *Helen VS* 82 B11, sec. 6. Note also Plutarch *Camillus* 17. But the convergence
in thought and language between 5.105.2 and 1.76.1-2 is sufficient to remind the reader of
correspondences within the *Histories* as well as between the *Histories* and ideas in the culture
as a whole. Note especially the following:

1.76.1 καὶ εἰ τότε ὑπομείναντες διὰ παντὸς ἀπήχθεσθε ἐν τῇ ἡγεμονίᾳ, ὥσπερ ἡμεῖς, εὖ
ἴσμεν μὴ ἂν ἧσσον ὑμᾶς λυπηροὺς . . . καὶ ἀναγκασθέντας ἂν ἢ ἄρχειν ἐγκρατῶς ἢ αὐτοὺς
κινδυνεύειν. οὕτως οὐδ' ἡμεῖς θαυμαστὸν οὐδὲν πεποιήκαμεν οὐδ' ἀπὸ τοῦ ἀνθρωπείου
τρόπου . . . οὐδ' αὖ πρῶτοι τοῦ τοιούτου ὑπάρξαντες, ἀλλ' αἰεὶ καθεστῶτος. . . .
5.105 οὐδὲν γὰρ ἔξω τῆς ἀνθρωπείας . . . πράσσομεν. ἡγούμεθα γὰρ τό τε θεῖον δόξῃ τὸ
ἀνθρώπειόν τε σαφῶς διὰ παντὸς ὑπὸ φύσεως ἀναγκαίας, οὗ ἂν κρατῇ, ἄρχειν· καὶ ἡμεῖς
οὔτε θέντες τὸν νόμον οὔτε κειμένῳ πρῶτοι χρησάμενοι, ὄντα δὲ παραλαβόντες καὶ ἐσό-
μενον ἐς αἰεὶ . . . εἰδότες καὶ ὑμᾶς ἂν . . . δρῶντας ἂν ταὐτό.

and self-interest that pervades these episodes, it also evokes the gradually changing Athenian rationales for their imperial power. When, for example, the Athenians tell the Melians: ''We believe that the divinity, insofar as one can tell, and mankind, quite evidently, in response to natural pressures dominate wherever they have the strength. We did not establish this law nor were we the first to use it once it was laid down; we received it in our turn, when it was already in existence, and having applied it, we will leave it as an inheritance that will endure for all time. We know that you too and others who come into the same power that we enjoy would do the same'' (5.105.2), they are restating a position already articulated during the Conference at Sparta just before the vote for war. The Athenian ambassadors told the Spartans that if they had retained the leadership of Greece after the Persian wars, they too would have provoked animosity:

We know that you would not have become less hateful to your allies [than we have become to ours] and would have been compelled either to dominate with strong measures or yourselves to run great risks. Thus we have done nothing surprising nor out of the ordinary way of mankind if we accepted domination when it was offered and refused to give it up, for we were overcome by the greatest considerations—honor, and fear and self interest. Nor were we the first to take the lead in this; rather it has always been the case that the weaker is restrained by the more powerful. (1.76.1-2)

The resemblances are also striking, however, to Hermocrates' comments at the Conference at Gela, reported in book 4: ''For it is the nature of what is human to dominate everywhere any one who yields and to ward off any one who attacks'' (4.61.5). Indeed the language of the Melian Dialogue repeats almost verbatim the first part of this important and central idea of Hermocrates' speech. But only the first part. As we have seen in the analysis of the Conference at Gela, this sentence is a highly significant one in the *Histories*, especially because it goes beyond the conventional formulations of the law of the stronger to examine a tendency equally grounded in nature to resist the assaults even of powerful aggressors. From this observation derive both the major point of Hermocrates' speech, the need to unite against Athenian aggression, and also the most important implication of the speech within the overall structure of the *Histories*: that the tendency of nature is two-fold, pressing toward the expansion of power but also toward self-defense and mutual protection against aggression.

The reader who bears Hermocrates' analysis in mind and who appreciates the connections within the text and their importance for our interpretation of the work approaches the Melian Dialogue from a position much closer to that of the Melians than to that of the Athenians. This does not mean that we fail to see the Melians' folly in attempting to resist the power of Athens. We know they have insufficient power and that neither the gods nor the Spartans will intervene to help them. But, whatever admiration we may feel for their determination to resist, the interest of the dialogue arises in large part from their attitudes and arguments, rather than from those of the Athenians. The Athenian speakers articulate in more rigorous and uncompromising terms a view that has long been part of Athenian imperialism. Their speeches are the culmination of the hard-headed realism so often encountered in Athenian argumentation. The Melians, on the other hand, present a combination of old-fashioned and rather naive ideas, with some that, in the context of the *Histories*, are relatively fresh: that a smaller state may find a way to resist an ostensibly stronger one and that self-restraint may be in the long-term interest of the more powerful. The first of the ideas, an extension of Hermocrates' argumentation in the fourth book, in the Melian situation is ill grounded. It turns out to be a naive hope for divine intervention or a change in the patterns of Spartan foreign policy. A true test of Hermocrates' ideas would be the cooperation of many smaller states against one or more great powers, not the dependence of a single island on the support of Sparta.

But the Melians also advance another idea. Forced by the Athenians to avoid arguments based on justice,[33] they attempt to point out the practical advantages of having generally observed standards to which to appeal:

The way it appears to us is that it is useful (a word we must use since you have made it the rule to talk about advantage rather than right) that you not abolish a common good but that the party that at any point finds itself in danger should have something reasonable to which to appeal and to gain some measure of assistance, even if his arguments are not rigorously compelling. This advantage applies even more in your case: if you fall, you will be subject to the greatest retaliation and become an example to other powers.[34]

That is an important idea within the *Histories* and much of the dramatic interest of the dialogue depends upon it. We wish to see whether this Melian counterattack will have any effect on the Athenians. We know, of

[33] 5.89. Cf. the Athenians at Corinth 1.76.2 and the Plataean and Mytilenean debates, *passim*. Note, however, the Periclean boast about Athens that only Athenians show true altruism in helping their friends: οὐ γὰρ πάσχοντες εὖ, ἀλλὰ δρῶντες κτώμεθα τοὺς φίλους (2.40.4).

[34] 5.90. I am persuaded by S. L. Radt, "Philologische Kleinigkeiten zum Melierdialog," *Mnemosyne* n.s. 29 (1976) 35 that G. Hermann, "Thucydides," *Philologus* 1 (1846) 370f. was correct in regarding καὶ δίκαια as a gloss on εἰκότα.

course, that the Melians' attempt to reintroduce considerations of right by pointing out their potential utility and advantage will not persuade the Athenians. The danger that worries them comes not from another imperial power such as Sparta but from their own subjects.[35] They point out that great powers can reach mutual understandings and accommodations but the example of Melian freedom is a threat to Athens' continued control of her empire. Hence Athens feels she must suppress Melos and continue a foreign policy unrtrammeled by considerations of right or convention.

For the reader, however, the Melian counterattack has greater effect. It changes the perspective from a narrow concentration on the events of 416 to the broader development of the war. In the immediate setting the Melian resistance is either folly or tragic heroism; it never becomes entirely clear which, since the focus moves to wider issues, perhaps even to the ultimate fate of Athens in the war, when the victors debated her destruction.

The Athenians appear in a most paradoxical light. On the one hand they are as tough minded, articulate, and rational as ever. No plague or passion afflicts their decision making; no demagogues lead the rabble to emotional responses; no long speeches delude. All is cool, deliberate, and rational. A small group of Athenian ambassadors meet with the officials and "the few" of the Melians (5.84.3) and insist upon the most sophisticated form of discourse, the dialogue. The short exchanges should eliminate the rhetoric and deception of speeches before a large group. "Fair names" are specifically excluded: arguments based on Athens' service to the Greeks at the time of the Persian War or on considerations of justice or the like (5.89). Everything specious or sentimental is eliminated; now if ever we should see pure *logos* in operation. Unbounded, unrestrained, it sweeps away all traditional constraints and inhibitions. Yet the Melians are unmoved and unpersuaded.

Whatever our reactions to what happens to the Melians, it is hard to escape a feeling of horror at what is happening to the Athenians. They remain in many respects as we have always seen them—clever, determined, vigorous, the fulfilment of the Corinthians' description of them as a people unaccustomed to choosing tranquility for themselves or allowing it to others (1.70). But now all is changed, for despite their clear mindedness, they fail fully to perceive the dangers that surround them.[36] They see the weakness of the Melians' position with total clarity but in important respects

---

[35] The outcome of the war partially confirms the Athenian assessment. Sparta rejected Theban demands for Athens' destruction, Xenophon *Hellenica* 2.2.3ff.

[36] Cf. Stahl, *Thukydides*, 158-71, and C. W. Macleod, "Form and Meaning in the Melian Dialogue," *Historia* 23 (1975), 385-400.

fail to realize who they are and the implications of their own words. The logic of their position compels them to suppress the freedom of island states. Yet the reader knows that another island, Sicily, will soon overcome an Athenian attack. As becomes clear in the sixth and seventh books, many of the themes of the Melian Dialogue continue into the account of the invasion of Sicily, and Athens ultimately comes very much to resemble Melos, forced to rely on hope, chance, and speculation about the gods (esp. 7.77.4).

The reader, to be sure, may as yet be only dimly aware of the extent to which the Sicilian Expedition will ultimately appear as the sequel to the destruction of Melos. But the dialogue looks backward as well as forward. It confronts us with one of the most important parts of Athens' past, precisely that part which the Athenian speakers are determined to leave out of consideration: Athens' role in the resistance against Persia. Her leadership in the Persian wars stimulated and justified the growth of Athenian power. Now such considerations are excluded, along with all other "fair names" (5.89). Yet the reader does not find it so easy to forget the Persian conflict. It was, after all, the struggle with Persia that made the Athenians "become nautical" (1.18.2 and 93.3) and thereby largely shaped their institutions and national character. They confronted in that struggle precisely the preponderance of power and the apparent hopelessness that Melos now faces. They were the saviors of Greece (Herodotus 7.139). And they succeeded with the help of Sparta and, if popular legends were to be believed, with the intervention of divinities and heroes. Melos, in other words, reminds us of the past of Athens and forces us to ask, "What if the Athenians had acted against the Persians as they now urge the Melians to act?"[37] But if the Melians resemble the Athenians of the early fifth century, the Athenians speak as Persians might have: "We know and you know that in human calculation considerations of justice apply when the pressures of necessity balance; those who excel in power do what they can and those who are weak submit" (5.89). Dionysius of Halicarnassus complained about this passage: "Words like these were appropriate to oriental monarchs addressing Greeks, but unfit to be spoken by Athenians to Greeks whom they liberated from the Medes."[38] Dionysius often judged Thucydides by inappropriate standards but his alertness to style has led him to

[37] I have learned a great deal about the Melian Dialogue from reading it and arguing about it with my students. George Ryan posed the question in the text. Keith Nightenhelser helped me by frequent discussions based on his forthcoming doctoral dissertation on the use of dialogue form in this period.

[38] Dionysius of Halicarnassus, *On Thucydides*, ch. 38, trans. W. K. Pritchett, p. 31.

notice an important part of this dialogue. He has noted, even if he has failed fully to understand, the despotic tone of the Athenian words. That is, of course, part of Thucydides' purpose—to show that in one important respect the Athenians have changed since the days of their resistance to the Persian invasion.

The contrast between the Persian and the Peloponnesian War runs through many sections of the *Histories*, a counterpoint or subtext to the surface narrative. We have encountered it already in the story of Plataea, in the association of Pylos and Thermopylae, and will meet it again with increasing intensity in the Sicilian Expedition. It now becomes evident in the Melian Dialogue as the Athenians restate the law of the stronger: "We did not establish this law nor were we the first to use it once it was laid down; we received it in our turn, when it was already in existence, and having applied it, we will leave it as an inheritance that will endure for all time."[39] The language is very similar to that in which Herodotus reports the words of a Great King of Persia at a crucial moment in his reign: "After Egypt was subdued, Xerxes, being about to take in hand the expedition against Athens, called together an assembly of the noblest Persians to learn their opinions and to lay before them his own designs. So, when the men were met, the king spoke thus to them: 'Persians, I shall not be the first to bring in among you a new custom—I shall but follow one which has come down to us from our forefathers. Never yet . . . has our race reposed itself. . . .' "[40] The reader who is aware of the Herodotean parallel recognizes that the traditional custom to which Xerxes alludes has in the Athenian world a counterpart in the law of the stronger on which the Athenians rely. The restless energy of the Athenians becomes a reflection of aggressive designs of the Persian monarch. Athens recreates Persian despotism, not only in its suppression of freedom and autonomy but in the arrogance of its language and in what Dionysius called the "depraved shrewdness" of its arguments.[41] And the Melians, in their folly and blindness, nonetheless resemble the Athenians at an earlier moment in their

[39] 5.105.2. The Athenians claim that the law of the stronger will endure for all time; Pericles claims the greatness of Athens' power will last forever (2.64.3); Thucydides claims it is his work that will achieve this immortality (1.22.4).

[40] Herodotus 7.8 alpha 1, trans. Rawlinson. On the relation to Thucydides see H. R. Immerwahr, *Form and Thought in Herodotus* (Cleveland 1966) p. 22, n. 40. Cf. also F. M. Cornford, *Thucydides Mythistoricus* (London 1907) 176-82.

[41] Dionysius of Halicarnassus, *On Thucydides*, ch. 41. On the *hybris* of the Athenians see W. Liebeschuetz, "The Structure and Function of the Melian Dialogue," *JHS* 88 (1968) 73-77.

history when they told Alexander of Macedon who had brought the king's demands for submission:

We know, as well as you do, that the power of the Mede is many times greater than our own. . . . Nevertheless we cling so to freedom that we shall offer what resistance we may. Seek not to persuade us into making terms with the barbarian—say what you will, you will never gain our assent. Return rather at once and tell Mardonius that our answer to him is this, "So long as the sun keeps its present course, we will never join alliance with Xerxes. Nay we shall oppose him unceasingly, trusting in the aid of those gods and heroes whom he has lightly esteemed, whose houses and whose images he has burnt with fire."[42]

For the reader of Thucydides the Melian Dialogue is thus one of the culminating points of the *Histories*. It attracts us by its unsentimental clarity in the analysis of power. Its force and appeal derive in large part from its avoidance of the hypocrisies and subterfuges of politics and its enlightened recognition of the importance of the natural processes in which history is grounded. These have been surgically detached from propaganda, moral justifications, and all "fair names" of rhetoric. Yet no persuasion results. The Melians are unable to make the Athenians recognize the advantages of arguments from justice or convention. The Athenians cannot convince the Melians to capitulate. *Logos*, despite its clarity and argumentative power, fails to avert the violence and destruction of war and is itself narrowed, distorted, and perverted.[43]

The Melians continue to resist. The reader too may find this the point at which he is unable to accept an analysis that sees only the power and self-interest of the stronger. The law of the stronger has been shown to be deeply rooted in human nature, but we have already glimpsed that it has another side—the natural tendency for smaller states to ally and resist aggression. And in the repudiation of their national identity as the opponents of despotism and of the enslavement of the Greeks we can begin to detect that the Athenians have cut themselves off from some of their sources of strength and come to resemble their ancient enemy, the Persians. Although the Melians are destroyed, the episode is never rounded off with a neat sentence of the sort that concludes the Plataean or Mytilenean affairs. We never hear "Such was the end of the Melian affair." Instead, with the destruction of Melos fresh in mind, we move directly to the great Athenian expedition against the island of Sicily.

[42] Herodotus 8.143, trans. Rawlinson. Cf. Deininger, *Der Melier Dialog*, p. 46, n. 65.
[43] Cf. C. W. Macleod, "Thucydides' Plataean Debate," *GRBS* 18 (1977) 233.

Book 6

THE DECISION TO INVADE SICILY

SUDDENLY the Athenians decide to invade Italy. The reader is plunged into a new undertaking of major proportions and awesome implications. Juxtaposed to the Melian episode,[1] without any discussion of the strategic background or the immediate circumstances of the decision, the first sentence of the book presents the Athenians' intentions in an extreme form: "The Athenians were wishing to sail against Sicily . . . and to subjugate it if they could."[2] The juxtaposition of this sentence with the Melian account is abrupt and powerful; there is no transition and, remarkably, no discussion of the strategic situation. Later we learn of Segesta's request for aid, of the plight of the citizens of Leontini, of the disputes that Syracuse had with other Sicilian cities, of the possibility that the Sicels and even the Etruscans might assist the Athenians.[3] When we

[1] The careful use of juxtaposition as a technique in book 3 lends plausibility to the view that Thucydides is deliberately emphasizing the connection between the Sicilian and Melian episodes. Cf. G. Murray, "Reactions to the Peloponnesian War in Greek Thought and Practice," *JHS* 64 (1944) 1ff. and R. Jebb, *Essays and Addresses* (Cambridge 1907) 436. It does not follow that Thucydides believed that Melos was the *hybris* and Sicily the *atē* in a cycle of cosmic retribution. See H.-P. Stahl, *Thukydides: die Stellung des Menschen im geschichtlichen Prozess* (Munich 1966) 160f., esp. n. 14 and W. Liebeschuetz, "The Structure and Function of the Melian Dialogue," *JHS* 88 (1968) 73ff.

[2] In 2.65.11 Thucydides argued that Athens' main mistake was not the decision to sail to Sicily but a failure to provide the expedition with the right kind of backing: οὐ τὰ πρόσφορα τοῖς οἰχομένοις ἐπιγιγνώσκοντες. The narrative of book 6 ultimately confirms this assessment. In the long run it becomes clear that the expedition itself would not have been a serious setback to Athens if subsequent decisions had not increased the scale and the risks. But at the opening of book 6 Thucydides emphasizes the folly of the decision itself. The tension with 2.65.11 is remarkable but must not be overinterpreted. As H. D. Westlake has shown ("Thucydides II, 65, 11," *CQ* 52 [1958] 102-110) the wording of 2.65 does not contradict book 6. In Thucydides' view it was a mistake to attack Sicily, but the subsequent decisions were even more pernicious. Thus there is no good basis for arguing about the relative time of composition of the two sections; what is clear is the difference in emphasis in the two settings.

[3] N.B. 6.6.2. The support of the Sicels, who controlled much of central and southern Sicily (6.2.5), could be especially important. The support of the Athenians by Archonides,

hear the language of the assembly's decision to send the expedition to Sicily, it is far more equivocal than Thucydides' own opening sentence. The decree enjoined the generals to bring aid to Segesta and to settle the Leontinian refugees if the war went well and "to arrange other matters in Sicily according to Athens' best interests"(6.8.2). In stripping away the pretenses of the decree and in emphasizing that Athens' objective was the subjugation of Sicily, Thucydides has considerable justification. As the first sentence of the book reminds us, Athens had long hoped to subjugate Sicily. This sentence binds together the simple, blunt statement of the objective of the expedition—"The Athenians began again to plan the subjugation of Sicily"—with a more complex and evocative statement about the type of expedition to be sent. They will sail with a greater force than that which Laches and Eurymedon had commanded some years before. That expedition, we remember, ended when the Sicilians arranged a settlement of their disputes, thereby eliminating any sound basis for continued Athenian intervention. When the assembly learned of this decision, it punished the Athenian commanders for failing to "subjugate" the island.[4] Thucydides' opinion of the Athenians' action was made fiercely explicit: "So using their present good luck they felt that nothing should stand in their way but that they could accomplish both the possible and the less feasible, either with a grand or equally well with a more deficient force. The cause was success on many counts beyond expectation, which gave them the underpinning of hope" (4.65.4). By alluding to the expedition under Laches and Eurymedon, Thucydides reminds his reader of Sicily's ability to unite when threatened. All parts of the sentence converge to emphasize the unreasonableness of Athenian ambitions. Thucydides further expands his sentence by introducing another important theme—the ignorance of the Athenians about the size and population of Sicily.[5] The first

---

the king of some of the Sicels, is not mentioned until the beginning of book 7 (7.1.4)—after his death. Etruscan support is requested in 6.88.6; they send the Athenians three fifty-oared ships in 6.103.2. The Athenians even have hopes of Carthaginian aid (6.88.6), perhaps not totally unreasonable in the light of later conflicts between Syracuse and Carthage. These episodes indicate the potential for a major anti-Syracusan coalition in the west. But Thucydides at the beginning of book 6 leaves this possibility obscure.

[4] 4.65.3. καταστρέψασθαι is the word used of the Athenian intentions in 6.1.1.

[5] The early books of the *Histories* emphasize the experience (*empeiria*) of the Athenians and rarely associate the word *apeiros* or its cognates with them. The Spartans are commonly represented as lacking the right kind of experience (1.141.3, cf. 1.72.1); the Athenians mock the Melians' *apeirokakon* (5.105.3). A thematic reversal begins with book 6, and by 7.61 Nicias' use of the old pattern of Athenian confidence in their experience is shown to be hollow and vain. Note also in presentations of the Persian invasion an emphasis on Xerxes' lack of experience, e.g. Lysias 2.27.

sentence, in other words, combines the sharpest and most unequivocal statement of the objective of the expedition with clear hints of Athenian folly.

It also leads directly into an excursus on the population and early history of Sicily and is, in effect, a second Archaeology setting the background for this new phase of the war.[6] The parallelism to the first book, however, heightens our awareness of an implicit contrast. The Archaeology, as we have seen, was a confident analysis of power, emphasizing the advantage enjoyed by naval and imperial states over continental land powers. It corroborates the observation, expressed by Pericles, "if we were islanders who would be more invulnerable?" (1.143.5). In the Sicilian narrative quite a different analysis of power is developed. The larger pattern of the sixth and seventh books, in which not only Athenian power but even the categories of analysis of power are confounded, is anticipated in the opening chapters of the sixth book. The contrast between island and continental powers, so central to the Archaeology, begins to break down. Athens, as was evident in the first book, is almost an island, separated from the surrounding countryside by its walls and deriving its strength primarily from naval power. Sicily, a vast island, is almost part of the Italian mainland, or, as Thucydides expresses it, "by approximately a twenty-stade measure of sea is kept from being a continent" (6.1.2). The antithesis, island versus continent, is thus broken down and we witness the conflict between a continental power that is almost an island against the major city of an island that is almost a continent.

No less significant is the impression of changeability in the first chapters of the book. The frequent migrations, the mingling of peoples, the instability of the Sicilian world is repeatedly illustrated. Again the categories of earlier Thucydidean analysis break down. The changeability of the Sicilian world, its lack of tranquility, *hēsychia*, invites the conclusion that the growth of its power would be impeded. Such would be the implications of the Archaeology in book 1 (e.g. chs. 2 and 12), and such is the inference drawn by Alcibiades, who argues that the changes and diversity of the island have prevented the development of military greatness (6.17.2-3). Eventually, however, it appears that the Sicilians, or at least the Syracusans, have an adaptability that allows them to develop effective naval techniques and to imitate and eventually surpass their innovative and bold attackers.

In describing the migrations, expulsions, and vicissitudes of Sicilian

[6] H. R. Rawlings III, *The Structure of Thucydides' History* (Princeton 1981) 62-67.

history, the narrative emphasizes, perhaps even exaggerates, the size of the island[7] and constantly leads the reader to look beyond the relatively narrow geographical limits of the earlier analysis to the more remote regions of the Mediterranean. The peoples of Sicily are migrants who have come from Troy, who have been driven out of Italy, or come from Spain or Phoenicia (6.2). The sense of vastness and unpredictability in the successive migrations and population movements and the feeling of the grandeur and magnitude of the west are highly appropriate indicators of the significance of the forthcoming actions.

The theme of the greatness of the war is reintroduced, a further link between the first and the sixth books. But a change in emphasis prepares the way for the grander reversal of the Sicilian narrative. Athenian power is unquestionably great, as its treatment of the island of Melos has made clear. But the emphasis has now shifted to the vastness of Sicily and the rashness of the hope to subjugate it; "Against Sicily, whose scale is such as has been indicated, the Athenians hastened on to make their expedition, craving as the truest reason to dominate all of it" (6.6.1). Throughout the account of the Sicilian Expedition the greatness theme continues its transformation until it is fully disassociated from the measurement of Athens' power and fully applied to the totality of its defeat.

Even at the outset, however, the reader is aware that what is in store for the Athenians is the greatest single disaster of the war. The prospect, moreover, is not entirely unwelcome. Melos is too fresh in our minds and Athenian severity too unmitigated. Such violence invited retribution. In the old Greek mythic world view the excesses of conquerors were often punished during their return over the high seas.[8] Their voyages change from triumphant celebrations to long wanderings, shipwrecks, and even annihilation. Something very similar to this, we know, will happen to the Athenians in Sicily. The Thucydidean reader, to be sure, is too enlightened to believe in any simple divine retribution, yet he realizes that the Athenians are about to overstep their proper boundaries, to set off over the high seas against an enemy whose strength has been misassessed. The reader also

[7] 6.1.2 says it takes a merchant vessel not much less than eight days to sail around Sicily. As Dover notes in *HCT* ad loc. (p. 197f.) this is excessive for a journey of roughly five hundred nautical miles, if the vessel sailed continuously with favorable winds. Ephorus (*FGrHist* 70 F 135) gave a shorter estimate. Is Thucydides exaggerating or is he simply using a more conservative figure based on a voyage that involved stops for rest or trade, or one that encountered adverse conditions?

[8] The pattern is generalized in Hesiod *Works and Days* 238-247, and evident in most accounts of the Greek return from Troy.

anticipates what will result: the suffering the Athenians have inflicted will be matched by the misery that awaits their expedition.[9]

Mythic patterns long established within Greek thought thus coincide with a rational and practical assessment based on the size and complexity of the Sicilian Expedition.[10] Nicias' speech urging reconsideration of the decision to go to Sicily, soon makes clear the difficulties and disadvantages of the expedition.[11] Nicias is introduced with language that emphasizes his reluctance to take on the command (a sharp contrast to Alcibiades' desire for advancement) and that echoes Thucydides' comments about the expedition's objectives and feasibility.[12] Nicias' rhetorical task is difficult, for he must urge inactivity on a people whose disposition is restless and active.[13] Much of the speech develops the obvious objections to an expedition of this sort: the Athenians still have many enemies in continental Greece and no secure settlement of their previous disputes; vital areas such as Chalcidice have not been brought back into the empire; even if Sicily were conquered it would be hard to hold on to. Up to this point we have

[9] Thus it may not be accidental that Thucydides, perhaps borrowing from Antiochus of Syracuse (K. J. Dover, "La Colonizzazione della Sicilia," *Maia* 6 [1953] 1-20), uses allusions to the most famous of the Greek returns home (*nostoi*), the return of Odysseus: 6.2.1 "Oldest of the inhabitants of the country are said to be the Cyclops and Laistrygonians." See also 6.2.2 with Dover's note in *HCT* ad loc. Surely the reader would here detect an allusion to *Odyssey* 11.107, the oxen of the sun. (Cf. 3.88.1 and 115.1) These allusions associate Sicily with the forces that impede Odysseus on his return to Ithaca.

The culmination of the *nostos* theme is of course the next to last sentence in book 7: πανωλεθρίᾳ δὴ τὸ λεγόμενον καὶ πεζὸς καὶ νῆες καὶ οὐδὲν ὅτι οὐκ ἀπώλετο, καὶ ὀλίγοι ἀπὸ πολλῶν ἐπ' οἴκου ἀπενόστησαν.

[10] On punishment in *nostoi* see L. Woodbury, "Neoptolemus at Delphi," *Phoenix* 33 (1979) 95-133, esp. 97.

[11] Why has Thucydides decided to present the reconsideration of the expedition rather than the initial decision itself? His choice creates a very dramatic scene by leading smoothly and without interruption through Alcibiades' counterarguments to Nicias' second rhetorical maneuver: an attempt to stop the expedition by pointing out how large a force would have to be equipped. But at the same time, Thucydides' selection of the second debate on the subject brackets this scene with the reconsideration of the decision about Mytilene (cf. 3.36.4). There second thoughts prove better; here the renewed deliberation simply compounds the initial difficulties. It also helps link the debate to the decision to ally with Corcyra (1.44.1).

[12] Note the echo of 6.6.1 in 6.8.4: in 6.6.1, ἐφιέμενοι μὲν τῇ ἀληθεστάτῃ προφάσει τῆς πάσης ἄρξαι, βοηθεῖν δὲ ἅμα εὐπρεπῶς and in 6.8.4, ἀλλὰ προφάσει βραχείᾳ καὶ εὐπρεπεῖ τῆς Σικελίας ἁπάσης, μεγάλου ἔργου, ἐφίεσθαι.

[13] His problem is very similar to that which confronted Pericles at the beginning of the war when the Athenians were tempted to leave the city walls and attack the invading Peloponnesians. Pericles had the *auctoritas*, and the audacity, to keep the Athenian assembly from meeting and thereby to prevent action under the influence of *orgē*: 2.22.1. Circumstances make it impossible for Nicias to use a similar method, but he is also much more reluctant than Pericles to come into direct conflict with the disposition of the Athenians and to risk their anger. From this reluctance come not only his devious rhetorical strategies but also his fatal decision to delay the withdrawal from Syracuse (7.48.4).

the sound arguments of a wise adviser,[14] who speaks honestly and forth-rightly, never concealing his own views, even if his opinions are likely to conflict with the natural disposition (*tropoi*) of his audience: "Nevertheless, neither in time past have I spoken other than my real opinion to win preferment nor do I now. I will talk in the way I think best. And my speech would be an ineffective response to your dispositions, if I advised you to keep what you have and not gamble with what is at hand for the uncertainties of the future. But I will show that your zeal is inappropriate and that it is not easy to control what you are hastening after" (6.9.2f.).

But as Nicias' speech continues, this one-dimensional portrait of him as the wise and disinterested adviser becomes more complex and ambiguous. The policies he urges are inappropriate and implausible—"We would be most likely to demoralize the Greeks in that area if we never came at all; second best would be to show the flag and leave soon thereafter" (6.11.4)—and completely in conflict with his audience's restless disposition. Nor does Nicias adequately deal with Athens' sworn treaty obligations to Segesta and its moral, if not legal, obligations to the refugees from Leontini.[15] Gradually he turns away from the problem of how to respond to a request for aid from allies in Sicily, to launch a personal attack on his opponents, and especially on Alcibiades: "If someone who likes to hold office advises you to sail, thinking of his own interests alone, especially if he is rather young to hold office, so he can be admired because of his stables and help pay for them from his official position, don't let such a person attain private splendor by risking the interests of the city" (6.12.2). The contrast between public and private interests so prominent in Nicias' speech functions in two ways. Nicias is represented as using it to criticize Alcibiades, as many politicians surely did. At the same time it has an ironic effect, for it also applies to Nicias himself. In Greek literature it is unusual for a wise adviser to indulge in personal attacks. His concerns and arguments are normally restricted to the public level. Lesser figures, as Thucydides has observed in his discussion of Pericles' successors, act "in accordance with their private ambitions and private profits" (2.65.7). In the same passage Thucydides looks ahead to the Sicilian Expedition and deplores the rivalries that "blunted the arrangements for the expedition and . . . threw the situation of the city into disarray" (2.65.11). Nicias' speech is a partial fulfilment of this analysis and thereby produces a strange dissonance. He advances telling objections

---

[14] On Nicias as an adviser figure see K. von Fritz, *Die Griechische Geschichtsschreibung*, vol. 1 (Berlin 1967) 728.

[15] 6.13.2 is his attempt to deal with the issue; Alcibiades' refutation is in 6.18.1.

to the proposed invasion, but his counterproposals and evident rancor raise doubts about the wisdom of his leadership and the well-being of the city.

Although Alcibiades' speech is, as oratory, a more brilliant performance, Thucydides' treatment is again by no means uncritical. Alcibiades is introduced with words that echo the comments about Cleon in book 4: "Alcibiades the son of Cleinias encouraged most enthusiastically this expedition."[16] Thucydides at first seems to be endorsing Nicias' criticism of Alcibiades and even to be adopting the ideas and language of Nicias' speech: "He [Alcibiades] wanted to oppose Nicias, both because he disagreed on other matters of civic policy and because Nicias had alluded to him in a personal attack. And in particular he desired the generalship and through that hoped to take Sicily and Carthage; and at a private level success would benefit him with funds and reputation. Since he had a position to maintain among his fellow citizens, he indulged in desires greater than his wealth would allow, in regard both to his stables and to other expenditures. This, more than anything else, later pulled down the city of Athens" (6.15.2ff.). But there is a typically Thucydidean change of expectation as the comments continue: "For the man in the street, fearing the extent both of his misconduct in his daily life in regard to his own body and of his plans about each specific matter he undertook, became hostile to him as someone who desired a tyranny. Even though at the public level he was most effective in the conduct of the war, at a private level they were annoyed at his way of life and turned to other leaders and before long tripped up the city."[17]

In these comments Thucydides shifts viewpoint and subverts Nicias' analysis. Alcibiades' extravagances and ambition are not the problem. Rather, we come to see that many Athenian citizens have confused private and public considerations. What damages the city is not Alcibiades but an inappropriate response to him. Even though Alcibiades' personal life may be reprehensible, his ability at public affairs is unequalled. This is precisely Alcibiades' own claim in the speech that follows: "Though there is a great

[16] 6.15.2. The same verb, ἐνῆγε, in 4.21.3 described Cleon's role in rejecting the Spartan peace initiative, as J. de Romilly points out in "Les problèmes de politique intérieure dans l'oeuvre de Thucydide," *Historiographia Antiqua* (*Commentationes Lovanienses in honorem W. Peremans*) (Leuven 1977) 83. This form of the verb occurs only in these two passages of Thucydides.

[17] 6.15.4. Excellent scholars have disagreed whether the allusion is to the failure of the Sicilian Expedition or to the ultimate fall of Athens. The phrase οὐ διὰ μακροῦ seems to me to support W. Schadewaldt's view (*Die Geschichtschreibung des Thukydides* [Berlin 1929] 11-12) that ἔσφηλαν refers to the Sicilian fall (which in turn foreshadows the ruin of Athens in 404). But see P. A. Brunt, "Thucydides and Alcibiades," *REG* 65 (1952) 60 and E. Kapp's review of Schadewaldt in *Gnomon* 6 (1930) 86.

sensation about my private life, ask if I am second to anyone in handling public matters" (6.16.6). Thucydides' introduction of Alcibiades thus moves from a restatement and apparent acceptance of Nicias' criticisms to a total reassessment of those criticisms. Simultaneously, it impels the reader, as so many Thucydidean reassessments do, to look at the long-range implications of individuals and their actions. The time-frame expands beyond the immediate situation to the ultimate effects of the loss of Alcibiades. In the long run the worst damage to Athens may have been caused not by the decision to go to Sicily, but by the repudiation of Alcibiades, by his subsequent withdrawal from Athens, and by his advice to the Spartans and later activities in Asia Minor. This suggestion is put forward so summarily and so obliquely that it cannot command immediate assent, but it leads the reader to view Alcibiades' speech with greater sympathy and a fuller appreciation of the brilliance that has always made Alcibiades such a powerful and controversial figure.[18]

The effect is strange and abrupt. We move suddenly from a recognition of the fundamental soundness of Nicias' advice on this occasion to an appreciation of the importance of Alcibiades' qualities and talents. This might be regarded simply as a transitional device or as a dramatic reversal to bring the reader over to Alcibiades' side. But in fact Alcibiades' arguments are far from compelling. When he deals with Sicilian power, for example, he propounds a glib and tendentious interpretation of the fact that the island had a great and diverse population. In his view the Sicilian cities are populated with "mixed rabbles" (6.17.2), constantly subject to changes and infusions of new populations.[19] In a sentence whose contorted syntax matches its devious logic, Alcibiades claims that the Sicilians have failed to develop a sense of civic loyalty but are constantly ready to move on after trying by rhetoric or *stasis* to aggrandize themselves (6.17.3). Obedience, common action, hoplite forces, he contends, are all likely to

[18] Thucydides emphasizes the brilliance of Themistocles by use of words built on the *lampr-* root in 6.12.2, 16.3, and 16.4. Rawlings in *The Structure of Thucydides' History*, 197 notes the echo of the description of Themistocles (and Pausanias) in 1.138.6. These "most brilliant men of their time," like Alcibiades, eventually fall into disgrace and collaborate with the enemy. On "brilliance" as a continuing claim of Alcibiades' family, see Lysias 14.25.

[19] Ἐπιδοχάς in 6.17.2 seems to me to compel the reading πολιτῶν, citizens, rather than πολιτειῶν, "constitutions." The latter, however, is defended by W. Peremans, "Thucydide, Alcibiade et l'expédition de Sicile," *AntCl* 25 (1956) 340 and by A. Masaracchia, "Tucidide VI 17, 2, 3," *Helikon* 17 (1977) 213-217. C. W. Macleod, "Rhetoric and History," *Quaderni di Storia . . . Bari* 2 (1975) 52 notes that Alcibiades' contemptuous allusions to the Sicilians as a mixed rabble might better apply to Athens' own force; cf. 6.69.3 and 7. 13.2.

be missing in such a society. Thus a probability argument, of the type often ascribed to the Sicilian founders of rhetoric, leads Alcibiades to a misinterpretation of the facts we have already learned in the opening chapters of the book. He is his own historian and infers weakness from evidence that we recognize is in fact indicative of power and grandeur. He allows the possibility of renewed Peloponnesian invasions without contemplating the possibility that Sparta might find new ways of applying her land power, as it had already done under Brasidas and as he would himself urge in recommending the occupation of Deceleia (6.91.6).

Thus the arguments of Alcibiades' speech are easily recognized as fallacious. His speech succeeds because his policies are grounded in the Athenian tendencies toward constant activity, expansion, and aggressiveness. Unlike Nicias, whose speech runs counter to Athenian dispositions, Alcibiades echoes Cleon in urging consistency with past practices and habits: "A city that has not avoided involvement, would seem to me most swiftly to be destroyed by a change to a policy of uninvolvement. A people that runs its city with the least divergence from established customs and habits, even if they are poor ones, lives most securely."[20] It is easy to see why Alcibiades' policies will appeal to the Athenians, not just on this point, but on the whole question of the expansion of the empire. More clearly than any other speaker, he articulates the rationale for continued expansion and the impossibility of establishing clear limits on Athens' empire: "We acquired this dominance, just as anyone else who has dominated, by coming enthusiastically to the aid of those who at any point called upon us, whether barbarians or Greeks. . . . It is not up to us to play accountant about how far we want to rule; since we are in this situation, we have to plot against some, hold on to others and recognize that there is a danger that we will be ruled by others if we do not ourselves rule them" (6.18.2f.). The significance of Alcibiades' speech, then, lies not in the force of its arguments for action against Sicily, but in its understanding and illumination of Athenian character.

Nicias is still not prepared to give in to the growing enthusiasm for the expedition. He makes a last attempt to stop it by using a technique well known from ancient rhetorical handbooks. If one cannot prevent an action by arguing it is wrong or not likely to succeed, one can urge that it is simply too troublesome or too expensive to undertake.[21] Nicias tries this

[20] 6.18.7; cf. 3.37.3

[21] Cf. the *Rhetorica ad Alexandrum* 1421 b 24f. urging that the speaker in such a situation should show if possible that the action he opposes is not just, lawful, expedient, honorable, pleasant and practical, "or failing this, that it is laborious and not necessary" (trans. H. Rackham in the Loeb Classical Library).

technique, elaborates the expense and the different types of forces that will be needed, urges the Athenians to view the expedition as a colonizing venture that must establish an unchallenged hold on the territory as soon as it arrives. Then, in characteristic fashion, he concludes his speech with a threat to resign if the assembly does not agree with him (6.23.3). He had used a similar threat in the debate on Pylos (4.28.1) when goaded by Cleon. His offer to resign his command had backfired badly when Cleon not only accepted the offer but brought off the coup at Pylos. Nicias has not learned. His management of the assembly is no better now than at the time of the Pylos debate. He has, moreover, abandoned his straightforward speaking for a more subtle rhetorical strategy, only to have it fail badly. Thus, instead of deflecting the Athenians from their rash plans, he has encouraged them to feel that such a large force ensures their safety: "They hastened on all the more and the reverse [of what he expected] happened to him. He seemed to give good advice and surely there would now be great security"(6.24.2). The irony of the comment simultaneously depends upon and reinforces the knowledge that the reader has and the assembly lacks. We are reminded of the disasters that will soon afflict the Athenians, the folly of their confidence, the magnitude of their miscalculation. We see them from an ironic distance and move, in effect, away from the assembly setting to view the forthcoming action from a broader perspective.

From this viewpoint mythic patterns emerge: "And Eros afflicted them all alike to sail forth" (6.24.3). The phrase is poetic, evocative of tragic drama, perhaps specifically modelled on the famous lines of Clytemnestra in Aeschylus' *Agamemnon* when she expresses her fear that some fatal desire for plunder and pillaging may have afflicted the Greek army at its moment of success and may have led it to impious acts before it began its journey home:

> Let not their passion overwhelm them; let no lust
> seize on these men to violate what they must not.
> The run to safety and home is yet to make; they must turn
> the pole, and run the backstretch of the double course.
> Yet, though the host come home without offence to high
> gods, even so the anger of these slaughtered men
> may never sleep. Oh, let there be no fresh wrong done![22]

---

[22] Aeschylus *Agamemnon* 341-347, trans. Richmond Latimore (Chicago 1953); cf. Euripides *Iphigenia in Aulis* 808, later echoed by Isocrates 10.52. F. M. Cornford, *Thucydides Mythistoricus* (London 1907) 214 pointed out the convergence with Aeschylus and asked, "Must not Thucydides have intended this dark allusion which so terribly fits the sequel?" I believe he must, but doubt that it implies, as Cornford argued, that Thucydides believed a process of retribution was at work whose agents were "disincarnate passions" (231) such as Eros and Elpis. This seems to me to overburden the text with an extraneous theology.

The echo of Aeschylus reminds the reader of the underlying mythic pattern and the traditional expectation of disaster for those who travel overseas after excessive violence. But a specific and highly analytical treatment of Athenian reactions accompanies this evocative and poetic language. Thucydides carefully catalogues the reactions of those of military age and of the older citizens and succinctly summarizes the factors that have in each group created confidence and enthusiasm. Mythic patterns and tragic language are juxtaposed with much more mundane descriptions of impulses, dispositions, and desires: the inveterate Athenian confidence, a yearning to see and visit new lands,[23] and the hope of good pay now and of power to produce state support for all time to come.[24] Thucydides does not hesitate to brand these desires as excessive.[25] It is easy to concur in this judgment. The ironic viewpoint adopted here, in which we are encouraged to look down from an Olympian height upon the mistaken plans and excessive desires of the Athenians, discourages any immediate sympathy for their plight. The sufferings of Melos, moreover, are still fresh in our minds. The Athenians will receive in Sicily what they gave in Melos. And they will deserve it. We assent; perhaps we even feel some pleasure in the foreknowledge of so just a punishment.

THE DEBATE AT SYRACUSE

The brilliant writing of much of the sixth and seventh books has been so widely acclaimed and the story of the expedition and its successive setbacks and failures is so well known that there is no point in retelling Thucydides' story. But within the narrative of the departure of the expedition, of its progress to Corcyra and then to Sicily, and of its eventual assault on

---

The reader is, to be sure, invited to recognize a paradoxical conviction in Thucydides, that some of what earlier Greek thought had affirmed about the *kosmos* still prevails, although in radically different ways, in the universe he describes. While recognizing the allusion to Aeschylean tragedy, we must not overlook the reference back to Diodotus' words in 3.45.5. Here too appears an emphatic use of *erōs*, identified as one of those forces that drive humans, despite laws and threats, to undertake grave dangers.

[23] 6.24.3: τῆς τε ἀπούσης πόθῳ ὄψεως καὶ θεωρίας. The expression evokes Nicias' warning in 6.13.1 not to be δυσέρωτας . . . τῶν ἀπόντων. Note also the use of *epithymia* in each passage and the fear that opponents of the expedition would be intimidated. Nicias' worst suspicions come true.

[24] The proposed invasion, by promising private gain at a risk to the state, is thus a further confounding of the public-private distinction so important in the work.

[25] 6.24.4. Τῶν πλεόνων is ambiguous: it can refer to the desires of the majority that intimidate those who are unconvinced; at the same time it hints at Athenian *pleonexia*, their frequent reaching out for more; cf. 4.65.4.

Syracuse (65.3) are three subordinate episodes, surprising for the elaborateness with which they are developed. Each deserves attention. The first
is a debate in Syracuse about what response should be made to the rumor
of the Athenian assault. The second is the unusual treatment of the events
that eventually result in Alcibiades' flight to Sparta. The third is a new
statement of the rationale for Athenian imperialism. Each of these episodes
interrupts a rapidly moving and coherent narrative and is developed with
a complexity that at first seems not entirely necessary for the understanding
of the expedition and its outcome. But ultimately these episodes are important in shaping the reader's response to the Sicilian story. Hence we
will deal with each in turn, while alluding only in passing to the well-
known main narrative of the expedition.

First, the debate at Syracuse. For a long time, Thucydides assures us,
the Syracusans consider the rumors of the Athenian expedition incredible.[26]
Eventually the Syracusan assembly convenes to decide whether any action
should be taken. Thucydides reports two speeches, one by Hermocrates,
the eloquent advocate of the pan-Sicilian settlement of 424 B.C. described
in book 4 chapters 58 through 65, the other by a Syracusan demagogue
named Athenagoras, who attempts to discredit the reports of Athenian
action. After much discussion no significant action results. A third speaker,
an anonymous member of the board of generals, intervenes and assures
the assembly that the generals will take whatever measures are necessary.
The most crucial part of Hermocrates' advice, to ask the Peloponnesians
to renew their attacks upon Attica, is not accepted at this time.[27] Nor do
the Syracusans adopt his daring, perhaps foolhardy, plan of an immediate
naval counterexpedition to stop the Athenians before they reach Sicily.[28]

The lengthy debate produces no practical result. Nor does it provide an

---

[26] 6.32.3 (cf. The Spartans' reactions on the occupation of Pylos, 4.5.1). Why should the
Syracusans consider the reports incredible? Athens had long been bound by treaty to various
states in Magna Graecia, as we know from inscriptions (especially *ML*37, also in *IG* i³ 11,
the Segesta decree and *ML* 64, also in *IG* i³ 54, the treaty with Leontini renewed in 433/2).
In the Archidamian War, only a few years after the devastation of the Great Plague, Athens
had sent an expedition of twenty ships against Syracuse (3.86) and later committed forty
more ships (3.115.4 and 4.2.2). Syracuse's expulsion of the commons of Leontini in 422
(5.4) could certainly be expected to provoke appeals to Athens such as those alluded to in
6.19.1. Could the Syracusans have been so confident that Athens would take no retaliatory
action? More likely the rumors of the scale of the expedition—134 triremes (6.43)—were
incredible.

[27] The ambassadors are only dispatched in 6.73.2.

[28] Dover's judgment of the likely outcome of Hermocrates' plan (*HCT* on 6.34.4; p. 299),
"The annihilation of the Siceliot fleets and the rapid imposition of Athenian rule on Sicily
and South Italy," is challenged by M. Cogan, *The Human Thing* (Chicago 1981) 281, n.
25.

especially helpful analysis of what is so crucial for the outcome of the
expedition: the political situation within Syracuse. The hope of *stasis* and
of eventual treason figures prominently in Alcibiades' argument (6.17.4f.)
and in the last days of the expedition leads Nicias to resist a decisive
withdrawal from Syracuse.[29] Any glimpse into the workings of the Syracusan government would be of great interest. But this debate provides only
partial and insignificant information. Athenagoras, for example, appears
as an individual speaker of great force, but is not associated with any broad
policies or with any identifiable faction or constituency.

But if the debate does not illumine the political situation within Syracuse,
it does perform two important purposes in the text. The first is evident in
both Hermocrates' and Athenagoras' speeches. Hermocrates argues: ''[The
Athenians] will not be more able to inflict damage on you than to suffer
it themselves. Nor is the fact that they are coming with a great expedition
without its advantage. Rather it is much better for our relations with the
other Siceliots—for their astonishment will make them more willing to
ally with you''(6.33.4).

Athenagoras makes a similar point even more brashly: ''For it is not
likely that they would willingly take on another greater war, leaving the
Peloponnesians and the war in that region incompletely resolved. My
opinion is they are very happy that we, cities of the size and number that
we are, have not moved against them'' (6.36.4). These comments remind
us that great actions are not necessarily successful ones and that the Athenians are themselves vulnerable. As Hermocrates says, ''Few great expeditions, whether of Greeks or of barbarians, have been successful in
operations far from home'' (6.33.5). But to emphasize the rashness of the
Athenian expedition and the strength of Sicily cannot be Thucydides'
principal purpose in this section. Those points have already been established at the opening of the book, especially through the scene in the
Athenian assembly. The debate at Syracuse reinforces the impression developed in the earlier assembly scene and, by paralleling it, breaks into
new ground. The similarities between the two debates are instructive. Both
concern preparation for war (*paraskeuē*); both are triads, rather than the
more common pair of speeches. Both utilize the themes of youth versus
age, personal attacks on political rivals, the importance of mixture or
balance in a properly run political system.[30] But on a more fundamental

[29] 7.48.2; cf. 6.103f. and 7.49.1.

[30] *Youth versus age*: Nicias' attack on Alcibiades 6.12.2 (answered in 18.6); cf. Athenagoras 6.38.5-39.2. *Personal attacks*: Nicias' attack on Alcibiades in 6.12; cf. 15.2 and
Athenagoras *passim*, also the general's comment in 41.2. *Mixture or balance*: Alcibiades'
digression on mixture in 6.18.6; cf. Athenagoras in 6.39.

level both are scenes within a democratic assembly. They underline thereby an essential similarity in the political life of the two cities. Up to this point we—and the Athenians—have seen Syracuse as a remote Dorian city and have never penetrated beyond the simple collective label, "the Syracusans," to look at the nature of political life within their city.[31] In the beginning of book 6, for example, we were told that Syracuse was founded by a Heraclid from Corinth, an emphatic reminder of its Dorian origin. And the fear that Dorian Syracuse would lend Sicilian support to Dorians in the Peloponnese provided a major basis for the Segestans' appeal for Athenian intervention in Sicily (6.6.2). Now, for the first time, we look behind the Dorian facade and discover something surprising—a democracy very similar to Athens'. Athenagoras, in particular, is introduced in language that evokes Cleon.[32] And his speech is the demagogue's characteristic blend of facile argument, personal invective, and self-advancement. We have traveled to Syracuse and found Athens.

Hermocrates' speech is quite different. He recognizes the Dorian nature of Syracuse—that is, its disposition to slowness, caution, and tranquility,[33] but he urges the Syracusans to break away from this disposition. He alludes to a "habitual tranquillity" among the Syracusans and calls upon them to abandon it for vigorous and immediate action. He advises them, as Harry Avery has pointed out, "to conduct themselves exactly as the Athenians would under similar circumstances, without, however, explicitly urging them to emulate the Athenians."[34] In effect, he exhorts the Sicilians to transcend their Dorian habits and inheritance and acquire the traits of their opponents. When Hermocrates speaks in this way, the idea seems remote and perhaps implausible. The reader wonders at first whether these traits are not inherent in their Dorian origin and whether other patterns will be easily acquired.[35] But in Athenagoras' speech the possibility seems less

[31] As often, the first mention is significant: 3.86.2, which emphasizes that Syracuse has most of the Dorian cities in Sicily as her allies against Ionian Leontini. This introduces the important theme of the threatened "ethnic" war that the ambassadors from Segesta exploit in 6.6.2. In book 7 (esp. chapters 57 and 58) the conflict along ethnic lines gives way to a more complex pattern of interest grouping.

[32] 6.35.2; cf. 3.36.6 and 4.21.3; see Dover in *HCT* on 6.36 (p. 311).

[33] On tranquility (*to hēsychon*), often a Dorian characteristic, see Wade-Gery's comments in appendix D to his article, "Thucydides the Son of Melesias," *JHS* 52 (1932) 224f.; also in *Essays in Greek History* (Oxford 1958) 265f. He emphasized its contrast with *stasis* and *polypragmosynē*.

[34] H. C. Avery, "Themes in Thucydides' Account of the Sicilian Expedition," *Hermes* 109 (1973) 6.

[35] The dispute about the roles of inherited versus acquired characteristics is a lively one in Thucydides' day. The topic is especially evident in the *Philoctetes* of Sophocles (e.g. lines 88, 475, 971, 1284, 1310). See the discussion in P. W. Rose, "Sophocles' *Philoctetes* and the Teaching of the Sophists," *HSCP* 80 (1976) esp. 154, n. 20 and 88f.

farfetched. He contradicts Hermocrates on the disposition of the Syracusans: "The truth is that our city is only rarely tranquil, but is constantly
fomenting many factions and rivalries, more of them directed against itself
than toward its enemies—yes and tyrannies sometimes, and unfair cabals"
(6.38.3). As Athenagoras' speech progresses his polemic becomes so strongly
reminiscent of Athens that we begin to suspect that Hermocrates may have
overstated the tranquil nature of the Syracusans. They are, after all, as
Nicias has pointed out, similar in major respects to the Athenians, and are
themselves an imperial power (6.18.3).

The view of Syracuse that is provided by this debate is like an unexpected
reflection in a mirror. We turn expecting to see a remote, alien antithesis
to Athens and find instead a close analogue.[36] Gradually Thucydides makes
this similarity explicit. Nicias has alluded to one aspect of it in noting the
resemblance in the military preparations and resources of the two states.
The word he uses to denote the resemblance, *homoiotropos*, "similar-in-
disposition," is a rare one that Thucydides uses on two other occasions
to clarify the nature of the power that Athens had attacked. The first of
these is his comment before the great battle in the harbor at Syracuse when
he observes that the Athenians had attacked cities that were *homoiotropoi*
(7.55.2). This usage stresses the democratic nature of some Sicilian cities,
especially Syracuse, as well as their military resources. The Syracusans
would not be intimidated by force, nor subverted by the attractiveness of
Athenian support for democratic factions. The final use of the term in the
Histories extends the generalization even further beyond the military application of Nicias' speech. In book 8 when Euboea revolts from Athens,
Thucydides remarks upon the characteristic Spartan failure to exploit this
opportunity: "And not on this occasion alone did the Spartans prove to
be the most convenient of enemies for the Athenians but in many other
instances as well. Since they were totally different in disposition—one
group swift, the other slow; one aggressive, the other lacking in boldness—
they were extremely helpful, especially in a naval empire. The Syracusans
demonstrated this. Since they were especially similar in disposition (*homoiotropoi*), they fought most effectively against them"(8.96.5).

The comment makes explicit what we have inferred from the debate in
the assembly at Syracuse. It is not, however, immediately evident from
the narrative of books 6 and 7 that the similarity of Syracusan and Athenian

---

[36] Thucydides is not suggesting that Syracuse is in all respects like Athens, but that certain
crucial similarities are to be detected. The two cities are analogues not duplicates. Thus
Athens is the city that is almost an island (1.143.5; cf. pseudo-Xenophon *Athenaiōn Politeia*
2.14); Sicily is the island that is almost a continent (6.12).

character is an important cause of Syracuse's success. In the early part of the war the Syracusan similarity to Athens is at first only partial or latent. Initially the reader does not find sustained and effective boldness but a willingness to undertake some hazardous and ill-conceived ventures, followed by discouragement and dismay when they fail. In one case their willingness to try a bold attack on Catana is exploited by the Athenians and provides an opportunity for an unimpeded landing on Syracusan soil.[37] Even after the Syracusan naval victory in the great harbor they are reluctant to exploit their advantage and Hermocrates must trick the Athenians, very much as they had tricked the Syracusans at the beginning of the Sicilian campaign. He sends some seemingly reliable informants to the Athenian camp to advise them not to withdraw on that night since the Syracusans are guarding the roads.[38] Only gradually do the Syracusans fully embody the old Athenian charateristics. In a similar way the Athenians find it increasingly difficult to sustain and apply their old qualities of boldness, decisiveness, swiftness. Their counsels are divided; they lack the cavalry necessary for effective campaigning in Sicily and hence are unable to follow up on their initial success around Syracuse.[39] Although Thucydides never says so in so many words, we can infer that the same deficiency accounts for Lamachus' assent to Alcibiades' diplomatic offensive and hence to the delays that later (7.42.3) seemed so damaging to the Athenian cause.[40] On these occasions the Athenians are unable, often for perfectly good reasons, to show their normal characteristics. As the expedition goes on they are increasingly impeded by Nicias' un-Athenian inclination to delay and temporize, and by his reluctance to confront the natures of the Athenians.[41]

Is it then the Athenians' failure to display their normal characteristics,

[37] 6.63-65. Superior Athenian military skill is initially able to counteract or even exploit Syracusan boldness.

[38] 7.73.3. Cf. Themistocles' false message to Xerxes after Salamis, Herodotus 8.110.

[39] On cavalry and its significance in this campaign see W. Liebeschuetz, *Historia* 17 (1968) 301.

[40] Lamachus at first urges an immediate assault on Syracuse, then shifts to support Alcibiades' plan. Although his reasons are never made clear, we can conjecture that he recognized that the Athenian deficiency in cavalry made it unlikely that his plan would succeed. He therefore concluded that a diplomatic offensive aimed at securing cavalry and other support for the Athenian force was a prerequisite to effective military operations. It is odd, however, that Thucydides does not explain Lamachus' reasoning.

[41] 7.48.4. Cf. 7.14.2 and 6.9.3. Nicias assumes that Athenian character is established by *physis* and hence cannot be changed. The Thucydidean role for *physis*, however, is more circumscribed. National characteristics (*tropoi*) are not the product of *physis* but of historical circumstances and decisions. Hence a leader like Pericles can shape and control the disposition of the citizenry, although he might thereby risk his personal position and private interests. See 2.65, esp. sec. 1-3 and 8-9.

rather than the similarity between Syracusan and Athenian disposition, that accounts for the Syracusan success? Does Thucydides' narrative contradict his comments in book 8 and the inference we have drawn from the debate at Syracuse? To answer the questions in the affirmative would be to neglect one important feature of the narrative. In Thucydides national characteristics are not unchanging. The Athenians themselves were not always as they are today. They "became nautical" at the time of Salamis, when the Persians attacked and they adopted the plan of leaving their city and going into their ships (1.18.2 and 1.93.3). Even within the narrative of the war we can observe developments as new leaders appear and as new circumstances confront them. In a similar way the Syracusans change as the expedition continues and as their own navy becomes successful against the Athenians. When the Athenians first sail against Syracuse, the citizens have not even manned their ships (6.52.1). But as the war continues, the Syracusans become more bold and gradually more expert in the techniques of naval fighting. They acquire the *technē* that Pericles emphasized had taken the Athenians so long to develop (1.142.7ff.). Throughout book 6 the Syracusans make no significant effort on the sea; but after Gylippus' arrival their confidence grows and soon they are willing to try to meet the Athenians on the sea as well as on the land (7.7.4). Although at first they are not successful, Gylippus and Hermocrates persuade them to keep trying. One of their arguments is that the Athenians' knowledge of the sea was not something they had acquired from their ancestors nor had always possessed. They argue that the Athenians had once been mainlanders and had been compelled by the Medes to become naval (7.21.3). The Syracusans' confrontation with the Athenians at sea is again unsuccessful for they are unable to maintain the proper order in their fleet and "handed the victory over to the Athenians" (7.23.3), but the simultaneous land victory at Plemmyrion presents the Syracusans with a great opportunity to harass the shipping of the Athenians and make it more difficult to supply the invading army (7.24.3). Syracusan confidence and skill grow (7.37.1) as the Athenians are tricked and beaten (7.40) and as the Syracusans become technical innovators in the design and operation of triremes.[42] Thus when Gylippus returns with further reinforcements, the Syracusans immediately prepare again to engage the Athenians in a land and sea battle (7.50.3). Success in this engagement leads to the bold and skillful plan of attempting to prevent the Athenian withdrawal from Syracuse (7.56.2).

As we trace through the Syracusan naval efforts we see the growing

[42] 7.36.3 and 40.5; cf. 1.13.2f.

confidence and the increasing assimilation to the qualities that in the early parts of the *Histories* have been ascribed to the Athenians. The Syracusans, like the Athenians, are forced to become naval, and as they do so they increasingly display the qualities of vigor and boldness that the Athenians showed in the second Persian invasion and in the years leading to the outbreak of the Peloponnesian War. This change results in a new relationship: the Athenians are to the Syracusans as the Persians once were to the Athenians themselves. The threat posed by the invading force drives the other power to take to the sea and to adapt its ways to new circumstances. The Melian episode had established an analogy between Athenian conduct and that of the Persians. The comparison of the Athenian expedition to the Persian invasion of Greece has already been hinted at in the description of its departure from the Piraeus.[43] Hermocrates makes the comparison more explicit: "Few great expeditions whether of Greeks or of barbarians have been successful in operations far from home" (6.33.5). As he continues he explores the causes and effects of this general rule and relates it explicitly to the Persian invasion of Greece:

For [the Athenians] are not more numerous than the inhabitants and their neighbors (all things stand together because of their fear). In addition, if they should fail through want of provisions in a foreign land, they leave a reputation to those against whom they have plotted, even if the responsibility for their stumbling is primarily their own. This is what happened to these very Athenians when the Mede unexpectedly had a great failure: They grew in power on the basis of the reputation that Athens had been the objective of their attack; it is not beyond hope that something similar will happen for us. (6.33.5f.)

Thus in Hermocrates' view Syracuse is embarking upon a course whose practicality is supported by the past experience of Greeks against Persians and whose implications are a growth of power and fame. This idea grows as Syracusan confidence rises and leads eventually to the plan of trying something the Greeks did not attempt against the Persians: preventing their withdrawal.[44] That plan changes everything. Up to now Athens has risked a serious military setback, the loss of some ships, much wealth, and many men, but it has always seemed reasonable to expect that the expedition as a whole could be extricated. Athens' command of the seas would surely guarantee a successful withdrawal if victory proved impossible (6.18.5). If naval supremacy were lost, the Athenians could in all probability with-

---

[43] 6.32. The race is similar to that described in Herodotus 7.44.

[44] Herodotus 8.108-110 indicates the idea was advocated by Themistocles but rejected. Hermocrates now surpasses the Athenian statesman in boldness.

draw by land to friendly cities within Sicily. After all, the Persians had been allowed to make their withdrawal from Greece after their defeats at Salamis and Plataea. But the new confidence and ambition of Syracuse leads to the unpredicted: the attempt to prevent the Athenian withdrawal, and ultimately to huge Athenian losses and the imprisonment in the quarries at Syracuse of the remnant of the Athenian army.

These long-range developments are not, to be sure, fully evident when the debate in the Syracusan assembly gives us our first glimpse inside this city. But, as we have seen, that debate does alert us to one important similarity between Athens and Syracuse, hints that Athens may be surprised by what she finds in Sicily, and reintroduces a theme that will prove of great significance as the Sicilian narrative develops: the parallelism between the Athenian and the Persian invasions. As this theme becomes more prominent, it reinforces the feeling that Athens has overstepped both geographical boundaries (6.13.1) and the limits of civilized behavior and entered a world of unbounded possibilities, either for aggrandizement, as Alcibiades suggested (6.18.2f.), or for loss, suffering, and destruction.[45]

THE OVERTHROW OF THE TYRANNY

As the city of Athens moves across moral and physical boundaries in its attack on Sicily, it is also moving chronologically backward to confront its own past.[46] The analogy between the Persian invasion and the Athenian attack on Syracuse, as we have seen, involves a recapitulation of a crucial episode in the history of the city, with a reversal of Athens' role. A similar movement may help explain a puzzling digression in the middle of the sixth book: the account of the overthrow of the sixth-century tyranny. Thucydides' version is in part a renewal of Herodotus' (5.55-65) refutation of the popular story that two bold Athenians, Harmodius and Aristogeiton,

[45] We naturally state this in the metaphor of boundaries, one fully developed in Greek civilization esp. for the Persian War (e.g. Lysias 2.29) and implicit in Thucydides' emphasis on the lack of geographical limits in Alcibiades' ambitions (esp. 6.90.2f.). But Thucydides also uses financial metaphors, e.g. Alcibiades' statement that it is not up to Athens to act like a treasurer about how far to dominate (6.18.3). This metaphor links the attack on Sicily to the "expenditure" of lives in the war. See also Chapter Seven, Note 11.

[46] Symbolically, the city itself, not an Athenian expedition, moves against Syracuse. The first adumbrations of this idea are introduced through the "colonization theme," i.e. the attack is compared to or represented as a colonizing effort rather than a normal military expedition. See 6.23.2 and 63.3 and Avery, *Hermes* 101 (1973) 1-13. Athens itself is eventually reduced to the status of a fort, *phrourion* (7.29.1), and the expedition identified with the city: 7.75.2 and 77.4 and 77.7.

liberated Athens from the hated Pisistratid tyranny by killing the tyrant Hipparchus.[47] It is also, however, an exploration of similarities between Athens' past and present conduct and at the same time an inquiry into a surprising and paradoxical connection between them.

The setting of this digression is the cause célèbre of 415 B.C., the mutilation of the herms, sacred stone images that stood in many places in Athens and were defaced shortly before the expedition was scheduled to sail to Sicily. Simultaneously rumors circulated that in private houses the Eleusinian mysteries had been parodied (6.28). Alcibiades was implicated but his guilt could not be determined before the departure of the expedition. After much discussion it was decreed that he should sail to Sicily, even though he might later have to return to Athens for trial (6.29).

Once Thucydides has related the arrival of the expedition in Sicily, he returns to the affair of the herms and the mysteries and reports a subsequent stage of the Athenian inquiry into the matter. Unnamed informers of dubious reputation,[48] he says, made accusations that were not critically evaluated. The citizenry became very suspicious and was inclined to investigate every charge, no matter how dubious the informant or how distinguished the accused: "For the people, who knew by word of mouth that the tyranny of Pisistratus and his sons had ended by being repressive and further that it had been overthrown not by themselves and Harmodius but by the Lacedaemonians, were constantly frightened and took everything suspiciously" (6.53.3). These introductory comments lead into a long digression on the fall of the tyranny and then, in ring composition, to a restatement of the suspicion of the Athenians, especially against Alcibiades.[49] Finally,

[47] Thucydides attacked one portion of the story in 1.20.1. Although Thucydides' account corrects Herodotus in some respects (cf. K. H. Kinzl, "Zu Thukydides über die Peisistratidai," *Historia* 22 [1973] 504-507), perhaps also Hellanicus (v. F. Jacoby, *Atthis* [Oxford 1949] 158-165), it emphasizes that it was the revised or more accurate version of the Pisistratid story that in 415 led to the exaggerated fear of renewed tyranny. It is not so much a false understanding of the past that misleads (although Stahl, *Thukydides* ch. 1 is correct in pointing out that the Athenians failed to understand the reasons for the increasing severity of the Pisistratid regime) as an awareness of the inadequacies of the traditional legend about Harmodius and Aristogeiton. The excursus thus serves, among its other purposes, as a comment on the dangers inherent in historical knowledge.

[48] Thucydides stresses the *ponēria* of those who accused individuals who were *chrēstoi*. On class attitudes in the passage see Rawlings, *The Structure of Thucydides' History*, 101-115; contrast the Spartan response to a similar situation: 1.132.5.

[49] The ring structure has been noted and variously schematized by K. H. Kinzl, "Mehr zu Thukydides über den Peisistratidai," *Historia* 25 (1976) 478-480, and Rawlings, *The Structure of Thucydides' History*, 108, n. 65. In my opinion the organization is best represented by the schematization in Appendix Six.

The ring composition facilitates the interpretation of the passage. The framing of the Harmodius and Aristogeiton episode, for example, alerts the reader to the personal and

we learn of Alcibiades' recall from Sicily, his flight to Sparta, and his condemnation, *in absentia*, to death (6.60-61).

The common scholarly tendency to assume that all digressions in Thucydides are irrelevant to the main purposes of the narrative has led many excellent scholars to regard the story of the overthrow of the tyranny as extraneous—a mere interlude, a youthful essay inappropriately injected into the *Histories*, an insertion by Thucydides' editor, or a pedantic correction of his predecessors.[50] There is, however, an ostensible connection to the events of 415 B.C.: the use in the Athenian assembly and perhaps elsewhere of arguments of the sort, "Beware, men of Athens of the would-be tyrant: for nothing is easier than to give yourselves into the hands of a tyrant, but nothing harder than to escape him again. Why not even the tyrannicides. . . ."[51]

This connection, however, fails to account for the length and complexity of the digression. Nor is the reader likely to be content with the superficial link provided by the political use of the story of the tyrannicides. At the very beginning of the digression comes a clear warning to be cautious and skeptical about popular attitudes. These are said to derive from word of mouth transmission, *akoē*, always a hazardous source of information.[52] The use of ring composition and the interpretation of the conspiracy of Harmodius and Aristogeiton as an act of erotic boldness link the digression to the theme of *erōs* so prominent in the work. We are reminded thereby of the comment in 6.24.3 on the widespread enthusiasm for the expedition, "And *erōs* afflicted them all alike to sail forth."[53] The influence of *erōs*

---

accidental elements in the plot against the tyrants. In a similar fashion, the modulation in the treatment of the theme of "severity/repression" (C in the schematization) emphasizes the prominence of this theme and its ultimate transference from the enemies of the *dēmos* to the *dēmos* itself. In general the careful repetitions of language closely link the story of Harmodius and Aristogeiton to the situation in 415 B.C.

[50] C. Schneider, *Information und Absicht bei Thukydides* (Göttingen 1974) 62, n. 111 and items 345-354a in his bibliography (197f.) provide a convenient introduction to the scholarship on this point. Note especially E. Schwartz, *Das Geschichtswerk des Thukydides*, 2nd ed. (Bonn 1929), 180-186. Dover in *HCT* on 6.54-59 (p. 329) is unwilling to allow the passage any great significance; he feels that Thucydides yielded "to the temptation before which all historians . . . are . . . weak, the temptation to correct historical error wherever they find it, regardless of its relevance to their immediate purpose."

[51] The phrasing is Dover's in *HCT* on 6.54-59 (p. 329).

[52] 6.53.3; cf. 6.60.1 and 1.20.1, introducing the first excursus on the Pisistratids. *Akoē* can be useful if subjected to careful examination, but that is missing in 415 B.C., as οὐ δοκιμάζοντες τοὺς μηνυτάς (6.53.2) emphasizes. See also Rawlings, *The Structure of Thucydides' History*, 115f.

[53] The association between tyranny and *erōs* is strong in fifth-century literature, e.g. Herodotus 6.62 and Euripides fr. 850 Nauck *TGrF*[2]: ἡ γὰρ τυραννὶς πάντοθεν τοξεύεται/ δεινοῖς ἔρωσιν, ἧς φυλατέον πέρι. Note also Alcibiades' association of himself with

provides the motivation for Harmodius and Aristogeiton's conspiracy. They are not political reformers or liberators, but lovers, threatened by the intervention of a member of the Pisistratid house into their erotic relationship, and offended by Hipparchus' insult to one of their families.[54] Their conspiracy emerges out of personal considerations, although it swiftly impinges upon the public realm. The analogy to 415 B.C. is evident, for there too private considerations shaped public events (e.g. 6.28.2). Once the reader begins to look beneath the surface connection of digression to main narrative, further thematic affinities swiftly appear. Both the conspiracy against the Pisistratids and the invasion of Sicily, for example, are presented as acts of inappropriate or misdirected boldness, *tolma*.[55] Perhaps the most significant of these thematic links is the emphasis on severity and repression. In each case the result of boldness is an unexpected increase in repression. The burdens of the Pisistratid tyranny were at first quite light and its accomplishments substantial (6.53.5f.). The effect of Harmodius and Aristogeiton's act was not liberation but increasing repression (6.59.2). Fear that a new tyranny, with Alcibiades as its leader, would prove repressive motivates the Athenians' intense concern about the alleged conspiracy of 415 B.C. (6.53.3). But as the reader moves through the ring structure, the surface analogy between the Pisistratid tyranny and Alcibiades' role, is recognized as facile, misleading, and pernicious. As it is subverted, new relationships emerge. The Athenians, like Harmodius and Aristogeiton, are under the influence of *erōs* and engaged in an act of unwarranted boldness.

At the end of the digression, when the ring composition leads back to the situation of 415, a further shift takes place. The structure again calls attention to the theme of severity or repression, but in a new and surprising way. The Athenian citizenry, which initially feared a recurrence of tyrannical severity, is now depicted as *chalepos*, severe and repressive, against its own citizens and as conducting a frenzied and ill-advised search for the guilty parties (6.60.1-61). Athens comes to resemble the tyrants, in their

---

Eros (Plutarch *Alcibiades*, esp. 16f.; cf. W. Arrowsmith, "Aristophanes' Birds: The Fantasy Politics of Eros," *Arion* n.s. 1 [1973-74] esp. 141-143). Since erōs and tyranny can both be represented as sicknesses, we have a close convergence of some of the main metaphorical systems of the *Histories*.

[54] The narrative in 6.56.2-58.2 contains several indications that Thucydides may have played down the extent to which there was a serious political opposition to the tyrants. Their fellow conspirators (6.56.2, 57.2; cf. 1.20.2) may have been motivated more by a desire to end Pisistratid rule rather than by the desire to avenge the grievances of Harmodius and Aristogeiton.

[55] Note the use of *tolma* and its cognates in 6.54.1 and 59.1; cf. 6.31.6 and 33.4.

last stages, when fear and suspicion led them to repression. And in a culminating irony, Alcibiades flees to the Peloponnese, as Hippias had fled to the court of the Persian King Darius.[56] He is not a tyrant, but is led by Athens' increasingly tyrannical mood to act as an enemy of his city. The digression thus anticipates the future course of Alcibiades' actions, including his crucial role as an adviser to the Lacedaemonians in their renewed operations against Athens.

After Athens' defeat in Sicily, Thucydides again emphasizes the repressiveness and suspicion in the city.[57] The reader is thus led to see that Athens is losing one of the qualities, its avoidances of suspicion, that distinguished it at the beginning of the war—or so at least Pericles claimed in the Funeral Oration: "Our civic relations are based on freedom both in respect to public business and as regards suspicion toward one another concerning the habits of our daily life. We do not hold our neighbor in anger if he does something to please himself nor do we impose burdens upon one another that, although not official penalties, are nonetheless grievances to behold."[58] The efforts to avoid a tyranny have resulted in a loss of some of the most essential features of the free civic order Athens prized so highly. In seeking to protect itself from a tyranny Athens begins to become a tyrant and a tyrant whose effects are felt not so much by its subjects as by its own citizens.[59]

THE CONFERENCE AT CAMARINA

The comparison of Athens to a tyrant occurs once more in book 6, in a very significant context. Athens' success in Sicily, it becomes clear, will

[56] Hippias: 6.59.4; Alcibiades: 6.61.7, cf. L. Pearson, "Note on a Digression of Thucydides," *AJP* 70 (1949) 186ff.

[57] Cf. the echoes of 6.60-65 in 8.1.1f. Cf. W. R. Connor, "Tyrannis Polis," in *Ancient and Modern: Essays in Honor of G. F. Else*, ed. J. H. D'Arms and J. W. Eadie (Ann Arbor 1977) 95-103.

[58] 2.37.2. Text, interpretation, and translation are all difficult. In the last phrase, for example, does τῇ ὄψει go with προστιθέμενοι (Classen) or with λυπηράς (Steup)? Word order and the Thucydidean attitude that ὄψις is an agent for λύπη (6.75.2f.) suggest that Thucydides means expressions of mutual animosity, the sight of which causes grief among citizens. Textual doubts have often been expressed about ὑποψίαν; see Gomme in *HCT* ad loc. (p. 111) and J. N. Madvig, *Adversaria Critica*, vol. 1 (Hauniae 1871) 310, since the sense is clearly that Athenians were free from suspicion. But the reader does not need to emend; the phrasing is a typical Thucydidean ellipsis for "the extent of suspicion."

[59] There is a further paradox. By an ostensibly rational and logical use of historical analogy the Athenians become impassioned (ὀργιζομένων, 6.60.2; cf. the action of Harmodius and Aristogeiton δι' ὀργῆς in 6.57.3).

in large measure depend upon which of two views of the Sicilians turns out to be correct. Hermocrates in book 4 urged, and even temporarily achieved, a settlement of the disputes that had divided the Greek cities of Sicily. In his view Sicily could and should combine to resist external intervention. His speech at Syracuse (6.33.5) had reaffirmed this view of his island. Alcibiades in the Athenian assembly (6.17) had drawn the opposite conclusion and argued that the Sicilians were a rabble incapable of concerted action.[60] His strategy, which is adopted by the other Athenian commanders (6.50.1), begins with diplomatic efforts to win allies in Sicily and to prevent any concerted action on behalf of Syracuse. It becomes difficult to implement this strategy, however, when its author flees to the Peloponnese (6.61.6). Yet during the winter of 415-414 the Athenians continue their diplomatic offensive. A debate at Camarina provides an opportunity to examine the progress of their efforts and to investigate again the conflicting views about the Sicilians. Although the ostensible subject of the debate is the Athenian appeal for Camarina's support, just below the surface is the question of Sicilian unity. Its advocate is again Hermocrates who attempts to repeat his earlier accomplishment of persuading the Sicilian states to resist Athenian interference. His approach, however, is quite different from the one he adopted at Gela. Now he emphasizes the ethnic conflict between Dorian and Ionian, as well as the record of Athenian imperialism.

The Athenian reply to Hermocrates is delivered by an otherwise ill-attested Euphemus,[61] and it is he who introduces the comparison of Athens to a tyranny. His case depends on two main arguments. One is that Syracuse herself is an imperial power and, hence, a likely threat to Camarina. The other is that Athens will not attempt to deprive the Sicilian cities of their independence. The second is a most difficult point to establish, given Athens' conversion of the Delian league into an Athenian empire. The reader, moreover, knows that Athens' ambitions are to subdue Sicily, if they are able (6.1.1). But in support of his call for an alliance with Athens Euphemus uses original, powerful—and revealing—arguments. His case turns on a comparison of Athens to a tyranny: "For a man who is tyrant or for a city that has an empire nothing is irrational if advantageous and there is no bond except reliability."[62] Euphemus implicitly accepts the

---

[60] Cf. Note 19 above.

[61] 6.81-87. On his speech see especially H. Strasburger, "Thukydides und die politische Selbstdarstellung der Athener," *Hermes* 86 (1958) 17-40.

[62] 6.85.1. The sense is perfectly clear but an English translation is difficult. Οἰϰεῖος is commonly rendered with "kin" or some cognate—an overtranslation. Ἄλογον answers Hermocrates' charge οὐ γὰρ δὴ εὔλογον in 6.76.2. (On the correspondences between

charge that Athens is like a tyranny, but dilutes its force by suggesting that any imperial power shares the essential mark of a tyranny—a reliance on self-interest in determining policy. By establishing that principle, Euphemus is able to attack a major point in Hermocrates' speech: that it is not reasonable (*eulogon*) to expect that the same power that uproots and subjugates cities in eastern Greece would benignly seek a settlement for the Leontinians in western Greece (6.76.2). Hermocrates wishes his audience to draw the obvious conclusion that Athens will be a destroyer of freedom in Sicily as in the Aegean. But Euphemus, by accepting what seems a very dark assessment of Athenian character and motives, can argue that there is a consistency in Athenian actions, for self-interest dictates that his city support the freedom of cities in Sicily while elsewhere denying autonomy:

> Our advantage here is not that we should harm our friends, but that our enemies should be unable to inflict that harm because our friends are strong. Do not refuse to believe this; for even there our leadership of the allies is adapted to their individual utility. The Chians and the Methymnaeans are independent through their contributions of ships. Many others we lead more forcefully by the imposition of tribute; still others are quite free allies because they are located in convenient spots around the Peloponnese, even though they are islanders and easily seized. (6.85.1f.)

At the same time the levelling of all imperial powers into tyrannies provides an easy transition to Euphemus' condemnation of Syracuse and his confident assertion about her intentions: "They desire to dominate you and hope by rallying you in suspicion of us to dominate Sicily by force or by default, if we withdraw without having accomplished anything."[63]

This sentence is perhaps the most explicit of many statements in the *Histories* about the domination of imperial policy by considerations of advantage. But unlike other such statements—Diodotus' speech or the Melian Dialogue—the argument from advantage here coalesces with an argument from justice. The two considerations, so often radically opposed, converge, but converge in an unexpected fashion. Euphemus argues that

---

Euphemus' speech and Hermocrates' see J. de Romilly, *Histoire et raison chez Thucydide* [Paris 1956] 189ff.). At the same time ἄλογον suggests the important theme of the use of *logos* in the *Histories*, and the progression from the shaping of policy by rational analysis (Pericles) to the gradual subversion of *logos* by considerations of advantage (e.g. Corcyra 3.82) and thence to the identification of reason with advantage in this speech, the implications of which become clear in the subsequent narrative.

[63] 6.85.3 Syracusan imperialism undoubtedly was a threat to Sicilian states; but a more serious danger was posed by Carthage whose interventions soon put both Syracuse and Camarina on the defensive. Camarina fell to Carthage in 406 B.C. Athens seeks Carthaginian support (6.90.2), but Alcibiades sees that success in Sicily would entail eventual conflict with Carthage (6.15.2, 90.2).

Athens is justified in dominating her subjects, and justified precisely by the radical antithesis between Ionian and Dorian that Hermocrates used to persuade the Camarinans to adopt a pro-Syracusan policy: "We come for the renewal of the previously existing alliance but since the Syracusan has touched on the matter, we must also argue that it is to be expected that we should have the dominance we enjoy. The most important evidence he himself supplied—the Ionians are eternally hostile to the Dorians. And that is indeed the case. Since we are Ionians, we planned in what way we would be least subject to the Dorians in the Peloponnese who were more numerous than we" (6.82.1f.).

The speech adapts a very succinct version of the usual account of the growth of Athenian power to the newly emphasized thesis of inveterate enmity between Ionians and Dorians. The ideas, and even some of the phrases, are ones that we have heard before, especially in the speech of the Athenian ambassadors at Sparta before the outbreak of the Archidamian War.[64] But soon the speech takes a new turn. The argument shifts from the familiar line that the allies themselves chose the Athenians as their leaders and that Athens was then compelled to develop its position of leadership to its present extent. Euphemus proceeds to develop a totally new argument—that Athens, having been chosen leader by these allies, did nothing wrong in subjugating them:

For they came against their mother city—against us—along with the Persians and did not have the boldness to break away and destroy their own holdings as we did when we abandoned our city [at the Battle of Salamis]. But they wanted enslavement and wanted to bring it upon us. As a result we deserve our dominance—because we supplied the largest fleet and the most unhesitating enthusiasm among the Greeks and because they willingly acted for the Persians and harmed us. Furthermore we were seeking strength against the Peloponnesians. (6.82.4-83.1)

The novelty of the argument is made all the more emphatic by its initial resemblance to, and then divergence from, a similar passage in the speech of the Athenian ambassadors at Sparta. They too adduced three of their accomplishments in the Persian wars: "We supplied three most useful things in it—the largest number of ships, the cleverest man as general, and an unhesitating enthusiasm" (1.74.1). Two of these three considerations are repeated in similar language in Euphemus' speech. But the third—the allusion to Themistocles as the cleverest general—is replaced

---

[64] Note the following similarities between 6.82.1, ὡς εἰκότως ἔχομεν, and 1.73.1, οὔτε ἀπεικότως ἔχομεν; between 6.82.2, τὸ μὲν οὖν μέγιστον μαρτύριον αὐτὸς εἶπεν, and 1.73.5, τεκμήριον δὲ μέγιστον αὐτὸς ἐποίησεν; and between 6.82.3, αὐτοὶ δὲ . . . ἡγεμόνες καταστάντες, and 1.75.2, τῶν ξυμμάχων καὶ αὐτῶν δεηθέντων ἡγεμόνας καταστῆναι.

by the new argument that because some Ionian cities contributed (under duress) contingents to the invading Persian force, Athens was justified in later reducing them to servitude. We recognize this as specious and realize how radically Athenian views of their past have changed since the earlier debate at Sparta. The Athenians on that occasion were, to be sure, tough-minded and unsentimental. They did not deny the operation of fear, honor, and advantage in their development of the empire nor did they pretend that all was kindness and affection in their rule. But they allowed some role for justice and mutual accomodation and some element of self-restraint (1.76.3-77.3). The pressures working against that restraint are evident throughout the *Histories*, not least in the second book in which Pericles, after emphasizing in the Funeral Oration the services which Athens renders to "her friends,"[65] turns in his last speech to the famous comment about the empire: "You now hold this as if a tyranny—to have seized it seems wrong but to give it up is dangerous" (2.63.2). A similar phrasing, as we have seen, was later adopted by Cleon in his famous criticism of the Athenians: "You do not consider the fact that you hold your empire as a tyranny, against the will of subjects who are plotting against you" (3.37.2). The gradual hardening of attitude and the gradual disappearance under the pressures of war of the relaxed self-confidence of Athens, is now reaching its fulfillment. The confidence and restraint envisioned in the Funeral Oration are replaced by the suspicion and repression described in the sixth book.

Thucydides' technique is one he often uses. He does not speak out directly or explicitly. Instead he records the change by noting gradual, almost imperceptible, shifts in language and argument. There are few sudden breaks in mood or attitude, but rather a progressive hardening, as imperial dominance and the argument from advantage are freed from re-straints and extended into new areas. This technique is the infinitesimal calculus of power, a vast series of changes, each minute, fully understand-able, perhaps even inevitable, but cumulatively producing an unanticipated result. Euphemus' speech reinforces the feeling that dominates the sixth book—that Athens has crossed the boundaries of restraint and has embarked upon a venture that is already profoundly changing her.

----

[65] 2.40.4. This passage is soon followed by a remarkable contrast to Eupemus' exaltation of the profitable: "We alone help someone not so much by the calculation of advantage as by unfrightened confidence in freedom" (2.40.5). In this assertion Pericles minimizes the calculation of advantage and reflects a feeling of confidence (τῷ πιστῷ) diametrically opposed to Euphemus' insistence that bonds are determined by "reliability"—πιστόν (6.85.1).

Book 7

THE MARGIN OF ESCAPE

THE SIXTH BOOK led the reader through a major progression. It began ironically; the knowledge of the outcome of the Sicilian Expedition shaped reactions to the decision to invade Sicily with a large expeditionary force. Our foreknowledge of the ultimate disaster informed our judgments about the speeches and actions of the participants in the assembly at Athens, at Syracuse, and in the council of Athenian generals. But gradually the ironic perspective was replaced by a much more immediate focus on the operations of the expedition. From this point of view Athenian success no longer seemed so farfetched. Despite the delays and initial setbacks—the removal of Alcibiades and the failure of other Sicilian states to render the hoped-for support—it seemed increasingly possible for the Athenians to defeat the Syracusans. Alcibiades' analysis of the strategic situation prepared the reader for the new perspective: "Next let me point out that the situation there will not stabilize unless you bring aid. The Sicilians are ill-trained, but if they all cooperate they might yet survive. But take the Syracusans alone—their full force has already been defeated in a battle, and if they are blockaded by the navy, they will be unable to hold out against the Athenian force already present there. And if this city is captured, the rest of Sicily is taken and soon Italy as well" (6.91.1-3). From this point until the end of the sixth book the narrative focuses increasingly on the growing strength of the Athenians and the exacerbating situation of the Syracusans. The Peloponnesians, to be sure, are sending aid to Syracuse, but the nature of this assistance is left vague;[1] its progress is slow and its significance eclipsed by the excitement of the operations at Syracuse where the Athenians are enjoying consistent victories. They capture Epipolae, the heights overlooking the city (6.97.4); they construct a valuable fort at Labdalon (6.97.5). The arrival of additional cavalry bolsters Athe-

[1] N.B. the vagueness of 6.93.2. The exact composition of the force does not become clear until 6.104.1 and 7.1.5.

nian strength in this crucial service (6.98.1). They now even win a cavalry
engagement (6.99.4). With surprising speed, demoralizing to the Syracusans, the Athenians build walls with which they expect to isolate and
besiege the city. The Syracusans are now unwilling to commit all their
forces in a single engagement.[2] Their strategy, and hence the narrative,
now concentrates on the harassment of the Athenian building operations
and on constructing a counterwall to block the Athenian wall. The "race
of the walls" distracts us from any contemplation of the eventual Athenian
defeat. The apparent success of the Athenian efforts and the growing
discouragement of the Syracusans command our attention.[3] The Syracusans
are represented as astonished (6.98.2), frightened (6.101.5), and after a

---

[2] The word πανδημεί ("in full force") helps mark the stages in Syracusan response to
the Athenians. They are induced to engage πανδημεί in 6.67.2 (cf. 6.64.1 and 64.3).
Alcibiades uses the term to refer to the ensuing Syracusan defeat in 6.91.2; in 6.96.3 it
describes the Syracusan preparations for the battle over Epipolae. In 6.99.2 the Syracusans
decide to forego further battle πανδημεί.

[3] Again routine military terminology helps us understand the morale of the belligerents.
Thucydides is normally very careful in the Sicilian narrative to record the defeated party's
request for the return of the bodies of the dead and the victors' setting up of a trophy to
commemorate the victory. Elsewhere he sometimes omits such details, but in this portion of
the work he lists ten Athenian *tropaia*: 6.70.3; 94.2; 97.5; 98.4; 100.3; 103.1; 7.5.3; 23.4;
34.8; and 54. The Syracusan *tropaia* begin at 7.24.1 (3); 41.4 (2); 45.1 (2); 54; 72.1. He
does not, however, mention any Syracusan *tropaion* for the defeats inflicted on the Athenians
in the final retreat nor any general commemoration at the end of the campaign. Surely there
was some such monument, but by this time the focus is entirely on the sufferings of the
Athenians.

This formulaic reporting is modified and shaped to measure the psychology of the participants; cf. e.g. 7.34.7 where Corinthian psychology is contrasted with Athenian. In the last
of the series (7.72) the Syracusans set up a trophy but the Athenians are so demoralized that
they fail even to ask for the recovery of their dead (cf. 3.113.5).

An Athenian epigram ascribed to Euripides, reported in Plutarch *Nicias* 17.4 (see W. Peek,
Griechische Grabgedichte [Berlin 1960] no. 13; also in *Griechische Versinschriften*, vol. I
[Berlin, 1955] no. 21), alludes to eight Athenian victories. Thucydides lists ten *tropaia*.
Perhaps the epigram does not commemorate all those who died in Sicily but only those who
died from summer 414 to the end of the campaign, i.e. the eight *tropaia* listed from 6.97.5
to 7.54.1.

Pausanias 1.29.11 refers to another Athenian monument commemorating the Sicilian Expedition—a *stēlē* that listed those who died on Euboea and Chios and "on the remote areas
of the Asian continent," and, if the text is sound, in Sicily, although it did not include Nicias'
name. Pausanias concluded that Nicias was deliberately omitted and cited Philistus in support
of his view. Philistus' testimony need not be challenged, but was Pausanias correct in assuming
that the monument was for the year 413 B.C.? The operations in Chios, Euboea, and Asia
make better sense in 411 B.C. (cf. 8.60.2ff.) at which time some of those who were still
missing in Sicily might have been officially listed as dead.

See also S. N. Koumanoudes, *Archaiologikē Ephēmeris* (1964) 83-86 for a discussion of
an epigram and monument ascribed by the author to the Sicilian Expedition but more plausibly
associated with the campaigns of 447/6 (D. W. Bradeen, "Athenian Casualty Lists," *Hesperia*
33 [1964] 26).

brief revival of their spirits (6.102.1) suspicious of one another and despondent of Peloponnesian aid (6.103.3). All events progress toward the
Athenians' hopes (6.103.2). The rumors that reach Gylippus lead him—
and the reader—to infer that the Athenian walls have cut the Syracusans
off and that there is now no hope of rescuing the city (6.104.1).

After the expectations that have been developed in the sixth book, the
beginning of the seventh book is surprising. Gylippus finds he has mis-
understood the situation; the walling is not yet complete; there is still a
chance of rescuing the Syracusans.⁴ He gathers added forces while Gongylus, one of the Corinthian commanders, is sent ahead and stops the
Syracusan assembly from considering a proposal for ending the conflict
with the Athenians.⁵

The mood then changes totally. The Syracusans gather their entire army
to engage side by side with the new forces that Gylippus will bring.⁶ He
appears, ascending Epipolae, just as the Athenians had when they attacked,
and moves against the Athenian wall. Suddenly it is all over. Syracuse is
safe: "By such a margin did Syracuse escape from danger" (7.2.4).

This sentence, echoing the narrow escape of the Mytileneans from the
Athenian execution order (3.49.4), is one of the most astonishing in the
Histories. The danger to Syracuse is at this point far from over. It is by
no means certain that Gylippus' troops, diverse in background, still without
an opportunity to train together, will be successful in an assault on the
Athenians—and in fact they are not. Athenian victories continue a while
longer (7.5.3), as does the focus on the "race of the walls." But the
sentence sets the continuing action in a different perspective. We are
reminded now that any Athenian success will not be lasting. Our foreknowledge is again invoked, as we return to an ironic perspective. We
know what the participants can only guess. Syracuse is safe.

This remarkable sentence, then, serves in part to mark a decisive moment

---

⁴ The misunderstanding derives from grammatical categories. 6.103.1 reports the Athenian
building of the walls in the past progressive, "they were walling off the Syracusans as far
as the sea with a double wall." This is ambiguous—it could mean that the walls were in an
advanced stage of completion or that much work still remained. The report that reaches
Gylippus resolves the ambiguity by using a perfect: Syracuse is παντελῶς ἀποτετει-
χισμένοι "entirely walled off" (6.104.1). 7.1.1 repeats the phraseology using the perfect
with a negative. Gylippus then turns his attention back to rescuing Syracuse. The exact
situation is described in 7.2.4.

⁵ 7.2.1. Gongylus does what Eucles was unable to do at Amphipolis—gain enough time
for his fellow commander to arrive with additional forces and thereby turn the mood of the
citizenry. Cf. 4.106.1: οὐ προσδεχόμενοι βοήθειαν ἐν τάχει.

⁶ The word is now πανστρατιᾷ, not πανδημεί; cf. Note 2 above. Gylippus uses it in
his instructions to the Syracusans, 7.1.3, and they comply, 7.2.2.

in the military narrative, but also to jolt the reader out of the mood and approach that were so carefully developed in the last part of book 6. It ends the fantasy of Athenian success and returns the reader to the perspective adopted at the beginning of the sixth book: the ironic recognition of the ultimate outcome of the expedition. Gylippus' arrival does make a difference; the Athenians, we know, will not succeed.

An equally abrupt change occurs a few chapters later when the Syracusans' third counterwall finally prevents any further Athenian circumvallation (7.6.4). Nicias, ever worried about the mood of the Athenian assembly, decides to use a letter to convey the full gravity of the situation; he fears that a messenger might fail to report precisely and effectively, either through failure of memory, inability to speak effectively, or, most significantly, from a desire to say what the assembly wanted to hear (7.8.2). Just as Nicias uses the letter to achieve an unmediated presentation of his views, Thucydides, by reporting that letter, is able to bring his reader directly into touch with the situation in the Athenian camp without any apparent authorial intervention. We confront the distress of the army directly, through the eyes of the commander, not through the description of the historian.

The letter's vividness of detail and its insistence on the possibility of defeat make both assembly and reader aware of new problems. Nicias' illness is no temporary indisposition, but nephritis (7.15.1). The ships cannot be hauled from the water and properly maintained (7.12.4); some of the forces are deserting (7.13.2), and captives from the Athenian enslavement of Hykkara (6.62.3) have been purchased to replace free rowers (7.13.2). The trierarchs have allowed this deterioration in the quality of their crews.

Most intolerable of all is that I am not able, even though the commander, to prevent such things. Your natures are not easy to rule! And further we have no source for replacement crews—which the enemy has from many quarters. Rather we have to meet present and past losses from the forces we had when we came, for our allied cities, Naxos and Catana, are unable to help. If one more factor shifts to our enemies' side—namely, if the regions of Italy that supply us with food, when they see what situation we are in and that you do not send further help, go over to their side—the war is over for them without a battle and we leave like people whose city has been taken by siege.[7]

---

[7] 7.14.2-3. The translation of the last phrase expands a compressed metaphor in the Greek. The idea in ἐϰπολιορϰηθέντων ἡμῶν is not simply "famine would compel us to evacuate" (Crawley) or "we shall be starved out, and they will have made an end of the war without striking a blow" (Jowett) or "hunger will force us to submit, and Syracuse will win the war

The deterioration in the situation, emphasized by the reversal of the colonization theme, leads to Nicias' recommendation that the Athenians either recall the expedition or send out another force, no smaller than the first one, and with it a new commander. This is the third time in the *Histories* he has offered to resign his command; once again his actions, however well intended, magnify his city's problems.[8]

The Athenians react to this powerful letter exactly as one would expect from a city that boasted to the Melians that it never withdraws from a siege (5.111.1). They keep Nicias in command—after all he is a skilled and experienced commander whose knowledge of the situation in Sicily will be invaluable—but they immediately send out Eurymedon to join him while they prepare a larger expedition that Demosthenes will command at the beginning of spring. The decision is perfectly reasonable and would not have appeared especially risky. The new force should continue to command the seas and hence to guarantee the safe return of the entire expedition, if withdrawal proved necessary. Yet the shift in perspective at the beginning of book 7 forces the reader to an assessment quite different from that of the assembly. We see clearly that this decision will simply increase the losses for Athens. The scale of the disaster will be greater if additional forces are sent and the chances for successful withdrawal are lessened by continuing Nicias in command. Once again the Athenians have failed to make "the additional decisions that would be beneficial to those who had gone to Sicily."[9]

THE NECESSITY OF WITHDRAWAL

The next unit in the narrative (7.16-46) largely concerns Demosthenes and his attempt to bring about a decisive resolution to the Sicilian campaign. His progress toward Syracuse, like that of Gylippus, is reported in stages

---

without having to strike a blow'' (Warner), but that the process whereby the Athenian besiegers have become the besieged (7.11.4) would result in their withdrawal from Sicily just as citizens of a city taken in siege withdraw from their homes. The prediction comes true in 7.75.5.

[8] The previous offers are in the Pylos debate, 4.28.3, and in the debate on the Sicilian Expedition, 6.23.3.

[9] 2.65.11. The usual interpretation of οὐ τὰ πρόσφορα τοῖς οἰχομένοις ἐπιγιγνώσκοντες is that it refers to the decision to recall Alcibiades. This seems to me partially correct but if it is the only content of the phrase then the expression is needlessly vague and opaque. More likely, I believe, it covers several decisions made after the initial expedition departed—one to recall Alcibiades, another not to recall the entire army (or at least Nicias) at this stage in the operations. Very general language is utilized to cover both occasions.

and seems agonizingly slow. Episodes in Sicily and other theaters interrupt the story of Demothenes' expedition and indicate the increasing gravity of the war and the urgency of Demosthenes' mission. Almost as soon as the vote to send him is passed (7.16), we are reminded that the Lacedaemonians are going ahead with their plans for an invasion of Attica;[10] they follow Alcibiades' advice to build a fort at Deceleia in the Attic countryside (7.19). While Demosthenes is still in home waters, Gylippus arrives at Syracuse (7.21.1). Although his hopes for a naval victory do not materialize, the strategic fort at Plemmyrion falls to the Syracusans (7.24). Meanwhile, Demosthenes is sailing around the Peloponnese, attempting to repeat his success at Pylos (7.26.2) by establishing a fort in Spartan territory. The effects of the war at home are brought out through an elaborate ring composition juxtaposing the operations at Deceleia to a massacre at Mycalessus in Boeotia.[11] Finally, Demosthenes reaches Syracuse—just after the Athenians have been outnumbered and defeated in a naval battle.[12]

The battle is part of a sequence that culminates later in the book in the great battle in the harbor of Syracuse. Its importance is underlined by the use of day-to-day narrative. Although its military effects are considerable, its significance lies less in the number of ships sunk or in the total casualties (7.41) than in the advancement of our understanding of the psychological balance between the two forces. In the naval engagement that had immediately followed Gylippus' arrival the courage and boldness of the Syracusans were already amply clear.[13] But the Syracusans could not match the skill and experience of the Athenians. In the engagement immediately before Demosthenes' arrival their boldness is undiminished but new skill and innovation are to be seen in their redesign of their triremes (7.36.2f.) to make them more effective against the Athenians. In this battle the Athenians fall into disarray and are defeated, just as the Syracusans had been in the previous engagement.[14] We are witnessing the process, alluded

[10] The invasion is reported in 7.19 using the formulas that have become familiar in the account of the Archidamian war, e.g. 2.19.1; 2.47.2; 2.71.1; 3.1.1; 4.2.1. Some of the variations, e.g. the use of terminology (ἐτείχιζον, κατὰ πόλεις διελόμενοι) normally used for siege narratives, evoke Plataea (2.78.1) and Melos (5.114.1). The effect is to remind the reader that Athens has now returned to the situation of the earlier war. This is reinforced in 7.20.1, when the dispatch of the naval expedition is reported with language reminiscent of 2.23.2, 3.86.1, and 4.2.2—the old strategy of naval assaults on the Peloponnese.

[11] The ring composition from 26.2 through 31.1 is schematized in Appendix Seven.

[12] 7.42. His slow progress is reminiscent of the delay of the Nicias who in 429 B.C. had been sent to bring aid to Phormio, 2.85.5 and 92.7. Cf. Chapter Two, Note 62 above.

[13] 7.21.3-23. On Hermocrates as a representation of *tolma* see V. Hunter, *Thucydides, The Artful Reporter* (Toronto 1973) ch. 9.

[14] N.B. the echo in 7.40.3 of οὐδενὶ κόσμῳ in 7.23.3 and of the description of the plague

to in the first book, of a nation "becoming nautical," the fulfillment of Hermocrates' observation that "they do not have their naval skill as an ancestral or eternal possession; they are in fact more continental than the Syracusans and were forced by the Persians to become nautical."[15]

As the struggle about Syracuse grows more intense we witness the acceleration of naval innovation and the increasing assimilation of Syracusan *tropoi* to those of the Athenians.[16] In Sicily the Athenians have encountered a new psychology, quite unlike that of their continental, conservative Dorian opponents in mainland Greece: "These were the only cities they attacked who had *tropoi* similar to their own, who were governed by democracies, just as they were, and who had ships and cavalry and great size."[17] Syracuse comes increasingly to resemble the old Athens described by the Corinthians in the first book as innovative, bold, and determined to take every advantage of victory. The Athenians at the same time lose these characteristics, at least temporarily, and become demoralized and despondent.[18]

But this is to anticipate. Although the opening of the seventh book prepares the reader for great changes not only in the military fortune of the two opponents but also in their psychology and characteristics, attention is kept focused on Demosthenes. When at length he reaches Syracuse, the reader knows what to expect. We have seen him in action often enough to predict his strategy. In particular his Ambraciot campaign (3.102.3-114.4) and his brilliant success at Pylos (4.29-40) have shown him to be a commander who believes in swift and decisive action and who recognizes the advantage of surprise. He is likely to move at or before dawn (3.112.3 and 4.31.1), to make a sudden rush (4.31.1), to catch the enemy unaware (3.42.1 and 4.36.2), perhaps still in their beds (3.112.3 and 4.32.1), to take advantage of allied troops who use the enemies' Doric dialect (3.112.4 and 4.33, cf. 4.41.2), and thereby astonish and demoralize the enemy (3.112.5 and 4.34.2f.). This strategic pattern provides the background to Demosthenes' operations at Syracuse. As soon as he arrives, Thucydides leads us into Demosthenes' assessment of the situation, blurring the usually sharp line between authorial assessment and the opinions and expectations of his characters; he lets us see the gradual shaping of the timing (7.42.3)

---

in 2.52.2. On this portion of the narrative see especially Hunter, *Artful Reporter*, ch. 5 and J. de Romilly, *Histoire et raison chez Thucydide* (Paris 1956) 151-60.

[15] 7.21.3. Cf. 1.18.2 and 93.3.

[16] 7.53.4; 62; 70.4. Cf. the importance attached to naval invention in book 1, esp. 13.2f.

[17] 7.55.2. Cf. 6.20.3 and 8.96.5.

[18] N.B. 7.72.4. Cf. Hunter R. Rawlings III, *The Structure of Thucydides' History* (Princeton 1981) 89f.

and direction of Demosthenes' plan.[19] We are taken into Demosthenes' confidence and share his analysis. Then Thucydides returns to a more detached narrative as we are told, "he hastened to apply himself to the attempt." The following sentence is heavily ironic, as disjunctive predictions often are in Thucydides: "He thought it would be the most direct route to a resolution of the war, for one of two things would happen. He would be successful and capture Syracuse or he would evacuate the force and not allow a purposeless attrition of the Athenians, their fellow expedition members, and the whole city"(7.42.5). The reader knows that the disjunction is specious for a failure in the attack will not result in swift and decisive withdrawal.[20]

When Demosthenes puts into effect his plan for a night attack on Epipolae, all seems at first to go very much as he hopes, and as the familiar pattern leads us to expect. The first outposts are seized. Then: "The Syracusans and their allies and Gylippus and those with him brought aid from the outposts. Since this bold attack was quite unexpected in the night time, they were demoralized when they engaged the Athenians and under the assault of the enemy they gave way."[21] But a sudden reversal follows. The Boeotian troops hold their ground. Soon the Athenians are routed and suffer what they had hoped to inflict. The darkness works to their disadvantage (7.44.1); the sounds confuse them (7.44.3, cf. 4.34.3), and they are especially frightened by the Dorian battle hymn sung both by the enemy and by some of their own allies (7.44.6). At length in total disarray and confusion, fighting with their own troops, rushing away from the enemy,

---

[19] In 7.42.3 the syntax of νομίσας reporting Demosthenes' assessment of the situation is interrupted by a long parenthesis, introduced by γάρ. It begins by explaining what Demosthenes meant by his criticism of Nicias and expands to give a general analysis of the first phase of the Sicilian operation. The parenthesis has caused protracted, and indecisive, discussion. Does it represent Thucydides' own view or the assessment of Demosthenes? Dover in *HCT* ad loc. (p. 419) insists that the form of the parenthesis (finite verbs, etc.) establishes it as a report of Thucydides' own views, and not a mere representation of Demosthenes' opinion. The point is well taken, but when the sentence resumes with ταῦτα οὖν ἀνασκοπῶν ὁ Δημοσθένης (*OCT*, line 14ff.), a shift in attitude is evident. Dover has oversimplified, as C. Schneider, *Information und Absicht bei Thukydides* (Göttingen 1974) p. 56, justly observes. The reader, having been encouraged to accept Demosthenes' analysis, is now sharply detached from these views and reminded that the strategy will not succeed.

E. C. Kopff, "An Unrecognized Fragment of Philistus," *GRBS* 17 (1976) 23-30 has urged another solution: the passage is an interpolation from Philistus, i.e. a marginal note by a learned reader that has found its way into the text. See the criticism by M. W. Dickie, "Thucydides, Not Philistus," *GRBS* 17 (1976) 217-19 and the rejoinder by Kopff, "Philistus Still," *GRBS* 17 (1976) 220-21. Andrewes' assessment is contained in *HCT* on book 8, app. 2, p. 425, n. 1.

[20] Cf. 4.28.5.

[21] 7.43.6 on the role of *ekplēxis*. Cf. 4.34.2 and 7.42.3.

throwing themselves over the cliffs, they flee, as best each individual can, back to their camp. Demosthenes' brilliant strategy has failed and inadvertently recreated not Pylos,[22] but the Aetolian disaster of 426 B.C.[23]

This episode provides a reminder of the awesome swiftness of military defeat. The transition from a carefully—and quite persuasively—planned assault to disarray, chaos, and rout is almost instantaneous. The army dissolves into its constituents and then engages against itself: "And so finally falling on one another in many sections of the battle, once the confusion had started, friend with friend and citizen with fellow citizen, they not only were reduced to terror but were so locked in hand to hand combat that they could hardly be separated" (7.44.7). The narrative replicates the military process by showing that the elements of Demosthenes' past campaigns produce unexpected results, and a new pattern of conflict.

Demosthenes had presumed that an immediate withdrawal would follow if his assault on Epipolae miscarried.[24] He had every reason to believe that despite the deteriorating condition of the original fleet, the reinforcements brought by himself and Eurymedon should ensure Athenian command of the seas and guarantee the extrication of the army. Any analysis based on material resources would predict a safe withdrawal. Further, there was no reason to think that the Syracusans would attempt more than minor harassments of a withdrawal. What could be more welcome to them than the departure of the Athenians and what more hazardous than a large and desperate army attempting to force a retreat? In the Persian wars the Greeks had wisely allowed Xerxes' army to withdraw and rejected the proposal to cut the line of retreat over the Hellespont.[25] Surely the same strategic considerations would apply in this situation.

But such an assessment is quite mistaken. The withdrawal, we know, will not be immediate, unopposed, or successful. Demosthenes' false confidence invites the reader to view this section from an ironic perspective. Thucydides immediately provides the details about Demosthenes' operation, and rather than distracting us from the known outcome of the ex-

[22] The closest equivalent to Pylos in this section of the narrative is the Spartan fort at Deceleia that enables slaves to escape from Attica as helots had from Spartan territory (4.41.3). The Pylos analogy is reintroduced, explicitly, at 7.71.7.

[23] 3.97-98, e.g. the echoes of 3.98.2 in διαμαρτόντες τῶν ὁδῶν in 44.8 and the emphasis on ἐμπειρία in the escape 3.98.1. There are also verbal echoes of the Plataean counterattack on the Thebans in 2.4 e.g. 7.44.4, κραυγῇ οὐκ ὀλίγῃ χρώμενοι and 2.4.2, κραυγῇ τε καὶ ὀλολυγῇ χρωμένων.

[24] 7.42.5. The disjunction, ἢ γὰρ κατορθώσας ἕξειν Συρακούσας ἢ ἀπάξειν τὴν στρατίαν, is similar to the ironic treatment of the assembly's reactions to Cleon's proposal about Pylos, 4.28.5.

[25] Herodotus 8.97 and 108f., also 9.106 and 114.

pedition, these reinforce our foreknowledge and increase our awareness
of the dangers confronting the Athenians.

The difficulties are of two sorts: divisions of counsel within the Athenian
command, and the growing determination of the Syracusans to prevent the
withdrawal. The first of these becomes clear in another council of the
commanders, reminiscent of the debate in book 6 (chs. 46-50) about the
best strategy of attack. The earlier council led directly to the implementation
of the plan backed by a majority of the commanders: Alcibiades' diplomatic
offensive. In this council two of the three commanders agree that a swift
withdrawal is required, but Nicias' pleas induce hesitation and delay.[26]
Nicias is now heir to Alcibiades' belief (6.17.4) that Syracusan factions
will ensure Athenian success.

During this delay Gylippus returns to Syracuse with additional forces
(7.50.1), and the Syracusans begin to plan a double assault on the Athenians, by land and by sea. The Athenians' delay is presented as a serious
mistake. But it is a subsequent delay that catches the reader's attention.
On August 27, 413 B.C., an eclipse of the moon induced the Athenians
further to postpone the withdrawal.[27] The strategic significance of this
decision, soon abandoned, is not great but the episode does have an important role to play in Thucydides' account. It reminds the reader of the
Syracusan mood at the time of their first engagement with the Athenians.
Thunderstorms and lightning helped frighten the Syracusans while the
Athenians recognized the purely natural phenomena to be expected at that
time of year.[28] Now, a natural phenomenon, an eclipse, provokes an irrational reaction in the Athenians and further contributes to the delay.

The second obstacle to the safe withdrawal of the Athenians is the
Syracusans' growing determination to stop them. The full measure of their
resolve is not immediately evident. Their initial concern is largely to
prevent the Athenians from establishing another naval base in a strategically
superior location (7.51.1). But gradually a bolder plan, to prevent the
Athenian escape from Sicily, emerges. An initial naval engagement helps
demoralize the Athenians and encourage the Syracusans. At the end of it
follow reports of the Athenians' discouragement (7.55.2) and of a new

---

[26] The debate of the commanders is presented in a very complicated pattern schematized
and discussed in Appendix Eight.

[27] It is sometimes said that the superstitious Nicias decided to postpone the withdrawal.
In fact a majority of the troops insists that the generals not withdraw (7.50.4); Nicias merely
accepts the soothsayers' interpretation that the expedition should wait twenty-seven days.
Confronted with this mood in the army and this interpretation by the soothsayers no Athenian
commander would find it easy to urge an immediate retreat.

[28] 6.70.1. There is a second and even closer parallel in 7.79.3.

Syracusan plan to close off their great harbor so the Athenians cannot escape (7.56.1). No longer are the Syracusans content with safety for themselves; they begin to think that it would be a wonderful victory prize (7.56.2) if they could control the Athenians and their allies both by land and by sea. The plan is still ambiguous: to "overcome" can be either to defeat or to capture the Athenians. But as the forces are mustered, it is restated in clearer form. Now the Syracusans consider it a wonderful victory prize (7.59.2) if, in addition to the former naval victory, they can actually capture the entire Athenian expedition, grand as it was, and allow it to flee by "neither by land nor by sea." They then proceed to close the mouth of the harbor (7.59.3). The Athenians continue in their discouragement (7.60.2) while preparing to fight their way out.[29]

In the middle of this ring composition stands a catalogue of the allies on each side. By marking the moment at which each side had received all the support forthcoming in the Sicilian campaign, it contributes to Thucydides' argument for the greatness of the Sicilian Expedition and reminds the reader of the scale as well as the importance of the battle soon to take place in the harbor.[30] "This was the largest number of peoples to come together before a single city except for the whole total in this war between the city of Athens and of Sparta" (7.56.4). In these respects it is an elaborate but quite conventional piece of writing. One other feature, however, is much more surprising. The catalogue is organized in part on the basis of the motives of the participating states,[31] or more precisely on a classification of status that seems intended to clarify why the individual states participated. The combination of this principle with geographical and ethnic criteria results in a very complex organization. But the general pattern is made clear at the outset: "The alignments were formed not on the basis of legal or moral obligations nor on the basis of kinship but more as circumstances—either advantage or compulsion—applied to each party" (7.57.1). As we read through the catalogue, the reason for this unusual principle becomes clear. The picture that emerges is a recurring one throughout the work—the dissolution of the normal bonds and ties of human relationships. One instance has recently appeared in the confounding of the

[29] The narrative is another elaborate ring composition and is schematized and discusssed in Appendix Nine.

[30] The placement of the catalogue has perplexed some commentators, F. Solmsen, *Intellectual Experiments of the Greek Enlightenment* (Princeton 1975) 217, notes that "a sequence has been interrupted" but he has not observed the ring composition that serves as the setting for the catalogue and draws attention to the significance of the forthcoming battle.

[31] Cf. H. P. Stahl, "Speeches and the Course of Events," in *Speeches in Thucydides*, ed. P. Stadter (Chapel Hill 1973) 70ff.

Dorian-Ionian distinction during Demosthenes' assault on Epipolae and a much grander example will be found in the account of the final withdrawal. But in the catalogue the process can be seen affecting a wide range of Greek states. The ethnic and cultural ties that normally determine alliances fail to hold. Boeotians fight Boeotians (7.57.5); Dorians confront Dorians; Corcyreans fight their mother city of Corinth and their fellow colony of Syracuse (7.57.7). Exiled Megareans fight with citizens of the Megarean foundation, Selinus (7.57.8).

Only now does the digression at the beginning of book 6 on the early settlement of Sicily become fully significant. The information provided there is vital for an understanding of the expected relationship among states; it helps clarify who is Dorian and who Ionian and hence which states are tied by blood or colonization ties. These relationships should make it possible to predict the alliances and loyalties of states. But although the rhetoric of the speakers sometimes pretends that this is the case (e.g., 6.77.1), the reality is quite different. The pressures that imperial powers exert on their subjects, the appeals of self-interest and advantage, and the compulsion of hatred prevail:

Argives, though Dorians, joined Ionian Athenians, less because of their alliance than because of their animosity toward Spartans and their immediate individual advantage. Mantineans and other Arcadian mercenaries who were accustomed to attack those who on any occasion were pointed out to them as their enemies were induced by financial gain to consider the Arcadians who had come with the Corinthians as no less hostile. Cretans and Aetolians also joined for pay. It turned out that the Cretans, who had joined the Rhodians in founding Gela, marched voluntarily [i.e., for pay] not with, but *against*, their colonists. (7.57.9)

This catalogue thus serves in part as a counterpiece to the comments on the Corcyrean revolution where the dissolution of normal ties culminates in the slaughter of son by father (3.81.5). Now the same process is projected onto the international scene with a similar result, the dissolution of old relationships and the triumph of advantage and profit over traditional ties and loyalties. One of the oldest and most traditional forms of narration, the catalogue, is thus transformed to convey the unprecedented disruption (*kinēsis*) brought about by the war.

Of the battle in the harbor at Syracuse little need be said. Although modern scholars have often complained that the strategy receives insufficient attention, the passage is powerfully written, and one of the best examples of Thucydides' technique of vividness (*enargeia*).[32] Plutarch's

---

[32] W. S. Ferguson in *The Cambridge Ancient History*, vol. 5 (Cambridge 1927) 308 is

comment on the passage points the way to an appreciation of this aspect of Thucydides' work: "The most effective historian is the one who makes his narrative like a painting by giving a visual quality to the sufferings and characters. Thucydides certainly always strives after this vividness in his writing, eagerly trying to transform his reader into a spectator and to let the sufferings that were so dazzling and upsetting to those who beheld them have a similar effect on those who read about them" (Plutarch *On the Fame of the Athenians* ch. 3, *Moralia* 347 Af.). The technique moves the reader beyond tactics and strategy to an awareness of the psychological importance and implications of the battle.

To recognize the visual and emotional power of the passage is not, however, to exhaust it. Underneath the surface of the text are other layers of significance, latent perhaps at this moment, but progressively developed and increasingly important. The first of these, the comparison to Pylos, is eventually made explicit.[33] But more important is the implicit comparison between the Athenian invasion of Sicily and the Persian invasion of Greece. The battle in the harbor inevitably evokes the Battle of Salamis—the decisive naval engagement of the Persian invasion, fought in narrow quarters, and resulting in a victory that brought special glory to Athens. The Athenian role is, of course, now totally reversed, since the victors of Salamis have become the defeated of Syracuse.

The sequel to the battle brings out the full significance of the comparison

---

sharply critical of Thucydides' presentation: "Thucydides fails even to suggest the factors that determined the outcome. Instead, he dwells on certain typical incidents in the confused fighting that followed, and then turns our attention to the spectators on the shore, and leaves us to infer the manifold vicissitudes of the protracted struggle from the agony of fear, joy, anxiety." Such criticisms neglect, however, the importance of the passage in clarifying the mood and psychology of the two rival forces. Since morale is the crucial factor in the remaining chapters of the seventh book, Thucydides' description is well adapted to his narrative purpose.

[33] 7.71.7. Cf. also the echoes of 4.33f. in 7.70.5-71.4.

The similarity between the great naval battle at Syracuse and the Pylos operation includes another detail and raises thereby an important, if perhaps unanswerable, question. Both at Pylos and at Syracuse there is a plan to blockade the entry to the harbor (4.8.7 and 7.56.1). Whereas the Spartans at Pylos fail to follow through on their plan (4.13.4) and thereby allow the Athenian fleet to surround their force on Sphacteria, the Syracusans implement their strategy (7.59.3) and thereby put the Athenians at a disadvantage and eventually demoralize them. Critics have long been puzzled by the Pylos account: some have doubted whether the Spartans ever intended such an ambitious plan; almost all readers wonder why the idea of blockade is abandoned. Has the parallelism to Syracuse (even the size of the harbor openings are said to be approximately the same, if R. Bauslaugh, "The Text of Thucydides IV. 8.6," *JHS* 99 [1979] 1-6 is correct) shaped the Pylos account by leading Thucydides to accept and emphasize a report of an unrealized Spartan plan to block the entrance to Pylos bay? The implicit contrast between the Spartan failure to follow through on their plan and the Syracusan vigor and boldness reinforces an important theme in this portion of the *Histories*.

to the Persian War. Once the battle itself is over, attention turns from the Athenians to the Syracusans and commander narrative replaces collective narrative. Hermocrates now (ch.73) appears in the central role, for the first time since chapter 21. His objective is to exploit the advantage presented by the battle and to prevent the swift escape of the Athenians. To achieve his goal he devises a stratagem—messengers, who claim to be from the pro-Athenian fifth column inside Syracuse, warn Nicias not to withdraw by night since the Syracusans are guarding the roads.[34] In fact, the Syracusans are celebrating their victory and are in no condition to block an Athenian withdrawal. The stratagem is the counterpiece to the earlier Athenian manipulation of the Syracusans by the false story that Catana could still be rescued (6.64.2). But it is also strongly reminiscent of the story in Herodotus 8.75f., Themistocles' false message to the Persians inviting them to engage at Salamis.[35]

The simple analogy between the Athenians at Syracuse and the Persians at Salamis breaks down, however, as Hermocrates implements his plan. After the victories at Salamis the allies, despite Themistocles' urging, decided not to sail immediately to the Hellespont and cut off Xerxes' line of retreat (Herodotus 9.108-110). Hermocrates, by contrast, manages to block the Athenian withdrawal and achieve the "wonderful victory prize" to which the Syracusans have aspired. This new Themistocles achieves what has hitherto seemed unlikely or impossible—the actual capture of the invading force. This achievement, and the immense loss and suffering that attend it, are the measure of the greatness of the Syracusan victory, and of Thucydides' own subject matter.

THE WITHDRAWAL

Perhaps no passage of ancient prose narrative is as powerfully written and as immediately accessible to the modern reader as the account of the Athenians' withdrawal after their defeat in the harbor at Syracuse.[36] Of all

---

[34] 7.72.2. The story is rather too apt for most historians who will not find in a two-day delay (in 75.1 τρίτῃ is based on inclusive count; see Dover in *HCT* ad 74.1, pp. 450f.) an excessive amount of time for an army of this size to regroup and prepare for a withdrawal by land.

[35] The parallel between Hermocrates and Themistocles has often been recognized; see most recently V. Hunter, "The Composition of Thucydides' *History*," *Historia* 26 (1977) 287.

[36] T. B. Macaulay called this section "the *ne plus ultra* of human art," *Life and Letters*, vol. 1 (New York and London 1875) 387; cf. J. Grant, "Toward Knowing Thucydides," *Phoenix* 28 (1974) 81ff.

the *Histories*, this section least needs explication—indeed here the critic's intervention may distract and impede the reader's comprehension of the text. Yet if sustained explication is inappropriate, attention to some of the techniques and implications of the passage is still essential to appreciate fully the progress of thought and feeling in the work.

The treatment of Nicias provides a good example. We have seen him temporarily eclipsed when Demosthenes arrived with the relief expedition, then dominating the council of the commanders that followed the unsuccessful assault on Epipolae. His confidence that subversion might yet bring victory detains the Athenians, and his willingness to follow the soothsayers contributes to further delay. Before the battle in the harbor, his speech, not Demosthenes' or Eurymedon's, is quoted (7.61-64) as is his second appeal, an emotional outburst evoking Aeschylus' description of the battle of Salamis.[37] And it is Nicias who addresses the Athenians and attempts to revive their despondent spirits just before the withdrawal begins (7.77). During the retreat Demosthenes never speaks in direct discourse and never emerges with great clarity, despite the importance of his role and the more frequent harassments directed at his force. Although the last stand of his troops is described in a moving and richly evocative passage, Demosthenes himself slips into the background, as the passage turns back from commander to a staccato collective narrative: "[Demosthenes] did not push on but rather made ready for battle, until delaying he is surrounded by them. Both he and the Athenians with him were in great confusion. They were pressed together in some spot that a wall encircled—a road on either side; it had olive trees, not a few of them; they were shot at from all sides" (7.81.4).

The picture of the surrounded force reminds us of the annihilation of Leonidas' Spartiates at Thermopylae, but Demosthenes is no Leonidas, nor do his troops refuse to surrender;[38] there may also be a hint of Demosthenes' criticism of Nicias for wasting time, since he, not Nicias, is the one who now delays.[39] But all this disappears in the nightmare quality of the passage as the view becomes simultaneously more vivid and more

---

[37] 7.69.2 based on Aeschylus *Persae* 402-405.

[38] The connection with Thermopylae may be underlined by περισταδόν in 7.81.4. This rare word occurs in *Iliad* 13.551 and in Herodotus' account of Thermopylae 7.225.3. Cf. C. F. Smith, "Traces of Epic Usage in Thucydides," *TAPA* 31 (1900) 74.

[39] In 7.81.4. Ἐνδιατρίβων is gratuitous but evokes διατρίβειν in 7.42.3, 43.1, and 47.3, τρίβειν in 49.2, and τρίψεσθαι in 42.5—all Demosthenes' views of the situation in Syracuse. Nicias in 7.48.6 uses the word to describe his proposed strategy against the Syracusans. Nicias' delays were not primarily of his own choosing, but were forced upon him by circumstances, as Demosthenes perhaps now appreciates.

abstract. The focus moves away from Demosthenes to his men and to their surroundings, which we see with growing clarity and awareness of their meaning. The individual drops out of sight. At first we see Demosthenes in a vague location, "some spot" (7.81.4); the force is encircled; then we glimpse the wall, and the road—now inaccessible—that loops around it on either side. And for protection, only some olive trees, as the barrage from all sides continues. Such scenes of encirclement recur in varying forms in Thucydides and take on a cumulative terror—a nightmare of being surrounded, with the enemy on some wall or cliff shooting down in steady annihilation.[40] The details of Demosthenes' surrender are not reported, nor do we hear of his attempt at suicide.[41] Later we learn of his murder by the Syracusans, but Thucydides reserves comment. His final valedictory is for Nicias (7.86.5).

Although some readers have suspected that Thucydides had a personal animosity against Demosthenes, the account is shaped not so much by hostility to Demosthenes as by fascination with Nicias. We now encounter one of the most remarkable progressions of thought and feeling in Thucydides' work. In the fourth book Nicias' attempt to outmaneuver Cleon in the assembly failed, and eventually contributed to the increasing power of the demagogue. In the sixth book his efforts to turn the Athenian assembly away from the Sicilian Expedition were equally inept. Thucydides presented him not as a tragic prophet but as a misguided leader whose advice exacerbated an already dangerous situation. Throughout the expedition he has again compounded Athenian difficulties, above all by discouraging a decisive withdrawal. His speeches are usually unconvincing and characterize him as "a leader as incapable of good planning himself as of inducing it in others."[42] Finally Thucydides is quite sardonic:

[40] The pattern begins in 1.106, the slaughter of Corinthian troops in a withdrawal from the Athenians. The similarities between this passage and 7.81 are remarkable: the place is at first simply ἐς του χωρίον ἰδιώτου; then attention is called to the ditch surrounding it, ᾧ ἔτυχεν ὄρυγμα μέγα περιεῖργον; and escape is cut off, οὐκ ἦν ἔξοδος. The force is encircled (κύκλῳ), and shot at from all sides. Also cf. the episode in 4.48 (Corcyra). Elements of the pattern appear in 4.35-36 (Pylos) and of course at the Assinarus 7.84.3f.

[41] Pausanias 1.29 and Philistus *FGrHist* 556 F 53.

[42] A. Parry, "The Language of Thucydides' Description of the Plague," *BICSL* 16 (1969) 109. One example of Nicias' oratorical ineptitude is characteristic: In 7.62.3 he draws attention to an important technological breakthrough in the equipment of the ships—something that should be very helpful in encouraging his dispirited troops. After alluding to it he adds the demoralizing phrase "if the marines should work the stuff" (ἢν τὰ ἐπὶ τούτοις οἱ ἐπιβάται ὑπουργῶσιν). He then desribes the strategic situation in a totally discouraging way: "We have been driven to the point that we are fighting a foot battle from ships" and goes on to point out that control of the shoreline, vital for rescuing sailors if their ship is sunk, is now in the enemies' hands! It is hard to imagine a speech less likely to be effective.

Nicias was demoralized by the immediate situation and when he saw the danger they were in . . . called again on each one of the trierarchs, mentioning the name of their fathers and their own name and their tribe urging each one who had some claim to distinction not to betray it and not to blacken the ancestral valor from which their ancestors were so famous, reminding them of their country, the freest in the world, and of the lack of regimentation that all enjoyed in it and saying all the other things that men would say in a situation like this if they did not care about seeming to speak in an old-fashioned way—things brought forth on all occasions about wives and children and ancestral gods they shout out thinking them useful in the dismay of the moment.[43]

Thucydides' tone is very similar to the one he adopted in the parenthesis on Nicias' willingness to delay after the eclipse: "for he always was somewhat—yes, too much—disposed to prophetic utterance and the like."[44] In each case we are invited to detach ourselves from the immediate situation and to view from some distance the circumstances that lead to Nicias' responses. Thucydides' comments reinforce our feeling of intellectual superiority, of being too sophisticated to identify with Nicias' words or actions.

But in the withdrawal, Nicias begins to appear in a different light. He has one more speech, in some ways the most unimaginative of all his addresses.[45] The words, especially if the reader remembers the Melian Dialogue, are heavily ironic. He urges the Athenians and their allies to derive hope[46] even from the present situation and bases his argument in part on theology: "Perhaps there will be some alleviation. The enemies have enjoyed ample good fortune and if we provoked the hostility of any god by sailing here, we have now been sufficiently punished. One can think of certain other forces who have moved against their opponents and having erred, as humans do, suffered what humans can bear. We too can reasonably hope to have more gentle treatment from the gods, for from

[43] 7.69.2. On ἀρχαιολογεῖν see H. L. Hudson-Williams, "Thucydides, Isocrates and the Rhetorical Method of Composition," *CQ* 42 (1948) 79f. and *HCT* ad loc. (p. 446). Nicias' speech is the most extreme departure in the *Histories* from the fifth-century insistence on freshness and ingenuity in argument: 1.73.2; 2.36.4 et alibi. The echo of Aeschylus' *Persae* 402-405 in the last few lines emphasizes how old-fashioned Nicias' approach is and reminds the reader of the continuing, usually implicit, comparison between the Sicilian Expedition and the great Persian invasion of Greece.

[44] 7.50.4. Τῷ τοιούτῳ is surely condescending. The cluster τι καὶ ἄγαν occurs only here in Thucydides and is not adequately paralleled by 7.63.3 or 4.63.2 often adduced by the commentators. On Thucydides' attitude to omens etc. see S. I. Oost, "Thucydides and the Irrational," *CP* 70 (1975) 186-96. and N. Marinatos, "Thucydides and Oracles," *JHS* 101 (1981) 138-140.

[45] Demosthenes is said (7.78.1) to have spoken in a similar way.

[46] 7.77.3; contrast the Athenian disparagement of *elpis* in the Melian Dialogue, 5.103.

them we are now more deserving of pity than of hostility."[47] In addition
to the theological argument, Nicias derives confidence from an historical
precedent, very vaguely mentioned because of its sensitive nature. The
"other forces" that "moved against their opponents," were defeated and
"suffered what humans can bear" must refer euphemistically to the great
Persian expedition against Greece, which, having done terrible deeds and
made terrible mistakes, was yet able in large part to escape to Asia. Nicias
feels the Athenians can hope that their withdrawal will experience no
greater severity. These naive and old-fashioned arguments are grounded
in a theology and a view of history that has nowhere else been affirmed
in the *Histories*. Parallel to them is another—and no more compelling—
line of thought. Nicias feels that his own way of life, above all his performance of all the conventional acts that express reverence for the gods
and avoid ill feeling among men, gives reason to be confident about the
future. He believes, we can see, that he lives in a universe in which some
divine power keeps prompt and careful count of the acts of men and nations
and sees that regular balances are reached. It is a *kosmos* with swift
recompense and recovery. Through his speech we recognize that Nicias
has never fathomed the Thucydidean world of grand and impersonal processes in which the scale of events and the measure of suffering are far
beyond the limits of human comprehension or endurance. We are reminded
simultaneously of the extent of his personal decency and of its inability
to ensure civic success.

Nicias' last words enjoin the soldiers to acquit themselves well and to
remember what has become clear in the narrative of Sicily, that they are
the city and that they have no refuge except their own valor: "The city is
men, and not walls or ships emptied of men" (7.77.7). Nothing could
be more trite. The sentiment has been expressed by Alcaeus (fr. 112.10
L.-P.), Sophocles (*Oedipus Tyrannos* 56f.), Themistocles and Mardonius
in Herodotus (8.61.2 and 100), and Euripides (fr. 828 Nauck *TGrF*[2]). And
yet this time Thucydides ventures no disparaging comment, shows no sign
of contempt or superiority. In their context the words become part of a
powerful thematic progression in the work and mark the transformation of
the expedition from a mighty fleet leading out a city as if on a great
colonizing venture, to a collection of individual and vulnerable human
beings. Nicias' apparent cliché completes the inversion of the calculus of
power in the Archaeology with its emphasis on the physical and quantitative

---

[47] 7.77.3-4. The echoes of Melos continue, evoking now 5.104. The scholiast notes a
parallel to Pindar *Pythian* I 164 (85), κϱέσσον γὰϱ οἰκτιϱμοῦ φθόνος—a proverbial
expression, undermining as much as confirming Nicias' view! Cf. Herodotus 3.52.

bases of power, especially walls and ships. In the last ironic analysis all depends on men, not on material resources.

For Nicias now there is perhaps even a hint of sympathy, a recognition that he has for once spoken with true eloquence.[48] As the withdrawal continues, his deeds bring out his concern, his courage, his compassion. When Nicias is separated from Demosthenes' force, Thucydides justifies his decision not to try to return to help Demosthenes but to push on as rapidly as possible. We are at Nicias' side, and can even read his thoughts: "Nicias led on quickly, thinking that security consisted not in being willing to remain in such a situation and to fight, but to withdraw as rapidly as possible, fighting only when forced to it" (7.81.3). The endurance of Nicias and his men surpasses all precedent.[49] In depicting the final slaughter at the Assinarus River, Thucydides implicitly rejects the version of his surrender that was widely believed in Athens—that Nicias had surrendered of his own choice—and presents instead a brave and honorable commander in a situation of unsurpassed difficulty and horror:[50]

Nicias, when day came, led on his army. The Syracusans and their allies kept up the pressure in the same fashion—shooting from all sides and attacking with javelins from high ground. The Athenians hurried on to the Assinarus River, under constant attack on all sides from the large cavalry force and the light-armed troops. It would

[48] A sudden transition to direct discourse was recognized by some critics in antiquity as a sign of emotion; see Longinus *On the Sublime* 27. The speech is introduced (7.76) without the usual ἔλεξε τοιάδε (cf. 7.60.5 and 65.3).

[49] This endurance is brought out by the expansion of a narrative pattern already developed in earlier sections, esp. 3.97.3-98; 112; and 4.32-40. In this pattern an army is attacked by mobile troops, often light-armed forces (*psiloi*) or cavalry. These shoot at it from the sides (προσέβαλλον e.g. 3.97.3) and direct javelin fire at it (ἐσηκόντιζον) or use rocks and arrows etc. When the army moves against the forces harassing it, they give way only to resume the attacks on its withdrawal. They control the roads or other means of access. Despite the pressure, the heat, the misery, the thirst etc., the army holds out for a time (ἀντεῖχον; e.g. 3.98.1) but finally breaks into a rout or surrenders. There then follows a statistic or some assessment of the size of the defeat and a superlative marking out the distinctive nature of the engagement.

This pattern is elaborated in a day-to-day narrative in 7.78-87 with much attention to the hunger and thirst of the army, and with repetitions of variations of phrases such as προσέβαλλόν τε πανταχῇ. . . κύκλῳ (7.79.5; 82.1; 83.3; 84.1 and 84.2). Note especially the verbal similarity of 7.79.5 to 2.79.6; 3.97.3; 4.32.4. Thucydides notes the division of the army into two forces with separate descriptions of each defeat. The figure for the number of captives in Demosthenes' force is given (with some precision) at 82.3; for Nicias' force the figures are imprecise (85.3). The superlative in 85.4 must apply to the expedition as a whole.

[50] Pausanias 1.29 and Philistus *FGrHist* 556 F 53; see also Dover in *HCT* on 7.86.5 (p. 463). D. H. Kelly, "What Happened to the Athenians Captured in Sicily?," *CR* 20 (1970) 129, n. 2 suggests that Thucydides was reacting to the hostile treatment of Nicias in contemporary discussion or in Philistus' history. By the time of the Aristotelian *Athenaion Politeia* (28.5) Nicias' reputation had recovered; cf. Lysias 18.2.

be easy for them if they could cross the river, or so they thought in their misery and lust to drink. And as they come to it they throw themselves in, all discipline now gone, each one wanting to be the first to cross, and their enemies pressed in to make their crossing difficult. They were forced to crowd together as they moved, stumbled over one another and trampled each other down. Amid their spears and equipment some were swiftly destroyed; others were entangled and swept down the river. On the other bank the Syracusans stood in line (there were steep banks) and shot down at Athenians, while the greater part of them were happy to keep on drinking, there at the bend in the river, in total disarray among one another. (7.84)

This is the consummation of the lust to conquer Sicily. In the midst of the destruction of the army, at the most horrible moment, our eye moves across a scene of destruction reminiscent of the Great Plague and picks out Nicias: "Finally, with bodies piled on bodies in the river and with the expedition ruined, part near the river, part—if anyone could escape from there—cut down by the cavalry, Nicias hands himself over to Gylippus, trusting him more than the Syracusans. And he urged Gylippus to treat him in any way he and the Spartans wanted, but to stop the slaughter of the rest of the army."[51] In our last glimpse of Nicias we see him, however reluctantly, however belatedly, in a new light, asking no quarter for himself but an end to the senseless slaughter of his troops. His famed good fortune has come to this.[52]

---

[51] 7.84.1-85.1. The passage is richly evocative not only of earlier scenes of fighting, and the encirclement narratives (cf. Note 50 above), but also of the plague as described in the second book: 84.2, τοῦ πιεῖν ἐπιθυμίᾳ, recalls 2.52.2, τοῦ ὕδατος ἐπιθυμίᾳ; 84.3., οὐδενὶ κόσμῳ, recalls 2.52.3, οὐδενὶ κόσμῳ; and 85.1, νεκρῶν τε πολλῶν ἐπ' ἀλλήλοις ἤδη κειμένων evokes 2.52.2, νεκροὶ ἐπ' ἀλλήλοις ... ἔκειντο. The parallels are all to the passage that marks the transition from the description of the physical symptoms of the plague to the discussion of the psychological and ethical disintegration that accompanied it.

There is a further group of echoes. In some respects the description of the withdrawal calls to mind the view of the underworld contained in Orphic tablets, largely found in Magna Graecia. See G. P. Carratelli, "Un nuovo testo orphico," *Parola del Passato* 29 (1974) 110-26 and most recently S. G. Cole, " New Evidence for the Mysteries of Dionysus," *GRBS* 21 (1980) 223-38. The tablets describe what those who have died should do when they reach the underworld. They will see a spring (κρῆνα) on the right but are not to go near it. Further on is the λίμνη of memory from which cold water flows. Opposite and above (ἐπ' ὑπέρθεν) are guards but they will have mercy and allow those to drink who know the correct thing to say: "I am the son of Barea and starry Heaven. I am parched with thirst and I perish." After drinking one may proceed on the sacred road with the other Mystai and Bakchoi. At the Assinarus the Orphic pattern is reversed. The Athenians fall upon themselves in their eagerness to drink the first water they see. The Syracusan guards show no mercy; no words are reported until Nicias hands himself over to Gylippus. The water turns bloody amid death. The Athenians' further movement is only to slavery or imprisonment. The reader need not assume that Thucydides is constructing a conscious contrast between his story and the Orphic myths to recognize the extent to which his narrative touches on deeply held fears and utilizes images of great emotional power within the culture.

[52] 6.24.2; cf. 6.17.1 and 5.16.1.

His death brings out a final irony. One reason he had wanted to stay on a little longer at Syracuse was his hope that subversion would bring the city over (7.48.2; cf. 49.1). After his capture, the story had it, his Syracusan sympathizers, afraid that he might reveal their communications with him and thereby inject some "disarray into their success" (7.86.4), joined with the Corinthians to bring about his death and that of Demosthenes: "He died for such a reason or something very close to it—a man who of all the Greeks of my time least deserved to come to such misfortune through his commitment to what is considered complete *aretē*."[53] This brief valedictory is no encomium; it makes no attempt to express the author's final assessment of Nicias as a person or of the effectiveness of his policies. It is not even a true authorial judgment, but rather a way of making the reader pause at this most horrible of moments and contemplate the un-

[53] 7.86.5. The passage is difficult and the manuscripts disagree; the agreement of adjective with noun is not easy to determine; a satisfactory English phrasing is almost impossible. The textual problem, however, can be resolved with a high degree of certainty since the manuscripts that omit πᾶσαν ἐς ἀρετήν almost certainly reflect an early haplography. Which adjectives modify which nouns is less easily determined. Dover in *HCT* ad loc. (p. 463) argues that πᾶσαν goes with ἀρετήν ("in the sense 'complete virtue' ") and νενομισμένην with ἐπιτήδευσιν (to denote the practice which Nicias observed). The result of Dover's views, however, is very strange: "through his practice all observed into goodness," a translation which immediately requires a very free paraphrase ("because he had ordered his whole life by high moral standards").

The scholiast supports Dover's interpretation of πᾶσαν (cf. Aelius Aristeides XLVI 268 = Dindorf, vol. 2 [Leipzig 1829] p. 349) but takes νενομισμένην with ἀρετήν. The first point is easily accepted. For the word order, preposition surrounded by noun and adjective, cf. 2.36.4 and perhaps 2.40.2; the effect is elevation of tone. The syntax and sense of νενομισμένην is more difficult. Here I find it hard to share Dover's confidence that νενομισμένην cannot agree with ἀρετήν and must modify ἐπιτήδευσιν. What does it add—indeed what does it mean?—when added to ἐπιτήδευσιν? The only reason I can see for writing it is to allow reader and author to detach themselves from disputes about the word ἀρετή. The point, Thucydides implies, is not whether Nicias' conduct was true *aretē*, but that he acted in ways that he and his society considered to be *aretē*. This is not malice, as J. B. Bury, *Ancient Greek Historians* (New York 1909) 119 suggested, nor a sneer at Nicias' merely "conventional" virtue, but a way of emphasizing the failure of Nicias' own expectations (7.77.2f.).

An equally significant, and much less discussed, ambiguity is whether the unit διὰ . . . ἐπιτήδευσιν modifies ἀφικέσθαι (he came to this misfortune through his conduct), or ἥκιστα . . . ἄξιος (he did not deserve this fate because his conduct was so upstanding). The latter is widely assumed, but the Greek is ambiguous; word order perhaps favors the former alternative. I believe the reader is encouraged to contemplate both aspects. Nicias' dutiful willingness to command the expedition, his refusal to adopt any course that might seem cowardly etc. all contributed to his disaster. The same qualities make us feel he does not deserve the treatment he receives. This ambiguity reflects the fundamental irony of Nicias' situation, that the qualities that make him admirable are also ones that contribute to his destruction.

Important recent discussions of the passage include L. Edmunds, *Chance and Intelligence in Thucydides* (Cambridge, Mass. 1975) 141f. and A.W.H. Adkins, "The *Aretē* of Nicias," *GRBS* 16 (1975) 379-91.

fairness of Nicias' end. He wagered all on presumptions that have turned out to be mistaken. He acted as best he could by his own values and by those of his society. And his mistakes were, after all, not vicious ones, but ones that he shared with his fellows—pride in courage, confidence in piety and integrity, and a reliance on the calculations of ships and money that had seemed so plausible and reassuring. Whatever we think of him or his policies, he did not deserve this.

Nicias has, morever, been a spokesman for and a representative of the cause of self-restraint and moderation so strongly, if tacitly, articulated in many of the earlier parts of the *Histories*. His death marks the destruction not only of the army, and symbolically of the city, but also of the constraints that convention and traditional morality sought to place upon appetite and self-aggrandizement.

For the reader too all way of retreat has been blocked. There is now no shadow of turning; we are forced to stare at the unrelenting circles of unallayed suffering, the quarries of Syracuse.

The Syracusans treated those in the quarries severely during the first stages. Since so many were crowded in a place hollow and small, they were afflicted by the sun and the heat even though it was late in the summer. There was no shelter. As autumn came on and the cold nights, the change ran riot with health. There was so little space that everyone did everything in the same spot, and even corpses were heaped all together one on the other. They died from wounds and the change and the like. The smell was unbearable; hunger and thirst together tormented them. (For eight months the ration per person was a half pint of water and a pint of grain.) Every form of suffering that you would expect to find afflicting men who had fallen into such a spot beset them; there was nothing that did not come upon them. For some seventy days they lived together in this fashion. Then they sold the others—all except the Athenians and their Sicilian and Italian allies. The total number captured is hard to state with precision, but certainly not less than seven thousand.

This Hellenic[54] accomplishment turned out to be the greatest in this war and it

---

[54] Editors since Krüger have commonly deleted Ἑλληνικόν as "stylistically objectionable" (Dover in *HCT* ad loc. p. 464). It is indeed remarkable in the same sentence as ὧν ἀκοῇ Ἑλληνικῶν ἴσμεν. But the manuscripts are unanimous and it is hard to see why the alleged mistake would be made. Would a copyist be tempted to gloss ἔργον or πόλεμον? Since this seems to me unlikely, the unanimous reading of all the major manuscripts should, I believe, stand, and our efforts should be directed at understanding the whole remarkable phrase ἔργον . . . Ἑλληνικόν. After the description of the quarries we would expect not ἔργον but πάθος; cf. 7.30.3. Ἔργον evokes Nicias in 6.8.4 (τῆς Σικελίας ἁπάσης, μεγάλου ἔργου, ἐφίεσθαι) and Hermocrates in 6.33.4 (κάλλιστον δὴ ἔργον ἡμῖν ξυμβήσεται, in turn an echo of Herodotus 8.75). The Athenians have failed in what they

would seem to me also the greatest of those Hellenic actions that we have heard about—most brilliant for the victors, most unfortunate for the ones who were annihilated. Defeated in all ways on all sides and afflicted to no small degree, in no small measure, with what has been called "total annihilation" of both infantry and fleet, there was nothing that was not annihilated. Few out of many ended their wanderings at home. These are the events concerning Sicily. (7.87)

Nicias' death, however horrible, was but the anticipation of the greater annihilation in the quarries. What we observed in his case at the personal level takes on an even more universal, and more horrifying application. For the reader cannot entirely disassociate himself from the suffering Thucydides describes. We too are implicated in the violence. Our observation of this expedition began from a lofty and ironic viewpoint, with the Athenians' confident suppression of Melos fresh in mind. Confronted with such arrogance it was easy to anticipate with some satisfaction the eventual defeat and punishment of Athenian aggression in Sicily. The arrogance of power would provoke its proper retribution, a sign of some residual justice and order. Now we have what we wished but it is a suffering greater than anyone could have imagined or willed. Our former emotions turn upon us. However great the injustice or arrogance of the Athenians, they did not deserve this.

Before the horror of the quarries measurement, individuality, and even language give way. The passage evokes at first the physical circumstances of the captives in the quarries—the cold, the hunger, the thirst, the smells— all in a long, almost shapeless, sentence. But the suffering is not the total of such details nor is it to be seen through any individual. All is collective; the unit has become the quarry and the suffering greater than any emotion. It is *meizō ē kata dakrya* (7.75.4)—too great to be measured by tears. Ultimately it is comprehensible only as the conflict between and the fusion of two extremes—the aggregate of physical torment, and death, negation, and extinction. Between these two whatever is separate or individual is reduced, first to the generic, then to a statistic and finally to nothingness. Stylistically the extremes are represented by an alternation between the accumulation of words for the aggregate, such as *pollous* ("many"), *homou*

---

hoped to accomplish and Hermocrates' analysis of the vulnerability of great expeditions (6.33.4f.) is confirmed. The language also combines an elegiac with an ironic tone. A comparison to the verses in the Eurymedon (or possibly Cyprus) epigram (W. Peek, "Die Kämpfe am Eurymedon," *HSCP*, supplementary vol. 1, *Athenian Studies Presented to W. S. Ferguson* [1940] 97-120 show the elegiac elements. The contrast to Eurymedon, however, also brings out the irony of the situation—the greatest accomplishment of the Greeks is now to destroy other Greeks. The repetition of "Hellenic" underlines this point, evokes 2.64.3, and should be retained.

xynnenēmenōn ("heaped all together") and multiple negatives, such as
the litotes *ouden hoti ouk epegeneto autois* ("there was nothing that did
not come upon them"). This is reinforced by contrasting patterns of alliteration: "p" sounds for words indicating much and many and "o"
sounds for negatives and words indicating annihilation. In the penultimate
sentence, before the epic echo of *apenostēsan* ("they ended their wanderings") lets us look away, the stylistic conflict becomes harsh and intense—*kata panta gar pantōs* ("in all ways on all sides") and *ouden oligon
es ouden* ("and afflicted to no small degree")—until the two extremes
merge in a cascade of phrases that combine the two elements and fuse the
two alliterative systems: *panōlethriai* ("total destruction"), *pezos kai nēes
kai ouden hoti ouk apōleto* ("of both infantry and fleet there was nothing
that was not annihilated"), and *oligoi apo pollōn* ("few out of many").[55]
The first of these is a combination of "all" (*pan-*) and a word for destruction
or annihilation (*olethria*).[56] The compound is an expression as awesome
as paradoxical, so unusual that it calls forth its one famous use in earlier
literature, Herodotus' comment on the fall of Troy: "When some divine
power contrives that all should perish with total annihilation, they [the
gods] make this clear to men, that for great wrongdoings great also are
the punishments from the gods."[57] That Thucydides, stern skeptic, enlightenment man, should contemplate such a theodicy surprises and per-
plexes. Are we suddenly to conclude that behind the immense suffering

---

[55] Ὀλίγοι ἀπὸ πολλῶν evokes Darius' ghost in Aeschylus *Persae* 800, who refers to
the survivors of the expedition against Greece as παῦροί γε πολλῶν.

[56] Note the alliterative pattern of "o" sounds and "p" sounds: (7.87.1) ἐν γὰρ κοίλῳ
χωρίῳ ὄντας καὶ ὀλίγῳ πολλοὺς οἵ τε ἥλιοι τὸ πρῶτον καὶ τὸ πνῖγος ἔτι ἐλύπει
. . . ; (87.2) πάντα τε ποιούντων . . . ἐμπεπτωκότας κακοπαθῆσαι, οὐδὲν ὅτι οὐκ
. . . ; (87.6) κατὰ πάντα γὰρ πάντως . . . καὶ οὐδὲν ὀλίγον ἐς οὐδὲν κακοπαθήσαν-
τες πανωλεθρίᾳ . . . οὐδὲν ὅτι οὐκ ἀπώλετο, καὶ ὀλίγοι ἀπὸ πολλῶν . . . ἀπενόστησαν.

[57] Herodotus 2.120.5, τοῦ δαιμονίου παρασκευάζοντος ὅκως πανωλεθρίῃ ἀπολό-
μενοι καταφανὲς τοῦτο τοῖσι ἀνθρώποισι ποιήσωσι, ὡς τῶν μεγάλων ἀδικημάτων
μεγάλαι εἰσὶ καὶ αἱ τιμωρίαι παρὰ τῶν θεῶν. Cf. Herodotus 4.205. N. Marinatos
Kopff and H. R. Rawlings, "*Panolethria* and Divine Punishment," *Parola del Passato* 182
(1978) 331-337, convince me that the allusion in Thucydides is specifically to Herodotus
and not to some proverb or commonplace. The Herodotus passage poses precisely the question
that was implied but swiftly suppressed at the beginning of book 6. Was this expedition an
instance of divine retribution? Kopff and Rawlings assume that the question is answered in
the affirmative by the evocation of Herodotus. I believe they are on the right track (pace
Dover in *HCT* ad loc., p. 465, who seems to me to beg the question: "if Thucydides had
recalled the Herodotean passage he would have taken some trouble to avoid the appearance
of subscribing to its theology"), but I am unable to go quite as far as they do. The passage
seems to me to raise the question of theodicy but to leave it quite open. It is not a statement
of Thucydides' theology, but a way to lead an enlightened and sophisticated audience to
confront the awesome possibility that there may be a divine dimension to human history.

that we are witnessing there stands some divinity requiting past offenses, not with the careful calibration that Nicias assumed but with an immensity that baffles and confounds? If so, what divinity is it, benign or demonic? Readers will here part ways and conclude as their theologies or dispositions dictate. Thucydides withdraws and provides no guidance. He is no theologian and will not play at it. The possibilities themselves are awesome enough and converge in a common recognition, that the destruction of the expedition has reached—and surpassed—the limits of human experience and comprehension.

Book 8

MOST READERS of Thucydides have found the account of the Sicilian Expedition to be the culmination of the work with the eighth book a disappointing sequel. Whereas the seventh book draws together many of the major themes of the work—ships, finances, walls, the dissolution of ethnic ties, and the greatness of the war[1]—and transforms them into a rich and moving unity, the eighth book is diffuse, fragmented, and incomplete. The narrative, in Cornford's words, seems "unfinished, dull and spiritless" and "the historian . . . seems to grope his way like a man without a clue."[2]

The reason for this reaction to the eighth book is in large part to be found in a conflict between the symbolic and the factual levels of the work. At the symbolic level the account of the Sicilian disaster has developed an equation between the large expeditionary force and the city, while Athens itself has become "instead of a city, a fort" (7.28.1). The destruction of the expedition is thus emotionally the destruction of Athens itself, and the virtual end of the war. In fact, however, the nineteenth year of the twenty-seven-year war is not yet over. There is much more, and much worse, to come.

The eighth book is thus another example of a familiar pattern in the *Histories*, reopening after apparent closure. As we have seen, Thucydidean narratives, especially those focussed on the *pathos* or suffering of the war, often seem to draw to a close and then open up again to explore a new instance or effect of the suffering.[3] This pattern is now transferred from

---

[1] L. Pearson, "Thucydides as Reporter and Critic," *TAPA* 78 (1947) 48.

[2] F. M. Cornford, *Thucydides Mythistoricus* (London 1907) 244. Recent scholarship has moved cautiously in the direction of a more sympathetic assessment of Book 8; see for example the discussions in P. Pouncey, *Necessities of War* (New York 1980); M. Cogan, *The Human Thing* (Chicago 1981); and J. de Romilly, "Les problèmes de politique intérieure dans l'oeuvre de Thucydide," in *Historiographica Antiqua (Commentationes Lovanienses in honorem W. Peremans)* (Leuven 1977) 77-93.

[3] Such reopenings are characteristic of Thucydides' *pathos* narratives, for example: (1) *The plague*, Apparent conclusion in 2.51.1 reopened to explore the psychological and moral effects of the affliction; (2) *Corcyra*, Completion and generalization in 3.81.5, followed by

the relatively short narratives in which it has most often appeared to the larger architecture of the work. In this reopening the reader swiftly encounters themes that had not been significantly treated in the Sicilian narrative, especially Athens' great endurance and the tendency of her allies and opponents to underestimate her strength and determination. The second book had already introduced this theme and anticipated the tension between it and the emphasis on the magnitude of the Sicilian disaster:

They took a fall in Sicily both with the rest of their force and with the greater part of their navy, and in the city they were now in *stasis*. Yet despite their attrition, they still held out against their former enemies, and against the reinforcements that came from Sicily, and as well against the majority of their allies who revolted, and later in addition against Cyrus, the son of the great king, who supplied funds to the Peloponnesians for their navy; they did not give in until, by entangling themselves in domestic disagreements, they took a fall.[4]

The passage begins and ends with the same wrestling metaphor ("took a fall"), conveyed by the same verb (σφάλλω), but the cause of the "fall" is transformed by the intervening analysis.[5] Neither Sicily, nor the Spartans, nor the revolt of Athenian allies, nor the intervention of Persia, but Athens' own political dissension, causes the ultimate defeat. This passage establishes that the disaster in Sicily, however important symbolically, is not the end of the Peloponnesian War nor the true cause of Athenian defeat. A further stage of analysis is required that must involve an investigation of material often lightly treated in some earlier sections of the work—the sources of Athens' continuing strength and the relation between Athenian domestic politics and the city's foreign affairs. The opening chapters of the eighth book thus serve as a modulation from the immensity of the Sicilian disaster to a new and even greater struggle for survival. The violence of the war now comes home to Athens, not only through the incursions of the Spartans from their fort in Deceleia but also through an internalization of violence in the political struggles and *stasis* of the period.

The difficulties that beset Athens after the Sicilian disaster have a double function. They are steps on the road to her ultimate defeat but also mark

---

further examples of atrocities and discussion of *staseis* in other cities; (3) *Mycalessus*, Total destruction of the town described in 7.29.4 followed by generalization about Thracians and a summary of the destruction in 7.29.5, then a further detail (destruction of the children in the school) and resumption of narrative with the account of the withdrawal of the Thracians and the Theban attack.

[4] 2.65.12. On the text see above, Chapter Two, Note 29.

[5] Other sentences beginning and ending with forms of the same word are found in 3.42.3 and 3.45.6, and Gorgias *Palamedes*, *VS* 82 B 112, sec. 3.

out her continuing strength and determination. A certain blurring or opacity
results, all the more troublesome because we cannot follow through the
larger development of which the book must be a part. The narrative ends
abruptly in the middle of a paragraph concerning events of the twenty-first
year of the war. Despite this incompleteness, the general development of
this section of the work can readily be detected. The initial despair following the news of the losses in Sicily gradually gives way to a determination to resist; amid grave difficulties Athens holds out, overcomes
revolution at home, and the revolt of her dependencies abroad, and even
defeats the enemy fleet at Cynossema (8.102-106). But this story of a slow
and unsteady movement from despair to endurance, from defeat to recovery, must be viewed with the foreknowledge of Athens' eventual defeat.
The recovery is an ascent leading to a greater fall.

The eighth book is thus a modulation abruptly terminated, hence inevitably unsatisfying. It begins, moreover, with a technique easily misun-
derstood if the reader is not alert to Thucydides' occasional tendency to
represent as fact the mood and expectations of the characters he portrays.
He does not stop to qualify or correct the Athenians' assessment of the
news from Sicily:

For they were grieved, both individually and as a city, by the loss of so many
hoplites and cavalry and of a crack force the like of which they had not seen. At
the same time they despaired of any salvation in their present situation for they
saw that the ships in reserve, the funds in the treasury, the crews for the ships
were insufficient. They expected that their enemies from Sicily would immediately
sail against the Piraeus with their navy, especially since they had won so decisively,
and that their enemies in Greece proper would then make double efforts and attack
them in force from both land and sea, and that their allies would revolt and join
them. (8.1.2)

Very swiftly, however, the mood changes and the recognition grows, both
among the Athenians and in the reader, that the situation is by no means
as desperate as had at first been thought. Even the passage we have just
quoted continues with a sentence reporting Athenian determination:
"Nevertheless, as best they could under the circumstances they resolved
that it was essential not to give in."[6] The idea and the language evokes

---

[6] 8.1.3. Note ὡς ἐκ τῶν ὑπαρχόντων echoes 7.76.1 and invites the expectation of some
statement about their improving attitude or encouragement. Abruptly μὴ ἐνδιδόναι sums
up the decision. See also 2.12.1 and 12.4, 18.5, and the Melians' refusal to give in in 5.86;
cf. 5.114.
   Failure to note that the account is constructed to lead the reader to share in the Athenians'
initial despair and then to participate in the recovery of their spirits can easily lead to false

the statement of the theme of Athenian endurance in 2.65.12. Soon we learn the measures the Athenians take to continue the struggle and gradually we share in their realization that the situation is not hopeless. The desire for revolt is not universal among Athens' subjects (8.9.3); the Sicilian contribution to the Peloponnesian military forces is not large (8.26.1); Spartan actions are characteristically slow and cautious; a reserve fund of one thousand talents, set aside at the beginning of the war (2.24.1), but not mentioned in the account of the initial Athenian despair, is now utilized (8.15.1). In retrospect the reactions to the Sicilian disaster, as reported in the first chapter of the book, are easily recognized as excessive.

The reader thus participates in the gradual revival of Athenian spirits. Many other Greeks, on the other hand, persist in their elation and over-confidence. They repeat, in effect, the miscalculation of Athenian power that had been made earlier in the war.[7] As the eighth book continues, we see the effects of this misassessment. The Chians, for example, despite their remarkable caution and careful preparations, underestimate Athenian power, are unsuccessful in their revolt and, for the first time since the days of Persian dominance, have their land ravaged (8.24.3f.). Thucydides emphasizes that their policies were typical of those adopted by many other Greek cities.

If this were the full measure of the book, it would be a relatively straightforward narrative and relatively easy to assess. The reader would expect, for example, that its techniques would not differ very significantly from those we have already encountered, and that behind the complex and scattered events of the war a clear and coherent shaping of material should be evident. There is, however, a new dimension to the eighth book, one which, I believe, transforms the narrative into something unlike the earlier portions of the *Histories*. This new dimension is already implicit in the

---

inferences about the work. R. Meiggs, *The Athenian Empire* (Oxford 1972) 351, for example, seems to imply that Thucydides overstated the danger to the empire and then provided facts that refuted his own view: "The empire meanwhile, according to Thucydides, threatened collapse as the allies competed fiercely to be the first to revolt, now that Athens' power was broken. His detailed narrative does not fully bear out this gloomy analysis." A similar approach is taken in *HCT* on 8.2.2 (p. 8): "Thucydides' preoccupation with Athens' unpopularity . . . seems to have run away with him once more."

[7] 8.2.1. The overconfidence of the Hellenes evokes two earlier episodes: The first is their enthusiasm at the beginning of the war for the Spartan cause, as reported by Archidamus in 2.11.2 (N.B. ἡ γὰρ Ἑλλὰς πᾶσα . . . ἐπῆρται) and in Thucydides' own words in 2.8.4. The second episode is the reception accorded Brasidas by Athens' allies in northern Greece (N.B. ἐπήρθησαν in 4.108.3). The second of these episodes anticipated the reaction after the Sicilian defeat: 4.81.2f. The Peloponnesians also misassess Athenian naval strength in 8.8.4 and 8.10.2.

first chapter, when Thucydides notes the Athenians' decision to establish a group of *probouloi*, or councillors, "and, as the populace often does, they were ready to put everything into disciplined order in response to the present fearful situation" (8.1.4). This sentence introduces an important topic in the eighth book—the connection between domestic political structure and the successful conduct of the war. As the book progresses, this topic becomes increasingly central, for the energy of the book comes to concentrate more on the struggle for stable and sensible political direction than on the military and diplomatic maneuvering. These are often swiftly recounted, with only passing attention to the underlying strategy, while the political conflicts, especially those leading up to the governments of the Four Hundred and the Five Thousand in Athens, are some of the most powerfully written portions of the book.

The political dimension of the war, now more fully developed than in any preceding portion of the *Histories*, transforms the book from a relatively simple story of Athenian endurance and recovery into a much more complex narrative. It points, moreover, to what Thucydides has already indicated was the source of Athens' ultimate defeat: "they did not give in until, by entangling themselves in domestic disagreements, they took a fall" (2.65.12). The real threat to Athens, we recognize, is not the Sicilian disaster, nor the revolt of her allies, nor the power of Sparta and Persia, but the dissolution of her political coherence.

The concern with political dissolution has a further effect upon the literary form of the book. A narrative convenience disappears. Until this point it has almost always been possible for Thucydides to represent the Athenians either as a unit in civic or collective narrative, or to select one or two individuals whose ideas and policies eventually shape civic action. In *stasis*, however, narrative units, as well as political coherence, disintegrate. We can no longer consider the Athenians as a unit, nor the city's political life as a series of choices between the policies of a few dominant leaders. The city is torn between oligarchic and democratic factions; it is physically divided between the military forces on Samos who claim to be the true city (8.76.3) and the oligarchs in Athens. Among the oligarchs there is a split between the more extreme and the more moderate factions and a strong tendency toward individual rivalries and struggles for preeminence (8.89.3).

The book has a large and brilliant cast of characters. We might expect that one or two of them—Alcibiades, Agis, or Phrynichus—might serve as a center of focus around which the events of the book might be arranged and given form. But no figure in the eighth book takes on the role that Brasidas performed in the fourth book or Nicias and Demosthenes in the seventh. Individuals appear with momentary prominence and then swiftly disappear in disfavor, obscurity, or death.

In this respect the book records the tendency toward civic disintegration or moral atomism that almost any student of history recognizes in the last decade of the war. More than any other book in the work it moves to the level of individual choices and motives. We see many individuals elaborately planning and plotting, sometimes quite desperately seeking their own advancement or survival. Yet for all the brilliance of the characters, there is no permanence or stability. Events are out of civic or individual control. We can appreciate in this another aspect of the *pathos* of the war, not just the pain and suffering so vividly depicted in the earlier parts of the work, but the other sense of the Greek word *pathos*, the inability to control events. In war individuals and states lose their ability to make things happen; things happen to them.

The literary analogue to this loss of individual and civic control is a disintegration of the units and techniques upon which so much of the earlier portions of the work is built. The reader can no longer assume civic unity or the centrality of any individual or place. The convenient concentration on a single theater, so well utilized in book 7, is now impossible. The war extends to wider and wider boundaries and involves simultaneous operations in Attica, Euboea, the Hellespont, Chios, Lesbos, Samos, and elsewhere. Chronologically, as we shall see, the division of the war into summer and winter campaigning seasons is no longer well suited to the lengthy and interconnected developments taking place in this phase of the war.

Nor can Sparta or Persia any longer be treated as monolithic units. Divisions and rivalries within each of these states have major effects on the course of the war. The tension between King Agis of Sparta and the authorities at home helps shape Spartan foreign policy, just as the conflicting objectives of Tissaphernes and Pharnabazus effect Persian conduct in the war (8.5-6).

Thucydides' normal confidence in the assessment of motives and strategies, moreover, gives way to a more meditative approach. If in the earlier books Thucydides was "determined to do all the work himself and to present only the finished product to the public, as the artist does. Wren showed St. Paul's Cathedral to the world, not his plans for it; so does the painter his picture; so did Pheidias his sculpture."[8] But now he seems to think out loud and invite the reader to analyze alternative explanations

---

[8] A. W. Gomme, *The Greek Attitude to Poetry and History* (Berkeley 1954) 119, following Gilbert Murray and others. Cf. L. von Ranke, *Weltgeschichte* (Leipzig 1896): I, ii, ch. 8, p. 52: "Die Ansichten des Historikers treten selbst als Historie auf."

with him, often labeling his conclusions as one man's opinion.[9] We are invited into Thucydides' study and allowed to watch him making up his mind. In chapter 87 for example, he deals with the question of why Tissaphernes, when he had at his disposal 147 Phoenician ships, in addition to other forces, refused to engage the Athenian navy. Elsewhere in the work we might have found a simple statement of Thucydides' conclusion, presented as fact. Here we witness the weighing of the evidence:

Various accounts are given and it is not easy to know with what intention he came to Aspendus and, having come, failed to lead on the ships. That Phoenician ships, 147 of them, came to Aspendus is agreed, but why they did not proceed is diversely conjectured. Some say it was so that by going away he might wear down the Peloponnesian side, as indeed he intended. (Tamos, in any event, who was following his orders, did not provide better, but actually worse, provisions for them.) Some say it was in order to make money by bringing the Phoenician fleet to Aspendus and selling the crews their discharges. (The implication is that he never intended to use them.) Still others say that it was because of the outcry that had arisen in Sparta so that it would now be said that he was not acting improperly, but had indeed indisputably gone after ships that were really manned.

To me it seems most evident that his reason for not leading on the ships was to wear down and hinder the Greek cause. He wasted their strength as long as he was travelling there and delaying; he kept them evenly balanced to avoid making one party stronger by throwing his weight on either side. Since, had he wanted to, it is evident that he could of course unequivocally have ended the war. For if he had brought on the fleet he would in all probability have bestowed the victory on the Spartans, whose navy at that point faced the Athenians more as an equal than as an inferior. What convicts him most decisively is the reason he gave for not bringing on the fleet. For he said that he had a smaller number of ships than the king had ordered him to collect. But he would of course have won still greater gratitude if expending less of the king's funds he had achieved the same results from fewer resources. Tissaphernes then, with whatever intention arrives in Aspendus and joins the Phoenicians.[10]

The earlier books of the *Histories* contain no precise parallel to a passage such as this. Here the reader and the author share a common inquiry and break beyond the surface narrative to the arguments and decisions that shape it.

In this new pattern of narrative we are much more aware of the author

---

[9] E.g. 8.56.3 and 87.4. Cf. J. de Romilly, *Histoire et raison chez Thucydide* (Paris 1956), 84, n. 1, and Andrewes in *HCT* on book 8, app. 2, p. 399f.

[10] 8.87.2-6. For similar examples see 8.46.5 and 56.2. There are useful discussions in Andrewes, *HCT* ad loc. (p. 290f.; cf. p. 455f.) and in D. Lateiner, "Tissaphernes and the Phoenician Fleet," *TAPA* 106 (1976) 267-290.

and his activities and less likely to be drawn into the illusion that the events of the war are reporting themselves. The omniscient narrator is replaced by a fellow inquirer who, at least from time to time, stops to look more closely at motives, admits his uncertainties and explains his reasoning.

Thus many of the characteristic features of Thucydidean narrative are shattered or changed in the eighth book. The result is a doubly difficult problem: not only is the book concerned with complex and diverse events, but also some familiar techniques and devices seem no longer fully adapted to the demands of the narrative. Few will want to argue that Thucydides fully solved this problem. But the reader does well to concentrate on the nature of the difficulty and the changes in literary technique rather than to rely on the conventional explanation that Thucydides died before completing the book and would radically have modified it if he had lived on. To be sure, the fact that the book breaks off in the middle of the account of 411/410, makes this common, if unverifiable, idea seem plausible. Corroboration is often drawn from the absence of speeches in direct discourse, the presence of directly quoted documents, for example the treaties quoted in chapters 18 and 37, and the omission of some major events, notably the Athenian alliance with Amorges.[11] Throughout there are loose ends and a lack of coordination of individual trains of events.[12] Although the book is less complete and far less polished than the others, it would be dangerous to assume that the cause lies purely in the length of Thucydides' life. As the discussion of book 5 has shown, the presence of documents and the absence of speeches in direct discourse do not provide reliable indications of "incompleteness." The two books that have quoted documents as well as speeches in indirect rather than direct discourse are ones that confront especially difficult narrative problems: source problems, the complex diplomacy involving Argos, Arcadia, and Thebes as well as Athens and Sparta in book 5, and in book 8 the connection between widely scattered military operations and the political events with which they are so intimately joined.

The reason for their distinctive shape may be found in the problems posed by these phases of the war rather than in the length of Thucydides' life. When we note the variations in narrative technique even in other

[11] The evidence for the incompleteness of the eighth book is admirably set forth by A. Andrewes in app. 1 of *HCT* on book 8, esp. pp. 369-375; cf. also Andrewes' introduction pp. 1-4. On the alliance with Amorges see Andocides 3 (On the Peace) 29, A. Andrewes, "Thucydides and the Persians," *Historia* 10 (1961) 1-18 and H. D. Westlake, "Athens and Amorges," *Phoenix* 31 (1977) 319-329.

[12] Cf. K. von Fritz, *Griechische Geschichtsschreibung* (Berlin 1967) I, a 757-778.

sections of the work, it becomes more likely that Thucydides was adapting his approach to the narrative opportunities and problems of these years. Among them are not only themes such as the breakdown of civic unity, the internalization of violence, the close connection between domestic and foreign policy, and the struggles for prominence by politicians of every persuasion, but also a special need to control the length of this part of the work. The complexity of events, the conduct of the war in many different theaters, the large number of prominent individuals all encourage the expansion of the narrative. The account of the twentieth year of the war consumes fifty-four chapters, well beyond the average for earlier parts of the war. The twenty-first year, if complete, would have been even longer. A desire to control this tendency toward disproportionate length may account for some of the features of the eighth book, and some of its resemblances to the fifth book where, for quite different reasons, Thucydides may have wished to avoid overexpansion. A preference for indirect over direct discourse may be the result, for example, of an effort to control the length of these portions of the work. Similarly the compression evident in the accounts of some of the military operations and the relative obscurity of strategic considerations may have a similar origin. At the outset, for example, we are left to conjecture that the control of the Hellespont is the key to defeating Athens and that the Peloponnesians lack the naval force to sail there and immediately dominate the area. From this starting point, we can understand why the one island that retains a significant independent navy, Chios, will be crucial to Peloponnesian operations (cf. 8.15.1). If Chios joins in a concerted attack on the Athenian grain route, the Peloponnesians will have a good chance of rapid success. If not, Athens may still find a way of successfully weathering the war. Such conjectures are vital for an understanding of Spartan strategy. They help explain the Spartans' reluctance to accept Pharnabazus' invitation to move directly against the Hellespont (8.6.1) and the considerable concern shown for Chios. Yet Thucydides' highly compressed narrative provides little space for the analysis of the background to military events.

Amid such compression more fully developed material stands out with great prominence. Again, as in book 5, the absence of speeches in direct discourse contrasts sharply with the presence of a series of documents quoted practically verbatim. The treaties and alliances in the earlier book, we argued, served an important purpose. They emphasized the breakdown of oaths and other restraints and brought out the instability of foreign relations during a period of ostensible peace. The documents in the eighth book, three understandings between the Spartans and the Persians (8.18,

37, and 58), serve a similar purpose. They reveal, more clearly than any generalization or indictment, the willingness of the Spartans to sacrifice the Greeks of Asia Minor in order to win the support of the Persians. The first of these treaties contains the astonishing agreement that the Great King of Persia is to own whatever land and cities he currently holds and whatever his fathers held (8.18.1). The phrase is not qualified or explained, but its implications would be momentous for the Greeks of Asia Minor, and even for those in the areas once held by the Persians in northern Greece. This objection is made explicit by the Spartan Lichas (8.43.3) shortly after the second understanding between the Spartans and the Persians is reported (ch. 37). He criticizes the treaties as a kind of slavery and as refutation of the Spartan claims to be liberators of Greece. The third treaty (ch. 58) is subject to the same strictures.[13]

The documents, then, carry forward another theme of the *Histories*: the enslavement of Greece. In the early books the Athenians are the enslavers (e.g. 1.98.4) and the Spartans promise freedom (e.g. 2.8.4). The fraudulence of that Spartan claim is progressively exposed as the work goes on, never by direct challenge from Athenian speakers, but by the criticisms of others and by the words and deeds of the Spartans themselves.[14] Eventually even Lichas accepts the need for some limited and temporary submission to the Persians; he "said it was proper that the Milesians and others in the king's territory act to a moderate extent as slaves to Tissaphernes and to tend to his whims until they could set the war in good order" (8.84.5).

The documents in book 8 have an important role in the development of the enslavement theme. Here we can conjecture that Thucydides has adapted a technique also used in book 5 and used it to good advantage. Another departure from the general compression of the book, however, is without a close parallel or precedent. This is the use of "flashbacks" or simul-

[13] Cf. H. Erbse, "Argos und Melos im fünften Buch des Thukydides," *Würzburger Jahrbücher* N.F. 1 (1975) 66. *HCT* on book 8 (e.g. pp. 86ff.) seems to me unpersuasive in its efforts to minimize the Spartan concessions in these documents.

[14] Opponents of Athenian rule introduce the enslavement theme in book 1.68.3; 69.1; 124.3. In 1.98.4 Thucydides adopts this language. Athenian speakers do not directly challenge these charges nor do they attempt to refute the Peloponnesian claim that they are acting for the liberation of Greece (1.122.3; 124.3; 139.3; cf. 2.8.4). Spartan words and deeds reveal the speciousness of their claim, e.g. 3.32.2 and the proposal in 4.17-20, esp. 20.4. On the themes of liberation and enslavement in the account of Brasidas' expedition see the discussion in Chapter Four. Book 8 resumes these themes, provides a more detailed view of the relationship between Athens and her allies, and points to dangers inherent in Spartan rule. The harmost system, for example, is alluded to in 8.52 (anticipated in 4.132.3).

taneous narration at two points in the book.[15] The development is not a
surprising one considering the overlapping action of the war in several
theaters. But the flashbacks of book 8 are not perfunctory glances at material
that might otherwise have been forced out of the narrative by more pressing
events. They take on a life of their own and carry forward some of the
most important themes and ideas of the book.

The first of the two flashbacks of book 8 begins in chapter 45 with the
awkward phrases, "in this time and even earlier, before they moved off
to Rhodes, the following things were done." The next ten chapters are a
series of dramatic episodes, told with a rich enjoyment of their ironies and
reversals, all focussed on Alcibiades. The effect is to break out of the
surface progression of events and to look more closely at the motives and
psychology of the characters. Alcibiades' personality emerges with great
clarity as the reader sees him maneuvering with Tissaphernes and Phrynichus. His desire to return to Athens shapes his advice to Tissaphernes
(47.1) and leads him to collaboration with oligarchical conspirators (48.1).
Eventually the flashback blends in with the narrative of continuing military
and diplomatic events.

The prominence of Alcibiades in this section has naturally led to speculation about Thucydides' sources and to the suggestion that Alcibiades
himself may have been one of them.[16] Whatever the merits of this suggestion, it has had one pernicious effect. Scholarly attention has tended
to focus on the source problem and to regard the narrative technique of
this flashback as the result of Thucydides' informants rather than of his
own shaping of material. Thus Delebecque's important observations about
the "recit nouveau" of this book have been excessively focussed on source
and compositional questions and have failed fully to appreciate the literary
originality of this book.[17]

A second flashback (8.63.3) replicates the concern with individuals and

---

[15] 8.45.1 and 8.63.3. The closest analogies are in book 4, 46.1 and 78.1. In Herodotus
note 5.108.

[16] P. A. Brunt, "Thucydides and Alcibiades," *Revue des études grecques* 65 (1952) 59-
96 and E. Delebecque, *Thucydide et Alcibiade* (Publication des annales de la faculté des
lettres . . . no. 49, Aix-en-Provence 1965). Andrewes provides a useful survey of scholarship
on this and related points in his introduction to book 8 in the *HCT*. Note, however, the
approach taken by P. Pouncey in *Necessities of Power* (New York 1980) esp. p. 42.

[17] Delebecque (above, Note 16) provides an elaborate analysis of book 8 based on the
contrasts among "old narrative" (e.g. 8.1-44), "new narrative" (e.g. 8.45-56, 63.3-77) and
"unified narrative" (8.83-109). I am persuaded by many of Delebecque's observations but
believe that the innovations of the eighth book arise primarily from Thucydides' engagement
with the literary problems posed by this phase of the war rather than from differing periods
of composition and differing sources of information.

their motives, and with the tensions within Athens, both of which were evident in the first flashback, but is even more elaborate in its development. The opening sentence echoes its predecessor in chapter 45 and points to its main subject: "About this time and even earlier the democracy in Athens was overthrown." This flashback, then, carries forward one of the major topics of the eighth book, the revolutionary activity within Athens, and further explores the important theme of the connection between domestic and foreign policy. Its technique, moreover, is innovative and its effect surprising. The increasing concern with individuals and their motives, already evident in the first flashback, is now used to assess Athenian political factions and their leadership. The result is a shift to a very critical view of the oligarchic movement. As Westlake has argued, Thucydides shows that, "Most of the leading oligarchs, or at least the most influential of them, were interested only in their own advancement and adopted unscrupulous and oppressive methods in seeking to achieve their selfish aims. Accordingly they ruined the oligarchical cause and nearly ruined Athens as well. On the other hand the democrats at Samos were, he maintains, for the most part genuine patriots who were prepared to make sacrifices in order to preserve the security of Athens under democratic government."[18]

The shift in attitude is surprising given Thucydides' coolness to democracy in earlier portions of the work. But the criticism of oligarchy is inescapable, and cleverly executed. Early in the account of the oligarchic movement at Athens, Thucydides had introduced a powerful critique of its claims. The spokesman through whom the analysis was presented was Phrynichus, of hated memory to the Athenian democrats, but whose admirable canniness was demonstrated in chapter 27.[19] Phrynichus examined one by one the claims of the oligarchs, exposing the weakness of each; he showed that Alcibiades had no interest either in oligarchy or democracy but only in his own return from exile (8.48.4), and argued that the Great King was not likely to attach himself to his old enemies, the Athenians, when he could co-operate with the Spartans, nor were the cities of the empire likely to be more easily controlled under a democracy. They had, he pointed out, ample grounds to fear the so-called "gentlemen" (*kaloi k'agathoi*), that is, government by the upper classes. Phrynichus' critique

[18] H. D. Westlake, "The Subjectivity of Thucydides," *Bulletin of the John Rylands Library* 56 (1973) 214.

[19] Note the echo of Pericles (1.144.1) in 8.27.3. After his death (8.92.2) Phrynichus was posthumously condemned for treason. See also Andrewes ad loc. in *HCT* (pp. 309f.) and H. D. Westlake, "Phrynichus and Astyochus," *JHS* 76 (1956) 99-104.

is logically compelling, and its major points are confirmed by the narrative. Alcibiades' single-minded devotion to his own return has already been indicated in chapter 47, and his lack of ideological commitment to oligarchy is as clear in the subsequent narrative as his contempt for democracy has been in the earlier portions of the work.[20] The king's interest is clearly to grind down the two Greek belligerents through their mutual conflicts, as Alcibiades has already argued (ch. 46). The reader can expect, then, that whatever temporary success Alcibiades might have with Tissaphernes (ch. 52), in the long run Persia will not significantly help Athens (ch. 56). Finally, Phrynichus' perception that the subject cities would be no more securely controlled by an Athenian oligarchy than by a democracy, is confirmed almost as soon as the flashback begins by the example of Thasos. The point is made quite explicitly: "On Thasos the opposite happened to what the Athenians who established the oligarchy expected; in my opinion this also happened among many other subjects. The cities, once they received "Moderation" and immunity for their [oligarchic] activities, moved toward the opposing "freedom," not preferring the suppurating "law and order" of the Athenians.[21]

The account of the revolt of Thasos to which this comment is appended completes the confirmation of Phrynichus' arguments against the oligarchy. With the deceptive claims of the oligarchs stripped away, it is easy to look below the surface of the events, and particularly at the terror and intimidation that accompanied the introduction of the oligarchy.[22] The next chapter begins this exposure. First it recounts some of the murders that preceded the establishment of the oligarchy,[23] and then turns to the oligarchic prop-

[20] Especially 6.89.6, his comment in Sparta describing democracy as an "acknowledged folly."

[21] 8.64.5. The passage is difficult but provides a good example of Thucydides' exploitation of the slogans and language of the various factions. On *sōphrosynē* (moderation) as a slogan of the Athenian oligarchs, cf. Peisander in 8.53.3 and H. North, *Sophrosyne* (Ithaca, N.Y. 1966) 111f.; on *eleutheria* (freedom) see 64.3 (cf. 2.8.4). The reading εὐνομίας (law and order) is attested here by the Vatican manuscript and is probably to be preferred to the more common (and less paradoxical) αὐτονομίαν; see Andrewes in *HCT* ad loc. (p. 160f.). Either term is likely to be an oligarchic slogan or propaganda claim.

Westlake (above Note 18) 193-218, esp. p. 200, points out the affinities between this passage and the account of the revolution in Corcyra. The use of slogans and the emphasis on the transvaluation of language are paralleled in 3.82.4f.

[22] The contrast between surface and deeper reality is suggested by the adjective ὑπούλου (suppurating) applied to *eunomias* (or *autonomias*) at the end of chapter 64. This adjective occurs only here in Thucydides; it properly applies to putrefaction setting in under a scar. The implication is that the surgery of *eunomia* does not work and the wound it causes becomes badly infected.

[23] Young supporters of the revolution killed Androcles both because of his past demagogy and because they thought that his death would be pleasing to Alcibiades "who was returning

aganda: "They devised an account for public consumption that state pay would be given only to the troops on duty, and that participation in public affairs would be restricted to not more than five thousand, and these would be the ones who were most able to come to the city's aid financially or through military service" (8.65.3). This was attractive to many citizens, since it implied that those who supported the move to oligarchy would have a voice in subsequent affairs. But Thucydides makes it clear that the claim was specious,[24] and that argument against the oligarchs, formerly (ch. 53.2) so vehement, was now suppressed. No one dared to speak against the oligarchy, or if someone did, he "immediately died from some suitable means."[25] The description of the terror in the city echoes earlier passages describing moments of political extremism in Athens: the crowd psychology when the Sicilian Expedition was voted,[26] the hysteria at the investigation of the affairs of the herms and mysteries,[27] and the mood of the Pisistratids after the attempted coup by Harmodius and Aristogeiton.[28] It

---

to Athens and making Tissaphernes a friend" (8.65.2). But we know Alcibiades has by this time failed with Tissaphernes (ch. 56) and the leaders of the revolution are no longer eager for his return (63.4).

[24] 8.66.1. ἦν δὲ τοῦτο εὐπρεπὲς πρὸς τοὺς πλείους, ἐπεὶ ἕξειν γε τὴν πόλιν οἵπερ καὶ μεθίστασαν ἔμελλον.

[25] 8.66.2. The phrasing utilizes the oligarchic language of the period and hints at its underlying distortions and violence. An *epitēdeios*, "a suitable one," was someone you could rely upon, a good friend. The word becomes a feature of oligarchic language, meaning someone who was suited to the oligarchy, that is who could be relied upon to support it, 8.48.2; 54.3; 63.4; 64.4; cf. 5.76.2. Hence opponents of the oligarchy were the "unsuitable ones" (8.65.2). To say that someone died "from some suitable means" catches the tone of oligarchic speech while showing how widely it can be extended to mask the violence of the conspirators. Cf. 8.70.2: "Suitable to be put out of the way."

[26] Cf. 6.24.4, δεδιὼς . . . ἡσυχίαν ἦγεν, with 8.66.2, δεδιὼς . . . ἡσυχίαν εἶχεν ὁ δῆμος.

[27] In the herms affair everything was regarded with suspicion (6.53.2), so much so that the democracy suspended its normal deference to "respectable" people and normal distrust of the *ponēroi*. A most detailed inquiry, *zētēsis* (6.53.2), was conducted but everything was quite incorrectly interpreted as a sign of an oligarchic and tyrannical conspiracy (6.60.1). In 8.66.2 when there really is an oligarchic conspiracy, there is no *zētēsis* at all and no one is arrested even when suspicion is strong. Suspicion works against the *dēmos* by encouraging distrust (8.66.5).

[28] In 6.58 Hippias is with his *doryphoroi* (foreigners who served as a bodyguard) when he hears of the murder of Hipparchus. He orders the citizen hoplites who are a little distance away (ἄπωθεν), armed and ready for the procession, to leave their arms and to withdraw to a certain spot. He instructs his bodyguards to seize the weapons (τὰ ὅπλα ὑπολαβεῖν, 6.58.2) and then conducts his own examination of the citizens to see if any has a hidden dagger.

In 8.69 we see an inversion of this pattern. The citizens are again in arms but are allowed to go on their way to their military assignments. Those who are part of the conspiracy and some supporters from other Greek cities are instructed to remain a little ways off (ἄπωθεν, 8.69.2) and to take up their own weapons if anyone moves against them (8.69.2, λαβόντας

also becomes clear that the oligarchy is not to be composed of the promised group of approximately five thousand citizens, but of a council of four hundred co-opted members, who can rule with full authority (*autokratoras*) and convene the Five Thousand when and if they so decide (8.67.3). The Five Thousand, thus, would have no regularly scheduled meetings and the Four Hundred would have full power to act without consulting them. Despite their protestations (8.72.1), the Four Hundred clearly have no intention of diluting their power by convening the Five Thousand.

Nowhere in the account are we encouraged to admire or even to sympathize with the oligarchic regime. In the midst of the exposure of its specious claims, Thucydides lists the men behind the conspiracy (8.68). Peisander, of course, was the most visible of these, but behind him stood three other highly influential figures. One was Phrynichus, now converted to the oligarchy because of his fears of Alcibiades and his recognition that the oligarchy was the best way to prevent Alcibiades' return to Athens. Another was Theramenes, first mentioned here, but later of great prominence both at the time of the Four Hundred and among the Thirty. Most attention, however, is paid to Antiphon, "a man who of the Athenians of his time was second to none in *aretē* and who was most adept at developing ideas and at expressing what he had in mind" (8.68.1). These words and the following tribute to Antiphon's ability as a speaker and as an adviser in law cases have often been taken as showing that Thucydides' "sympathies went along with the oligarchical party; and that while the exaggerations of opposition speakers or demagogues, such as those which he imputes to Kleon and Hyperbolus, provoked his bitter hatred, exaggerations of the oligarchical warfare, or multiplied assassinations, did not make him like a man the worse."[29] But closer examination suggests grounds for caution. Antiphon's *aretē* need be nothing more than his ability to obtain many of the goals he set for himself, above all rhetorical effectiveness.[30]

τὰ ὅπλα). The Four Hundred, armed with small swords and accompanied by some of their young supporters from abroad, then take over the council house and administer the city "by force" (κατὰ κράτος, 8.70.1, only here in a nonmilitary context), killing some, imprisoning others. Note also the use of τοιούτῳ . . . τρόπῳ in 6.59.1 and τρόπῳ τοιῷδε in 8.69.1.

[29] G. Grote, *A History of Greece* (London 1888) pt. II, ch. lxii, p. 313, n. 1.

[30] *Aretē* in Thucydides is used in a very wide range of senses. In addition to military valor (2.34.5), it can be used to indicate conformity to the reciprocal obligations imposed by the *charis* and *philia* ideals (cf. J. L. Creed, "Moral Values in the Age of Thucydides," *CQ* n.s. 23 [1973] 213-231, and J. T. Hooker, "Χάρις and Ἀρετή in Thucydides," *Hermes* 102 [1974] 164-169) and even such mundane qualities as the fertility of land: 1.2.4. It is a mistake, I believe, to infer that the word indicates Thucydides' own moral approval. See also E. Lange, "Die Bedeutung von *aretē* bei Thukydides," *Jahrbuch für kl. Philologie* 145 (1892) 827-840. As Andrewes points out in *HCT* ad loc. (p. 171f.) Thucydides' praise and

"Skill" may here be the best translation. It is true that the wording used to praise Antiphon's rhetoric, echoes Pericles' description of himself as someone "inferior to none both to devise what is necessary and to communicate it" (2.60.5). But Pericles immediately added two further considerations; he was, he said, "devoted to my city and incorruptible. For the person who devises a plan but cannot instruct others in it, is no better than one who failed to develop any idea. But he who has both of these qualities but is ill-disposed to his city, would not advise with its interests equally close to his heart." The implicit comparison to Pericles helps us assess Antiphon's accomplishments and deficiencies. His rhetorical skill is almost Periclean, but to stop the comparison at this point draws attention to Antiphon's lack of devotion to his city. By now the reader recognizes the contrast with Pericles, a topic implicitly developed in the rest of the discussion of Antiphon. Unlike Pericles, who was willing to confront directly the people's suspicions and passions, Antiphon worked behind the scenes counselling those in legal or political difficulties. Thucydides' admiration for his ability is evident, but he does not conceal the ultimate direction of Antiphon's activities: treason.

The treatment of the other conspirators is similar. They are talented men who have undertaken an immensely difficult task—the overthrow of a well-established democratic government: "Thus the deed having been undertaken by so many clever men progressed, despite its magnitude. For it was a difficult thing to deprive the people of Athens of their freedom, in approximately the hundredth year since their suppression of the tyranny. Not only had they been subject to no one, but for over half this time they were used to ruling others" (8.68.4).

Although the main point in this passage is the difficulty encountered by the conspirators, the language shows no sympathy for their cause. The overthrow of the democracy is not represented as an essential step in Athens' recovery nor as the elimination of democratic excesses but as the suppression of long-cherished freedom. The form of the statement recalls the *pathos* statements that sometimes accompany moments of loss and suffering in the *Histories*.[31]

This passage leads to increasing clarity about the deceptiveness and deficiencies of the oligarchy. The culmination of this analysis comes somewhat later when the tensions within the oligarchy have become evident

---

admiration for Antiphon's gifts did not extend to approval of his politics. In a similar way Thucydides applied the term *aretē* to Nicias (7.86.5) but clearly did not approve of all aspects of Nicias' policy.

[31] Cf. 1.110; 3.68.5; 5.112.2; 8.24.3.

and its own demise is imminent. Some members of the Four Hundred now urge that the Five Thousand become a reality, not just a name. In Thucydides' view however, this was mere sloganeering:

Through their own private rivalries most of them inclined to the policy by which an oligarchy that comes about from a democracy is destroyed. For its members spend each day thinking themselves worthy not of equality but of how each can gain distinct pre-eminence. In a democracy when an election takes place, the loser takes the outcome more easily, since he feels he was not defeated by his equals. What raised their confidence most firmly was that the situation of Alcibiades on Samos seemed secure and that the oligarchy did not seem to them likely to endure. Each one individually struggled therefore to gain first place as protector of the people.[32]

These comments clarify a dynamic within the oligarchy. The striving for first place, which in book 2, chapter 65 was seen as a cause of mistakes made by the Athenian democracy, now emerges as a feature of oligarchy. Indeed the implication is that oligarchy may be even less stable than democracy, for in a democracy the unsuccessful politician can always console himself that his merits were not appreciated by an unsophisticated populace, while in an oligarchy rejection means repudiation by those of high status.

The criticism of the oligarchy of the Four Hundred prepares the way for an important new step. Until this point in the work, it has been easy to adopt a contemptuous attitude toward democracy and to assume that its opposite, oligarchy, would be an improvement. Surely the weaknesses and problems of democratic leadership in Athens have been amply exposed and there has been little encouragement of sympathy for democracy. Even in the Funeral Oration, where the reader might have expected an explicit link between Athens' national characteristics and the city's democratic institutions, the familiar distinction between name and reality mutes the connection. The civic pattern of Athens, Pericles said, was in a name democracy, since administrative power resided not with the few but with

---

[32] 8.89.3f. Note the echoes of book 2, chapter 65 in the passage:

8.89.3, κατ' ἰδίας δὲ φιλοτιμίας ... προσέκειντο ... ἀλλὰ καὶ πολὺ πρῶτος αὐτὸς ἕκαστος εἶναι. 89.4, ἠγωνίζετο οὖν εἷς ἕκαστος αὐτὸς πρῶτος προστάτης τοῦ δήμου γενέσθαι.

2.65.7, κατὰ τὰς ἰδίας φιλοτιμίας ... κακῶς ... ἐπολίτευσαν 65.10, ὀρεγόμενοι τοῦ πρῶτος ἕκαστος γίγνεσθαι 65.11, περὶ τῆς τοῦ δήμου προστασίας.

The passage also evokes the theory expressed in Darius' speech in Herodotus 3.82, that oligarchy is subject to fierce competition. The outcome, however, is not a monarchy, as suggested by Darius' analysis, but a mixed constitution.

the many (2.37.1). But he immediately went on to explain that this form of government gave due recognition to ability, *aretē*, suggesting thereby that it was, in effect, an unusual form of aristocracy. Thucydides' comments on Pericles made a similar point: "What came about was a democracy in name, but in fact the rule of the first man" (2.65.9). Thus in the second book whatever sympathy or admiration the reader feels for Athens is deflected from her distinctively democratic political institutions and associated with elements of aristocracy or the unique leadership of Pericles.

The tendency to expose the faults and pass swiftly over the accomplishments of democracy is continued in the early parts of the eighth book. There Thucydides sounds patronizing in his admiration of the Athenian populace's ability to rally and to rise to the challenge posed by the Sicilian disaster (8.1.4). Something close to disdain of democracy is encouraged by the comment in chapter 48.3 on the reaction of the citizenry to the plans for the establishment of the oligarchy: "And the rabble, even if it was to some extent initially annoyed at these activities, remained tranquil because of the plausibility of the hope of financial support from the King."[33]

Until well into the eighth book, in other words, political analysis, when it has appeared at all, has tended to reinforce doubts about democracy. In the eighth book the focus shifts, and oligarchy is shown to be subject to the same strictures as democracy. With the shift in viewpoint comes a shift in the use of the distinction between word and reality. In chapter 65, for example, Thucydides emphasizes the difference between the public claims (*logos*) of the Four Hundred and the actual conduct of their government. The leadership of this group, moreover, as analyzed in chapter 68, provides a further example of the radical disassociation between intelligence and civic loyalty among Athenian politicians. Peisander, Antiphon, and Theramenes are all shown to be able and skillful men, but there is no hint of their willingness to risk personal advantage for civic good.

The shift evident in the eighth book is not a sudden conversion to democracy. Rather, as so often in the work, we find a facile equation subverted and broken down. The easy inference that if democracy has proved pernicious, oligarchy must be beneficial is implicitly shattered through the treatment of the Athenian oligarchs. The book even goes one step further, in pointing to an alternative to both democracy and oligarchy. An elaborate and emphatic superlative praises the government of the Five

---

[33] 8.48.3. Note the use of the word *ochlos* ("rabble") in this passage (versus *dēmos* in 8.1.4) and the suggestion of venality. The passage also echoes Diodotus' comments on the destructiveness of *elpis*, "hope," in 3.45.5. Cf. 5.102.

Thousand that succeeded the regime of the Four Hundred: "And not least—
for the first time in my experience—do the Athenians appear to have
governed themselves well."[34]

To the implicit question of why this government proved so effective
Thucydides provides an immediate, albeit tantalizing, answer: "For a
balanced mixture of the few and the many came about, and this above all
raised the city out of the difficulties that had beset it" (8.97.2). The
"balanced mixture" is most likely an allusion to some of the theorizing
about a "mixed constitution," prominent in later antiquity, but already
being developed in Thucydides' day.[35] Its precise application, however,

[34] 8.97.2. The translation and interpretation of this sentence are extremely difficult. For a
good exposition of the difficulties and references to the principal discussions see Andrewes
in *HCT* ad loc. (pp. 331-339). His translation "The initial period [of this regime] was one
of the periods when the affairs of Athens were conducted best, at least in my time," is quite
different from that presented above. He takes οὐχ ἥκιστα δὴ as a very tame expression,
resolves the ambiguity inherent in εὖ πολιτεύσαντες into an allusion to the manner in
which political affairs were conducted (excluding thereby any allusion to the form of the
constitution) and limits the praise to an unspecified first period of government of the Five
Thousand (whose rule in any case cannot have extended beyond nine months) and leaves
"in my time," as he admits, "out on a branch" (p. 339). The philological parallels adduced
are not compelling ones, in my opinion. For example, since τὸν πρῶτον χρόνον occurs
only here in Thucydides, Xenophon, Plato, or Demosthenes (the plural occurs in Thucydides
7.87.1 and Demosthenes 18.249), arguments about the difference between πρῶτον and τὸ
πρῶτον do not help resolve the question why Thucydides avoided both these familiar expressions and chose this unique phrasing. The peculiarity of the phrase has been given insufficient
weight. The words demand some clarification; and clarification is precisely what is offered
by the next phrase, ἐπί γε ἐμοῦ. Hence the translation above: "for the first time in my
experience."

Some of the problems in interpreting this passage may be caused by efforts to reconcile
the passage with the generally positive impression of Pericles in book 2 and with the praise
of Athens in the Funeral Oration. If Thucydides admired Pericles and his government, how
can he say what the Greek seems to say in this passage: that now for the first time the
Athenians seem to have governed themselves well? To make this passage consistent with
book 2 the reader must soften the litotes in οὐχ ἥκιστα δὴ (not least) and construe it not
as a very strong assertion implying a comparison with Pericles' day, but as a way of saying
they had a "particularly good government." And the reader may wish to narrow ἐπί γε
ἐμοῦ to the period before 431 B.C. or narrow εὖ πολιτεύσαντες to refer to administrative
arrangements rather than the actual structure of the *politeia*, or take τὸν πρῶτον χρόνον
as "during the first period of the Five Thousand's rule." I find none of these plausible. If
the reader rejects the premise that the eighth book must reflect the same attitude as the
second, and if we allow that attitudes have modified in the interim, then it is possible to
avoid these strained interpretations and accept the passage as part of a major development
of attitude in the work.

[35] On the mixed constitution in antiquity see K. von Fritz, *The Mixed Constitution in
Antiquity* (New York 1954) and F. W. Walbank's commentary on Polybius 6.3.7 (pp. 639-
641). The origins and early development of the idea are difficult to trace but passages such
as Alcmaeon of Croton *VS* 24 B 4, Aristotle, *Politics* 1267 b 22ff., and Thucydides 6.18.6
strongly suggest that some theory of the mixed constitution had already been developed by
the late fifth century. Note also Andocides (?) 4.15, Euripides, *TGF*² 21, and Aristotle *Politics*
1273 b 35ff.

is much more difficult to determine. It may allude to the desirability of a moderate restriction in the franchise, to cooperation between those in power in the city of Athens and those of Samos, to a reallocation of political power among various social classes, to a balancing of various institutions of government, or to some combination of these. Readers can argue at length—and excellent scholars have—whether it alludes to an essentially democratic or oligarchic form of government.[36]

But the metaphor itself, with its rich connotations of medical practice and symposium ritual, conveys the essential message: the domination of either the few or of the many is likely to be pernicious.[37] A moderation of their conflicts can help the distressed city. Thucydides offers no further clarification and swiftly resumes the story of the war. His decision is understandable, however much the reader would like to find a fuller ex-plication of his thinking about the "balanced mixture." The war, after all, still has many years to go, and the government of the Five Thousand did not last for long. But the glimpse provided by Thucydides' new, more explicit technique is revealing and characteristic. Thucydides provides no remedy or prescription, will not even pause to expound his own views about balance and mixture. He seems content to have directed our attention for a minute to something beyond the familiar conflicts and antitheses. He has exposed the deficiencies, and strengths, of democracy and shattered the facile illusion that oligarchy can somehow succeed where democracy has failed. The favorable comments on the Five Thousand point to a stage of political analysis beyond the partisan claims for democracy or oligarchy. It would overburden those comments to make to them a prescription or political program. The possibility of a balanced mixture is merely a glimpse, an evanescent ray of hope in the increasing bleakness of the war.[38] But

---

[36] G.E.M. de Ste. Croix argued in *Historia* 5 (1956) 1-23 that the constitution of the Five Thousand was essentially a democratic one. Andrewes in *HCT* 8.97.1 (pp. 323-328) advances several considerations that show that "for Thucydides there was a substantial distance between the Five Thousand and democracy" (p. 328). The two discussions are a good introduction to the problems of explicating the passage. A sharp distinction between the form of government and the quality of administration (e.g. Gomme, *Greek Attitude to Poetry and History*, 152, n. 3) is likely, however, to be anachronistic.

[37] For the setting of the idea in Greek thought see J. de Romilly, "Alcibiade et le mélange entre jeunes et vieux: politique et médecine," *Wiener Studien* n.s. 10 (1976) 93-105. This essay is very suggestive about the use of the idea of mixture to link together several of the metaphorical systems in the work: ideas of measure and balance, the sickness metaphor, especially as extended to political life (e.g. 6.14; cf. Plato *Republic* 556 e), and the use of food and drink terminology to represent ides of civilization and justice.

[38] The principal attraction of theories of mixed constitutions in antiquity seems to have een their promise of long-lasting political stability. Thucydides may have been skeptical bout this part of the promise. The government of the Five Thousand was not long lived. ence we must not overestimate the amount of hope in the comment in 8.97.2. Note that

even here, in the midst of the least satisfactory of his books, Thucydides has managed to lead his reader beyond clichés and conventionalities to a deeper understanding of the war. The book, whatever its problems and deficiencies, however incomplete it may be, sustains the freshness and the originality we have come to expect in Thucydides' work.

---

in 4.74.4 he emphatically calls attention to the long endurance of the narrow oligarchy at Megara.

Conclusion

Books are to be call'd for, and supplied, on the assumption that the process of reading is not a half-sleep, but, in the highest sense, a gymnast's struggle; that the reader is to do something for himself, must be on the alert, must himself or herself construct indeed the poem, argument, history, metaphysical essay—the text furnishing the hints, the clue, the start of the frame-work. Not the book needs so much to be the complete thing, but the reader of the book does. That were to make a nation of supple and athletic minds, well train'd, intuitive, used to depend on themselves and not on a few coteries of writers.—Walt Whitman[1]

THUCYDIDES' history has no conclusion; half way through the account of the twenty-first year of the war, in the middle of a paragraph, at a semicolon, it abruptly stops. Many themes that we have encountered throughout the work find no completion; many of its tensions lack resolution; the author makes no final appearance and provides no summing up to indicate what we should conclude about his work or how we should react to it.

We crave something more than this incompleteness: some resolution, some clearer sense of the writer's own responses and conclusions. Yet the ending is in many respects appropriate to a work that throughout resists encapsulation and demands, in Walt Whitman's words, that the reader "do something for himself . . . , must himself or herself construct . . . the . . . history." We wish, of course, that Thucydides had completed his work, but there is no reason to expect that he would ever have explained or resolved the complexities of his text. Everything we know about the work points to its resistance to paraphrase and summation.

The price of such resistance has been high. Critics who concentrate on Thucydides himself find it easy to depict him as a cold and detached observer, a reporter concerned with the exactness of his account rather than an artist who responds to, selects and skillfully arranges his material,

---

[1] Walt Whitman, "Democratic Vistas," *Prose Works 1892*, ed. Floyd Stovall, vol. 2 (New York 1964) 424f.

and develops its symbolic and emotional potential. As long as historical writing was judged by "objective" or "scientific" standards, such as prevailed in the late nineteenth and early twentieth centuries, Thucydides' work could be seen, and admired, as a precursor to modern academic history.

Now, in a different intellectual climate, with a less naive conception of history, the work appears in a different light, and a new participant enters into the discussions of how the text works and what it means. As the reader comes into view, a new set of relationships and new interpretive possibilities demand consideration. The discussion expands to include the reader's reactions as well as the author's views. "Not the book needs to be the complete thing, but the reader of the book does," as Whitman said. At the same time the "objectivity" of the text can be understood in a new way, not as a goal or standard, but as a means by which the reader is drawn into the work, and made "to do something for himself."

The difficulty in such an approach is very clear: it is not easy to identify or characterize this reader, or to distinguish the reactions of the ancient audience from those of modern critics. The problem is indeed difficult, but not insuperable, for the reader is in part the product of the text itself. The conflicts and contradictions of belief, value, and attitude that affect us all are shaped by the work until some are dominant and articulate, while others, temporarily at least, are muted or forgotten. This, I believe, is part of what Henry James meant in his famous comment: "In every novel the work is divided between the writer and the reader; but the writer makes the reader very much as he makes his characters. When he makes him ill, that is, makes him indifferent, he does no work; the writer does all. When he makes him well, that is, makes him interested, then the reader does quite half the labor."[2]

From a recognition of the importance of the reader in the understanding of Thucydides two consequences follow. The first is that the emotional power of the work is not to be denied, repressed, branded as modern sentimentality or condemned as a form of "brain-washing."[3] The ancient critics recognized Thucydides' ability to recreate the *pathos* of events, that is, to lead his readers to participate vicariously in the sufferings of the war. That experience is at the center of any reading of Thucydides and is the product of the shaping of the text to involve and implicate the reader, both mentally and emotionally. The result is the intensity of engagement

---

[2] Henry James, "The Novels of George Eliot," *The Atlantic Monthly*, October 1866, 485.
[3] See, for example, the criticisms by W. P. Wallace in "Thucydides," *Phoenix* 18 (1964) 251-261.

that so many readers experience as they struggle with the *Histories*. If we want fully to appreciate Thucydides' work, we must give the emotional power of the work its place and shape our reactions by its development.

The second consequence of keeping the reader constantly in view is a change in perspective on the use of the work as historical evidence. Thucydides' authority can intimidate, especially at this remove when so much evidence has disappeared, when alternative and dissenting versions of events have been lost, when many controversies of his age have been forgotten. He was a contemporary, an eyewitness, a man of unchallengeable intelligence. His work commands assent. As we investigate the relation between author and reader, however, his authority comes to seem less intimidating. This is not to say that he is to be dismissed as partisan or self-seeking but simply to remember that he demands a reader of independent judgment. We can even suspect that Thucydides was sometimes inviting challenge and reassessment, a historical rereading of his text in which details and reactions postponed or minimized in his narrative are given a second look and then seen in a new relationship, with a new weighting. Certainly he knew that his treatment of almost every major figure, Pericles, Cleon, Demosthenes, Nicias, Alcibiades, would in his own day be controversial and would cut against conventional wisdom and judgments. His is sometimes a revisionist, often a polemical work, designed to provoke rather than suppress dissent.

Behind both the emotional power of the work and its historical persuasiveness stand the techniques by which the author guides his readers, or even, if we follow Henry James, creates them. Many of these are the familiar devices of ancient poetry and rhetoric: for example, the selection and emphasis of relevant details, coloration of language, concentration on one aspect of an action, selection and shifting of viewpoint, interpretations of the motives of the various actors. The major types of narrative that I have identified, "commander," "civic," "day-by-day," all have their role to play. But perhaps most distinctive is the Thucydidean shaping of the work through progressions, or narrative chains—series of episodes or speeches each of which resembles the other. Similar situations recur; the narrative is organized and the language chosen to establish the resemblances; we are led to observe the similarities and assess the effects of apparently minor contrasts and variations among them. The author needs to say little or nothing in his own voice; the reader is there, witnessing the unfolding of events, listening to the analyses offered by the speakers, participating as a contemporary might.

The procedure is admirably suited to assessing the tactics and strategies for military operations. As plans are tested against outcomes, the assumptions behind them are exposed and clarified. The technique can easily be extended to the identification of the factors that shape the outcome of the war. But in Thucydides it is also used to trace changes of attitudes and values. This is especially evident in the speeches. A phrase, argument, or even a distinctive word is introduced by one speaker: later the language recurs, echoed or adapted by other speakers in a new situation, and its implications are progressively exposed and clarified. In their second speech at Sparta (1.122.3 and 124.3), the Corinthians, for example, allude to Athens as a tyrant city: πόλις τύραννος. This highly colored phraseology helps persuade the Peloponnesian allies to undertake what appears as a war of liberation for Greece. Pericles in the last of his speeches reported by Thucydides utilizes similar language but for quite a different purpose. He tells the Athenians that they have an empire that is like a tyranny (2.63.2), ὡς τυραννίδα γὰρ ἤδη ἔχετε αὐτήν, which it seems wrong to have taken but is dangerous to let go. Again the language is effective, for through this speech Pericles succeeds in stopping what he regards as premature and inappropriate negotiations with the Peloponnesians. Later Cleon adapts the phraseology when he urges the execution of the citizenry of Mytilene. "You hold an empire that is a tyranny," (3.37.2)—τυραννίδα ἔχετε τὴν ἀρχήν—he says, abandoning the slight but crucial qualification that Pericles had used in his statement that the empire was like a tyranny. Cleon's policies do not fully carry the day, but are blocked by Diodotus' skillful exploitation of the argument from self-interest. But in the recurrence of the comparison of imperial Athens to a tyranny, we begin to sense a change in Athens' self-conception, a willingness, at least on the part of Cleon and his followers, to accept their enemies' description of their city and to act with the repression and violence that often characterized the ancient tyrants.

Our suspicions are strengthened as the dangers of Athens' expansionism are analyzed, especially when in book 6 the Athenian speaker Euphemus explains to a Sicilian audience that they can readily gauge Athenian intentions because "for a man who is tyrant or for a city that has an empire nothing is irrational if advantageous and there is no bond except reliability" (6.85.1). In this progression, language becomes reality—the polemics of the Corinthians become part of the Athenians' perception of themselves and Athenian conduct assimilates itself, albeit for very complex reasons, to the characterization of their city as a tyrant. Euphemus' speech is one of the ways by which the author guides his readers to an understanding of the implications of the Sicilian invasion. It is also a reminder of the parallelism between tyranical action and the domination of policy by considerations of self-interest (*to xympheron*) rather than of right (*to dikaion*)—another major theme within the work. At the same time it carries forward another theme—the dissolution under the pressure of the war of loyalties based on personal bonds and the ties of kinship. The city of Athens, properly the culmination and harmonization of the ties among its citizens, is, in Euphemus' view, the correlative of the man who defines his conduct by self-interest and his associations by "reliability."[4]

Throughout the *Histories* episode recalls episode and language echoes earlier phrases and ideas. Such recurrences shape not only the form of the work but also the responses and attitudes of its readers. We pause, interrupt the forward movement of our reading, break through the surface linearity of the text to recognize underlying patterns and structures. This recognition, however, is not a purely formal or aesthetic experience. For from it follow reassessments of old attitudes and the development of new responses as the complexity and implications of the patterns become clear. To a hostile critic this is part of the "brainwashing" imposed by a text that behaves as historical texts ought not, affecting attitudes, values, and feelings rather than conveying data. A more supple view of the nature of historical writing recognizes the advantages, as well as the dangers, in Thucydides' technique, above all its ability to represent the complexity of historical developments and the cumulative effects of changes that are individually almost infinitesimal. Euphemus' echoes of earlier justifications of the empire, for example, help us recognize that Athens' venture in Sicily is tied to her image of herself, to the domination of advantage over right and of profit over the bonds of loyalty and kinship.

These recurrences inevitably confront the reader with questions of judgment and evaluation. But they pose these questions in an especially historical way. Judgments within the *Histories* are commonly concerned not with clear-cut contrasts but with minimal variations. We are presented with cases that are ostensibly very similar, but that on closer examination contain significant differences. Cleon echoes Pericles; his policies, like those of Pericles, insist on the control of the empire even if stern measures are needed. Yet his policy in the Mytilenean debate is only superficially Periclean. It runs deeply counter to Pericles' sense of restraint, his high valuation of the intellect, and his ability to attune immediate policy to the achievement of long-range goals. Diodotus' speech clarifies these contrasts.

---

[4] Cf. 3.82.6, which emphasizes the relative weakness of kinship bonds compared to loyalty to factions in the Corcyrean revolution.

And by the end of the debate we can see how great a difference separates Pericles and Cleon.

All this is done without explicit comment from the author. Individual reactions and assessments may vary, but the underlying process is the same. The reader follows the progression, is drawn into the action of the war, and finds that his assessments and reactions broaden and deepen. The emotional power of the text is the agent for changes in the reader's evaluations and responses. Thus readers may feel themselves changing as they work through the text, and some may feel distressed or annoyed. But whatever change occurs results from an artistic experience, not from the manipulations of an ideologue. The text leads the reader back to events and individuals, not away toward abstractions or dogmas. It respects rather than reduces the complexity of events and invites rather than dictates the reader's reaction. It is, in other words, simultaneously thoroughly artistic and thoroughly historical.

Perhaps then criticism should imitate its subject matter and having analyzed as best it can the development of the work through the twenty-first year of the war, should simply stop, without summary or generalization. Since the literary power and moral authenticity of the work derive in large part from its respect for the complexity and irreducibility of events, the challenge to the critic—and his duty—is to illumine the richness of the text, not to impose a neat interpretation or final judgment. We must, for that reason, resist summarization or the reduction of the work to a series of propositions—Thucydides' view of imperialism, Thucydides' view of Pericles or of Alcibiades, Thucydides' political philosophy, or the like. But something remains to be said, if only to challenge the tendency, so persistent and so pernicious, to view the text as homogeneous and the attitudes it engenders as static and undeviating.

Repeatedly we have detected changes and shifts in attitudes and evaluation as the history progresses. These are most obvious, perhaps, in the case of the individual characters within the work. In the treatment of Brasidas, for example, the development of the narrative exposes the rashness of the northern Greeks, the deceptiveness of Spartan policy, and the moral ambiguity of Brasidas' own actions in his brilliant campaign in the Thraceward regions. The account is not, as has often been thought, written in simple admiration of Brasidas, nor does it seek to condemn him. Rather it is a way of leading the reader to deeper and more alert responses to the situation—to a far more cautious and complex reaction than the one the historical Brasidas attempted to induce.

The role of Nicias in the Sicilian Expedition also shows a remarkable development, although of a different sort. His role in the Athenian debate on the invasion of Sicily is developed with a high sense of irony—for although he attempted to be the wise adviser and to discourage what the reader knows will be a disastrous undertaking, the strategy he employed in the debate led to a larger and more vulnerable expedition. His leadership in the field compounded Athens' problems; it is presented as uninspired, unimaginative, ineffective, or even worse. At the end, when swift withdrawal is essential, Nicias temporizes, the victim of false hopes and a source of bad advice and fatal delay. At this crucial stage, moreover, we recognize that, although Nicias was brave in battle, he is frightened by the thought of facing the Athenian assembly, and, unlike Pericles, unwilling to stand up to it, preferring death on the battlefield to condemnation and disgrace at home (7.48.4). Thucydides' description of Nicias' attitude marks another stage in the confounding of public and private values within the work and a low point in our assessment of Nicias. But, as we have seen, during the retreat, Nicias shows a devotion to his men, a personal integrity, an uncomprehending bravery that we cannot fail to respect even if we cannot fully praise. His death is as undeserved as it is ironic. He is destroyed by the collaborators on whom he had based his false hopes for the betrayal of Syracuse. He falls at the point in the narrative where we have become fully aware of another dimension to his character and when we have abandoned our own disposition (and that of the Athenians) to condemn him.

As can be seen from these examples, the questions concerning Thucydides' attitude to one or another of his characters rarely admit simple or summary answers. Indeed, if our approach is correct, such questions are falsely formulated. The attempt to summarize Thucydides' judgments of individuals is bound to be unsatisfactory, a reductionist search for a least common denominator. The issue is not Thucydides' views, but ours. The reader's reactions are not static or simplistic. Our response to almost all the major characters undergoes great changes as the work develops. The characters do not, to be sure, grow and change like those often encountered in modern literature, but changing circumstances reveal progressively more about them and evoke a constant broadening and deepening of response.

If we turn from individual characters to political phenomena, the similarities are evident. Again critics and scholars have expressed the most divergent views. Thucydides was by disposition a democrat "incapable of conceiving a great progressive city except as a democracy";[5] he was an

---

[5] John Finley, *Thucydides* (Cambridge, Mass. 1942) 237.

advocate of a mixed constitution;[6] he ended "his life as he had begun it, a confirmed oligarch who had never renounced the creed of his fathers."[7] Hobbes was convinced that Thucydides "least of all liked democracy. . . . Upon divers occasions he noteth the emulation and contention of the demagogues for reputation and glory of wit: with their crossing of each other's counsels, to the damage of the public; the inconsistency of resolutions, caused by the diversity of ends and power of rhetoric in the orators; and the desperate actions undertaken upon the flattering advice of such as desired to attain, or to hold what they had attained, of authority and sway amongst the common people."[8] But Hobbes recognized that Thucydides was no friend of oligarchy: "Nor doth it appear that he magnifieth any where the authority of the few, amongst whom he saith every one desireth to be chief, and they that are undervalued beare it with less patience than in a democracy; whereupon sedition followeth, and the dissolution of the government."

Unless the reader is willing to accept Hobbes' tendentious conclusion that Thucydides was an advocate of monarchy, or attach a very specific meaning to his comments about the "balanced mixture" in 8.97.2, his political views remain a puzzle. Typically, behind the puzzle is a tension in the text: "If Thucydides regards the constitution of the Five Thousand as the best Athens had during his life (8.97.2), what becomes of the attitude of apparent approval and even profound admiration of the Periclean democracy expressed in the Funeral Oration?"[9] We have sufficiently studied Thucydidean techniques to recognize a familiar problem, the resistance of the text to summaries and formulations. This does not mean, of course, that Thucydides the Athenian had no consistent or readily articulated political views, but it does suggest that he did not use the *Histories* to express or advocate those views. Yet the work is, in every sense of the word, a highly "political" text, as well as a fully historical one, and hence ought to be amenable to some explication of its political implications. This, I believe, is possible, if we are again prepared to look at the progressions within it and to bear in mind the relationship between text and audience.

---

[6] J. de Romilly, "Alcibiade et le mélange entre jeune et vieux: politique et médecine," *WS* 10 (1976) 93-105.

[7] M. McGregor, "The Politics of the Historian Thucydides," *Phoenix* 10 (1956) 102. Cf. the influential article by H. Vretska, "Perikles und die Herrschaft des Würdigsten—Thuk. II 37, 1," *Rh. Mus.* 109 (1966) 108-120.

[8] Thomas Hobbes, "On the Life and History of Thucydides," the preface to his translation, ed. R. Schlatter (New Brunswick 1975) 13; cf. Schlatter's own preface xxivf.

[9] G. Kirkwood, "Thucydides' Judgement of the Constitution of the Five Thousand," *AJP* 93 (1972) 94.

We know that Thucydides' contemporaries did not always fully share the excitement of earlier generations at the overthrow of outmoded and often repressive governments and the development of more democratic patterns. His own generation grew up after the battle for democracy in Athens had been won and when the problems and contradictions of this form of government were becoming apparent. The war intensified that process and imposed great burdens upon the Athenian system of government. The strains became evident to all citizens as the war went on. Thucydides' audience, moreover, was no representative cross section of the Athenian citizenry or of Greeks in general. It was enlightened, well-educated, and affluent—not disposed to revert to the aristocratic patterns of the archaic age, but distrustful of the populist strain in contemporary democracy. It had reason to be worried that democracy might become the weapon of the poor against the wealthy—as it often did in the late fifth and fourth centuries—and saw more immediate provocations in the policies and rhetoric of many popular politicians.

Thucydides addresses, in other words, an audience that saw in Athens' defeat a confirmation of their doubts about democracy. Through much of the *Histories* there is no significant challenge to these attitudes. The difficulties of leadership in Athens are made abundantly clear, whereas no equally penetrating critique is directed toward the problems, also intense, that afflicted Spartan political life during the period.[10] The problems of Athenian democracy become very evident in the *Histories*; its accomplishments (for example, the cultural and artistic flourishing of Athens) are through much of the work either omitted or are alluded to in language suggesting that the city was only nominally a democracy but in fact an unusual form of aristocracy, or under Pericles, "the rule of the first man" (2.65.9). The treatment of the populist leaders of Athens seems to confirm this low valuation of democracy. Hyperbolus (8.73) is treated with open contempt; to Cleon the work is overtly hostile. In these respects the work reflects and reinforces the attitudes of the class into which Thucydides was born and from which its readership was largely drawn.

But our analysis, for example of the fourth book, has indicated that Thucydides sometimes had a subtle relationship to the political attitudes of his class. He structured his account of Cleon's success at Pylos first to encourage the reader's identification with the merriment at Cleon's discomfiture when Nicias offered to resign his generalship and pressed Cleon

[10] There are, however, hints of the difficulties in Sparta: 2.18.3; 4.80.3; 5.16; book 8 also exposes many of the effects of the tensions within Sparta.

to take the command. Having shared in the merriment, we also share in the amazement and dismay when Cleon succeeds, contrary to all expectation, and his promise "although it had seemed quite crazy" (4.39.3) was fulfilled. Here Thucydides exploits a class antagonism against Cleon to construct a narrative that draws forth from the reader reactions analogous to those felt at the time of the events. But felt by whom? Surely not by Cleon and his supporters, but by members of precisely the class from which the audience of the *Histories* was in large part drawn. Thucydides' writing here is double-edged, as acerbic in his treatment of the mistaken merriment of the audience as of Cleon's apparent dismay.

The episode illustrates both the strengths and the weaknesses of Thucydides' approach to the writing of history. It is carefully shaped to develop and exploit the reader's reactions and eventually to subvert them. The result is a vigorous and powerful narrative, but by no means an unchallengeable version of events. Today's historians can—indeed, must—be skeptical about its interpretation of Cleon's motives and about his apparently casual relationship to Demosthenes. They must recognize that in political judgments, as in so many other ways, Thucydides is often at play with his readers, challenging and subverting attitudes, including those widely held within his own socioeconomic class and those which had initially been assumed, affirmed, or sympathetically represented within the *Histories*. As we have seen in the treatment of Cleon, Brasidas, and Nicias, the narrative frequently seems at first to accept or justify one assessment—often a conventional one—then new considerations emerge and new responses are evoked.

So too the treatment of the government of Athens. Having seen the difficulties and failures of Athenian democracy, having despaired of its ability effectively to wage the war or to achieve a peace, we are led in the eighth book to note the vigor, endurance, and determination of the Athenian people and their achievement, even if only temporarily, of a form of government of which Thucydides can say: "And not least—for the first time in my experience—do the Athenians appear to have governed themselves well. For a balanced mixture of the few and the many came about and this above all raised the city out of the difficulties that had beset it" (8.97.2). The government that he praises is the so-called rule of the Five Thousand, a "mixed constitution."[11] Modern critics have argued over the best classification of such a government, whether it should be viewed as a form of democracy or a modified oligarchy. Thucydides' point is

---

[11] See above Chapter Eight, Note 36.

rather different. For him it is neither one nor the other but a blend that avoided the excesses and deficiencies of each. His praise of the Five Thousand is representative of a tendency within the work to subvert and break down conventional antitheses and categories and to look for fresher approaches and conclusions. The passage, of course, should not be over-burdened. It does not imply that the work is a crypto-democratic tract, any more than the treatment of Cleon implies that Thucydides secretly admired him. But it again reminds us how reluctant Thucydides is to live with cliché.

Nothing would have been easier than to continue exposing the difficulties and ineffectiveness of democracy in the years following the Sicilian disaster. But to do so would have been misleading in several important respects. It would have invited the conclusion that oligarchy could some-how have solved or alleviated the problems that afflicted Athens. And it would have obscured a paradox that underlies the *Histories*, for much of the work, especially the Periclean Funeral Oration, shows the connection between the relatively free and open system of Athens and the city's greatness. The Funeral Oration, as has often been pointed out, deviates from the other examples of the genre by substituting a discussion of the social and civic patterns of Athenian life for the usual encomiastic survey of her history. The speech thereby establishes a connection between these patterns and the extraordinary energy that earlier Athenian history often illustrated. Pericles is made to equivocate on whether this government should be called a democracy, but the connection between the pattern of Athenian civic life and her vigor and success in foreign affairs is evident. Against Spartan tranquility these characteristics prove immensely effective. Athenian vigor, however, leads to a reluctance to give up expansionism, a tendency to reject peace offers when successes have been attained, and an inability to accept tranquility. Ultimately it engenders the hopes that lead to the Sicilian Expedition and convert it into a disaster. In Sicily the Athenians, for the first time, confront another democracy, and a people of a disposition similar to their own. Athens, it appears, is defeated not by Sparta's conservative disposition and military strength but in large part by the democratic qualities of the Syracusans.

In the seventh book this is at best implicit, perhaps because Thucydides still wishes to focus on the deficiencies and failure of Athenian leadership. But in the eighth book, shortly before the comment on the government of the Five Thousand, it becomes explicit: "And not on this occasion alone were the Lacedaemonians the most convenient of enemies for the Athe-nians, but in many other instances as well. Since they were totally different in disposition—one group swift, the other slow; one aggressive, the other lacking boldness—they were extremely helpful, especially in a naval empire. The Syracusans demonstrated this. Since they were especially similar in disposition, they fought most effectively against them'' (8.96.5). This observation is closely coordinated with the explicit praise of the Five Thousand in the following chapter. The first passage points out that the failure in Sicily was not so much a triumph for Spartan conservatism as the success of one innovative state against another, while the comment on the Five Thousand carries the same progression of thought one stage further to a recognition of the accomplishments of a government that was neither a democracy nor an oligarchy. Thucydides, in other words, refuses to let us be trapped into the neat antitheses and binary oppositions so common in Greek thought. He allows no room for fashionable upper-class Lacedaemonophilia and he exposes the tendency of oligarchy, no less than of radical democracy, to subordinate public good to private advantage. An attentive reader, in other words, is encouraged to move beyond conventional upper-class attitudes and to rethink the facile condemnation of democracy. The literary form of the *Histories* and the intellectual openness of the work prevent any conclusion that this is the last word in the assessment of politics. At the end of the work, the reader is left alert and engaged, freed from cliché, and ready for the continuing assessment of political decisions and forms.

One other progression within the work demands consideration, not only because it is so central to current scholarly controversies about the *Histories* but because so much of our understanding of the nature of the text depends upon it. The opening of the work, we have noted, implies a highly rational view of history, a confidence in the ability of reason to uncover the past and determine the sources and patterns of power. The confidence in the historical method of the Archaeology is the analogue to Pericles' assurance that Athens can succeed in the war if it is willing to follow his policies. Reason seems very much in command and to justify both Athenian strategy and the claim of the *Histories* to offer useful knowledge (1.22.4). The reader naturally concludes that ''Since Thucydides presents his work as useful . . . he must have regarded human nature, political and military affairs, and perhaps even the natural environment as liable to rational prediction and control, at least to some degree.''[12] Thucydides' concern with reason in its many forms and his obvious admiration for Pericles

---

[12] Lowell Edmunds, *Chance and Intelligence* (Cambridge, Mass. 1975) 145. Some of the necessary qualifications to such a bald statement are suggested in the subsequent pages of Edmunds' book.

make a fully rationalist interpretation of the work seem plausible. We are tempted to read it as a document of the Greek Enlightenment, a reminder of the importance of reason, and, despite all the irrationality and horror it reveals, as a work ultimately optimistic about the future, if only man will learn fully to use reason.

In recent years this view of the work has repeatedly been challenged by critiques pointing out the frequency with which irrational forces in the work are shown to overpower rational planning or expectation. Highly pessimistic interpretations have emphasized the bleakness of vision in passages such as the plague, the Corcyran *stasis*, and the Sicilian disaster. Such views leave little room for reason or prediction, still less for the control or shaping of the future. The knowledge of history is the awareness of the domination of the irrational.

The analysis in the preceding pages has, I hope, shown that this approach to Thucydides, while it may be one-sided or overstated, is not an aberration or a mere product of the *Zeitgeist* of the late twentieth century. It is deeply grounded in the text and accounts for features that are likely to be neglected or undervalued by more rationalist or optimistic critics. Its adequacy as an interpretation of Thucydides, however, is perhaps best assessed by looking at one part of the problem: the utility of historical knowledge in the *Histories*. Three statements are commonly cited on the topic, each linked to the others in what can readily be recognized as an important progression. The first of these statements (1.22.4) is the comment at the end of the Archaeology that despite the difficulties of the task, the work will prove useful for the understanding of events that are likely to recur in the future.[13] Taken in isolation the passage indicates a confidence in historical method, a belief in an ability to recognize recurring patterns, even to predict and thereby in some degree to control events.

But Thucydides does not pause to explore such implications. Instead he immediately turns to natural disturbances, earthquakes, eclipses, and the like, to the human sufferings of the war, and thence to the causes of its outbreak. The recurrences in history are not reintroduced as a significant topic until the opening of the account of the plague in the second book. In this passage, Thucydides refuses to speculate about the causes of the illness. Others can speak about those matters, he says, "but I will discuss

---

[13] For an explication of the passage see above Chapter One, Note 28. In its immediate context it is a very confident statement. To reconcile it with the rest of Thucydides and thereby to construct a single static statement of his position on the utility of history one must adopt, as many interpreters have, a very restrictive explication of the words, denying the natural implication that Thucydides' work will be very useful.

what the process was like and I will clarify those factors from which, if the affliction ever again occurs, one might, by having some advance knowledge, not fail to recognize it" (2.48.3). Thucydides' virtual agnosticism about the cause of this disturbance and the restraint and comparative modesty of this statement contrast sharply with his confident comments at the end of the Archaeology that led directly to his identification of the "truest cause" of the war. Here he not only abjures any certainty about the causes of the plague, but also shows considerable caution in his allusion to the idea of recurrence—"if the affliction ever again occurs"—and even greater equivocation about the knowledge that his account offers—"one might, by having some advance knowledge, not fail to recognize it." But most remarkable is the absence of any explicit claim, however qualified, to parallel the assertion in 1.22.4 of the utility of the work. Indeed, the account of the plague, as has often been pointed out, makes clear that no remedy or treatment is effective against the malady: "Some died for want of attention, others even though they received the best of medical care. No treatment, no, not one, was there whose application would help. What benefited one person, harmed the next" (2.51.2). In reading the account of the plague we are forced to confront what Hans Diller has called "the brutal fact . . . that according to Thucydides absolutely nothing helped against the plague. . . . Thucydides explicitly emphasizes that neither an indication of a specific means of treatment nor a prognosis for a specific type of physical constitution was provided. . . . One could really only feel sorry for the ill or become infected oneself."[14] We are told in effect that the plague may recur and that with the help of the *Histories* we may be able to recognize it, but not that we will thereby cure its victims. In the second book the confidence in the possibility of predicting and controlling the future at which the author's comments in the first book seem to hint erodes.[15]

The third book, as we have seen, takes up another theme, the subversion of *logos* in its many forms and its transformation into an instrument of

---

[14] H. Diller, review of K. Weidauer, *Gnomon* 27 (1955) 14; cf. E. Kapp, review of W. Schadewaldt, *Gnomon*, 6 (1930) 93, n. 2.

[15] If the reader concentrates too narrowly on the treatment of the disease, it is easy to exaggerate the pessimism of the account. Thucydides' recognition of the contagious nature of the disease, as J.C.F. Poole and A. J. Holladay have pointed in "Thucydides and the Plague of Athens," *CQ* n.s. 29 (1979) 282-300, was a major contribution. Even more important is the recognition of the psychological effects of the illness and their implications for the political life of the city—the despair, the demoralization, and the consequent inflammation of feelings against Pericles' leadership. See also K. von Fritz, *Griechische Geschichtsschreibung*, vol. 1 (Berlin 1967) 530f.

violence. The account of the Corcyrean *stasis* is a major statement of this theme and does not exempt knowledge of the past from its bleak view. As we read the account both its ideas and its verbal reminiscences of the account of the plague remind us of that great affliction.[16] But the view has become even bleaker. The recurrence of events holds out no hope of benefits or control: "Many atrocities afflicted the cities in *stasis*, things that continue to happen and will keep happening as long as there is the same *physis* for human beings, though more intense or more tranquil or more adapted in their manifestations as individual changes of circumstances appear" (3.82.2). After explaining that in war the attendant circumstances exacerbate attitudes and assimilate men's dispositions to their harsh conditions, Thucydides notes that the later instances of *stasis* were worse than the earlier ones: "Those at later stages by learning of what had gone before, achieved new excesses in the innovation of planning both by the perfection of the design of plots and by their unparalleled acts of vengeance" (3.82.3). Now knowledge of the past has a new role. In 1.22.4 there was the strong suggestion that it would prove useful and might advance man's control over his future; in 2.48 it is much more an intellectual abstraction—the recognition of similarities without medical application. In 3.82, familiarity with the past becomes a way of perfecting the atrocities of *stasis*. The next sentences discuss the transformation of language under the pressure of *stasis* and its role in the intensification of violence. Thus language and history, as parallel systems, contribute to the destructiveness and horror of war.

The three passages we have so far examined—the introductory comments on the utility of the work, the observations of the Great Plague, and the analysis of the *stasis* at Corcyra—are bound together by language and theme and by their common interest in the recurrence of events. They invite comparison, but not homogenization or levelling. They are not statements of a single theory or attitude, but a progression that leads the reader to a deeper understanding of the complexity and ambiguity of historical knowledge. Nor do they exhaust Thucydides' exploration of the utility of historical knowledge. The sixth book contains a long excursus on the Pisistratid tyranny, introduced by the comment that the Athenian citizenry at the time of the Sicilian Expedition learned that the tyranny had become oppressive in its last days and had been overthrown not by Har-

---

[16] Note the following verbal connections between 3.82.2 and earlier links in the chain:

3.82.3, καὶ ἐπέπεσε πολλὰ καὶ χαλεπὰ . . .	2.48.3, εἴ ποτε καὶ αὖθις ἐπιπέσοι
γιγνόμενα καὶ αἰεὶ ἐσόμενα, . . .	1.22.4, τῶν τε γενομένων . . . καὶ τῶν μελλόντων ποτὲ αὖθις . . . ἔσεσθαι
ἕως ἂν ἡ αὐτὴ φύσις ἀνθρώπων ἦ	1.22.4, κατὰ τὸ ἀνθρώπινον.

modius and the efforts of the Athenian citizenry but by Spartan intervention. In this episode (6.53-60) the knowledge of an essentially correct version of the overthrow of the sixth-century tyrants exacerbates the Athenians' fears and eventually contributes to a serious mistake: the recall of Alcibiades from Sicily. The episode is not directly linked to the three passages discussed above but by its transformation of the earlier discussion of Harmodius and Aristogeiton (1.20.2) breaks the linear and irreversible time of historical writing. It brings the reader full circle, back to the first book—back, however, with a new perspective on history and a deeper awareness of its limits and ironies.

Yet as we mentally return to the first book we encounter again the claim of the permanent value of the work—its boast that it will be a possession forever. How can this claim be justified if the utility of historical knowledge is progressively undermined and if belief in rational prediction and control erodes as the work continues? This question poses one of the most important problems in the analysis of Thucydides and points to one of the most distinctive features of the text. For the progressions within the *Histories* transform but do not destroy their elements. As we progress from confidence in prediction and rational analysis to a growing awareness of the power of the unexpected and unpredictable, we recreate the experience of many of those Athenians who were convinced by Pericles at the beginning of the war and lived to see its sorry end. We focus increasingly upon the *pathos* of war—not just its emotional power, but its way of undermining planning, outmaneuvering prediction, and making sufferers out of those who thought they would be in control.

But this bleak progression does not refute or destroy the analysis of power in the Archaeology, nor does it result in a work of pure pacifism or pessimism. The anatomy of power in the first book remains valid within limits of which we become increasingly aware. It is not rejected but transformed. Naval power and financial strength continue to be important throughout the work but they result not in progress and security but in expansion and vulnerability. Walls come to symbolize not security but siege and defeat. Boldness and innovation are crucial constituents of Athens' growth but also of her overextension and defeat. Greatness characterizes the war throughout, but comes to describe suffering, not accomplishment. Thus we are constantly led to see the other side, the unexpected application of qualities and terms. This is evident as well in the treatment of the so-called law of the stronger. We encounter this law in the first speech by an Athenian speaker in book 1. The Athenian delegates to the Conference at Sparta say that in acquiring and developing her empire

Athens was merely following a principle that had always been established, that the weaker was restrained by the more powerful (1.76.2). The idea, widespread in the Greek Enlightenment, is plausible and reasonable in this initial setting, an appeal to the Spartans to think twice before they commit themselves to war. But the Athenians come to apply the law to new situations. It underlies the demand for the punishment of Mytilene and is part of the argument against the Melians (5.105.2). Soon, all restraint abandoned, it is embodied in the Athenian attack on Sicily. Our reactions, however, are shaped not only by the context and progressive extensions of the law, but by another explicit statement of it. This comes in the fourth book, during Hermocrates' address to the Sicilian delegates at Gela. "There are ample grounds for excusing the Athenians for such planning and such self-aggrandizement. My criticism is directed not against those who wish to dominate but against those who are more disposed to yield. For it is the nature of what is human to dominate everywhere anyone who gives way and to ward off the attacker" (4.61.5). Through Hermocrates' words, and the temporary unification of Sicily which he achieves, we recognize another side to the familiar law of the stronger. It is not simply an explanation and justification of great power domination of the small, but a principle that, if properly understood and applied, can lead to alliance, mutual assistance and resistance to aggression. This transforms the familiar Athenian approach to power, and reminds us that in Hermocrates and his city they will meet their match.

The ideas of the *Histories* are in constant transformation. We constantly become aware of new applications and implications and, above all, of ironies and paradoxical results. From our heightened awareness derives the true utility of the work. We learn from it not how to predict the future or to control events but their complexity and the consequent vulnerability of civilization and order. Human reason does not foretell the future, but can lead to a stance and a response to complexities that cannot fully be measured by our intellects. Hermocrates at Gela again makes explicit a pattern implicit throughout the *Histories*: "The unpredictability of the future exercises the greatest control and, although it is most hazardous, it nevertheless can be seen to be most useful. For if we share an equal fear, we are more inclined to approach each other with forethought" (4.62.4). History does not teach us how to control human events, nor enable us to cure plagues or prevent potential tyrannies, but it reminds us how easily men move from the illusion of control over events to being controlled by them—from action to *pathos*.

The claim for the utility of historical knowledge is not so much refuted as the work progresses as it is transformed. It is not shown to be false, but true in a quite unexpected sense. The result is not a repudiation of the study of the past but a different approach to it.

It is not, however, only the ideas of the *Histories* that are transformed. The style reflects the interconnectedness of events and the constant unexpected shifts in balance and construction. Indeed, the work transforms itself. It begins as a paradoxical combination of a theme said to be of unparalleled greatness and a form that seems devoid of conventional grandeur. The opening of Thucydides' history is far less elevated than that of Herodotus, reminiscent of the works of more modest prose writers and the less pretentious historians. Its style is as far from the ornamented prose of the rhetoricians as from the elegancies of poetry. The verb chosen for the author's writing is *xynegrapse*, a prosaic word, appropriate for the technical manuals on architecture, medicine, rhetoric, and cookery that we know became common in the late fifth century. Like them the work seems to offer exact and useful information—a way of analyzing and reconstructing the past. The Archaeology, as we have seen, is not a comprehensive narrative of early Greece but an anatomy of power and hence a source of immensely valuable knowledge. At its conclusion we see a radical change. As the greatness of the war is reaffirmed the unpretentious prose of the author gives way to the more exalted tone of a new narrator, the war itself: "This war will nevertheless make clear to those who examine the actions themselves that it was greater than all that went before" (1.21.2). It thereby mocks the pretensions of the poets and orators and advances its boldest claim. While admitting it will not offer the pleasure that comes from storytelling, it claims to be something far more than a contest entry or fading laurel and olive wreath prizes. It is a possession forever, an heirloom received from the past and transmitted to the future. A further transformation follows. The final chapter of the introduction again restates the theme of greatness, but in doing so redefines it. The greatness of this war is now seen to consist not in the number of men, ships, and talents, but in the length and intensity of the suffering concentrated in it.

The Introduction represents in miniature a transformation to be found in the work as a whole. As we have seen, Thucydides' history progresses from a confident analysis of power to an exploration of the destructive misery of war. The reader's confidence in the Archaeology's analysis of the past has its counterpart in Periclean rationalism and the confidence that the war can be managed and a successful outcome achieved. This confidence is subverted and gives way to the recognition that: "In peace and in good times both cities and individuals have better dispositions since they are not afflicted by pressures over which they have no control. But war, by taking away the prosperity of everyday life, becomes a teacher of violence and assimilates most men's impulses to their circumstances" (3.82.3). Eventually, we are implicated in the greatest suffering reported in the work, the epic and tragic story of the Sicilian Expedition. In this account is to be found the explanation of the rivalry with the epics and with Herodotus and the justification for the claim that this war "was greater than all that went before" (1.21.2): "This Hellenic accomplishment turned out to be the greatest in this war and it would seem to me also the greatest of those Hellenic actions that we have heard about—most brilliant for the victors, most unfortunate for the ones who were annihilated" (7.87.5). Even here the development does not stop. In the eighth book we encounter new possibilities, above all a growing awareness of the internalization of violence and a renewed exploration of the link between war and *stasis*.

Any attempt to encapsulate these transformations is likely to result in misrepresentation and oversimplification. The work cannot be summed up as advocacy of Periclean rationalism, the law of the stronger, a tragic pessimism, or any of the other formulations so popular in Thucydidean scholarship. It defies reduction and resists simplification, for a very good reason. Any encapsulation stops our rethinking and re-examination of our own premisses and values. If, as we have often conjectured, the war and the narrative are counterparts, then the *kinēsis* of the war has as its analogue the constant shifts and transformations of the text and its sustained assaults on the complacency of the reader. The style too is analogous, constantly shifting its emphasis, breaking into new ground, subverting old antitheses. There is no justification for dismissing the style as unpolished, or for viewing it as the result of mechanical application of principles such as *variatio* or for condemning it, as Collingwood once did, as a sign that Thucydides "has a bad conscience."[17] The style is the perfect expression of the true narrator of the work, the war itself (1.21.2). It forces us to engage, attacks our assumptions, lays siege to our certainties, and grants no quarter or settlement.

Yet at every stage we resist. Like the Melians, we feel there must be some possibility, however remote, of rescue or escape. The unexpected, we know, has a great role in war—immense for the belligerents as well as for the reader of the *Histories*. In hope of the unanticipated, we refuse accommodation. More than that, we envision something better. The Funeral Oration projects before us an image of a society shaped by law,

---

[17] R. G. Collingwood, *The Idea of History* (New York 1956) 29.

reason, mutual respect, self-restraint, and self-sacrifice. We know it is not
a description of the historical Athens. Nor is it to be explained as mere
Periclean propaganda or Thucydides' manipulation of his readers. Rather
it is the symbolic standard of order and stability to which Greece in any
other condition must be compared, just as the paradigmatic *stasis* on Corcyra, an inversion of the Athens of the Funeral Oration, is the festal and
amateur world turned upside down, destroying the dispositions that lead
to civic strength and individual attainment, and producing those that debase
and degrade: "Thus every form of base disposition imposed itself through
these *staseis* on the Hellenic world. And simplicity, of which nobility in
no small measure consists, was laughed off stage and, in the absence of
mutual trust, man's intelligence served to spread conflict far and wide"
(3.83.1). In passages such as this we come very close to the source of the
intense emotional power of the work. Thucydides' history is perhaps unique
among historical writings in its uncompromising demonstration of how
deeply the sufferings of the war are rooted in human nature and in its
simultaneous insistence that they are mistakes that ought to be avoided.
The work provides no resolution to this tension. There are, perhaps, some
hints—the awareness that the right of the stronger implies as well the right
of the weaker to unite against domination and enslavement; the identification of a dynamic whereby fear of the powerful can generate counter-
forces that may ultimately, slowly, with immense difficulty, displace
oppression; and above all, a sense of the uncertainty of events and an
awareness that the unpredictability of the future may itself instruct us in
the way of caution and restraint. As Bernard Brodie has said: "What we
have done must convince us that Thucydides was right, that peace is better
than war not only in being more agreeable but also in being very much
more predictable. A plan and policy which offers a good promise of
deterring war is therefore by orders of magnitude better in every way than
one which depreciates the objective of deterrence in order to improve
somewhat the chances of winning."[18] But ultimately the *Histories* defy
resolution. Those who are not content with the limits of history as a form
of literature and as a mode of thought will always be dissatisfied with such
restraint and either reject Thucydides' work or seek to impose upon it
grander constructions. But for those who are willing to listen, it speaks
still with honesty, reason, and compassion.

[18] B. Brodie, *Strategy in the Missile Age* (Princeton 1965) 408f.

Appendix One

RING COMPOSITIONS IN THE ARCHAEOLOGY

(see Chapter One, Note 29)

1. Before the Trojan War (1.2-8)
   Troy (13.4)
      Minos (1.4.1)
         Piracy (1.4.1-5.2)
            Carrying of weapons etc.
         Piracy (1.8.1)
      Minos (1.8.2)
   Troy (1.8.4)
2. The Trojan War (1.9-11), ending in a ring composition:
   Insufficiency of financial reserves, ἀχρηματία (1.11)
      Farming, γεωργίαν (1.11.1 line 30)
         Piracy, λῃστείαν (1.11.1 line 30) λῃστείας (1.11.2 line 3)
      Farming, γεωργίας (1.11.2 line 3)
   Insufficiency of financial reserves, ἀχρηματίαν (1.11.2)
3. After the Trojan War (1.12-18.2)
   Initial hindrances to growth: μὴ . . . αὐξηθῆναι (1.12.1)
      Growth of naval power: (1.13-15.3) ναυτικά τε ἐξηρτύετο ἡ Ἑλλάς
      (1.13.1); τὰ μὲν οὖν ναυτικὰ τῶν Ἑλλήνων τοιαῦτα ἦν (1.15.1)
   Subsequent hindrances to growth: (esp. Persia) κωλύματα μὴ αὐξηθῆναι
   (1.16.1)

Appendix Two

RING COMPOSITION IN THE CENTRAL
PART OF BOOK 2

A. The challenge of *orgē*

   Archidamus' last reported speech (2.11): The attempt to provoke Athens to engage

   Periclean *pronoia* and confidence (2.13)

      B. Bad feeling against Pericles and his response (2.21-22): The Athenian desire to engage the enemy

      Pericles' response: Assembly prohibited (2.22.1)

         C. The Funeral Oration (2.34-46)

         C. The Plague (2.47-54)

      B. Bad feeling against Pericles and his response (2.59-64): The Athenian desire to negotiate with the Peloponnesians

      Pericles' response: Assembly convened (2.59.3) and Pericles' last reported speech (2.60-64)

A. The challenge of *orgē* partially met (2.65)

   Periclean *pronoia* and confidence

This necessarily oversimplifies a very rich and complex grouping of material; it does not show, for example, the similarities between Archidamus' situation and that of Pericles (cf. 2.18.5 and 2.21.3). It emphasizes, however, the persistence and development of the theme of *orgē* in this portion of the work.

Appendix Three

STRUCTURAL PATTERNS IN THE
CENTER OF BOOK 3

A. The stasis at Notium (3.34)
   Athenian intervention
   Settlement
     First stage
     Later stage (3.34): καὶ ὕστερον Ἀθηναῖοι οἰκιστὰς πέμψαντες
     B. The decision concerning Mytilene (3.36-49)
       Cleon's speech (3.37-40)
       Diodotus' speech (3.42-48)
       Outcome (3.49-50)
         Apparent closure (3.49.4): παρὰ τοσοῦτον μὲν ἡ Μυτιλήνη ἦλθε κινδύνου
         Reopening (3.50.1): τοὺς δ' ἄλλους ἄνδρας
         Settlement
           First stage
           Later stage (3.50.2): ὕστερον δὲ
           Dedication to the gods
         Rounding off sentence (3.50.3): τὰ μὲν κατὰ Λέσβον οὕτως ἐγέ-νετο.
     B. The Decision concerning Plataea (3.52-68)
       Plataean Speech (3.53-59)
       Theban Speech (3.61-67)
       Outcome (3.68)
         Settlement
           First stage
           Later stage (3.68.3): ὕστερον δὲ
           Dedication to the gods
         Rounding off sentence (3.68.5): καὶ τὰ μὲν κατὰ Πλάταιαν ἔτει τρίτῳ καὶ ἐνενηκοστῷ ἐπειδὴ Ἀθηναίων ξύμμαχοι ἐγένοντο οὕτως ἐτελεύτησεν.
A. The stasis at Corcyra (3.69-85)
   Athenian intervention
   No settlement: (3.85.1)
     First stages: τοιαύταις ὀργαῖς ταῖς πρώταις ἐς ἀλλήλους
     Later stage: ὕστερον δὲ

Appendix Four

THE PLACE OF DOCUMENTS IN THE
NARRATIVES OF BOOKS 4 AND 5

(see Chapter Five, Note 16)

	Athenian setbacks:
	Delium
	Loss of Amphipolis
4.118-119	*Truce between Athens and Sparta*
	Athenians' inability to recoup losses
	Brasidas' further successes
	Athens' failure to recover Amphipolis
	Deaths of Cleon and Brasidas
5.18-19	*Treaty between Athens and Sparta*
5.23-24	*Alliance between Athens and Sparta*
	Shifts in Spartan and Argive foreign policy
	Alcibiades' manipulations
5.47	*Treaty and Alliance between Athens and Argos*
	The Battle of Mantinea
5.77	*Treaty between Sparta and Argos*
5.79	*Alliance between Sparta and Argos*
	Further shifts in foreign policies

Appendix Five

MAJOR SIEGE NARRATIVES IN THUCYDIDES

(See Chapter Five, Note 24)

PLATAEA	*MYTILENE*	*MELOS*
	PRELIMINARIES	
2.71-74	3.2-18	3.91 First attack
Mini-dialogue	Background information	5.84 Renewed hostilities
	POLEMOS BEGINS	
2.75.1: καθίστη ἐς πό-	3.4.1: ἐς πόλεμον κα-	5.84.2: ἐς πόλεμον φα-
λεμον	θίσταντο	νερὸν κατέστησαν
	BEGINNING OF SIEGE	
2.78.1: περιετείχι-	3.18.4: περιετείχι-	5.114.1: διελόμενοι
ζον τὴν πόλιν κύκλῳ,	ζουσι Μυτιλήνην ἐν	κατὰ πόλεις περιε-
διελόμενοι κατὰ πό-	κύκλῳ	τείχισαν κύκλῳ Μη-
λεις		λίους
2.78.2: καταλιπόντες	—	5.114.2: φυλακὴν . . .
φυλακὰς		καταλιπόντες
	3.18.5: καὶ ἐκ γῆς καὶ	5.114.2: καὶ κατὰ γῆν
	ἐκ θαλάσσης εἴργετο	καὶ κατὰ θάλασσαν
2.78.2: ἀνεχώρησαν τῷ	—	5.114.2: ἀνεχώρησαν τῷ
στρατῷ		πλέονι τοῦ στρατοῦ
	INTERVAL	
2.79	3.19	5.115.1-3
	RENEWED HOSTILITIES; GRAIN GIVES OUT	
3.20.1: τῷ τε σίτῳ ἐπι-	3.27.1: ὁ σῖτος ἐπελε-	5.114.4 Melians get grain!
λείποντι	λοίπει	
SOME PLATAEANS ESCAPE		

INTERVAL

3.25   —   5.116

SURRENDER AGREEMENT

3.52.1: ξυνέβησαν   3.28.1: ξυμβάσεως . . .   5.116.3: ξυνεχώρησαν
                          ποιοῦνται

DEBATE

3.53-67 Antilogy   3.37-48 Antilogy   No debate!

DECISION AND IMPLEMENTATION

3.68.1: ἀπέκτεινον . . .   3.50.1: τοὺς δ' ἄλλους   5.116.4: ἀπέκτειναν
διέφθειραν . . .   ἄνδρας . . . διέφθει-   Μηλίων ὅσους ἡβῶν-
                          ραν   τας ἔλαβον

3.68.2: γυναῖκας δὲ   —   5.116.4: παῖδας δὲ καὶ
ἠνδραπόδισαν   γυναῖκας ἠνδραπόδι-
                                                       σαν

3.68.3: ὕστερον δὲ . . .   3.50.2: ὕστερον δὲ . . .   5.116.4: ἀποίκους ὕ-
τὴν δὲ γῆν . . . ἀπε-   κλήρους δὲ ποιήσαν-   στερον πεντακοσίους
μίσθωσαν   τες τῆς γῆς . . . κλη-   πέμψαντες.
                          ρούχους . . . ἀπέπεμ-
                          ψαν

ROUNDING OFF SENTENCE

3.68.5: καὶ τὰ μὲν κατὰ   3.50.3: τὰ μὲν κατὰ   —
Πλάταιαν . . . οὕτως   Λέσβον οὕτως ἐγένε-
ἐτελεύτησεν   το.

This comparison makes clear both the similarities between the Melian episode and
those of Plataea and Mytilene and also the major contrasts, especially the early
and dominant position of the dialogue (chs. 85-112) and the absence of a final
rounding off sentence.

Appendix Six

RING COMPOSITION IN BOOK 6

A. The Salaminian galley comes for Alcibiades and others. (6.53.1): τὴν Σαλαμινίαν ναῦν . . . ἐπί τε ᾿Αλκιβιάδην καὶ ἐπ᾽ ἄλλους . . . τῶν . . .
μεμηνυμένων.
  B. Knowledge of the Pisistratid tyranny affects the mood in Athens (6.53.3):
  ἐπιστάμενος γὰρ ὁ δῆμος ἀκοῇ . . . πάντα ὑπόπτως ἐλάμβανεν.
    C. The tyranny was severe in its last phase (6.53.3): τὴν . . . τυ-
    ραννίδα χαλεπὴν τελευτῶσαν γενομένην
      D. The tyranny was overthrown not by the Athenians but by the
      Lacedaemonians (6.53.3): οὐδ᾽ ὑφ᾽ ἑαυτῶν . . . ἀλλ᾽ ὑπὸ
      τῶν Λακεδαιμονίων
        E. Boldness through erotic circumstance (6.54.1): τόλμημα
        δι᾽ ἐρωτικὴν ξυντυχίαν
        THE STORY OF HARMODIUS AND ARISTOGEITON
        E. Through erotic grief . . . boldness (6.59.1): δι᾽ ἐρωτικὴν
        λύπην . . . τόλμα
    C. The tyranny was severe in its last phase (6.59.2): χαλεπωτέρα
    μετὰ τοῦτο ἡ τυραννὶς
      D. The tyranny was overthrown by the Lacedaemonians (6.59.4):
      παυθεὶς . . . ὑπὸ Λακεδαιμονίων
    C. The Athenians become severe (6.60.1): ὁ δῆμος . . . χαλεπὸς
    ἦν
  B. Knowledge of the Pisistratid tyranny affects the mood in Athens (6.60.1):
  ῟Ων ἐνθυμούμενος ὁ δῆμος . . . καὶ μιμνησκόμενος ὅσα ἀκοῇ περὶ
  αὐτῶν ἠπίστατο . . . ὑπόπτης
A. The Salaminian galley comes for Alcibiades (6.61.4): τὴν Σαλαμινίαν ναῦν
. . . ἐπί τε ἐκεῖνον καὶ ὧν πέρι ἄλλων ἐμεμήνυτο.

Appendix Seven

RING COMPOSITION IN BOOK 7

A. The Athenian fortification in Laconia (7.26.2): τῆς Λακωνικῆς . . . ἐτεί-
χισαν
  B. Demosthenes sails to Corcyra (7.26.3): ὁ μὲν Δημοσθένης . . . παρ-
  έπλει ἐπὶ τῆς Κερκύρας
    C. Late arrival and dismissal of Thracians (7.27.1f): Θρακῶν . . . ὡς
    ὕστεροι ἧκον . . . ἀποπέμπειν.
      D. Deceleia and effects (7.27.2-28 ad fin.)
    C. Late arrival and dismissal of Thracians (7.29.1): Θρᾷκας τοὺς
    . . . ὑστερήσαντας . . . ἀπέπεμπον
      D. Mycalessus (7.29.2-30 ad fin.)
  B. Demosthenes sails off to Corcyra (7.31.1): Ὁ δὲ Δημοσθένης τότε
  ἀποπλέων ἐπὶ τῆς Κερκύρας
A. The Athenian fortification in Laconia (7.31.1): μετὰ τὴν ἐκ τῆς Λακωνικῆς
τείχισιν

The effect is to establish a close and deliberate parallelism between the two episodes, Deceleia and Mycalessus. Deceleia's effects could be discussed with appropriateness at any of a number of points in books 7 or 8 and Mycalessus was
not of such strategic significance that it demanded any mention whatsoever. The
two, however, are brought into a powerful collocation, all the more remarkable
by the transfer of vocabulary between the two episodes. The financial expenditures
in Deceleia are reported in part by the use of language normally used for human
death: 7.27.3, χρημάτων τ' ὀλέθρῳ and 28.4 ad fin., αἱ δὲ πρόσοδοι ἀπώλ-
λυντο. Conversely, the deaths in Mycalessus are reported with financial metaphors, conventional at 29.4, φειδόμενοι, but more unusual in 30.3, μέρος τι
ἀπανηλώθη. (Cf. Pericles in 2.64.3.) This is more, I think, than elaborate architecture. It suggests the incommensurability of two thematic systems within the
work—financial resources/expenditures and human resources/expenditures.

Appendix Eight

STRUCTURE OF 7.47-49

A. Demosthenes' first position (7.47.3-4): Quick withdrawal dictated by
　1. Time of year: ἕως ἔτι τὸ πέλαγος οἷόν τε περαιοῦσθαι
　2. Naval superiority: ταῖς γοῦν ἐπελθούσαις ναυσὶ κρατεῖν
　3. Finances: χρήματα πολλὰ δαπανῶντας
Conclusion: οὐδ' αὖ . . . εἰκὸς εἶναι προσκαθῆσθαι.
　B. Nicias' position (7.48)
　　1. Equivocal attitude (7.48.1-2)
　　　a. Recognizes Athenian affairs are πόνηρα
　　　b. Syracusan affairs may be πονηρότερα (7.48.2)
　　　　(i) Finances: χρημάτων . . . ἀπορίᾳ
　　　　(ii) Naval superiority of Athens: ταῖς ὑπαρχούσαις ναυσὶ
　　　　　θαλασσοκρατούντων
　　　　(iii) Subversion promised: τι . . . βουλόμενον τοῖς 'Αθη-
　　　　　ναίοις τὰ πράγματα ἐνδοῦναι
　　2. Speech (7.48.3-5)
　　　a. Attitude of the Athenians (secs. 3 and 4)
　　　b. Syracusan situation (sec. 5)
　　　　(i) Financial distress: χρήμασι . . . ἀπορεῖν
　　Conclusion: τρίβειν . . . χρῆναι προσκαθημένους
　　　C. Authorial comment (7.49.1): Nicias was correct about:
　　　　1. Finances: χρημάτων ἀπορίαν
　　　　2. Subversion: πολὺ τὸ βουλόμενον τοῖς 'Αθηναίοις
　　　　　γίγνεσθαι τὰ πράγματα
　　　　3. Naval superiority: ταῖς γοῦν ναυσὶ . . . κρατήσειν
A. Demosthenes' second position (7.49.2): rejects τοῦ προσκαθῆσθαι and urges
　move to Catane
Outcome: Eurymedon agrees with Demosthenes
　B. Nicias induces delay (7.49.4): ἀντιλέγοντος δὲ τοῦ Νικίου ὄκνος
　τις καὶ μέλλησις ἐνεγένετο

The structure results from two modifications of an A-B-A (Demosthenes I-Nicias-Demosthenes II) pattern. The first is the overlay of an authorial comment pointing out one irony: Nicias was correct in his information about Syracuse: finances were difficult; there was a faction in correspondence with Nicias. But Nicias' inference that they should therefore stay on is known to be wrong. The second is a *logos/ergon* division in the presentation of Nicias' views. Thucydides distinguishes Nicias' own view, which is based on a recognition of the gravity of the Athenian situation, from his speech, which, as often with Nicias, does not represent his actual thinking. The speech is a very confident one (ἰσχυρίζετο, 49.1; cf. ἰσχυρίζηται, 49.4). It plays up the political difficulties that are likely to await the expedition on its return to Athens—a sensitive topic for Demosthenes who has had some acquaintance with the results of unsuccessful expeditions (3.98.5), but it says nothing of a more compelling reason for Nicias' hesitation: his *elpis* (48.2) that subversion would take place. The end of the episode brings out a final irony: Demosthenes and Eurymedon agree. The vote is two to one but Nicias' confidence (ἰσχυρίζηται 49.4; cf. 49.1) induces delay.

Appendix Nine

RING COMPOSITION IN 7.50-71

A. Initial naval battle (7.50-54)

  B. Athenian discouragement (7.55) ἠπόρουν, 7.55.2

      C. Initial statement of Syracusan plan (7.56.1f.): τὸ στόμα αὐτοῦ διενοοῦντο κλῄσειν . . . κρατῆσαι Ἀθηναίων τε καὶ τῶν ξυμμάχων καὶ κατὰ γῆν καὶ κατὰ θάλασσαν

         D. The wondrous victory prize (7.56.2): καλὸν σφίσιν ἐς τοὺς Ἕλληνας τὸ ἀγώνισμα φανεῖσθαι

           CATALOGUE OF ALLIES (7.57-58)

         D. The wondrous victory prize (7.59.2): καλὸν ἀγώνισμα σφίσιν εἶναι

      C. New statement of Syracusan plan (7.59.2): ἑλεῖν τε τὸ στρατόπεδον ἅπαν τῶν Ἀθηναίων . . . καὶ . . . μήτε διὰ θαλάσσης μήτε τῷ πεζῷ διαφυγεῖν

      Closing of the harbor (7.59.3): ἔκλῃον οὖν τόν τε λιμένα . . . ἔχοντα τὸ στόμα . . .

  B. Athenian discouragement (ch. 60): πρὸς τὴν παροῦσαν ἀπορίαν, 7.60.2

A. Second naval battle (7.60.3-71)

As so often in Thucydides, ring compositions do not simply reiterate the constituent elements, nor are they static or always fully symmetrical. Frequently, they modulate and mark shifts in attitude or theme. In this case the structure is part of a steady crescendo. The second engagement is much larger and more significant than the first and the plan behind it has changed in one major respect. The Syracusans now no longer aim at mere victory and dominance (*kratēsai*, 56.2) over the Athenians by land and by sea, but at the much more difficult task of actually capturing the Athenian expedition (*helein*, 59.2).

Index

Passages and characters discussed in the text at the place they occur in Thucydides' narrative are not included in the index. References below are largely confined to discussions that occur outside the order of the text.

Library of Congress Cataloging in Publication Data

Connor, W. Robert (Walter Robert), 1934-
Thucydides.

Includes bibliographical references and index.
1. Thucydides. History of the Peloponnesian War.
2. Greece—History—Peloponnesian War, 431-404 B.C. I. Title.

PA4461.C58 1984   938'.05   83-43066
ISBN 0-691-03569-5 (alk. paper)